The
BOSTON
SYMPHONY
Cookbook

BOSTON
SYMPHONY
ORCHESTRA
SEIJI OZAWA
*Music
Director*

The BOSTON SYMPHONY Cookbook

*The Council
of the
Boston Symphony Orchestra*

HOUGHTON MIFFLIN COMPANY BOSTON 1983

Library of Congress Cataloging in Publication Data

Main entry under title:

The Boston Symphony cookbook.

Includes index.

1. Cookery, International. 2. Boston Symphony Orchestra. I. Boston Symphony Orchestra. Council.

TX725.A1B69 1983 641.5 82-21267

ISBN 0-395-33118-8

Printed in the United States of America

V 10 9 8 7 6 5 4 3 2 1

Photo credits: page 1, Ted Dully; page 69, Walter Scott; page 101, © 1981 Peter Schaaf; page 143, © 1982 Donald Dietz; page 161, © Milton Feinberg; page 181, Charles Leavitt; page 217, Donald Curran; page 245, Story Litchfield; page 273, Ted Dully; page 309, Béla Kalman. All photographs are courtesy of the Boston Symphony Orchestra.

Endpapers: When the old Boston Music Hall was threatened with demolition, it became clear that the Symphony needed a home of its own. Founder Henry Lee Higginson formed a corporation to construct a new hall. The building was designed by the eminent architectural firm of McKim, Mead and White; Wallace Clement Sabine, assistant professor of physics at Harvard, was the acoustical consultant. The result was the first concert hall in the world to be built in conformity with known scientific principles, and it is now generally reckoned to be one of the best concert halls in the world. The endpapers are adapted from the architect's rendering, circa 1900, the original of which is part of the Boston Symphony's permanent art collection.

A Message from
the Music Director

Aside from music, one of my passions, along with tennis, is excellent cooking. I love to try different cuisines in cities throughout the world. With this marvelous assortment of recipes, some wonderful dishes — exotic or very simple — can be created at home.

I would like to thank the incredibly dedicated and hard-working Council of the Boston Symphony for its tremendous effort in producing this book. The Orchestra and I need the love and support of our volunteers, who undertake so many fantastic projects in Boston, in New York, and at Tanglewood. In my tenth year as music director, I am especially honored to be associated with such a distinguished institution, and I am very proud of our great Boston Symphony family.

As for this book, bravo and *itadakimasu!*

Seiji Ozawa
Music Director

March 1983

Foreword

Dedication to the arts implies dedication to gastronomy, one of the minor though indispensable arts practiced by mankind. It is, therefore, a pleasure to introduce *The Boston Symphony Cookbook*, which carries overtones of international flavor brought to it quite naturally by the contributors from the international musical world of the Orchestra and its friends. Even small regional touches are vital and inspired in their effects. Witness the chili peppers in a Texas corn pudding which totally confirm its origin and perfect its flavor.

The symphonic character of this delightful cookbook truly reflects the title. According to Webster, the word *symphonic* implies "interweaving of themes, harmonious arrangements," which surely have their place in describing flavors and ingredients.

The careful blending of one flavor with another to form still a third entity of distinctive taste becomes the definition of a recipe. When we have formed a series of such formulas — whether merely pedestrian or extending to the symphonic in style — we have contributed a cookbook to gastronomic history.

Narcissa G. Chamberlain

Preface

The broth which has resulted in *The Boston Symphony Cookbook* simmered for several years before it came to a full boil in 1980. By the summer of 1981, approximately thirteen hundred recipes had been collected from the players and their families, the Orchestra's distinguished visiting artists, the staff, and members of the various support groups. For over a year a dedicated band of amateur chefs tested, tasted, culled, and refined these contributions. The caliber of the final selections was so high that the book was enlarged from the projected three hundred–plus recipes to some five hundred "absolute musts." These were written to a formula by a team of writers, edited, rewritten, and re-edited until the results were satisfactory to us. The book in your hands is the culmination of this enormous effort on the part of people too numerous to name here, most of whom are listed in the Acknowledgments. It is a tribute in print to the strength, imagination, determination, and plain hard work of the volunteers who toil for the orchestra they love.

This is a book for music lovers who like to cook and for good cooks who love good music. We have tried to make the directions simple and logical. All recipes may be made from scratch using hand tools, but labor-saving equipment is a boon to the busy. Any exotic ingredients or unusual methods are given straightforward explanations. Unless otherwise specified, all eggs are U.S. "large" (2 ounces), all flour is unbleached white, all sugar is granulated, and, of course, all ingredients are fresh and of the finest quality available. Recipes are indexed by title (where appropriate), chief ingredients, and general category.

The Boston Symphony is of Boston and New England: it is also of the world. The book that bears its name is influenced by both its regional roots and its international character, and reflects the many aspects of the Symphony's life. As you use this book, you will see, we hope, something of what the Orchestra means to the city, the region, the nation, and the world.

On behalf of the Cookbook Committee and the Council of the Boston Symphony, I wish to thank all of our generous contributors, whose expertise and ingenuity made the book possible. We had fun working with their culinary offspring, and we hope that you, who now hold the result, will enjoy using these recipes as much as we have enjoyed preparing them. And remember, recipes are only road maps — they point the way to your destination, but you must choose the route. Experiment, and have fun in the kitchen!

Bon appétit!

Judy Gardiner
Chairman of the Cookbook Committee
Council of the Boston Symphony Orchestra

Editor's Note: A ◆ following a recipe title in the text indicates that the recipe itself appears elsewhere in the book and may be located by consulting the index.

Contents

APPETIZERS AND SOUPS

A symphony orchestra is a complex living entity made up of some dozens of individuals who retain their own independent artistic techniques while serving the overall concept of the master architect of the performance, the conductor. Seiji Ozawa *(overleaf)* was born in China of Japanese parents, and received his first musical training in Japan, where he took prizes in composition and conducting. In 1959 he won first prize at the International Competition of Orchestra Conductors in Besançon, France, where one of the judges, Charles Munch, promptly invited him to Tanglewood for the following summer. There he won the Berkshire Music Center's highest honor, the Koussevitzky Prize for outstanding conductor, and his career skyrocketed, with posts in San Francisco and Toronto. He became an artistic director of the Berkshire Music Center in 1970 and was named music director of the Boston Symphony in 1973. During his decade in this post, he has led the Orchestra on highly acclaimed tours of the United States and Europe, Japan, and China, and during the Symphony's centennial season (1981–82), around the world.

NORWEGIAN PINWHEEL

Serves 12 as an hors d'oeuvre,
8 as a first course,
4 to 6 as a main course

Soprano Phyllis Bryn-Julson has been a frequent and always welcome guest with the Boston Symphony since 1966. Her recipe is a showstopper: it is handsome, delicious, and can be prepared considerably ahead of serving.

1 15-inch cooked Pizza Crust,◆ cooled
1 pound cream cheese, softened
2 cups flaked cooked salmon, or
coarsely chopped smoked salmon or
lox
1½ cups chopped green peppers

1 cup chopped red onion
1 cup chopped black olives
1 cup chopped green olives
6 "extra large" hard-boiled eggs,
yolks and whites chopped separately

Spread the pizza crust with the cream cheese. Starting at the outside, make a circle of salmon, then circles of green pepper, onion, egg white, black olive, egg yolk, green olive, salmon, and so on. The order is immaterial, except for the fact that there is more salmon than the other ingredients. Beginning and ending with salmon makes a very pretty combination. Chill the pinwheel until ready to serve. Cut into small wedges for hors d'oeuvres, larger portions for a light summer luncheon or supper dish.

Note
Packaged crescent roll mix, spread on a pizza pan and baked, is an easy alternative to pizza dough, which can also be bought partly baked.

Variation
Smaller amounts of red and/or black caviar may be substituted for the salmon. Serve with lemon wedges.

Phyllis Bryn-Julson, soprano

TEA STICKS

Makes about 36 sticks

Mrs. Cronkhite, the former dean of Radcliffe College for whom the Cronkhite Graduate Center is named, was given this simple recipe during one of her many visits to Mexico. It has been a feature of her teas ever since, and it provides a welcome change of tastes at a cocktail party.

*6 to 8 slices oatmeal bread, crusts
  removed*

*2 tablespoons peanut butter
2 tablespoons mayonnaise*

Preheat the oven to 350°.

Mix the peanut butter and mayonnaise thoroughly and spread thinly on both sides of the trimmed bread slices. Cut into uniform ½- to ¾-inch-wide sticks and place on a buttered cookie sheet. Bake for about 5 minutes; then turn the sticks over for about 5 more minutes, until they are crisp and golden brown.

Serve hot, warm, or cold with tea, wine, or cocktails.

Note
The better the bread, the better the sticks.

Variation
Sprinkle with sesame or poppy seeds.

Mrs. L. W. Cronkhite

EASY TIROPITA (Greek Cheese Appetizers)

Serves 12 to 14

*1 loaf (20 slices) soft, fine-textured
  sandwich bread, crusts removed
½ pound butter, melted
Sour cream*

*½ pound cream cheese, softened
Salt
Curry powder
2 ounces sesame seeds*

Preheat the oven to 350°.

Place the bread slices on the work surface in four or five rows and roll them thin with a rolling pin. Brush both sides of each slice with melted butter. Beat enough sour cream into the cream cheese to make a soft mixture that spreads easily. Add salt and curry powder to taste.

Spread a thin layer of the cheese mixture on each slice of bread, covering it completely to the edges. Firmly roll up each slice like a jellyroll and set aside, seam side down. Cut each roll into thirds, and toss the pieces in the sesame seeds. Place the pieces (again seam side down) on a buttered cookie sheet and bake for 30 minutes, or until golden brown. Serve hot.

To freeze for later use, place the pieces (seam side down) close together on a cookie sheet, with waxed paper between the layers. Seal with plastic wrap or foil. Remove from the freezer 1 hour before baking as above.

Mrs. Ralph B. Seferian
Council of the BSO

CHEESE AND MUSHROOM MORSELS

Makes about 60

BSO assistant personnel manager Harry Shapiro, former horn player with the Orchestra, is also a devotee of opera and ballet. His wife is a member of the Subscription Office staff, an excellent cook, and a valued member of the Cookbook Committee.

½ pound mushrooms, chopped
2 tablespoons butter
½ pound cream cheese
1 tablespoon grated onion
Salt

Freshly ground black pepper
15 slices thin white bread, trimmed
and quartered
Mayonnaise
Paprika

Sauté the mushrooms in the butter until all their liquid has evaporated. Remove from the heat. Add the cream cheese and stir until well blended. Add the grated onion, as well as salt and pepper to taste. Toast the bread slices on one side only. Spread the untoasted side first with mayonnaise and then with the mushroom mixture. Place on a lightly buttered cookie sheet and sprinkle with paprika. Refrigerate until serving time.

Preheat the oven to 400° and bake for 8 to 10 minutes, or until the morsels are hot and crisp. Serve immediately.

Frances Shapiro

BRAZILIAN CHEESE WAFERS

Makes about 6 dozen

Bernard Kadinoff is a solo viola recitalist, a member of the Boston Fine Arts Ensemble, a teacher, and a member of the BSO viola section. His wife, who sings with the Tanglewood Festival Chorus, is a fine cook, though she gives the credit for the following recipe to Gilda Pinto, wife of Ayrton Pinto, the versatile and talented Brazilian violinist who played with the Boston Symphony for several years.

1¼ pounds butter, softened
1 cup milk
4 cups flour
½ teaspoon salt

1 tablespoon baking powder
½ pound freshly grated Parmesan
cheese
Cayenne pepper (optional)

Using a food processor or electric mixer, combine half the butter with the milk, flour, salt, and baking powder and beat until smooth. Divide the dough into three equal parts and chill while making the filling.

Cream together the remaining butter and the Parmesan cheese. Season to taste with cayenne pepper, and divide into three equal parts.

On a sheet of waxed paper, roll one part of the dough into a rectangle about ⅛ inch thick. Spread with one part of the cheese mixture and roll up like a jellyroll. Repeat the process with the remaining parts of the dough and filling. Wrap the rolls in waxed paper and chill, seam side down, overnight, or freeze for at least several hours. Frozen dough is easier to slice than chilled.

Preheat the oven to 375°.

Cut the rolls into very thin slices, no more than ¼ inch thick, and bake on an ungreased cookie sheet for 10 to 12 minutes, or until the wafers are crisp and golden brown. Serve hot, warm, or at room temperature with wine or cocktails. Store in an airtight container, or wrap and freeze. Frozen wafers must be crisped in a 300° oven for several minutes.

Frances V. Kadinoff
Tanglewood Festival Chorus

JUDY'S SESAME ROUNDS
(Hungarian Hot Pastry)

Makes 50 to 60

1 pound butter, softened
1 pound cottage cheese
3½ cups flour

2 egg whites, lightly beaten
⅓ to ½ cup sesame seeds
Coarse salt

Beat the first three ingredients together until smooth. Form the dough into a ball and refrigerate for several hours or overnight.

Preheat the oven to 425°.

On a lightly floured board, roll out the dough to a thickness of ⅛ to ¼ inch and cut it into 1½- to 2-inch rounds. Place on an ungreased cookie sheet. Brush the rounds with egg white and sprinkle them with sesame seeds and salt. Bake for about 10 minutes, until they are lightly browned and crisp on top but soft inside. Place the rounds on a warmed platter and serve with wine or cocktails.

These may be made ahead and reheated.

Variation
Add 1 teaspoon of salt to the dough and substitute caraway or poppy seeds and raw sugar for the sesame seeds and coarse salt.

Mrs. David Dustin Tuttle
Council of the BSO

CHEESE BEUREG

Makes about 50 pieces

*1 pound Muenster cheese (skin
  removed), finely chopped*
¾ pound cream cheese
¼ pound cottage cheese

2 eggs, beaten
½ cup chopped fresh parsley
1 pound phyllo dough
½ pound butter, clarified

Preheat the oven to 400°.

Mix together the cheeses, eggs, and parsley. Take one leaf of dough from the package at a time, keeping the rest covered with a damp cloth, and cut it into four or five strips. Using a pastry brush, butter each strip lightly. Working with two strips at a time, one on top of the other, place 2 tablespoons of the cheese filling on one corner. Pick up the corner and fold it toward the opposite side to form a triangle. Continue folding the dough down the whole strip as if you were folding up a flag, flipping from side to side. This makes one triangular pastry. Continue in this manner until all the filling has been used.

Place the triangles on a lightly greased baking sheet, and brush the tops with butter. Bake for 15 to 20 minutes, or until the pastries are golden brown, and serve warm as hors d'oeuvres.

The triangles may be frozen, uncooked, in a tightly sealed container. Remove from the freezer several hours before baking as above.

Phyllis Dohanian
Junior Council of the BSO

SHRIMP DIP

Serves 6 to 8

1 7-ounce can tiny shrimp
½ pound cream cheese, softened
2 teaspoons chili sauce
2 teaspoons fresh horseradish

⅓ cup Blender Mayonnaise◆
1 teaspoon lemon juice
Salt
Freshly ground white pepper

Drain the shrimp and add to the cream cheese. Stir in the other ingredients and mix well. Chill until ready to serve. Serve with potato chips or crackers.

Variation

Other canned seafood such as lobster or crab meat may be substituted for the shrimp.

Mrs. Richard E. Hartwell
Junior Council of the BSO

DILL DIP OR SPREAD

Makes 2½ cups dip,
3½ cups spread

1 cup sour cream
1 cup mayonnaise
6 scallions, finely chopped
2 tablespoons chopped fresh dill, or 1
  tablespoon dried dill weed

2 tablespoons chopped parsley
½ teaspoon lemon juice, or to taste
8 ounces chive cottage cheese (for
  spread only)

For dip: beat together the first six ingredients. Serve, chilled, with vegetables or chips.

For spread: mix as above. Beat in the cottage cheese to a suitably spreadable consistency and serve with crackers.

Beverly G. Sweeney

MOCK CHOPPED LIVER (Kosher)

Serves 6 to 8

1 medium-sized onion, coarsely
  chopped
1 tablespoon butter
4 ''extra large'' hard-boiled eggs
16 walnuts (4 for each egg)

3 or 4 saltine-type crackers or an
  equivalent amount of matzo
Salt
Freshly ground black pepper
Mayonnaise

Lightly brown the onion in the butter.

Chop the eggs, walnuts, crackers, and cooked onion, using the steel blade of a food processor or the fine blade of a meat grinder. Season with salt and pepper to taste. Add enough mayonnaise to make the mixture spreadable. Serve with toast or crackers.

Mrs. Jerome S. Hertz
Council of the BSO

MARINATED HADDOCK WITH CHIVES

Serves 8 as a first course,
12 to 16 as an hors d'oeuvre

2 pounds haddock fillets, boned and
  skinned
Milk
Freshly ground black pepper

¼ cup chopped chives
2 tablespoons olive oil
Lemon wedges
Capers

The day before you plan to serve, place the haddock fillets in a shallow container, cover them with milk, and refrigerate for 24 hours. The next day, drain the fish and pat it dry. With a very sharp knife, cut the fish across the grain into fine diagonal slices. Sprinkle them with the pepper, chives, and olive oil.

Serve as one would serve smoked salmon — with lemon wedges and capers, plus toast or thinly sliced whole-wheat or dark rye bread spread with sweet butter.

Hotel Meridien, Boston
Gérard Vié, guest chef
Proprietor and chef, Les Trois Marches
Versailles, France

MOUSSELINE DE POISSON TAMARA

Serves 3 as a main course,
6 to 8 as a first course,
10 to 12 as an hors d'oeuvre

Both Mrs. Dufresne and her husband, retired BSO double bass Gaston Dufresne, are famous in the Symphony family for their elegant French cuisine, of which the following recipe is a good example.

1 pound haddock, cod, or flounder
fillets, skinned
1 tablespoon Dijon mustard
1 cup Blender Mayonnaise◆

Lemon juice
Salt
Freshly ground white pepper
Salad greens and parsley (for garnish)

Court Bouillon

2 tablespoons butter
1 medium-sized onion, sliced
1 medium-sized carrot, sliced
1 rib celery, sliced
5 cups boiling water
4 parsley sprigs

6 peppercorns
2 whole cloves
½ bay leaf
¼ teaspoon dried thyme
Salt
Freshly ground white pepper

Pick over the fish carefully, removing all the bones, and set it aside. Stir the mustard into the mayonnaise and refrigerate the mixture.

Prepare the court bouillon: Heat the butter in a large pan and sauté the vegetables over medium heat until they are limp but not brown. Add the water and all the seasonings; cover and simmer for 30 to 45 minutes. Correct the seasonings, strain the bouillon, and return it to the heat. Simmer the fish in the court bouillon for about 10 minutes, until it flakes when tested with a fork. Remove, drain well, and cool.

Combine ½ cup of the mustard mayonnaise with the fish and work with a pestle until the fish is reduced to a paste. (This can be done in a food processor.) Add lemon juice, salt, and pepper to taste, and refrigerate for several hours or overnight.

Just before serving, mound the fish on a chilled serving platter, small individual plates, or shells. Mask with the remaining mayonnaise, and draw a decorative design with a fork. Garnish with crisp greens and top with parsley sprigs.

Coda
The court bouillon may be reduced, strained, and frozen for future use in recipes calling for fish stock.

Martha C. Dufresne

JOANNA'S SEVICHE

Serves 8 to 10 as a first course,
12 to 14 as an hors d'oeuvre

Mezzo-soprano Joanna Simon has sung the music of Beethoven, Berlioz, and Mozart with the Boston Symphony. Joanna's seviche is a colorful and pungent treat for scallop lovers, and it's guaranteed to convert those who think they dislike raw fish.

2 pounds bay scallops, picked over
¾ cup lemon juice
1 large tomato, coarsely chopped
12 large black Greek olives, pitted and
* coarsely chopped*
1 medium-sized onion (red or white),
* minced*

5 tablespoons olive oil
1½ teaspoons dried chili pepper
½ teaspoon salt
Perfect lettuce leaves
1 ripe avocado, peeled and sliced

Toss the scallops with the lemon juice, and marinate them in the refrigerator for 2 hours, until they turn white. Add all the remaining ingredients except the avocado and lettuce, and mix well. Refrigerate for 24 hours, turning occasionally.

Just before serving, drain off the marinade and dip the avocado slices in it to retard discoloration. Discard the marinade. Arrange the lettuce leaves on a chilled platter or individual plates, and heap the scallops on the leaves. Serve immediately, garnished with the avocado slices.

Joanna Simon, mezzo-soprano

SALMON LOG

Serves 10 to 12

2 teaspoons grated onion (see
* instructions)*
1 teaspoon white horseradish (see
* instructions)*
1 16-ounce can red salmon, drained,
* skinned, and flaked*

½ pound cream cheese, softened
1 tablespoon lemon juice
2 to 3 teaspoons liquid smoke flavoring
¾ cup chopped pecans or walnuts
¼ cup chopped parsley

Before measuring, squeeze the onion and horseradish in a paper towel or cheesecloth to extract all the juice. Discard the juice.

Beat together all the ingredients except ½ cup of the nuts and all the parsley. When the mixture is well blended, form it into a log, wrap it in waxed paper, and refrigerate it for several hours or overnight. Just before serving, roll the log in the reserved nuts and parsley.

Serve with crackers or sliced French bread.

Mrs. Samuel Boxer
Tanglewood Council of the BSO

PICKLED SHRIMP

Serves 4 to 6 as a first course,
8 to 10 as an hors d'oeuvre

This delicate and original shrimp dish must be prepared at least two days before serving.

1¼ cups salad oil	*2 bay leaves*
¾ cup white vinegar	*1 medium-sized onion, sliced*
1½ teaspoons salt	*Tabasco*
2½ teaspoons celery salt	*1 pound shrimp, shelled and deveined*
2½ teaspoons capers	

Mix the first seven ingredients in a large glass container, and add Tabasco to taste. Add the shrimp and stir well. Cover tightly and refrigerate for 48 hours, stirring five or six times each day. Before serving, drain the shrimp thoroughly and pat them with paper towels to absorb any excess marinade. Serve very cold without additional sauce.

Mrs. Lewis P. Cabot
Junior Council of the BSO

SKÅNE SENAPSILL (Scania Mustard Herring)

Serves 8 as a first course,
12 to 15 as an hors d'oeuvre

This sauce is the same as that used for Swedish gravad lax.

8 large herring fillets in wine sauce	*4 tablespoons white vinegar*
½ cup brown mustard	*Coarsely ground black pepper*
8 teaspoons Dijon mustard	*1 cup salad oil*
3 tablespoons sugar	*Fresh or dried chopped dill*

Drain the fillets, cut them into 1-inch pieces, and set aside. Mix the mustards, sugar, vinegar, and pepper, and beat in the oil very slowly. Add dill to taste (the amount cannot be given, as dill differs in strength) and mix well.

Fold the fish into the sauce and refrigerate for at least 4 hours, or overnight. (The herring will keep for up to two weeks if refrigerated.)

Variation
Serve with steamed new potatoes for a light luncheon dish.

Marianne S. Lipsky
Tanglewood Council of the BSO

BSO MARATHON BOURBON HOT DOGS

Serves 16 to 20

1 pound frankfurters (preferably
  kosher)
¾ cup bourbon

1½ cups ketchup
½ cup brown sugar
1 tablespoon minced onion

Cut the frankfurters into ½-inch slices, and place them in a large frying pan. Stir in all the other ingredients, bring to a boil, and simmer for 1 hour. Serve in a chafing dish with toothpicks.

Mrs. Charles L. Odence
Council of the BSO

SMOKED SALMON PÂTÉ

Makes ¾ to 1 cup

This pâté keeps for several days in the refrigerator. Do not use a blender: it ruins the texture.

4 tablespoons butter, softened
1 tablespoon olive oil
¼ pound smoked salmon, bones
  removed (cheapest lox is fine)
¼ cup heavy cream

1 to 2 tablespoons lemon juice
Cayenne pepper
Capers (for garnish)
Lemon wedges (for garnish)

Beat the butter and the olive oil together until smooth. Gradually mix in the smoked salmon, and beat until the mixture becomes a smooth paste. Beat in the cream, the lemon juice, and cayenne to taste. Mix well and refrigerate until ready to serve — garnished, if desired, with capers and lemon wedges.

Thin fingers of lightly buttered whole-wheat or rye bread are traditional

with smoked salmon, but Melba toast or bland crackers also go very well
with this pâté.

Stephen R. Parks
Curator of the Osborne Collection
Beinecke Rare Book and Manuscript Library
Yale University

RIBBON PÂTÉ

Serves 25 to 30

Henry Portnoi, long-time principal double bass for the BSO, remained in
the bass section for several years after retiring from the first chair. Mrs.
Portnoi's pretty and delicious pâté takes time to make, but it's time well
spent.

2 tablespoons gelatin
1⅓ cups cold water
1 beef bouillon cube
1 pound cream cheese, softened
½ cup sour cream
1 tablespoon grated onion
2 4½-ounce cans deviled ham

¼ cup sweet relish
1 teaspoon prepared mustard
2 4½-ounce cans liver pâté
¼ cup mayonnaise
2 tablespoons chopped parsley
6 to 8 stuffed green olives, sliced

Lightly oil a 6-cup mold and set it aside in a pan of ice water. Soften the
gelatin in the cold water in a saucepan. Add the bouillon cube and stir over
low heat until both are dissolved. Combine the cream cheese, sour cream,
and onion, and stir in ⅓ cup of the hot gelatin mixture. Set aside at room
temperature.

Mix the deviled ham, relish, and mustard in a small bowl until well
blended, and stir in ⅓ cup of the remaining gelatin mixture. Set aside as
above.

Combine the liver pâté, mayonnaise, and parsley in another bowl, and
stir in ⅓ cup of the gelatin mixture. Set aside as above.

Stir an additional ⅓ cup of water into the remaining gelatin mixture to
make ⅔ cup, and pour it into the mold. When almost set, arrange the olive
slices decoratively in the aspic and chill it until firm.

Add layers (in this order: half the cheese mixture, all the liver mixture,
half the cheese mixture, all the ham mixture), chilling each until firm
before adding the next mixture. Keep the reserved mixtures at room temperature so they will not jell prematurely. Cover the mold with foil or
plastic wrap and refrigerate for several hours or overnight.

To serve, unmold onto a chilled serving plate and surround with Melba
toast, unsalted crackers, or bread.

Mrs. Henry S. Portnoi

BRANDIED CHICKEN LIVER PÂTÉ

Serves 8 to 10 as an hors d'oeuvre,
6 as a first course

½ pound chicken livers, picked over
and cut in half
½ pound mushrooms, thinly sliced
¼ pound butter
1 tablespoon gelatin

1 10-ounce can beef bouillon
1 teaspoon Worcestershire sauce
¼ cup brandy
Parsley sprigs (for garnish)

Sauté the chicken livers and mushrooms in the butter until they are lightly browned. Cool, chop, and set aside.

Meanwhile, soften the gelatin in the bouillon. Heat the bouillon until the gelatin dissolves, and remove from the heat. Add the liver-and-mushroom mixture; then add the Worcestershire sauce and brandy. Mix thoroughly and turn into a buttered shallow pan if the pâté is being used for hors d'oeuvres, or into small individual molds if it will be served as a first course. Refrigerate for at least 2 to 3 hours, or overnight.

Unmold the pâté and serve as follows: For hors d'oeuvres, cut the pâté into small squares and place on crackers or thinly sliced bread. For a first course, garnish the individual molds with parsley or other crisp curly greens.

Helene E. Strodel
Tanglewood Council of the BSO

GRANDFATHER ETTORE'S PÂTÉ

Serves 6 to 8 as a first course,
12 as an appetizer

This recipe from Melbourne, Australia, was the favorite appetizer of the late unlamented Benito Mussolini, who journeyed to Switzerland especially to enjoy it at Mrs. Darling's grandfather's inn.

½ cup unsalted butter
⅔ cup chopped shallots
1 7-ounce can tuna fish (preferably
Italian dark), drained

2 tablespoons sweet Marsala
⅛ teaspoon grated nutmeg
⅛ teaspoon freshly ground white
pepper (optional)

Melt the butter in a frying pan, add the shallots, and sauté slowly until they are soft but not browned. Add the tuna fish and stir for 1 minute. Spoon into a blender or food processor, add the Marsala and nutmeg, and blend until very smooth. Pack into a small crock and refrigerate at least overnight. Serve with crackers or toast.

Manuela Darling

CAPONATINA (Sicilian Eggplant Relish)

Serves 4 as a side dish,
8 as an appetizer

American soprano Benita Valente has been a frequent guest soloist with the Boston Symphony since her first appearances in 1969. Her contribution to this cookbook is especially welcome, for *caponatina* is a versatile dish that travels well to picnics and will keep for a week in the refrigerator.

1 large eggplant, diced but not peeled
Salt
1 cup diced celery
Olive oil
1 large onion, thinly sliced

½ cup Spanish olives, pitted and sliced
2 tablespoons capers
2 teaspoons sugar
½ cup red wine vinegar
1 cup tomato purée

Sprinkle the eggplant pieces generously with salt, and place them in a colander. Let stand for about an hour to drain. Rinse off the excess salt, and pat the pieces dry with paper towels. Meanwhile, blanch the celery for 10 minutes in unsalted water to cover and set it aside to cool.

Brown the eggplant in several tablespoons of olive oil in a deep heavy pan over medium heat, adding more oil as necessary. Remove the eggplant from the pan and lightly brown the onion. Return the eggplant to the pan with the celery and its liquid and all the remaining ingredients. Simmer for about 15 minutes, stirring occasionally. Serve hot as a side dish or cold as an appetizer or salad.

Benita Valente, soprano

MUSHROOMS À LA RUE GAMAGE

Serves 6

1 pound small mushrooms
1 medium-sized onion, sliced and
*   separated into rings*
2 tablespoons water
1 tablespoon sugar
1½ teaspoons salt

1 medium-sized clove of garlic, finely
*   chopped*
½ cup salad oil
⅔ cup tarragon vinegar
Freshly ground black pepper
Tabasco

Pick over the mushrooms and cut the larger ones into bite-size pieces.

Place the mushrooms and onions in a large bowl. Combine the remaining ingredients, using pepper and Tabasco to taste. Add to the mushrooms and onions, and stir. Chill, covered, for 8 hours or overnight, stirring several times.

Serve with toothpicks as an hors d'oeuvre, or as a relish at a buffet.

Mrs. Richard D. Hill, Overseer
Council of the BSO

MARINATED MUSHROOMS

Serves 6 to 8

1 pound button mushrooms, washed
 and dried
½ cup olive oil
½ teaspoon salt
½ teaspoon freshly ground black
 pepper

1 clove garlic, minced
1 teaspoon oregano
2 tablespoons lemon juice
1 tablespoon red wine vinegar
½ teaspoon sugar

Cut the mushroom stems off at the cap, and halve the larger mushrooms.

Combine all the remaining ingredients and pour over the mushrooms. Cover and marinate for at least 4 hours, or overnight, stirring occasionally. When ready to serve, pour off the marinade and pass the mushrooms with toothpicks.

Bonus
The marinade may be refrigerated for reuse.

Mrs. Robert E. Siegfried
Council of the BSO

MARVELOUS MUSHROOMS

Serves 12 or more

½ pound mushrooms, washed and
 dried
2 tablespoons butter
1 medium-sized onion, minced
1½ tablespoons lemon juice
1 teaspoon Worcestershire sauce
½ teaspoon salt

⅛ teaspoon freshly ground black
 pepper
2 tablespoons mayonnaise or sour
 cream
Parsley sprigs or other greens (for
 garnish)

Mince the mushrooms, and set them aside.

Melt the butter over medium heat and sauté the onion until it is transparent. Stir in the mushrooms; then add the lemon juice, Worcestershire sauce, salt, and pepper. Cook over medium heat for about 15 minutes, until the liquid evaporates, stirring occasionally. Cool, add the mayonnaise or sour cream, and chill.

Garnish with parsley or other decorative, curly greens. Serve with bland crackers or Melba toast.

Mrs. Donald G. Magill
Council of the BSO

THE BROTHERS' FISH CHOWDER

Serves 8

Chowder is always best when made a day ahead and reheated just before serving. The unconventional method in this recipe may well be the original one, when the fish came home with the fisherman. Approximately 3 pounds of skinned haddock fillets may be substituted for the whole fish, or a "fish rack" (the head, tail, and carcass from which the fillets have been removed) may be used with fillets. The fish rack is generally given away by fishmongers, which means that this very flavorful chowder can be made quite inexpensively.

1 whole 5-pound haddock or cod, with the fillets removed and skinned
1 to 2 quarts milk (see Note)
Sliced or diced potatoes (use an amount equal in bulk, not weight, to the fish)
1 pound salt pork, cut into ¼-inch dice

Sliced onions (use an amount equal to half the bulk of the fish)
Salt
Freshly ground black pepper
Powdered thyme (optional)
Butter (optional)
Common crackers or oyster crackers
Chopped chives (for garnish)

Place the fish bones, skin, and head in a large pot, and lay the fillets on top. Add enough milk almost to cover, and bring the liquid to a boil. Cover and simmer for about 15 minutes, or until the fish flakes. Remove the fillets and strain and reserve the milk. Set the fish aside to cool; then pick it over carefully, discarding the bones, skin, and head.

Meanwhile, cook the potatoes in a little boiling salted water until barely tender. Drain, and set aside. "Try out" (that is, render) the salt pork, drain the crisp scraps on paper towels, and set aside. Sauté the onions in 2 tablespoons of the pork fat and set aside.

To assemble: In a large stockpot, combine the fish, potatoes, onions, and fish milk. Season to taste with salt and pepper, and add a little powdered thyme. Add butter or pork fat to taste, and heat until just boiling. Pour in additional milk if the chowder seems too thick.

Serve with the pork scraps, crackers, and chives.

Note

A richer chowder may be obtained by substituting light cream for part of the milk, or by adding a large can of evaporated milk to the final mixture.

Variation: Layered Chowder

Using the proportions of ingredients given above, first simmer only the fish bones in 1 quart of milk. Meanwhile, try out the diced salt pork in the bottom of a large stockpot. Remove all but 2 tablespoons of fat from the pan, and drain and set aside the crisp pork scraps. Add, in layers, half the uncooked potatoes, half the fish fillets cut into several pieces, and half the onions. Dust with salt and pepper and repeat the process. Strain the simmering fish-bone milk over the layers until they are barely covered. Bring to a slow simmer over very low heat and cook, covered, until the onions are tender. Remove the chowder from the heat. Finish and serve as above.

Mrs. John A. Perkins
Council of the BSO

COLONNADE CLAM CHOWDER

Serves 4 to 6

36 medium-sized clams, about 3
   inches in diameter
4 cups water
3 tablespoons diced salt pork
½ cup diced onions
2 tablespoons flour
1½ cups diced potatoes

1 cup milk, scalded
1 cup light cream
1½ teaspoons salt
¼ teaspoon freshly ground white
   pepper
¼ teaspoon chopped fresh basil

Scrub the clams thoroughly and place them on a rack in a deep pot. Add the water, cover, and bring to a boil. Reduce the heat and simmer for 5 to 10 minutes, until the shells are all open. Remove the clams and set them aside to cool. Pour the broth slowly into another pot to filter out any sand that has settled at the bottom. Cover and keep hot.

Fry the salt pork in a large stockpot until crisp. Remove the pork scraps, add the onions to the rendered fat, and sauté them slowly until soft but not brown. Add the flour and stir the mixture for about 2 minutes. Carefully pour in the clam broth, stirring briskly. Discard any broth that appears to have a sandy residue. Bring the mixture to a boil and add the potatoes. Cover and simmer for 15 minutes, or until the potatoes are tender but not too soft.

Meanwhile, shuck the clams and cut out the soft centers. Remove and discard the necks, and rinse the bellies to remove any remaining sand. Add the clams, milk, cream, and seasonings to the broth. Stir well and heat thoroughly, but do not boil. Serve in heated bowls, with chowder crackers and the crisp pork scraps.

Variation

Substitute 1½ cups chopped fresh clams, or 1 cup canned clams, and 3 cups clam broth for the unshucked clams and their broth.

Zachary's at The Colonnade, Boston

OVEN CHOWDER ✓

Serves 6

This is a very sophisticated version of the old New England staple. Mrs. Bartlett says, "I learned to make it while living in Paris."

2 pounds haddock or cod (haddock is firmer)
2 cups peeled potatoes cut into ½-inch dice
¼ cup chopped celery leaves
3 bay leaves
2½ teaspoons salt
¼ teaspoon freshly ground white pepper
4 whole cloves
1 medium-sized clove of garlic, minced
½ cup melted butter
1 cup dry white wine or vermouth
2 cups boiling water
2 cups light cream
1½ teaspoons chopped fresh dill

Preheat the oven to 350°.

Place all the ingredients except the boiling water and cream in a large casserole. Pour the boiling water over all, cover, and bake for 50 to 60 minutes. The fish should flake but not be mushy, and the potatoes should be tender but firm.

Heat, but do not boil, the cream; add it to the fish mixture. Sprinkle the dill on top, and serve from the casserole with warm French bread.

Mrs. Charles W. Bartlett
Council of the BSO

NEW BRUNSWICK FISH SOUP ✓

Serves 8

A meal in a soup bowl, this recipe from a New Brunswick Friend is a delicious change from the ubiquitous New England chowder.

⅓ cup butter
1 cup thinly sliced onion
1 cup thinly sliced celery
1 clove garlic, minced or pressed
1 32-ounce bottle tomato-clam cocktail
1 cup clam broth
1 16-ounce can tomatoes, coarsely chopped, with juice
½ teaspoon dried thyme
1 large bay leaf, crushed
¼ teaspoon powdered saffron
1 pound haddock, cut into 2-inch pieces
1 pound cod, cut into 2-inch pieces
1 pound perch or flounder, cut into 2-inch pieces
1 pound scallops, carefully picked over
Salt
Freshly ground black pepper
Chopped parsley (for garnish)

Melt the butter in a large soup pot. Add the onion, celery, and garlic, and cook until the onion is transparent. Pour in the tomato-clam cocktail, clam broth, tomatoes, and herbs, and bring to a boil. When the vegetables are almost tender add the fish, reduce the heat, and simmer for 10 minutes. Add the scallops, cook until they are barely opaque, and remove the soup from the heat. Do not overcook the scallops. Season to taste with salt and pepper and set aside to cool; then refrigerate for 24 hours.

Reheat gently but thoroughly and serve immediately, garnished with chopped parsley.

Variation
To serve as a first course at a formal dinner, reduce the amount of fish by half.

Mrs. Carl G. Ericson
Tanglewood Council of the BSO

ABANDONED FARM MUSSEL STEW

Serves 25

Says Mrs. Myers, "We served this stew, at our daughter's request, for her prewedding luncheon."

10 quarts mussels (see Preparing
   Mussels◆)
3 cups dry white wine or vermouth
¾ pound unsalted butter
3 tablespoons dried thyme, ground

3 medium-sized cloves of garlic,
   minced
3 quarts whole milk, scalded
1 pint heavy cream
Freshly ground white pepper

Steam the mussels in 1 cup of the white wine. Drain and set aside to cool. Strain the broth through four layers of cheesecloth to remove all sand, and set it aside. There should be 2 cups of liquid: add more wine if necessary. Shuck the mussels, removing the "beards" when necessary.

Heat the butter until bubbling in a large soup pot over medium heat. Add the thyme and garlic, and simmer for 1 minute. Add the mussels and toss carefully with a wooden spoon to make sure they are well coated with the seasoned butter.

Pour in the hot milk, about 1 quart at a time, waiting for each addition to become very warm before adding more. Add the mussel broth, the remaining 2 cups of wine, and finally the cream. Heat thoroughly but do not boil, and add white pepper to taste. Remove from the heat and cool the stew uncovered; then refrigerate it for 24 hours. Reheat over low heat, but *never allow it to boil!* Serve very hot with French bread, sweet butter, and a garden salad or assorted crudités.

Julia Booth Myers

FAVORITE OYSTER STEW

Serves 8

3 to 4 cups shucked oysters, with their
   liquor
1 cup milk
3 cups light cream
¼ teaspoon freshly ground white
   pepper

¼ teaspoon Tabasco
1 teaspoon salt
8 tablespoons unsalted butter
Dry sherry
Oyster crackers

Drain the oysters, reserving the liquor. Heat the milk, cream, oyster liquor, and seasonings in a large saucepan until the mixture comes to a boil. Remove it from the heat. Heat the butter in a frying pan until bubbling, and toss in the oysters. Shake the pan vigorously until the oysters have plumped and are barely curled at the edges. *Do not overcook!*

    Combine the oysters with the simmering cream mixture and adjust the seasoning. Add sherry liberally to taste and serve immediately, in individual warmed bowls or from a large heated tureen, with plenty of warmed oyster crackers.

Valerie Horst

ARTHUR D. WESTON'S VINEYARD SCALLOP STEW

Serves 4

Prepare the scallops ahead of time, and this Martha's Vineyard specialty will be ready to eat in about 15 minutes.

1 quart milk, or 1 pint milk and 1
   pint half-and-half
1 tablespoon butter

1 pound Vineyard scallops, carefully
   picked over (see Note)
Salt
Freshly ground white pepper

Heat the milk in the top of a double boiler. Melt the butter in a frying pan, add the scallops, and sauté quickly until they are barely opaque. Add the scallops to the hot milk and continue to heat for about 5 minutes. *Do not overcook.* The scallops should be very tender. Season with salt and pepper to taste and add more butter if desired. Pour the stew into a heated tureen or individual bowls and serve immediately, with chowder crackers.

Note

Bay, Cape, or ocean scallops may be substituted, but ocean scallops must be cut to a uniform size.

J. V. Weston

CIOPPINO (Seafood Stew)

Serves 6

4 large cloves garlic, minced
1 small onion, chopped
2 tablespoons olive oil
2 cups tomato purée
1 tablespoon chopped fresh basil
1 teaspoon thyme
Salt
Freshly ground black pepper
2 cups dry white wine

1 pound white fish (cod, scrod, or
   haddock), cut into 6 pieces
2 pounds monkfish (lotte), cut into 12
   pieces
18 mussels (see Preparing Mussels♦)
12 cherrystone clams in the shell
12 "medium" shrimp, shelled and
   deveined
½ pound crab meat
Pernod

Sauté the garlic and onion in the olive oil until the onion is transparent. Add the tomato purée, herbs, and salt and pepper to taste. Cover, simmer for 15 to 20 minutes, and adjust the seasonings.

Pour the sauce into a large stockpot, and stir in the wine. Add the fish, and place the shellfish on top. Cover and poach over low heat until the fish is just tender. Remove the seafood to individual heated soup bowls, placing the shellfish on top. Add Pernod to taste to the cooking liquid, pour the sauce over the seafood, and serve immediately, with plenty of bread and butter.

St. Botolph Restaurant, Boston
John Harris, proprietor
David Joyce, chef

SOUPE DE POISSON MEDITERRANÉE (Mediterranean Fish Soup)

Serves 6

¼ cup olive oil
1 large onion, chopped
1 whole orange, seeded and chopped
   (in a blender or food processor)
3 medium-sized cloves of garlic,
   minced
1 leek, carefully cleaned and chopped
3 carrots, chopped
3 ribs celery, chopped
1 teaspoon saffron threads
1½ teaspoons thyme
1 bay leaf
1 1-pound can peeled Italian tomatoes
   with basil

1 large tomato, peeled and chopped
1 cup dry white wine
2 cups clam broth
2 pounds firm fish (a combination of
   bass, cod, snapper, and monkfish),
   cut into serving-size pieces
Salt
Freshly ground black pepper
1 cup dry sherry
2 teaspoons Pernod
¼ cup chopped parsley
6 each cooked mussels, clams, and/or
   shrimp (for garnish)

Heat 2 tablespoons of the olive oil in a large saucepan. Add the onion, orange, garlic, leek, carrots, celery, and saffron. Cook, stirring, until the vegetables are limp but not brown. Add the thyme, bay leaf, tomatoes, wine, and clam broth. Bring to a boil and simmer, uncovered, for 45 minutes. Bring to a high boil, add the fish, cover, and simmer for 20 minutes. Season to taste with salt and pepper. Stir in the remaining 2 tablespoons of olive oil and the sherry, Pernod, and parsley. Cool the soup; then refrigerate for 24 hours. Reheat gently, and serve in heated bowls, garnished with the cooked shellfish and accompanied by garlic bread.

Restaurant Le Bellecour
Lexington, Massachusetts
Frans and Mita van Beckhout, owners

Reduce, strain, and freeze any cooking liquid from fish, chicken, or vegetables for later use in stocks. Date and label clearly.

Use a little instant mashed potatoes to thicken soups that may become lumpy if flour is added.

SHELLFISH BISQUE

Serves 8

Mrs. Wright uses the meat from a 4- to 5-pound deep-sea lobster, but if one is not available lobster meat is a very acceptable substitute.

Sauce

1 tablespoon butter	½ cup dry vermouth
1 tablespoon flour	Salt
1 cup milk	Freshly ground white pepper
2 cups heavy cream	

Bisque

1 pound lobster meat	1 pint Cape scallops, carefully picked over
2 tablespoons butter	12 large shrimp, peeled and deveined

Make the sauce, which should be very thin. Season with salt and pepper to taste, and keep warm in the top of a large double boiler.

Cut the lobster meat into bite-size pieces and add them to the sauce. Heat the butter until foaming, sauté the scallops until they are opaque, and add them to the sauce. Chop the shrimp and stir them into the sauce. Turn up the heat to bring the water in the bottom of the double boiler to a boil, and cook the soup for about 5 minutes, until the shrimp is thoroughly heated. Adjust the seasonings, cool, and refrigerate until 1 hour before serving time. Reheat over boiling water, and serve from a heated tureen or in individual soup plates.

Variation: Shellfish Béchamel

Thicken the sauce with an additional 3 to 4 tablespoons of flour and 1 to 2 tablespoons of butter. Season with tarragon or fennel and serve in patty shells, on toast, or over steamed white rice.

Mrs. Whitney Wright
Council of the BSO

Freeze ribs of celery, the tops of leeks, outer leaves of cabbage or lettuce, as well as other vegetables, in a large bag for future use in the creation of stock.

RUSSIAN CABBAGE SOUP WITH BOILED BEEF

Serves 8

Pianist Gilbert Kalish has performed with the Boston Symphony Chamber Players, and he has been head of keyboard activities at the Berkshire Music Center for a number of years. He and his wife, Diana, here contribute their version of a splendid and substantial soup, a peasant repast for which black bread, sweet butter, ice-cold vodka, hot tea, and tinkling balalaika music will set a very Scythian stage. This soup should be made at least 24 hours ahead.

*1½ pounds beef flanken "cut into
   chunks" (see Note)
3 cups tomato juice
4 cups water
½ cup grated raw beets
1 teaspoon basil
1 teaspoon tarragon
2 teaspoons salt*

*¼ teaspoon freshly ground black
   pepper
1¼ pounds cabbage, shredded
2 ribs celery with leaves, chopped
½ cup chopped green pepper
2 medium-sized carrots, sliced
1 large apple, peeled and chopped
3 tablespoons lemon juice
¼ to ½ cup sugar*

Place the first eight ingredients in a large stockpot and bring to a boil. Reduce the heat, cover, and simmer for about 1½ hours, until the meat is almost tender. Add the remaining ingredients, except for half the lemon juice and all the sugar. Simmer until the meat is tender; remove the meat and set it aside. Continue to simmer the soup until the vegetables are tender, which should take 30 to 40 minutes total. Add the remaining lemon juice and sugar to taste. Set the soup aside, uncovered, to cool. Refrigerate it overnight.

The next day, skim off the fat and reheat the soup, including the meat.
Serve the soup as a separate course, followed by the meat with boiled
potatoes, or serve it all together as a meal in a bowl.

Note
According to the U.S. Meat Board, "flanken" is chuck short ribs, cut in
strips across the bones rather than between the ribs as with American short
ribs.

Gilbert Kalish, piano
Diana Kalish

EGGPLANT SOUP WITH BEEF

Serves 8

Philip K. Allen, BSO Trustee emeritus, long-time member and vice-
president of the Board of Trustees, music-lover and raconteur, shares with
his wife a reputation for warm hospitality. Her hearty and unusual soup is
a sample of her excellent cooking.

2 tablespoons butter
2 tablespoons olive oil
1 medium-sized onion, chopped
2 medium-sized cloves of garlic,
  minced
1 pound lean ground beef
1 medium-sized eggplant peeled and
  cut into 1-inch cubes
1 35-ounce can plum tomatoes
1 rib celery, chopped
1 small carrot, chopped

5 to 6 cups beef stock
1/2 teaspoon nutmeg
Salt
Freshly ground black pepper
1/2 cup small pasta shells (No. 23),
  uncooked
1/2 cup grated Swiss or Cheddar cheese
  (for garnish)
2 tablespoons chopped parsley (for
  garnish)

Heat the butter and olive oil in a large covered saucepan. Sauté the onion
and garlic until wilted, and add the beef. Cook and stir until the meat
separates and loses its color. Add the vegetables, stock, and seasonings;
cover and simmer for about 30 minutes.

Add the pasta shells, return to the boil, and cook for 10 minutes more,
adding more liquid if desired. Correct the seasonings and serve in preheated bowls, sprinkled with the cheese and parsley.

Mrs. Philip K. Allen
Council of the BSO

*Freeze the cooking liquid from corned beef, tongue, or ham for later use as a base
for pea or lentil soup.*

ESCAROLE-SAUSAGE SOUP

Serves 8 as a first course,
4 as lunch

1 cup diced onion
2 cloves garlic, minced
4 tablespoons butter
1 large head escarole, washed and
　sliced
4 cups chicken broth

3 medium-sized carrots, sliced
3 medium-sized potatoes, sliced
1 to 1½ pounds kielbasa (Polish
　sausage), cut diagonally into ¼-inch
　slices
Chopped parsley (for garnish)

Sauté the onion and garlic in the butter until golden. Stir in the escarole, and cook until wilted, about 2 minutes. Transfer these vegetables to a large covered saucepan, and add the chicken broth, carrots, and potatoes. Bring to a boil, cover, and simmer for about 10 minutes.

Meanwhile, add the sausage to the sauté pan and toss until browned. Pour off any excess fat and add the sausage to the soup. Simmer, uncovered, for 10 to 15 minutes, until the vegetables are tender but not mushy. Correct the seasonings and serve very hot, garnished with parsley.

Judith C. Bertozzi, co-chairman
Rhode Island Council of the BSO

FIORELLINO IN BRODO (Artichoke Soup)

Serves 6

Pulitzer Prize—winning American composer Donald Martino has been a faculty member at Tanglewood. He is one of the twelve composers who were commissioned by the Boston Symphony to commemorate its centennial in 1981. Of his composition for artichokes he says, "As far as I know, this is my own invention."

6 artichokes, stems removed and tops
　carefully trimmed
4 cups cold water
2 tablespoons lemon juice
1 to 2 tablespoons olive oil
2 medium-sized cloves of garlic,
　quartered

12 whole cloves
6 to 7 cups chicken stock, heated
1 teaspoon salt
⅛ teaspoon freshly ground white
　pepper
Parsley sprigs (for garnish)

Carefully spread apart the leaves of each artichoke and scrape out the choke with a small spoon. Place the artichokes in the cold water and lemon juice as you finish preparing them.

Cover the bottom of a large saucepan (it must later hold all the artichokes in a single layer) with a thin film of olive oil. Use no more than 2 tablespoons, so the soup will not be greasy. Sauté the garlic until golden;

then discard it. Drain the artichokes and arrange them in the pan, with two cloves in the center of each one. Cook over low heat until the artichokes are lightly browned on the bottom. Pour in the chicken stock to cover, add the salt and pepper, and bring to a boil. Reduce the heat, cover the pan, and simmer until the artichokes are tender, about 30 to 40 minutes.

Center the artichokes in individual soup bowls, and discard the cloves. Pour broth over each artichoke, carefully spreading the leaves to form a flower effect. Place a parsley sprig in the center of each artichoke, and serve immediately.

The artichokes are eaten with the fingers, and the broth with a spoon. Small plates should be provided for the discarded leaves, together with finger bowls of warm water and an extra napkin per person.

Donald Martino, composer

MULLIGATAWNY SOUP

Serves 4 to 6

A great way to glorify a little leftover chicken!

2 tablespoons cooking oil
½ cup diced onion
1 large carrot, diced
2 ribs celery, diced
1½ tablespoons flour (preferably presifted granular flour)
1 to 3 teaspoons curry powder
4 cups strong chicken stock
½ cup diced cooked chicken

¼ cup peeled and diced tart apples
½ cup boiled rice
½ teaspoon seasoned salt, or more to taste
Freshly ground black pepper
⅛ teaspoon dried thyme
½ cup all-purpose cream, at room temperature
Parsley sprigs (for garnish)

Heat the oil in a large frying pan over medium heat, and sauté the onion, carrot, and celery until limp but not brown. Add the flour and curry powder, and cook and stir for about 3 minutes. Slowly pour in the chicken stock, stirring rapidly. Simmer for 30 minutes.* Add the chicken, apples, rice, and seasonings, and cook for about 15 minutes more. Stir in the cream immediately before serving, and reheat but do not boil. Pour the soup into a heated tureen or individual bowls, and serve garnished with parsley sprigs.

*May be prepared ahead to this stage.

Mrs. Frank H. Healey, Jr.
Council of the BSO

Frozen chicken does not make good stock. Quickly boil up bones and trimmings and freeze the resulting stock, which may be seasoned as needed.

KATHLEEN'S CORN CHOWDER

Serves 4 as a main dish,
6 as a first course

Mrs. Cabot's quick and easy chowder develops its full flavor when made at least a day ahead.

2 cups peeled and diced potatoes
1 cup diced carrots
4 small onions, chopped
2 tablespoons butter
1 can cream-style corn
1 can cream of mushroom soup

2 cups milk
1 teaspoon salt
¼ teaspoon freshly ground black
  pepper
6 to 8 strips bacon, cooked and
  crumbled (for garnish)

Cook the potatoes and carrots in water to cover until almost tender. Sauté the onions in the butter until limp but not brown. Add the potatoes and carrots, including the cooking liquid, to the onions. Cover and simmer until the vegetables are tender.

  Combine all the ingredients except the bacon in a large saucepan over medium heat and heat thoroughly, stirring frequently. Correct the seasonings if necessary and serve in heated bowls with the crumbled bacon sprinkled on top.

Mary Louise Cabot, Overseer
Founding co-chairman, Council of the BSO

AGNÈS SOREL SOUP

Serves 4

Agnès Sorel, sometimes called Mlle. de Beauté, is said to have exercised a good influence over Charles VII of France during the six years she was his mistress, from 1444 until her death in 1450. The soup named for her is a frequent good influence on the membership of The Somerset Club, a stronghold of proper Bostonians.

6 tablespoons butter
1 medium-sized onion, diced
½ pound mushrooms, finely chopped
4 tablespoons flour
2 cups chicken stock
1 cup milk, scalded

1 cup heavy cream
Salt
Freshly ground black pepper
3 tablespoons slivered cooked chicken
3 tablespoons slivered cooked tongue

Heat the butter in a heavy saucepan, add the onion, and cook slowly until it is tender. Add the mushrooms, sauté gently for 3 minutes, and remove from the heat. Stir in the flour until it is completely absorbed. Pour in the stock and milk, and return to the heat, stirring until the soup.is smooth and slightly thickened. Cover and simmer for 20 minutes; then add the cream.

Season to taste with salt and pepper.* Stir in the chicken and tongue, heat thoroughly, and serve immediately.

*May be prepared ahead to this stage and refrigerated for later finishing.

The Somerset Club, Boston

CREAM OF BROCCOLI AND LEEK SOUP

Serves 8 to 10

This is a good basic recipe, which may be varied by substituting zucchini, asparagus, spinach, or other vegetables for the broccoli.

1½ pounds broccoli	*10 cups chicken stock or broth*
¾ pound leeks	*1 cup heavy cream*
½ cup butter	*Salt*
2 medium-sized potatoes, peeled and cubed	*Freshly ground black pepper*

Trim the leaves from the broccoli and peel the coarse stalks. Chop the stalks and flowerets separately. Discard the green part of the leeks and chop the white. Rinse in several waters to remove all sand.

Melt the butter in a large soup pot and sauté the leeks and broccoli stalks for about 3 minutes. Add the broccoli flowerets and sauté for 3 more minutes. Add the potatoes and chicken stock. Bring the liquid to a boil, cover, and simmer for 20 minutes, or until the vegetables are tender. Remove from the heat and cool.

Purée the mixture in a blender or in a food processor fitted with the steel blade. Return the mixture to the soup pot and place over medium heat. Stir in the cream and season to taste with salt and pepper. Heat the soup until it is almost boiling, stirring occasionally. Pour into a large heated tureen or into individual heated bowls.

Variation
Cool the soup and refrigerate overnight. Serve very cold, sprinkled with chopped chives and topped with a dollop of sour cream.

Mrs. Alan J. Weyl
Junior Council of the BSO

JERUSALEM ARTICHOKE SOUP

Serves 4 to 6

A leading baritone with most of the world's great opera companies, Donald McIntyre has performed with the Boston Symphony in *The Damnation of Faust* by Berlioz. His soup uses an old-fashioned vegetable that is once again coming into its own.

2 cups scrubbed and sliced Jerusalem
    artichokes
4 cups peeled and sliced potatoes
2 cups sliced leeks, white part only
2 cups sliced onions
3 tablespoons butter
1 cup chicken stock

1 egg yolk, beaten
2 cups milk
½ cup heavy cream
Salt
Freshly ground black pepper
2 tablespoons chopped chives or
    parsley (for garnish)

Stir the vegetables and the butter for a few minutes in a large saucepan over medium heat. Pour in the chicken stock, cover, and simmer for 15 to 20 minutes, or until the vegetables are tender. Remove from the heat and cool slightly. Purée the mixture in a blender or a food processor, and return it to the saucepan. Beat together the egg yolk, milk, cream, and seasonings, and stir into the soup. Heat well but do not boil. Adjust the seasonings if necessary, and serve in heated bowls, garnished with chives or parsley.

Donald McIntyre, baritone

INDIAN POINT MUSHROOM SOUP

Serves 4 to 6

2 cups chopped onions
4 tablespoons butter
¾ pound mushrooms, cleaned and
    sliced
½ teaspoon dill weed
1 tablespoon tamari (Japanese soy
    sauce)
1 tablespoon paprika

2 cups chicken stock
3 tablespoons flour
1 cup milk
2 teaspoons lemon juice
½ cup sour cream
1 teaspoon salt
Freshly ground black pepper
¼ cup chopped parsley (for garnish)

Sauté the onions in 2 tablespoons butter until transparent. Add the mushrooms, dill weed, tamari, paprika, and ½ cup stock. Stir, cover, and simmer for about 15 minutes over low heat. Melt the remaining butter in a large saucepan, whisk in the flour, and cook for a few minutes, stirring constantly. Add the milk and whisk until the mixture is thickened. Stir in the mushroom mixture and the remaining stock, and bring to a boil. Reduce the heat, cover, and simmer for 15 minutes more.*

Just before serving beat in the lemon juice, sour cream, salt, and pepper to taste. Pour the soup into a heated tureen or individual bowls and serve garnished with parsley.

*May be prepared ahead to this stage and refrigerated for later finishing.

Mrs. David Soule

TASTER'S CHOICE MUSHROOM SOUP

Serves 6 as a first course,
4 as luncheon

This unusual mushroom soup is perfect for a light summer luncheon, accompanied by a salad and crisp bread. It should be prepared at least a day ahead.

¼ cup butter
1½ pounds button mushrooms, stems
  removed
2 cans jellied beef consommé

2 tablespoons dry vermouth
3 tablespoons dry sherry
Freshly ground black pepper
½ cup heavy cream, whipped

Melt the butter in the top of a double boiler and add the mushrooms. Coat with the butter, cover, and steam over simmering water for 25 to 30 minutes, stirring occasionally. Remove from the heat and stir in the consommé, vermouth, and sherry. Add pepper to taste, pour into a glass serving bowl or individual soup cups, and refrigerate overnight. Garnish with dollops of whipped cream when ready to serve.

Variation

This soup may also be served very hot, adding the wines at the last minute. Serve in heated bowls, garnished as above.

Mrs. Overton Phillips

CREAM OF SQUASH SOUP

Serves 4

1 cup cooked winter squash (such as
  Hubbard or butternut)
1 cup chicken stock
1 teaspoon curry powder
1½ cups milk
Marjoram (optional)

Salt
Freshly ground white pepper
3 tablespoons sour cream (for garnish)
1 tablespoon chopped parsley (for
  garnish)
Croutons (for garnish)

Place the first four ingredients in a blender, and blend at high speed for 1 minute. Season with marjoram, salt, and white pepper to taste, and heat in a covered double boiler over boiling water.

Serve in heated soup cups, garnished with a dollop of sour cream, a sprinkling of parsley, and a few croutons.

Variation

Chill for several hours or overnight and serve as above, very cold.

Mrs. Charles P. Lyman, Overseer
Council of the BSO

ROMANIAN ONION SOUP

Serves 8

4 tablespoons butter
4 cups coarsely chopped onions
5 cups beef stock
1 potato, sliced
½ teaspoon celery seed
1 cup dry white wine
2 tablespoons cider vinegar

2 teaspoons sugar
¼ teaspoon freshly ground black
   pepper
1 cup all-purpose cream
2 tablespoons chopped parsley (for
   garnish)

Heat the butter in a large saucepan and sauté the onions over low heat until golden brown. Add the stock, potato, and celery seed, and bring to a boil. Cover and simmer over low heat for about 30 minutes. Remove from the heat and cool.

Purée the mixture in a blender or a food processor, or force it through a food mill. Return it to the saucepan and stir in the wine, vinegar, sugar, and pepper. Bring to a boil and simmer for about 10 minutes; then stir in the cream and reheat, but *do not boil*. Serve very hot, garnished with chopped parsley.

*Elizabeth H. Valentine
Council of the BSO*

CURRIED TOMATO SOUP

Serves 8

Do not boil this delicate and delicious soup after the final assembly — it will curdle. Curry powders vary in intensity, so start with the smaller amount.

1 large onion, finely chopped
4 tablespoons butter
1 32-ounce can Italian tomatoes
   (including juice), chopped
1 tablespoon flour
1 to 3 teaspoons curry powder

2 cups chicken stock
3 cups light cream
Salt
Freshly ground black pepper
Cayenne pepper (optional)

Sauté the onion in 2 tablespoons of butter in a large saucepan. Add the tomatoes and simmer over very low heat, stirring occasionally, for 1 hour. Cool slightly, strain through a fine sieve, and season to taste. Set aside until ready to serve.

Meanwhile, melt the remaining butter in another saucepan, add the flour, and stir until the roux is golden. Stir in 1 teaspoon curry powder and beat in the chicken stock and cream. Bring the mixture to a boil, stirring constantly. Remove from the heat, adjust the seasonings to taste, and set aside until serving time.

Reheat each mixture separately just to the boiling point. Pour together into a heated tureen or large bowl, stir to combine, and serve immediately in heated soup bowls or plates.

Mrs. Frank G. Allen, Overseer
Council of the BSO

CURRIED PEA SOUP

Serves 4 to 6

2 potatoes, peeled and chopped
1 10-ounce package frozen peas
2 scallions, chopped
1 tart apple, peeled, cored, and
   chopped
1 can condensed chicken broth
¾ soup can water

1 cup light cream
½ teaspoon curry powder
Salt
Freshly ground black pepper
Milk (if necessary)
Chopped parsley or chives (for
   garnish)

Simmer the potatoes, peas, scallions, and apple in the chicken broth and water, covered, for about 10 minutes, or until the potatoes are tender. Remove the mixture from the heat and let it cool.

Purée the mixture in a blender or a food processor. Peas need a lot of blending, so it may be necessary to strain the purée. Stir in the light cream and curry powder, and salt and pepper to taste. Thin with milk, if necessary. Reheat the soup, without letting it boil; serve garnished with chopped parsley or chives.

Variation
Chill the soup instead of reheating it, and serve cold. In this case you may need to add more curry.

Elizabeth H. Valentine
Council of the BSO

BLACK BEAN SOUP

Serves 8

1 pound black beans
¼ pound bacon, diced
2 cups finely chopped onions
1 tablespoon minced garlic
2 cups diced green peppers
8 cups water, including the
   bean-soaking water

1½ pounds smoked ham hocks
1 teaspoon dried oregano
½ teaspoon Tabasco
½ cup dry sherry
Lemon slices (for garnish)

Soak the beans in water to cover for 1 hour, or overnight if more convenient.

Cook the bacon in a large soup pot until most of the fat is extracted. Discard all but 2 tablespoons of the fat and sauté the onion, garlic, and green pepper until wilted. Add the beans and all the other ingredients except the sherry and lemon slices. Bring to a boil; then reduce the heat and simmer gently for 2 hours, stirring occasionally. Remove from the heat and cool slightly. Remove the ham hocks, dice the meat, and discard the bones. Set the meat aside. Skim any accumulated fat from the soup. Purée half the soup, to give the whole a thicker consistency. Combine the purée, diced meat, and sherry with the remaining soup, and adjust the seasonings.* Reheat and serve immediately, garnished with lemon slices.

*May be prepared ahead to this stage, and refrigerated or frozen.

The Old Mill
South Egremont, Massachusetts
Terry and Juliet Moore, proprietors

VEGETARIAN SPLIT PEA SOUP

Serves 8 to 10

Viola Aliferis, now living in California, was a member of the Old Guard at Symphony Hall, where for many years she presided over the office of general manager and executive director Thomas D. "Tod" Perry. This simple "hambone soup without the hambone" was a favorite of her father's.

2 cups diced onions
1 teaspoon sugar
3 tablespoons olive oil
2 cups dried green split peas
6 cups water (see Note)
3 tablespoons oregano

2 teaspoons salt
1/4 teaspoon freshly ground black
  pepper
Croutons (for garnish)
Chopped parsley or mint (for garnish)

Sprinkle the onions with the sugar, and fry them in the olive oil in a large soup pot until they are golden but not brown. Add the peas and the water, or other preferred liquid, and bring to a boil. Grind the oregano, salt, and pepper in a mortar and add to the soup. Cover and simmer for 3 to 4 hours, or until the peas are soft. Stir occasionally, and add more liquid if necessary. Whip with a whisk to make the soup creamy, and adjust the seasonings. Serve in individual heated bowls with croutons and chopped herbs.

Note

Tomato juice, V-8 juice, or any kind of vegetable stock may be substituted for part of the water.

Viola Aliferis
Retired BSO staff

SUPER-CHARGED SOUP

Serves 2 or 3

This is a potent warming potable for tailgate picnickers, winter sailors, or shivering skiers.

1 soup can milk
1 can condensed tomato soup
¼ cup freshly grated Parmesan cheese
2 tablespoons butter

1 tablespoon Worcestershire sauce
Freshly ground black pepper
2 tablespoons vodka
½ cup dry sherry

Scald the milk and beat in the soup and all the other ingredients except the vodka and sherry. Return the soup to a boil; then remove it from the heat. Add the liquors, pour into a preheated Thermos bottle — and enjoy!

Allie Blodgett
Council of the BSO

SENEGALESE SOUP

Serves 8 as a luncheon main course,
10 to 12 as a dinner first course

This traditional cold soup makes an excellent summer luncheon dish, with a salad and hot bread. Curry powder varies in strength, so start with the smaller amount, but bear in mind that chilling makes curry seem milder.

1 whole chicken breast, including skin
  and bones
6 cups rich chicken stock
6 medium-sized potatoes, peeled and
  quartered
6 medium-sized white onions,
  quartered
1 tablespoon butter
1 tart green apple, peeled and chopped

1 small yellow onion, chopped
2 large shallots, chopped
1 medium-sized clove of garlic,
  chopped
1½ to 2½ tablespoons curry powder
1 cup heavy cream
Salt
Freshly ground black pepper

Poach the chicken breast in chicken stock to cover for 15 to 20 minutes, or until tender. Remove and cool the chicken; then remove and discard the skin and bones. Dice the meat, wrap it, and refrigerate.

Strain the cooking liquid into a large saucepan. Add the potatoes, white onions, and additional stock to cover the vegetables. Bring to a boil, cover, and simmer for about 5 minutes: the vegetables will still be very crisp. Remove from the heat and set aside.

Meanwhile, heat the butter in a large soup pot and sauté the apple, yellow onion, shallots, and garlic until soft but not browned. Add 1½ tablespoons curry powder and cook for 1 to 2 minutes longer. Pour in the remaining chicken stock and the potato-and-onion mixture, and bring to a boil. Reduce the heat, cover, and simmer gently for about 45 minutes. Set aside, uncovered, until cool enough to handle. Purée in several batches, using a blender or food processor, and pour into a large bowl. Add the cream, adjust the seasonings, and chill for several hours or overnight. Serve in chilled bowls topped with the diced chicken.

Mrs. Richard Schanzle
Council of the BSO

GAZPACHO

Serves 8

One of summer's glories, a Tanglewood picnic, is made even more glorious by this traditional distillation of summer. Haskell Gordon is a member of the Board of Overseers of the Boston Symphony.

4 cups peeled and chopped ripe
  tomatoes
2 cups peeled, seeded, and chopped
  cucumber
1 cup diced green pepper
½ cup finely chopped sweet onion
1 18-ounce can tomato juice

1 slice white bread, crust removed
3 tablespoons wine vinegar
3 tablespoons olive oil
½ teaspoon salt
1 clove garlic
Freshly ground black pepper

Combine half the tomatoes, cucumber, green pepper, onion, and tomato juice in a glass or stainless steel bowl. Place all the remaining ingredients in a blender and blend until smooth. Combine the blended ingredients with the vegetables in the bowl, cover, and chill for 4 to 6 hours or overnight. Serve very cold in chilled bowls.

Mrs. Haskell R. Gordon

LUBO'S BORSCHT

Serves 10 to 12 as a first course,
6 to 8 as a main course

Boris Goldovsky's is a name to conjure with in opera circles: past director of the Opera Department at Tanglewood, he is also the founder of the Goldovsky Opera Company. "Lubo" was his mother, the violinist Lea Luboshutz, about whom he tells the following story: "David Oistrakh won the highest award when he was graduated from Moscow's famous Music Academy. Mother had won the same prize and had received a splendid violin as a prize, which she sent to Oistrakh with her congratulations. When he first toured the United States, he accepted no social engagements except for dinner with Mother, at which she served this borscht for his pleasure."

4 bunches beets, scrubbed and
   trimmed but unpeeled
4 pounds beef shin bone with meat
2 large potatoes, diced
1 large onion, diced
1 large cabbage, finely shredded

1 46-ounce can tomato juice
1 6-ounce can tomato paste
Sugar
Lemon juice
Sour cream (for garnish)

Boil the beets in water to cover until tender, about 45 minutes. Remove the beets, and strain and reserve the cooking water. When they are cool enough to handle, peel and slice the beets and set aside.

Meanwhile, place the beef bones in a large stockpot and add water almost to cover them. Add the potatoes, onion, and cabbage and enough of the tomato juice to cover. Bring to a boil, cover the pot, and simmer until the cabbage is tender and the meat is cooked, about 2 hours. Remove the meat from the soup and set it aside to cool.

Add the beets to the stock along with enough strained beet water to give the soup the desired consistency and color. Chill the soup overnight, or until the fat solidifies on the surface. Skim off the fat and return the soup to the stove. Bring it to a boil, and add the tomato paste, as well as sugar and lemon juice to taste. Cut the cooled meat into bite-size pieces and add them to the soup, with additional beet water and/or tomato juice if necessary. Serve hot with a dollop of sour cream in each bowl.

Boris Goldovsky
Founder, Goldovsky Opera Company

GRANDMA'S BORSCHT

Serves 6 to 8

Award-winning pianist Malcolm Frager, who is also fluent in seven languages, has been a frequent and welcome guest with the Boston Symphony. His grandmother's recipe results in a light and delicate soup that may be served hot instead of chilled. Despite the variations he offers, Mr. Frager confides, ''I like it best with sour cream and a few chopped green onions.''

2 pounds red beets, peeled and cut into
   julienne
3 quarts boiling water
Salt
Freshly ground black pepper
1½ tablespoons lemon juice

1 tablespoon sugar
1 cup sweet cream or sour cream, or 2
   beaten eggs
Chopped hard-boiled egg and/or
   chopped green onion (for garnish)

Pour the boiling water over the beets in a large saucepan, and bring to a boil. Add 1 teaspoon salt and a little pepper, reduce the heat, and simmer, covered, for about 30 minutes. When the beets are tender, drain and set them aside, reserving the cooking liquid. Add the lemon juice and sugar to the liquid and cool; then chill. Add the cream, sour cream, or beaten eggs, and serve garnished with chopped egg and/or chopped green onion.

Variation
Serve Grandma's Borscht hot with boiled potatoes.

Coda
"Instead of discarding the beets left over from the soup, chop them rather coarsely and add 1 medium-sized clove of garlic, pressed, 1 to 2 tablespoons lemon juice, and about ½ cup chopped nuts. A little sugar may be added if desired. This makes an excellent beet relish."

Malcolm Frager, piano

ORANGE BORSCHT

Serves 4 to 6

5 large beets, parboiled, peeled, and
   sliced
4 cups beef stock
1 cup tomato juice
½ teaspoon salt
¼ teaspoon freshly ground black
   pepper

¼ teaspoon thyme
1 cup freshly squeezed orange juice
Sour cream
Chopped fresh dill or chives (for
   garnish)

Place the beets and beef stock in a large pot and bring to a boil. Cover and simmer until the beets are tender. Remove the beets. Return the stock to the heat and add the tomato juice, salt, pepper, and thyme. Boil for about 5 minutes, remove from the heat, and cool. When completely cool, add the orange juice, mix well, and chill for several hours or overnight. Serve in chilled bowls with a dollop of sour cream and chopped fresh dill or chives.

Variation 1
This light clear soup may also be served hot. *Do not boil it* (the orange juice will turn bitter), but reheat carefully and serve as above.

Variation 2
The beets may be chopped or puréed and added for a thicker soup.

Teddie Preston
Council of the BSO

PINK SOUP

Serves 12 as a first course,
8 as lunch

Descended from a marvelous Polish recipe, this pretty soup goes happily to picnics ashore or afloat, particularly when accompanied by black bread and unsalted butter, an assortment of cheeses, and sliced Polish sausage.

1 quart strong borscht, strained
1 quart buttermilk
1 quart tomato juice
Salt
Freshly ground black pepper
Cayenne pepper
1½ cups grated, unpeeled,
* seeded cucumbers, with the juice*
* squeezed out*

1½ cups thinly sliced celery
¾ cup chopped green peppers
½ cup chopped scallions
¼ cup chopped parsley
Sour cream or Double Yogurt◆

Mix the liquids thoroughly, season to taste with salt, pepper, and cayenne, and refrigerate until ready to serve. Prepare the vegetables and parsley and store them separately in sealed containers in the refrigerator. Serve the soup in chilled bowls. Pass the vegetables, parsley, and sour cream or yogurt in separate dishes to be spooned into the soup according to individual taste.

Variation
For a hot soup, omit the vegetables but use the parsley. Heat the soup almost to the boiling point, but *do not boil*, as the buttermilk will curdle. Serve in heated bowls, garnished with sour cream and parsley.

Mrs. Thomas Gardiner, Overseer
Council of the BSO

COLD ZUCCHINI SOUP

Serves 6

1½ quarts chicken stock
½ cup chopped onion
2 tablespoons butter
4 cups seeded and sliced unpeeled
* zucchini*

1 teaspoon basil
1 cup yogurt or sour cream
Chopped parsley or chives (for
* garnish)*

Heat the chicken stock in a large saucepan. Sauté the onion in the butter until transparent; add it to the chicken stock. Add the zucchini and basil and simmer for 30 minutes. Remove from the heat and set aside until the mixture is cool enough to handle. Purée it in a blender or food processor and refrigerate until ready to serve.*

Add the yogurt or sour cream, mix well, and pour the soup into chilled bowls. Garnish with chopped parsley or snipped chives.

*May be frozen at this stage. Defrost overnight in the refrigerator.

Mary Jo Boyer
Tanglewood Council of the BSO

FISH AND SHELLFISH

From the beginning the Orchestra's founder, Major Higginson, intended to provide concerts of "a lighter kind of music," especially during the warm-weather days of late spring and early summer. The first such concerts, billed as "Music Hall Promenade Concerts," took place under the direction of Adolf Neuendorff in 1885. The combination of light music and light refreshments immediately attracted enthusiastic audiences. The concerts, christened "Popular" (shortened almost at once to "Pops"), quickly became a tradition. During the first forty-five years of the Pops, there had been seventeen conductors — often two or three sharing a single season. On May 7, 1930, Arthur Fiedler took over as Pops conductor; he remained in charge for half a century, vastly increasing the popularity and renown of the Pops concerts. After his death in 1979, a wide-ranging search for a successor ended when John Williams *(overleaf)*, a classically trained pianist and composer with vast experience in jazz and unparalleled popularity as a composer of film scores, was named nineteenth conductor of the Boston Pops in January 1980.

ORIENTAL FISH

Serves 4

The wife of famed concert impresario Aaron Richmond, Mrs. Richmond has sampled the cuisines of the world during their travels. This is her version of a dinner served to her by friends in Japan. Warm *sake* and/or cold Japanese beer, which is readily available in the United States, add to the Oriental aura of this unusual dish.

2 pounds whole sea bass (or other whole fish)

1 teaspoon salt

1 teaspoon monosodium glutamate (optional)

1 tablespoon tamari (Japanese soy sauce)

4 tablespoons peanut or corn oil

1 clove garlic, crushed

1 tablespoon chopped cooked ham or bacon

4 tablespoons Chinese pickles, shredded very fine

2 scallions, white part only, quartered and cut into 2-inch lengths

2 tablespoons sliced preserved ginger

Salt the fish inside and out and place on an oiled rack. Cover and steam over boiling water (see Note) for 20 minutes, or until the fish flakes from the bone. Remove the fish and place it on a heated serving platter. Sprinkle with the monosodium glutamate and tamari and set aside but keep hot.

In a small pan, heat the oil until almost smoking; add the garlic and remove the pan from the heat. Leave the garlic in the hot oil for about 1 minute. Strain the flavored oil over the fish and sprinkle with the remaining ingredients. Serve with boiled rice or Oriental noodles, stir-fried Chinese cabbage, and more tamari.

Note

Add the discarded green part of the scallions, ½ teaspoon ground ginger, and 1 tablespoon tamari to the steaming water.

Mrs. Aaron Richmond

BAKED BLUEFISH

Serves 6

2 pounds bluefish fillets, skinned
Salt
Freshly ground white pepper
½ pound fresh or frozen crab meat
2 cups sour cream

2 tablespoons milk
1½ teaspoons chopped fresh dill or
   fennel
Lemon wedges (for garnish)

Preheat the oven to 400°.

Place the fish in a buttered shallow oven-proof serving dish and season with salt and pepper to taste. Spread the crab meat over the fish. Mix the sour cream, milk, and dill or fennel, and carefully spoon the mixture over the crab meat. Cover and bake for 15 minutes; then reduce the heat to 350°. Cook for 15 to 25 minutes longer, until the fish flakes when tested with a fork. Brown the top lightly under the broiler (if necessary), and serve immediately with lemon wedges.

Mrs. Thomas E. Jansen, Jr.
Council of the BSO

BLUEFISH GREAT POINT

Serves 2

1 fresh bluefish fillet, about 1 pound
1 to 2 tablespoons lemon juice
1 cup sour cream

Dill (fresh or dried)
8 to 10 tablespoons fine bread crumbs
Chopped parsley or chives (for
   garnish)

Marinate the fish in the lemon juice for about 1 hour before cooking.

Preheat the oven to 500°.

Place the fish in an unbuttered oven-proof dish or heavy frying pan, skin side down: the skin will stick to the bottom of the pan. Spread the sour cream thickly and evenly over the fillet. Sprinkle a delicate amount of dill over the sour cream and top with a light dusting of bread crumbs. Bake until the fish flakes when tested with a fork, 10 to 15 minutes. Serve immediately, sprinkled with chopped parsley or chives.

Mrs. George H. Simonds
Council of the BSO

CODFISH BALLS √

Serves 12 for hors d'oeuvres,
6 for a main dish

Codfish balls and Boston baked beans were made for each other, but that does not mean they must always be served together. These fish balls make excellent hors d'oeuvres, and they are also perfect for a leisurely Sunday breakfast.

½ *pound salt codfish*
Potatoes, unpeeled but thoroughly
  scrubbed (see instructions)
Oil for deep-frying, enough for about
  3 inches in a deep-sided pan
1 tablespoon butter
2 eggs, beaten

⅛ *teaspoon freshly ground black*
  pepper
¼ *teaspoon ground ginger*
2 tablespoons chopped chives or green
  onion (optional)
Cayenne pepper

Soak the codfish in cold water for about half an hour; then drain and rinse. Cover with cold water, and simmer, covered, until the fish flakes. Remove from the heat, drain thoroughly, and set aside to cool.

Meanwhile, boil the potatoes in their jackets. When they are cooked, peel and mash them: there should be three to four times more mashed potatoes than flaked fish. Set aside to cool, but do not refrigerate.

When ready to cook the fish balls, heat the oil to 375°. Beat together the fish, potatoes, butter, and eggs. Add the pepper, ginger, chives, and cayenne to taste, and beat until the mixture is light and fluffy. Drop it by teaspoonfuls into the hot fat, cooking only a few at a time. Keep the fat hot and work fast. When the fish balls are browned, remove them and drain on paper towels. When all are done, serve immediately.

To serve as hors d'oeuvres, pass with toothpicks and tomato and mustard dipping sauces.

To serve as a main dish, pass tomato sauce (see Tomato Coulis♦) in a separate sauceboat.

Note
Although they are never quite as good as when freshly fried, fish balls may be carefully sealed and frozen. Reheat on a cookie sheet in a hot (400°) oven for 3 to 5 minutes, depending on the size. *Do not overcook.*

The Cookbook Committee

HADDOCK SMETANA ✓

Serves 6

2 pounds thick haddock fillets, skinned
Salt
Freshly ground white pepper
3 tablespoons chopped scallions or
  minced onions

2 cups sour cream
Paprika
½ *cup capers with a small amount of*
  their vinegar

Preheat the oven to 350°.

Place the fish, skinned side down, in a buttered oven-proof serving dish, and season with salt and pepper. Mix the scallions and the sour cream and pour over the fish, covering it completely. Dust with paprika and bake for about 30 minutes, or until the fish flakes when tested with a fork. Remove from the oven and sprinkle with the capers and a little of the vinegar they were bottled in. Serve immediately, with a bright green seasonal vegetable.

Variation
Halibut steaks, 1 inch thick, or any other firm white fish may be substituted for the haddock.

Bonus
This sauce may be used on stronger-tasting fish, such as bass or bluefish.

Mrs. Thomas S. Morse
Tanglewood Council of the BSO

HADDOCK PRESTO

Serves 4

Helen Perry, the wife of Thomas D. Perry, Jr., former executive director of the Boston Symphony and now a Trustee, presides over large and small gatherings at their magnificent eyrie in the Berkshires with apparent ease and the grace of long experience. This quick fish dish was a favorite of the late Charles Munch, BSO music director from 1949 to 1962.

1 tablespoon bacon fat
1½ pounds haddock fillets, or other white fish, cut into serving-size pieces
1 tablespoon chopped onion
1 teaspoon celery seed
Salt
Paprika
½ cup sour cream
1½ tablespoons lemon juice

Heat the bacon fat in a large frying pan. Add the fish and sprinkle with the onion, celery seed, and salt and paprika to taste. Cover and cook over medium heat for 10 to 15 minutes, or until the fish flakes. Remove the cover and set the pan aside. Mix the sour cream and lemon juice and pour it over the fish. Place over low heat, uncovered, until the cream is hot. *Do not boil.* Serve immediately.

Mrs. Thomas D. Perry, Jr.

MEDITERRANEAN-STYLE BROILED MACKEREL

Serves 4

Violinist Amnon Levy was born in Tel Aviv, where Jascha Heifetz recommended that he come to study in the United States. He has performed as solo artist with the Boston Pops on the Esplanade, and with many orchestras in this country and Mexico.

4 small whole mackerel or 8 fillets (1½
to 2 pounds altogether)
⅓ cup olive oil
2 tablespoons lemon juice
⅛ teaspoon oregano
3 small cloves garlic, minced

½ teaspoon salt
Freshly ground black pepper
4 tablespoons chopped parsley (for
garnish)
Lemon wedges (for garnish)

Preheat the broiler.

Arrange the fish in an oiled broiler pan: the fillets should be skin side up. Mix all the remaining ingredients except the pepper, parsley, and lemon, and pour over the fish. Broil fillets for 6 minutes, whole fish for 10, basting once or twice. Turn and continue cooking and basting until the fish flakes when tested with a fork.

Remove the cooked fish to a heated platter and pour the pan juices over all. Sprinkle with pepper to taste and garnish with parsley and lemon wedges. Serve immediately.

Amnon Levy, violin

MAQUEREAU A L'ESPAGNOL
(Spanish-style Mackerel)

Serves 2

Vera Ozawa, the beautiful wife of BSO music director Seiji Ozawa, lives most of the year in Japan with their two children. Summers, however, see the whole family at Tanglewood. Mrs. Ozawa's international taste in food is exemplified by her quick, pretty, and delectable recipe for an often overlooked fish. If the fish is sautéed while the sauce is cooking, this dish will be on the table in about 15 minutes.

1 large or 2 small mackerel fillets (1 to
1¼ pounds)
Salt

Freshly ground black pepper
2 tablespoons olive oil
½ cup dry white wine

Sauce
1 tablespoon olive oil
2 cloves garlic, chopped
1 small onion, chopped

1 rib celery, chopped
3 small tomatoes, peeled and chopped

Season the fish lightly with salt and pepper and sauté it, skin side up, in the olive oil for 2 to 3 minutes. Turn the fish over and pour in the wine.

Simmer for 2 to 3 minutes more, until the fish flakes. Set aside and keep hot until the sauce is ready.

To make the sauce: Heat the olive oil and add the remaining ingredients. Stir over medium heat for about 10 minutes, until the vegetables are tender, and season with salt and pepper to taste. Pour the sauce over the fish and heat through. Serve on individual heated plates with steamed rice lightly flavored with saffron.

Vera Ozawa

SALMON MOUSSE

Serves 8

1 tablespoon gelatin	1 teaspoon salt
¼ cup cold water	2 cups cooked salmon, carefully picked
½ cup boiling water	over for bones
½ cup mayonnaise	1½ tablespoons chopped capers
1½ tablespoons lemon juice	½ cup heavy cream, whipped
1 tablespoon minced chives or grated	1 pound large-curd cottage cheese
onion	Cucumber sauce (optional)
½ teaspoon Tabasco	Lemon slices or wedges (for garnish)

Soften the gelatin in the cold water and dissolve in the boiling water. Cool it, then add the mayonnaise, lemon juice, chives, Tabasco, and salt. Chill until the edges begin to set, stir, and fold in the salmon and capers. Mix well and fold in the whipped cream. Turn into an oiled 8-cup ring mold and fill the ring with cottage cheese. Cover with plastic wrap and refrigerate for several hours or overnight. Unmold on a bed of greens, and fill the center with cucumber sauce, dressed greens, guacamole, or another filling. Garnish with lemon.

Variation

To serve as a first course, fill individual molds with the salmon mixture, without the added cottage cheese, and serve on individual plates, garnished as preferred.

Mayonnaise or a dill-flavored dressing may be substituted for the cucumber sauce.

Mrs. Elting E. Morison, Overseer

Boston Scrod: *Legend has it that scrod, or "schrod" as it is sometimes spelled, was a fillet cut from a small cod. Practically, the term has evolved to cover fairly thick fillets of any firm white fish, generally cod or haddock, prepared very simply. Dust the fillets with a little salt, pepper, and paprika, and dot them with butter. Broil without turning until the fish flakes and is slightly browned. Baste with the pan juices, and serve with tartar sauce and/or lemon wedges. Other recipes follow.*

 ## BAKED SCROD ✓✓

Serves 4

Barbara Lee is the daughter of violinist Pierre Mayer, who played with the Orchestra for many years under the batons of Serge Koussevitzky and Charles Munch.

½ cup butter
1 tablespoon minced onion
2 tablespoons lemon juice
1 teaspoon salt
¼ teaspoon freshly ground black
    pepper

4 pieces thick scrod for baking, each 3
    to 4 inches wide and weighing 6 to
    8 ounces
Seasoned bread crumbs

Preheat the oven to 350°.

Heat the butter in a small saucepan and sauté the onion for about 5 minutes. Remove from the heat; add the lemon juice, salt, and pepper.

Roll the fish in the bread crumbs and place in a buttered baking dish. Pour the lemon butter over the scrod and bake for 35 to 40 minutes, until the fish flakes when tested with a fork. Serve immediately.

Barbara M. Lee

PARTY SCROD

Serves 2 or 3

This is a low-calorie way to prepare a Boston staple.

1 pound fillet of scrod, or other firm
    white fish
1 large tomato, peeled and sliced
Butter
Salt
Freshly ground black pepper

½ cup dry white wine
1 to 2 tablespoons grated Parmesan
    cheese
Sprigs of parsley and/or basil (for
    garnish)

Preheat the oven to 325°.

Place the fish in a buttered shallow pan. Cover with the tomato slices, dot with butter, and season with salt and pepper. Pour the white wine over all and top with cheese to taste. Bake for 15 to 20 minutes, or until the fish flakes when tested with a fork. Serve immediately garnished with sprigs of parsley and/or basil.

Mrs. William F. Wiseman
Junior Council of the BSO

Frozen Fish: *Thaw frozen fish in milk — it removes the ''freezer'' taste.*

Smelts: *Smelts are easy and quick to prepare, and they taste delicious. Remove the heads and the innards, leaving the tail intact. Rub lemon juice and salt into the body cavities, and sauté the fish in a little butter for 2 to 3 minutes per side. When the fish flakes, remove to a heated platter and serve immediately with tartar sauce or lemon wedges. The backbone lifts out completely, along with the bones, which are so small they can be eaten with impunity.*

SOGLIOLA SEMPLICE (Simple Sole)

Serves 2

4 small sole fillets	Salt
4 tablespoons olive oil	Freshly ground black pepper
1 clove garlic, minced	¼ cup dry vermouth
2 shallots, chopped	Lemon juice
4 scallions, chopped	Parsley sprigs and lemon wedges (for
3 or 4 mushrooms, sliced	garnish)

Trim the fillets, pat dry, and set aside.

Sauté the vegetables lightly in the olive oil until limp. Add the fish and sauté quickly until lightly browned on both sides. Place the fish on a heated platter, season with salt and pepper, and set in a warm oven.

Add the vermouth to the vegetables in the pan and cook down until most of the liquid has evaporated, adding lemon juice to taste. Pour the sauce over the fish. Garnish with parsley sprigs and lemon wedges, and serve immediately.

Ciro & Sal's Restaurant, Boston and Provincetown
Ciriaco G. Cozzi, proprietor

SOLE MOUSSELINE WITH DILL SAUCE

Serves 4

1 pound fresh sole fillets	1 teaspoon salt
1 egg	½ teaspoon freshly ground white
1 egg white	pepper
4 tablespoons unsalted butter, softened	1 tablespoon snipped fresh dill
2¼ cups heavy cream	1 lemon cut into four wedges

Dill Sauce

3 tablespoons butter	½ cup light cream
3 tablespoons flour	Salt
1½ cups strong fish stock, heated	Freshly ground white pepper
2 tablespoons snipped fresh dill	

Trim the sole and cut it into 1-inch pieces. Purée the fish in a food processor, and force the purée through a food mill or a coarse sieve. Beat the egg and egg white together until just mixed, and add to the purée. Mix well. Cube the butter and add it in small amounts to the sole mixture, blending well after each addition. Very slowly stir in the heavy cream and add the salt, pepper, and dill. Refrigerate the mixture for 2 hours.

Start the sauce, using the butter, flour, and fish stock. Simmer it over low heat for 30 minutes and set aside.

About 1 hour before serving preheat the oven to 375°.

Spoon the chilled sole mixture into eight well-buttered small custard cups, filling them two-thirds full. Pat down firmly, and set the cups in an oven-proof pan containing ½ inch of boiling water. Bake for 30 to 35 minutes, until a knife inserted in the center of a cup comes out clean.

Meanwhile, reheat the sauce, adding the dill, cream, and salt and pepper to taste. Set aside and keep hot.

Invert the custard cups and unmold onto a warmed serving platter. Top with the sauce, garnish with fresh dill and the lemon wedges, and serve immediately.

Piaf's Bistro, Boston
Richard L. Pilla, proprietor

FILLET OF SOLE CLAUDIO ARRAU

Serves 4

World-famous pianist Claudio Arrau has been a welcome guest with the BSO since his first Symphony Hall appearance in 1924. He has also recorded the Grieg, Schumann, and Tchaikovsky concertos with the Boston Symphony and principal guest conductor Sir Colin Davis. The dish that bears his name was originally made for him by the chef at the Savoy in London, and is, as he says, "just right after a concert, substantial but not too heavy."

6 tablespoons butter	Freshly ground white pepper
1 large leek, halved lengthwise, washed and dried, cut in very thin slices	Sprig of fresh thyme
	4 thick sole fillets (6 to 8 ounces each), trimmed
2 carrots, thinly sliced	Chopped fresh dill
8 large mushrooms, thinly sliced	½ cup sweet sherry
Salt	1 cup cream

Heat the butter until foamy in a large deep frying pan that can later be covered. Sauté the leek slices for 2 to 3 minutes. Add the carrots and sauté for 5 minutes. Stir in the mushrooms, adding more butter if necessary; season to taste, and add the thyme. Sprinkle the fish with salt and pepper and roll up each fillet, skin side out; secure with toothpicks and arrange in the frying pan on top of the vegetables. If the rolls are placed close together, toothpicks may not be necessary. Sprinkle lightly with dill. Cover and simmer for 20 minutes.* Add the sherry and simmer for 5 minutes more. Pour in the cream, bring the liquid to a boil, and serve immediately in large soup plates.

Serve with boiled peeled new potatoes, and/or slices of garlic bread.

*May be prepared ahead to this point. Reheat before proceeding as above.

Claudio Arrau, piano

FILLET OF SOLE COLBERT

Serves 2

4 4-ounce white sole fillets
1 cup milk, scalded and cooled
1 teaspoon tarragon
1/4 teaspoon basil
1/4 teaspoon chervil
Salt

Freshly ground white pepper
1 cup fresh bread crumbs
2 eggs, beaten
1/4 cup olive oil
Lemon wedges and parsley sprigs (for garnish)

Maître d'Hôtel Butter
4 tablespoons butter, softened
2 teaspoons chopped parsley
2 teaspoons lemon juice
Tabasco

Worcestershire sauce
Salt
Freshly ground white pepper

Soak the fish in the cooled milk for at least 4 hours.

Meanwhile, make the maître d'hôtel butter: Beat the butter, parsley, and lemon juice together until well blended, and add the seasonings to taste. Form into four balls and refrigerate.

Combine the herbs, salt, and pepper with the bread crumbs in a shallow dish. Discard the milk and pat the fish dry. Dip the fish in the beaten eggs, coat it with the bread crumbs, and sauté it in the olive oil until lightly browned. Remove the fillets to a warm serving dish and top with maître d'hôtel butter. Garnish with lemon wedges and sprigs of parsley. Serve immediately.

The Country Club
Brookline, Massachusetts

MARYLAND-STYLE CRAB IMPERIAL

Serves 4

Wally Hill, BSO director of business affairs, was a member of the Cookbook Committee: he participated fully in all decisions, as well as guarding the finances. Fortunately, he also loves to cook.

*1 pound crab meat (back fin for
  authenticity)*
2 tablespoons butter
1 small onion, minced
*1 small rib celery, without leaves,
  chopped*
*4 medium-sized mushrooms, thinly
  sliced*

½ teaspoon salt
1 teaspoon English dry mustard
3 tablespoons mayonnaise
1 teaspoon chopped pimiento
1 teaspoon chopped parsley
Paprika

Preheat the oven to 350°.

Carefully pick over the crab meat, removing all traces of shell, and set aside.

In a small frying pan, heat the butter until foaming and sauté the vegetables until limp but not brown. Remove from the heat, add the salt, and cool slightly.

Mix the mustard with 2 tablespoons of the mayonnaise and add to the vegetable mixture. Fold in the crab meat, pimiento, and parsley. Taste, and adjust the seasonings if necessary. Spoon into lightly greased scallop shells or ramekins, top with a dab of the remaining mayonnaise, and dust with paprika.

Bake for 15 minutes, or until slightly browned and heated through. Serve immediately.

Walter D. Hill
BSO Director of Business Affairs

KING CRAB DORÉ WITH HOLLANDAISE SAUCE

Serves 6

Soprano Elizabeth Knighton performed with the Boston Symphony during the 1979–80 season, in Gluck's *Orfeo ed Euridice*. "This dish is served at my restaurant, The Blue Diamond, in San Francisco, skillfully prepared by our chef, Martin Hester," she says. Any hollandaise sauce can be used in this recipe, but Flornie's Blender Hollandaise Sauce◆ is an especially easy one to make.

*2 pounds cooked king crab meat, in
  large chunks*
1 cup flour
1 teaspoon salt
*½ teaspoon freshly ground white
  pepper*

3 eggs, lightly beaten
4 tablespoons butter
2 cups hollandaise sauce
*Lemon slices and parsley sprigs (for
  garnish)*

Dip the crab meat in the flour (which has been seasoned with the salt and pepper) and then into the eggs. Sauté in the butter until lightly browned, turning occasionally. Remove with a slotted spoon to a heated platter, draining off any excess butter.

Mound the crab on individual heated plates, mask with the hollandaise sauce, and garnish with lemon slices and parsley. Asparagus is a natural symbiote!

Elizabeth Knighton, soprano

TOMATO CRABBIT

Serves 4 to 6

½ pound grated or sliced Cheddar cheese
1 can tomato soup
2 eggs, beaten
1 cup light cream

½ pound crab meat, carefully picked over
1 ounce pimientos, sliced
Patty shells or toast points

In the top of a double boiler, melt the cheese in the tomato soup. Beat the eggs and cream together and add to the cheese mixture. Stir over simmering water until hot and thick. Gently stir in the crab and pimientos and heat thoroughly. Serve in patty shells or on toast points.

Priscilla Lingham
Council of the BSO

VIRGINIA BELT'S CRAB SUPREME

Serves 12 as a first course,
8 as a main dish

Born in Havana, Tchaikovsky Competition–winning pianist Horacio Gutierrez has performed the music of Prokofiev, Rachmaninoff, and Tchaikovsky with the Boston Symphony. His much-traveled crab dish is easy to prepare ahead. He says, "Once we even brought it from New York and had it for lunch in Los Angeles."

12 thin slices white bread, crust removed
1 pound crab meat, native or Alaskan king crab, cut into bite-size pieces
1 cup mayonnaise
1 cup minced onion

4 eggs
3¼ cups milk
Salt
Freshly ground black pepper
1 can cream of mushroom soup
2 cups grated mild Cheddar cheese

Cube five of the bread slices and place the cubes evenly in a buttered, deep 13-by-9-inch baking dish. Combine the crab, mayonnaise, and onions, and distribute over the cubed bread. Arrange the remaining slices of bread on top of the crab mixture. Beat the eggs with 3 cups of the milk until foamy, add salt and pepper to taste, and pour the mixture over the bread. Mix the remaining milk with the mushroom soup and pour over all. Set in the refrigerator for at least 1 hour, or overnight.

Preheat the oven to 350°.

Bake the "supreme" for 1 to 1¼ hours, or until it is lightly puffed and the center is almost set. Cover with the cheese and bake for 10 to 15 minutes more, or until the cheese is melted and lightly browned. Allow the dish to stand at room temperature for about 10 minutes before serving.

Horacio Gutierrez, piano

HOMARD AU GRATIN, NANTUA

Serves 3 or 4

Samuel Chamberlain was largely responsible for introducing Americans to the joys of French cuisine produced in their own kitchens. The following recipes do not appear in his *Bouquet de France*, but they do appear frequently on Mrs. Chamberlain's epicurean table.

3 1-pound lobsters, boiled for 12
   minutes and slightly cooled
5 tablespoons butter
½ cup sliced mushrooms
½ cup water
1 teaspoon lemon juice
Salt

½ cup dry white wine
1 truffle, sliced (optional)
1½ tablespoons flour
1 cup heavy cream
2 tablespoons Lobster Butter♦
½ cup grated Gruyère cheese

Remove the tails and claws from the lobsters, and sauté them, shells and all, in 4 tablespoons of the butter for several minutes, turning frequently.

Meanwhile, combine the mushrooms, water, lemon juice, and salt to taste in a small saucepan. Cover and steam over low heat for 5 minutes. Drain and set the mushrooms aside, reserving the liquid. Add the wine and mushroom liquid to the lobsters, cover, and cook over medium heat for 5 minutes. Remove and set aside the lobster, and reduce the liquid to ¾ cup.

When the lobsters are cool, remove the meat from the shells and cut it into bite-size pieces. Arrange in a buttered shallow oven-proof dish, and top with the mushrooms and truffle. Blend the remaining tablespoon of butter with the flour over low heat, and gradually beat in the lobster liquid, cream, and Lobster Butter. Simmer for 2 to 3 minutes, until the sauce is thick and smooth. Spoon the sauce over the lobster and mushrooms, sprinkle with the cheese, and brown delicately under the broiler. Serve with steamed rice and a bright green vegetable.

Narcissa G. Chamberlain

LOBSTER BUTTER

Makes approximately ½ cup

The frugal lobster cook will always have this delicately flavored butter in the freezer to use with any fish or shellfish.

Shells from a small boiled lobster
¼ pound butter (or more)

2 tablespoons cold water
Boiling water

Preheat the oven to 250°.

Place the lobster shells on a cookie sheet and dry them in the oven for a short time, or until somewhat brittle. Pound the shells in a mortar until pulverized. Place them in the top of a double boiler with the butter and cold water. Heat gently over simmering water and let steep without boiling for about 15 minutes.

Place a fine strainer over a small bowl and put the lobster mixture in the strainer, letting the liquid drip into the bowl. Pour a little boiling water over the shells remaining in the strainer to wash all the butter into the bowl. Place the bowl in the refrigerator until the butter hardens on the surface. Skim off the lobster butter and store it in a small jar in the refrigerator. Use it promptly or freeze it for future use.

Narcissa G. Chamberlain

HELEN BURKE'S NOVA SCOTIAN LOBSTER

Serves 2 to 4

Asparagus is a perfect accompaniment for this rich and delicate dish.

¼ to ½ pound butter
2 cups cooked lobster meat cut in
  medium-sized pieces
1 tablespoon flour

1½ cups coffee cream, or half-and-half
Salt
Freshly ground black pepper
Lemon juice

Heat ¼ pound of butter in a large, heavy frying pan. Add the lobster meat and toss over high heat until the redness is out, about 7 to 10 minutes. Add more butter as needed.

Sprinkle the flour over the lobster and mix well. Slowly stir in the cream, and cook for several minutes. Season to taste with salt, pepper, and lemon juice. Serve in patty shells or over toast points, mashed potatoes, or steamed rice. The finished sauce should be light, rich, and smooth — and not too thick.

Mary P. Hayes
Junior Council of the BSO

LOBSTER MOUSSE

Serves 12

3 tablespoons gelatin
½ cup cold water
3 cups chicken stock, heated
1 cup mayonnaise
4 tablespoons lemon juice
2 tablespoons grated onion
1 teaspoon paprika

Tabasco
¾ cup heavy cream, whipped
4 cups chopped cooked lobster meat
½ cup minced celery
¼ cup drained capers
Salad greens and cherry tomatoes (for
garnish)

Soften the gelatin in the cold water in a large bowl. Pour in the hot chicken stock and stir until the gelatin is dissolved. Set aside to cool.

When the gelatin is cool but not set, add the mayonnaise, lemon juice, onion, paprika, and two or three dashes of Tabasco. Chill until the mixture begins to thicken; then gently fold in the whipped cream, lobster meat, celery, and capers. Pour the mixture into an oiled 6-cup mold and refrigerate for several hours or overnight. Unmold onto a chilled platter, garnish with greens and tomatoes, and serve immediately.

Variation

King crab meat or frozen langostinos may be substituted for all or part of the lobster.

Mrs. Albert E. Pratley
Council of the BSO

Preparing Mussels: Mussels have been featured in most of the world's cuisines for many years but have only recently become popular in the United States, where they are now being grown commercially. Because so few cookbooks have any information about these nutritious, versatile, and inexpensive shellfish, we have provided our method for preparing mussels, which will suffice for the basics of almost any recipe.

Any mussels with damaged or open shells should be discarded. Because mussels grow on rocks, they are not sandy like clams, but "wild" mussels should be carefully scrubbed. Some gatherers of wild mussels recommend that they be refrigerated for 24 to 48 hours in salt water with a handful of cornmeal, which will cause them to eliminate any sand they may have ingested incautiously. The "beards" may be removed before or after steaming.

To steam mussels, place them on a rack in a steamer or deep pan with a tightly fitting cover — a pressure cooker without its final seal is perfect. Pour in ¼ to ½ inch of wine or water, add seasonings as preferred (mussels do not need any salt), and cook over high heat until the shells are open. Remove from the heat, discard any stubbornly closed mussels, and proceed as directed for cooked mussels.

OVEN-STEAMED MUSSELS

Serves 6

½ peck mussels (see Preparing
  Mussels ◆)
2 cups dry white wine
2 cups water
2 bay leaves
2 cloves garlic, minced

1 tablespoon chopped fresh oregano, or
  1 teaspoon dried
1 tablespoon salt (optional)
6 parsley sprigs
Freshly ground black pepper

Preheat the oven to 450°.

Place the prepared mussels in a 5- to 6-quart casserole, or divide them among six individual 1-quart casseroles. Combine all the remaining ingredients and pour the mixture over the mussels. Cover and steam in the oven for 15 minutes, or until all the shells are open. Serve immediately, with plenty of crusty bread, a tossed garden salad, and more of the same wine that was used to cook the mussels.

The Union Club of Boston
Kevin LeGault, chef

HUÎTRES EN PAQUETS (Oysters in a Package)

Serves 8 as an appetizer,
4 as an entrée

48 large fresh shucked oysters with
  liquid
24 very large spinach leaves, stems
  removed

1 pound butter, softened
6 tablespoons lemon juice
Salt
Freshly ground white pepper

Preheat the oven to 400°.

Pick over the oysters and strain, reserving the liquid.

Flatten the spinach leaves with the palm of your hand. Place two oysters on each leaf; roll it up and fold in the ends to make a neat package. Place the packages, seam side down, in a buttered flame-proof baking dish, and pour the oyster juice over the packages. Bring to a boil on the top of the stove; then transfer the dish to the oven for 5 minutes.

Place 1 tablespoon of butter in a saucepan over *very low heat* or in a double boiler over hot but not boiling water. Gradually incorporate the remaining butter, being careful that it does not melt. You should be able to touch the pan without burning your fingers. Beat in the lemon juice and salt and pepper to taste.

Place a layer of the lemon butter sauce on a warmed platter and arrange the packages attractively on top. Serve immediately on heated plates, and pass the remaining sauce.

Maison Robert, Boston
Georges Painault, guest chef

SCALLOPED OYSTERS

Serves 6

This is a cross between an oyster stew and a conventional escallop. It is a luncheon specialty of The Harvard Club.

¼ pound butter	*Tabasco*
60 freshly opened Cape oysters	*Worcestershire sauce*
1½ cups milk	*Salt*
1½ cups all-purpose cream	*Freshly ground white pepper*
1 cup crushed oyster crackers	*4 tablespoons melted butter*

Preheat the oven to 350°.

Melt the ¼ pound of butter in a large frying pan. Add the oysters in their liquor and simmer until the edges curl slightly. *Do not overcook.* Add the milk and cream, rotating the pan to mix well. Season to taste with Tabasco, Worcestershire sauce, salt, and pepper, and remove from the heat.

Divide the oyster mixture among six individual oven-proof dishes and sprinkle with the crushed oyster crackers. Top with melted butter and bake only until the dishes are very hot. Serve immediately with whole oyster crackers and a green salad.

The Harvard Club of Boston

ARTHUR D. WESTON'S VINEYARD BAKED SCALLOPS

Serves 2 or 3

This quick and easy recipe is almost infinitely expandable, and it presents scallops perfectly.

1 pound Vineyard scallops (see Note)	*⅔ cup cracker crumbs*
Salt	*2 tablespoons melted butter*
1 cup light cream	*Paprika*

Preheat the oven to 400°.

Place the scallops in a single layer in a buttered shallow baking dish and season them with a little salt. Pour in the light cream to a depth of ¼ inch. Mix the crumbs and butter and sprinkle the mixture over the scallops. Dust lightly with paprika and bake for about 10 minutes, or until the scallops are just firm and opaque. *Do not overcook.* Serve immediately.

Note

Cape or bay scallops, or ocean scallops cut to a uniform size, may be substituted.

J. V. Weston

BARBECUED SHRIMP

Serves 6

Marinade

1 cup olive oil
½ cup lemon juice
2 teaspoons crushed red peppers
2 teaspoons turmeric

1 tablespoon chopped fresh herbs (such
as dill, thyme, or rosemary) or 1
teaspoon dried herbs

24 "jumbo" shrimp in their shells
Salt

Fresh mint leaves and paper-thin
lemon slices (for garnish)

Mix the marinade and add the shrimp in their shells. Marinate overnight, turning occasionally.

Preheat the grill or broiler.

Remove the shrimp from the marinade and sprinkle with salt. Cook for 2 minutes on each side, or until they are pink. *Do not overcook.* Arrange the shrimp on a large platter and sprinkle with mint leaves and lemon slices. Serve with Sauce Aïoli.♦

Variation

Cook the shrimp ahead of time, and serve very cold.

Ruth Deeley

BAKED STUFFED SHRIMP

Serves 4

The Lunch Club is a downtown institution where Boston bankers, brokers, and businessmen meet in order, we are told, not to talk about business.

12 "jumbo" shrimp
1 medium-sized onion, minced
¼ pound butter
1 cup dry white wine
¼ pound lobster tomalley (green liver)

1 cup heavy cream
1 to 1½ cups dry bread crumbs
Parsley sprigs and lemon wedges (for
garnish)

Shell the shrimp, but do not remove the tail shells. Carefully split each shrimp in half without cutting completely through. Wash, dry, and refrigerate the shrimp until ready to cook.

Preheat the oven to 325°.

Sauté the onion until soft in a small amount of butter. Add the wine and reduce the mixture until almost dry. Add the remaining butter and melt slowly. Stir in the tomalley and the cream and bring to a boil. Remove from the heat and add just enough bread crumbs so the stuffing is moist but not wet. Stuff the shrimp and arrange them in a buttered oven-proof serving dish. Bake for 20 to 30 minutes, or until they are bright pink: shrimp should be tender, so *do not overcook*. Serve immediately, garnished with parsley and lemon wedges.

The Lunch Club, Boston
Pierre Tisserant, chef

CARIBBEAN CURRY

Serves 6

Beer is the traditional accompaniment for curry — wine does not complement its spicy taste.

5 tablespoons butter	*1¼ cups clam broth*
2 tablespoons curry powder	*1 tablespoon tomato purée*
1 medium-sized onion, minced	*1 teaspoon salt*
1 clove garlic, crushed	*Freshly ground black pepper*
¼ teaspoon chili powder	*3 medium-sized bananas, not too ripe,*
4 tablespoons flour	* sliced*
1¼ cups chicken broth	*1 pound cooked fresh shrimp, shelled*

Stir the first five ingredients in a saucepan over medium heat for 5 minutes. Gradually blend in the flour, and then the broths, the tomato purée, and salt and pepper to taste. Bring to a boil, stirring constantly. Reduce the heat and simmer the sauce for about 20 minutes, stirring occasionally.

Preheat the oven to 450°.

Pour a thin film of sauce into a buttered baking dish. Layer the bananas and shrimp over the sauce. Pour half the remaining sauce over the shrimp and bananas. Bake for about 5 minutes at 450° to heat the bananas; then lower the heat to 350°. Add the remaining sauce and bake for 20 minutes, until the top is slightly browned. *Do not overcook*. Serve over hot rice, with condiments — chutney, raisins, chopped nuts, or shredded coconut, for example.

Mrs. Drayton Phillips
Council of the BSO

TRINIDAD-STYLE CURRIED SHRIMP IN PINEAPPLE

Serves 4

Trinidad-born mezzo-soprano Lorna Myers sang in the Boston Symphony performances of Mahler's Eighth Symphony, including the 1980 Mahler Society Award–winning recording. It was very difficult to choose one from her collection of fascinating recipes.

¾ to 1 pound cooked shrimp or
   prawns
1 tablespoon lime juice
1 tablespoon water
Salt
Freshly ground black pepper
2 tablespoons olive oil
2 tablespoons chopped chives or
   shallots
1 medium-sized onion, chopped

2 tomatoes, peeled, seeded, and
   chopped
2 tablespoons curry powder
1¼ cups fish stock
1 tablespoon butter
1 tablespoon flour
2 small pineapples
Boiling water
3 cups hot cooked rice flavored with
   saffron or nutmeg

Stir the shrimp into the lime juice and water with salt and pepper to taste. Set aside and turn occasionally.

Heat the olive oil in a large frying pan; add 1 tablespoon of the chives, and the onion, tomatoes, and curry powder. Stir for 5 minutes over medium heat, add the stock, and bring to a boil. Cover and simmer over low heat for 15 minutes. Mix the butter and flour together and beat it into the stock. Stir until the sauce is thickened, about 3 minutes more. Adjust the seasonings, add the shrimp, and set aside but keep hot.

While the sauce is cooking, place the pineapples in boiling water to cover for 3 minutes. Drain and cut them in half lengthwise, keeping some leaves on each half for decoration. Using a melon-ball cutter or sharp spoon, scoop out about half the pineapple flesh and set aside. Fill the pineapple halves with the shrimp mixture and sprinkle with the remaining chopped chives. Garnish with the reserved pineapple, and serve with the hot rice.

Lorna Myers, mezzo-soprano

SHRIMP CURRY

Serves 4

This is a good chafing-dish recipe for a buffet, with the fruit served separately in a glass bowl.

1 large onion, chopped
1 clove garlic, crushed or minced
2 tablespoons butter
1 can cream of mushroom or celery
   soup
1 pound shrimp, cooked and shelled
¼ cup seedless raisins
1 tablespoon curry powder (adjust to
   taste)

¼ teaspoon salt
Freshly ground black pepper
1 apple, peeled and grated
Lemon juice
2 cups hot cooked white rice
1 cup cubed pineapple
2 oranges peeled and sliced
1 grapefruit peeled and cut into
   sections

Sauté the onion and garlic in the butter until lightly browned. Add the soup, shrimp, raisins, curry powder, salt, and pepper to taste. Heat thoroughly, but *do not boil*. Add the apple and lemon juice to taste just before serving. Serve over the hot rice, garnished with the fruit. Pass additional condiments, such as chutney, raisins, chopped nuts, or shredded coconut.

Mrs. Frederick Schecter

SHRIMP MARIO

Serves 2

Leo Panasevich joined the BSO's first violin section in 1951, after a varied career with many other musical organizations. An ardent golfer, he is also a fisherman, although he does not catch the shrimp that his wife prepares for *diner à deux*.

10 to 12 "jumbo" shrimp, shelled	2 tablespoons dry sherry (or to taste)
6 tablespoons melted butter	Paprika
4 cloves garlic, minced	Salt
2 tablespoons minced parsley	Freshly ground black pepper
1 tablespoon Worcestershire sauce	Croutons (optional, see Note)
1 tablespoon steak sauce	

Preheat the broiler.

Brush the shrimp lightly with the melted butter.

Combine the remaining ingredients except the sherry, seasonings, and croutons in a heavy oven-proof frying pan. Place the shrimp on top and sprinkle with paprika, salt, and pepper. Broil for 5 minutes, basting occasionally.

Remove the shrimp from the broiler and set aside. Add the sherry to the sauce and cook on top of the stove over medium heat for about 5 minutes. Taste and add more sherry and seasonings if necessary.

Place croutons on heated plates, top with the shrimp, and pour the sauce over all. Serve immediately.

Alternative

This may be cooked entirely on top of the stove. Mix the sherry with the other ingredients and simmer briefly; then add the shrimp and cook until tender, turning several times. Proceed as above.

Note

To make croutons, brush whole bread slices, with crusts removed, on both sides with melted butter. Fry over medium heat until golden on both sides, and keep warm until needed.

Eleanor Jones Panasevich
Former BSO staff

SHRIMP WITH SCAMPI SAUCE

Serves 8 to 10

Principal clarinet for the Boston Pops and clarinet for the BSO, "Patsy" Cardillo was born in western Massachusetts. A trout fisherman and a golfer in his few free hours, he is also on the faculty of Boston University. As the following recipe demonstrates, he is an innovative chef in the Italian manner.

1 cup butter	¾ cup chopped fresh parsley
½ cup olive oil	Salt
6 cloves garlic, pressed	Freshly ground black pepper
1½ cups dry sherry	2½ to 3 pounds "medium" shrimp,
1 tablespoon dry mustard	shelled, deveined, and cut in half
3 tablespoons lemon juice	lengthwise
2 slices lemon peel	2 tablespoons melted butter

Heat the cup of butter and the olive oil over low heat. Add the garlic and cook briefly, but do not brown it. Slowly add 1 cup of the sherry, and simmer for 10 minutes. Beat in the mustard and the remaining sherry, and continue to cook for 10 to 15 minutes more. Add the lemon juice and peel; simmer for 10 minutes, stirring occasionally. Remove the lemon peel, add the parsley, and season with salt and pepper to taste. Cover and simmer for 30 to 45 minutes, stirring frequently. Remove the sauce from the heat, cool, and refrigerate overnight.

The next day, preheat the broiler.

Heat the sauce over low heat. *Do not overcook.* Arrange the shrimp in a generously buttered pan, coat with the melted butter, and broil quickly. Drain thoroughly and place in a chafing dish over simmering water. Pour the sauce over the shrimp and allow to stand for about 15 minutes, stirring occasionally to blend the flavors.

Serve with warmed Italian bread to absorb the fragrant sauce.

Pasquale Cardillo
Boston Pops principal clarinet

SAKANA NO MIZUTAKI (Japanese Hot Pot)

Serves 6 to 8

Tokyo-born Ikuko Mizuno has played the violin almost all of her life. She joined the BSO in 1969, but still manages to spend some time each year in Japan. Solicited early by the Cookbook Committee, she contributed her version of a traditional Japanese dish, which, she says, "I have adapted for an American electric frying pan instead of the traditional Japanese hot pot." Japanese cuisine depends on the freshest of ingredients, painstakingly prepared and elegantly presented. The initial impact of this dish is the beauty of the ingredients. It may look like a lot of trouble, but it can all be prepared ahead of time, and it allows the host and hostess to be with their guests the whole evening.

1 pound mixed shellfish ("medium" shrimp, scallops, lobster meat)
1 pound mixed firm fish (swordfish, shark, cod, halibut)
1 small Chinese cabbage, sliced diagonally
2 small ribs celery, sliced diagonally
1 bunch scallions, trimmed
½ pound mushrooms, sliced
2 medium-sized carrots, sliced or cut into julienne
1 or 2 small zucchini, halved and sliced
1 cup bean sprouts, rinsed
1 large sweet potato, cut into julienne

1 cup snow peas or sugar snap peas
1 cup green beans, whole if small, cut up if large
1 package tofu (bean curd), drained, rinsed, and cut into 1-inch cubes
1 package harusame *(cellophane noodles), prepared according to package directions*
Dashi-no-moto *(see Notes)*
½ cup grated daikon, *or other strong radish*
¼ cup lemon juice
Soy sauce
2 to 3 cups cooked white rice

Pick over the seafood carefully, and cut it into bite-size pieces. Arrange the prepared vegetables on a large platter with the seafood and tofu. Refrigerate until ready to serve. Cut the noodles into 3-inch lengths, place in a handsome bowl, and refrigerate.

Set the table with individual plates, chopsticks, *sake* cups, and beer mugs. Chopsticks for serving are a refinement. Put the *daikon*, lemon juice, and soy sauce in separate small dishes, and place them on the table.

Half-fill a large electric frying pan with water and add the *dashi-no-moto*. When the "soup" is almost boiling, bring the frying pan to the table and plug it in. Seat your guests, and give each a small hot, wet towel with which to wipe his hands. Pour hot *sake* and/or cold beer; then bring in the gorgeous platter and the noodles. Guests help themselves from the platter, cooking each morsel as they please, and dipping it in lemon juice, soy sauce, and grated radish to taste. It is regarded as gauche to drop one's food in the pot, but it adds to the hilarity.

Toward the end of the meal, bring in the hot rice in individual bowls. The end of the meal is signaled by ladling the broth into bowls (rice bowls may be used) or cups.

A non-Japanese finale would be fruit and/or ginger ice cream for dessert.

Notes

Dashi-no-moto is available in Oriental specialty shops. Lightly seasoned chicken stock, thinned with water, may be substituted.

Almost any vegetables suitably prepared may be substituted for those listed here — spinach, watercress, broccoli, bamboo shoots, onions, turnips, even small pieces of corn on the cob or potatoes. But they must be *fresh!*

Ikuko Mizuno, violin

SHELLFISH CASSEROLE

Serves 2 to 4

In effect a hot salad, this is a quick dish for luncheon or supper, using ingredients generally on hand.

1 cup cooked shrimp (fresh, frozen, or canned)
1 cup crab meat (fresh, frozen, or canned)
1 cup chopped celery
¾ cup chopped onion
¾ cup chopped green pepper

1 5-ounce can water chestnuts, drained and sliced
Mayonnaise
1 cup coarse dry bread crumbs or prepared stuffing mix, buttered
1 10-ounce package tiny frozen peas, cooked and lightly buttered

Preheat the oven to 350°.

Mix the shellfish and vegetables with mayonnaise to the consistency of a salad. Place in a buttered casserole and top with the crumbs. Bake until browned and very crunchy, and serve with a border of peas.

Mrs. Curtis Buttenheim
Tanglewood Council of the BSO

SHELLFISH IN PERNOD CREAM

Serves 4

8 tablespoons butter
4 small lobster tails, split
20 "medium" shrimp, peeled and deveined
⅔ cup Pernod
4 cups heavy cream
1 large ripe tomato, peeled and chopped

¾ pound scallops of uniform size
4 tablespoons chopped chives
2 tablespoons chopped parsley
Salt
Freshly ground white pepper
3 cups hot steamed rice

Heat 4 tablespoons of the butter in a large saucepan. Add the lobster tails and shrimp and toss to coat thoroughly. Cover and cook over low heat, shaking the pan frequently until the shellfish are pink. Remove to a heated dish and keep warm.

Pour the Pernod into the hot pan, swirl it around, and carefully flame it.

When the flame subsides, stir in the cream and tomato and reduce the sauce by about half. Add the scallops and simmer for approximately 2 minutes. Return the lobster and shrimp to the pan and heat thoroughly. Remove the shellfish to a warm platter.

Quickly beat the remaining butter into the sauce; add the chives, parsley, and salt and pepper to taste. Strain the sauce, if desired, or pour it as is over the hot shellfish. Serve immediately with the hot rice.

Swiss Hutte Restaurant
Hillsdale, New York

BIRDS

Growing from a short series of concerts organized by music-loving summer residents of the Berkshires in 1934, the Berkshire Music Festival now runs nine weeks every summer at the beautiful estate known as Tanglewood, near Lenox. It draws more than three hundred thousand people annually for twenty-four concerts by the Boston Symphony Orchestra as well as performances by the Boston Pops, early Friday evening "Prelude" concerts, a Festival of Contemporary Music, a weekly chamber series, open rehearsals, and almost daily concerts by the young musicians of the Berkshire Music Center. No sight is more typical of a Berkshire summer than the thousands of people assembled before the Shed on the vast Tanglewood lawn to enjoy a Sunday afternoon concert *(overleaf)*.

FRUIT STUFFING FOR ROASTED BIRDS

Makes 3 to 3½ cups

Pianist and conductor Vladimir Ashkenazy has been a frequent and welcome guest of the Boston Symphony. The proportions given here will stuff a large (7- to 8-pound) chicken, six to eight Rock Cornish hens, or two 4-pound ducks. Suitably increased, the stuffing may be used for goose or turkey.

2 cups mixed pitted dried fruit (apples,   ⅛ cup slivered almonds
   pears, peaches, prunes, apricots)   Sugar or honey
¼ cup raisins   Salt
1 large onion, chopped   Freshly ground black pepper
3 tablespoons butter

Cover the fruit with water, bring to a boil, and simmer for 5 minutes, adding more water if necessary. Remove from the heat, stir in the raisins, and allow to stand, covered, until the fruit has softened but still retains its identity. Drain thoroughly, reserving the water.

Sauté the onion in the butter until golden, and add the fruit. Stir over medium heat for 3 to 4 minutes, add the nuts, sweeten, and season to taste. Stuff the bird(s), reserving any surplus stuffing. Roast the bird(s), basting with the reserved water, adding the surplus stuffing to the pan for the last half-hour of cooking.

Vladimir Ashkenazy, pianist and conductor

CHICKEN IN A FRIULIAN MODE

Serves 6 to 8

Friuli is a small town in northern Italy, an area where chicken is often stuffed with delicately seasoned polenta. This is an adaptation to suit American ingredients. The stuffing in this recipe can also be used for six to eight Rock Cornish hens, and it may be doubled or tripled to stuff a small or medium-sized turkey. It may be prepared one to two days ahead.

1 6- to 7-pound roasting chicken
4 cups coarse unsweetened Corn
  Bread, ◆ crumbled and lightly packed
1 teaspoon salt
⅛ teaspoon freshly ground black
  pepper
1½ tablespoons chopped fresh basil, or
  ½ teaspoon dried
1½ teaspoons chopped fresh chervil, or
  ½ teaspoon dried
¾ teaspoon chopped sage, or ¼
  teaspoon dried
¾ teaspoon chopped fresh oregano, or
  ¼ teaspoon dried

1 medium-sized onion, chopped
½ cup chopped Italian parsley
¾ cup melted butter
4 egg yolks, beaten
½ cup freshly grated Parmesan cheese
1½ cups ricotta cheese
4 large Idaho potatoes, peeled and cut
  into 1-inch dice
Salt
Freshly ground black pepper
3 tablespoons olive oil
Chopped parsley (garnish for the
  potatoes)
Parsley sprigs (garnish for the chicken)

Wash and dry the chicken inside and out, and refrigerate until ready to cook. Combine the crumbled corn bread with the salt, pepper, 1½ teaspoons basil, and the chervil, sage, and oregano, and dry for several hours in a preheated 225° oven. Do not allow the crumbs to brown, but they must be completely dry. Add the onion, parsley, butter, egg yolks, and cheeses. Mix well. Refrigerate the stuffing for at least 2 to 3 hours, until very cold.

Preheat the oven to 400°.

Combine the diced potatoes with the remaining basil and salt and pepper to taste. Coat them thoroughly with 2 tablespoons of the olive oil and place them in a lightly oiled covered baking dish (see Note).

Stuff the chilled bird with the chilled stuffing, brush it with the remaining olive oil, and set it on top of the potatoes. Cover tightly and bake for 1 hour, or until the potatoes are tender but not too soft. Remove the potatoes and reduce the heat to 350°. Continue to bake the chicken, uncovered, for another 1 to 1½ hours, or until the juice runs clear when the skin is pierced with a fork, basting occasionally. *Do not overcook.* When the bird is done, remove it to a heated platter and allow it to stand in a warm oven for about 15 minutes. Meanwhile, reheat the potatoes, sprinkle them with chopped parsley, and arrange them around the chicken.

Degrease the pan drippings, adding a little water if necessary, and strain the "sauce" over the bird. Garnish with parsley sprigs. Serve with a robust salad and Italian bread.

Note
This recipe lends itself nicely to a well-soaked clay roaster. Start it in a cold oven, set the thermostat for 425° degrees, and proceed as directed.

Marys Wright

HUEHNER FRICASSEE
(German-style Chicken Fricassee)

Serves 8

Emil Kornsand, now retired, was long a member of the violin section. His wife gives credit for this excellent do-ahead method for fowl to her mother-in-law, Luise Kornsand, who brought it with her from Germany. It has been slightly adapted — after all, where in the United States does one find "an old hen"?

1 fowl or capon, 7 to 8 pounds	*4 bay leaves*
½ cup coarsely chopped parsley	*8 cloves*
2 cups sliced celery	*½ cup butter*
2 medium-sized onions, sliced	*8 tablespoons flour*
4 carrots, sliced	*3 tablespoons capers in vinegar*
1 tablespoon salt	*Chopped parsley (for garnish)*

Place the bird, parsley, celery, onions, and carrots in a large pot with water to cover. Bring the liquid to a boil, reduce the heat, and simmer for about 20 minutes, or until the vegetables are barely tender. Remove the vegetables, cool, and refrigerate overnight. Add the salt to the pot and simmer until the bird is barely tender. Take the bird from the pot and set it aside until cool enough to handle. Remove the skin and bones, return them to the stockpot with the bay leaves and cloves, and reduce the liquid by about a third. Strain, cool, and refrigerate the stock overnight. Cut the meat into strips or large dice and refrigerate overnight.

The following day, remove and discard the fat and heat the stock. Melt the butter in a large saucepan, add the flour, and stir until well blended. Pour in the stock slowly, stirring constantly until the sauce has thickened. Add the capers and vinegar, and adjust the seasonings. Stir in the chicken and vegetables, and heat thoroughly. Serve very hot with noodles, rice, or biscuits.

Mrs. Emil Kornsand

CHICKEN BAKED WITH PARSNIPS

Serves 4

Dennis Helmrich, chief vocal coach for the Berkshire Music Center, is also an excellent cook. His chicken dish cooks superbly in a clay roaster.

1 3-pound chicken, quartered,	*1 large onion (or 16 shallots)*
* backbone removed*	*Salt*
2 medium-sized parsnips	*Freshly ground black pepper*
2 medium-sized carrots	*Paprika*
2 large ribs celery	*½ cup boiling water*

Preheat the oven to 400°.

Peel the vegetables and cut them into ¼-inch slices (leave shallots whole). Spread the pieces in a single closely packed layer in a buttered casserole. Place the chicken, skin side down, over the vegetables and sprinkle it with salt, pepper, and paprika to taste. Pour the water over all, cover, and bake for 45 minutes.

Remove the chicken and turn the vegetables. Replace the chicken, skin side up, and dust with more paprika. Bake uncovered for 10 to 20 minutes more, or until the chicken is tender and the skin is crisp and brown. Remove the chicken and keep warm. Pour off any excess fat. Return the casserole to the oven, and bake until the vegetables are lightly caramelized. Return the chicken to the casserole, and serve immediately.

Dennis Helmrich, chief vocal coach
Berkshire Music Center

AUNT KATE'S CHICKEN

Serves 4

Harold Wright, the Boston Symphony's esteemed principal clarinet, once played the cymbals in an army band before rising to the position of drum major. A lover of chamber music, he is a regular performer at the Marlboro Music Festival as well as the Casals Festival, and he obviously prefers dishes that are quick to prepare. Of this one he says, "It takes five minutes to put together and while it is cooking I can practice or fix reeds."

1 3-pound broiler, quartered,
 backbone removed
2 tablespoons melted butter
Salt
Freshly ground black pepper
1 large onion, slivered or chopped
1 cup rice

1 can cream of mushroom soup
½ cup strong chicken stock
½ cup cream or evaporated milk
¼ cup dry vermouth or dry sherry or
 water
Paprika (optional)

Preheat the oven to 350°.

Brush the chicken with some of the melted butter and season to taste with salt and pepper. Mix the onion with the remaining butter and the rice, and spread it in the bottom of a buttered 1½-quart casserole. Mix the soup and the liquids together and pour over the rice mixture. Arrange the chicken pieces over the rice, skin side up, and dust with paprika. Bake for 45 to 55 minutes, until the rice is tender but not mushy and the chicken is tender and lightly browned. Serve immediately.

Harold Wright
Principal clarinet

POULARDE EN PAPILLOTE
(Chicken in Parchment)

Serves 4

This dramatic chicken dish will appeal to those seeking a novel presentation of the versatile bird. It is much easier than it looks, and the chicken and the sauce may be prepared ahead for last-minute finishing.

1 3-pound chicken, quartered,
    backbone removed, and carefully
    trimmed
1 teaspoon salt
¼ teaspoon freshly ground black
    pepper
½ cup butter
1 tablespoon chopped shallots
¼ cup chopped mushrooms

½ cup dry white wine
¼ cup dry vermouth
½ cup brown stock
1 tablespoon flour
2 tablespoons finely diced ham
1 tablespoon chopped fresh tarragon,
    or 1 teaspoon dried
Cooking parchment

Season the chicken lightly with the salt and pepper. Reserve 1 tablespoon butter and sauté the chicken in the remaining butter over low heat until lightly browned on both sides. Set the chicken aside, but keep it warm.

In the same pan, lightly sauté the shallots until they are limp; then add the mushrooms and sauté for 5 minutes. Add the wine and vermouth and cook over medium heat until the liquid is reduced by about half. Add the stock and the chicken, and simmer, covered, for about 20 minutes. Remove the chicken breasts and set in a 200° oven to keep warm. Cook the dark meat for 5 to 10 minutes longer; then add it to the white meat.

Cool the liquid in the pan slightly, add the flour, and beat over low heat until the sauce is smooth and thickened. Stir in the ham and tarragon and adjust the seasonings if necessary.*

Preheat the oven to 400°.

Cut the parchment into four pieces large enough to wrap the chicken parts with plenty to spare. Rub the pieces on both sides with the reserved butter and fold each one in half. Place a piece of chicken on each piece of paper and top with 3 to 4 tablespoons of the sauce. Bring the edges of the paper together and crimp into a double fold. The packages must be tightly sealed. Place on a buttered shallow baking dish and bake for 10 minutes. Serve in the paper; each guest unwraps his package at the table.

*May be prepared ahead to this stage and refrigerated for later finishing. Refrigerated chicken and sauce should be brought to room temperature before wrapping, and should be allowed to bake for 15 minutes.

Eleanor Aronoff
Tanglewood Council of the BSO

BARBECUED CHICKEN

Serves 12

Marinade

1 12-ounce can frozen orange juice,
* thawed*
2 large garlic cloves, pressed
5 tablespoons soy sauce

2 tablespoons honey
1 tablespoon freshly grated gingerroot
1 tablespoon lime juice
¼ teaspoon rosemary

4 broiling chickens, quartered

Beat together the marinade ingredients and pour over the chicken. Cover tightly and refrigerate overnight.

When ready to cook, drain the chicken and reserve the marinade. Grill the chicken over hot coals for 30 to 40 minutes, turning and basting frequently with the reserved marinade. The chicken should be dark brown and tender but not dry.

Variation

The chicken may be cooked in the oven at 350° for about 45 minutes, turning and basting as above.

Note

Chicken pieces, breasts, or legs may be substituted with excellent results.

Mrs. Stephen Stone

CHICKEN IN BEER

Serves 4 to 6

4 tablespoons butter
1 chicken (3 to 3½ pounds), cut up
16 small white onions, peeled
¾ cup beer
¼ cup tomato sauce
1½ teaspoons salt

Freshly ground black pepper
¼ teaspoon thyme
1½ teaspoons paprika
1 bay leaf
¼ cup heavy cream

Melt the butter in a large frying pan and brown the chicken pieces. Add the onions and all the remaining ingredients except the cream. Cover and simmer for 30 to 40 minutes, or until the chicken is tender but still adhering to the bones.

Pour off the surplus fat, add the cream, and heat thoroughly; adjust the seasonings if necessary. Serve over noodles, rice, or unpeeled new potatoes.

Joan-Marie Peshin

BAKED DEVILED CHICKEN

Serves 4

Mrs. Pincus is the wife of the music critic of the *Berkshire Eagle;* he takes this chicken to Tanglewood with chilled white wine, a green salad, and a gently perceptive pen.

1 frying chicken, cut up
8 tablespoons melted butter
1 cup seasoned bread crumbs
2 tablespoons Dijon mustard
1 tablespoon Worcestershire sauce

2 teaspoons chopped fresh tarragon
  (optional)
Salt
Freshly ground black pepper

Preheat the oven to 350°.

Place the chicken pieces in a buttered baking dish that can later be covered.

Melt the butter in a small saucepan and add the crumbs and seasonings. Pat the crumb mixture over the chicken pieces. Cover and bake for 30 minutes. Remove the cover, and continue to cook until the chicken is tender but not dry and the coating is crisp and delicately browned.

Serve hot or cold.

Mrs. Andrew Pincus

POULET AU VINAIGRE

Serves 8

2 3-pound chickens, quartered and
  trimmed
Salt
Freshly ground black pepper
4 tablespoons butter

½ cup finely chopped onions
½ cup red wine vinegar
2½ cups heavy cream
1 tablespoon Dijon mustard
Parsley (for garnish)

Season the chicken with salt and pepper.

Heat the butter in two frying pans. Add the chicken, skin side down. Sauté, turning occasionally, until golden brown and cooked through, about 20 minutes: the dark meat may take 5 to 10 minutes longer. *Do not overcook.* Remove the chicken to an oven-proof serving platter, cover, and keep in a warm oven (200°).

Pour off all but about 2 tablespoons of the pan drippings and add the onions. Cook and stir over medium heat for 4 minutes. Deglaze the pan with the vinegar, and cook until most of the vinegar has evaporated.

Pour into the pan any juices that have accumulated around the chicken pieces in the oven. Add the cream and bring to a boil. Cook rapidly for about 7 minutes, and beat in the mustard.

Remove the dish of chicken from the oven and pour the sauce over all, coating thoroughly. Garnish with parsley and serve with rice or homemade noodles.

Mrs. Ames Stevens, Jr.

CHICKEN QUASI UNA FANTASIA

Serves 4

Pianist James Fields was a soloist with the Boston Pops several times, under the baton of Arthur Fiedler. His appropriately named chicken dish is quick, easy, and hearty — *una fantasia*, indeed!

1 3½-pound chicken, cut up	1 can cream of mushroom soup
Salt	1 can cream of celery soup
Freshly ground black pepper	2 cups milk
1 clove garlic, minced	2 cups steamed rice
3 tablespoons butter	2 tablespoons chopped parsley (for
¼ cup dry sherry	garnish)

Preheat the oven to 350°.

Dry the chicken pieces very thoroughly and salt and pepper them lightly. In a large frying pan, sauté the garlic briefly in the butter. Add the chicken and brown the pieces on all sides, turning often. Remove from the pan and place in a buttered casserole. Pour off any accumulated fat, and deglaze the pan with the sherry.

Mix the soups and milk, and add to the frying pan. Stir the sauce and pour it over the chicken. Cover and bake for 1 hour, or until the chicken is tender but not dry. Arrange the chicken on a heated platter around a mound of steamed rice. Season the sauce to taste, pour it over the chicken, and sprinkle parsley over all.

James Fields, piano

TANDOORI MURGHI (Indian Chicken)

Serves 4 to 6

The name *tandoori* comes from the Hindu word *tandor*, a tall cylindrical clay oven used in India to cook meat dishes and bread.

3 pounds chicken pieces, skinned	2 teaspoons garam masala (see below)
1½ teaspoons salt	1 teaspoon chili powder
⅓ cup cider vinegar	1 teaspoon paprika
2½ cups plain yogurt	1½ teaspoons ground coriander
2 large onions, quartered	Few strands saffron
4 cloves garlic	½ head iceberg lettuce, sliced
½ cup coarsely chopped unpeeled fresh	Lemon wedges, sliced red onion,
gingerroot	tomato wedges (for garnish)
1 lemon, seeded and quartered	

Make several ¼- to ½-inch cuts in the chicken flesh, but be careful not to cut so deep that the chicken will break up in cooking. Rub with the salt, especially into the cuts. Place the chicken pieces in an oven-proof glass or ceramic baking dish and set aside.

Mix the vinegar and half the yogurt in a blender at the lowest speed. Slowly add the onions, garlic, ginger, and three of the lemon quarters. Blend until smooth.

Pour half the yogurt mixture into another container and add the remaining ingredients except the lettuce and garnishes. Beat vigorously so there will be no lumps. Return the mixture to the blender, add the remaining yogurt, and blend for 30 seconds. This may have to be done in installments.

Pour the marinade over the chicken, cover tightly, and refrigerate for 24 to 48 hours.

Preheat the oven to 350°.

Remove the cover from the chicken, transfer the dish to the oven, and bake for 1 to 1½ hours, until the chicken is brown and crisp. Remove the chicken pieces from the sauce and serve hot on the cold lettuce, garnished with slices of red onion and tomato and lemon wedges.

Garam Masala (Indian Seasoning)

3 tablespoons whole black peppercorns	*8 black cardamom seeds*
2 tablespoons whole black cumin seeds	*6 bay leaves*
2 tablespoons whole cloves	*1 tablespoon mace*
1 to 2 inches stick cinnamon	

Pulverize all the ingredients in a blender, food processor, or mortar (the traditional utensil). Store in an airtight container, and use to season soups, chicken, and meats, especially pork and meat loaf.

Nancy K. Clough
BSO staff

BREAST OF CHICKEN ALGONQUIN

Serves 6

12 ounces cream cheese, softened	*Salt*
2 large shallots, minced	*Freshly ground black pepper*
6 small chicken breasts, skinned, boned, and pounded thin	*2 eggs, beaten*
	2 tablespoons water
12 small thin slices Muenster cheese	*Dry bread crumbs, plain or seasoned*
6 thin slices cooked ham, slightly smaller than the chicken breasts	*Paprika*
	Parsley or watercress sprigs (for garnish)
Flour	

Combine the cream cheese and shallots, and set aside a quarter of the mixture. Place the flattened chicken breasts, skinned side down, on a flat surface and proceed as follows:

1. Spread the breasts with about one third of the remaining cream cheese mixture.
2. Cover the cream cheese with half the Muenster cheese slices.
3. Spread the Muenster cheese with about half the remaining cream cheese mixture.
4. Cover the cream cheese with the ham slices.
5. Spread the ham with the remaining cream cheese mixture.

Roll each chicken breast into a neat bundle, being careful to enclose all the filling. Secure with toothpicks, strong thread, or light kitchen string. Preheat the oven to 375°.

Dredge the chicken in flour lightly seasoned with salt and pepper. Beat the eggs and water together and dip each breast in the egg wash. Coat well with bread crumbs and arrange, fold side down, in a lightly buttered baking dish. Bake for 30 minutes, until the chicken is firm to the touch and the crumbs are golden.

Spread the reserved cream cheese mixture over the chicken breasts, top with the remaining Muenster cheese slices, and dust with paprika. Return to the oven for several minutes, until the cheese melts. Remove the chicken from the oven, garnish as desired, and serve immediately.

Algonquin Club, Boston
John Ford, chef

CHICKEN BREASTS FLORENTINE

Serves 6

This spicy chicken dish, which calls for no salt, may be prepared considerably ahead of time and refrigerated until about 1½ hours before serving. Chilled chicken needs about 10 to 15 minutes' additional cooking time.

1 pound mushrooms, thinly sliced
1 cup minced Spanish onion
1 tablespoon chopped fresh oregano, or 1 teaspoon dried
1 tablespoon chopped fresh basil, or 1 teaspoon dried
½ teaspoon dried red pepper flakes, crushed fine
1 large or 4 small cloves garlic, pressed
2 tablespoons olive oil
1½ cups dry white wine

1 pound spinach, stems discarded, chopped
6 small whole chicken breasts, boned, with the skin intact
6 tablespoons freshly grated Parmesan cheese
6 slices Gruyère cheese
Melted butter
Parsley or watercress sprigs (for garnish)

Sauté the mushrooms, onions, and seasonings in the olive oil over medium heat until the onions are lightly browned. Add the wine and reduce the liquid by about half. Stir in the spinach and set the mixture aside to cool.

Preheat the oven to 400°.

Place the chicken breasts on a flat surface, skin side down. Sprinkle with Parmesan cheese, and fit a slice of Gruyère cheese on top of each breast. Divide the spinach mixture evenly among the pieces of chicken, reserving the pan liquid, and press it firmly into place on top of the cheese. Fold the edges in around the filling, and pull the skin tight so that it makes a neat package. Place the breasts, folded side down, in a buttered baking dish, and brush with melted butter. Bake for about 15 minutes; then lower the heat to 325° and continue baking for 20 to 30 minutes more, basting occasionally with the reserved pan liquid. When the chicken is firm to the touch and well browned, remove it from the oven and allow it to stand in a warm place for 10 to 15 minutes (or longer) before serving. The pan juices may be slightly thickened to make a sauce, if desired.

Ganesh Café
Lenox, Massachusetts
Olena Rajan, chef/manager

CHICKEN EMPRESS ZARIO

Serves 6

One of the world's most highly regarded mezzo-sopranos, Frederica von Stade has performed music by Berlioz, Mahler, Mozart, and Ravel with the Boston Symphony. Her amusingly named and unusually sauced chicken will please her many fans almost as much as her singing does.

6 small chicken breasts, boned,
  skinned, and split
Salt
Freshly ground black pepper
4 tablespoons butter
1 cup dry vermouth, white wine, or
  Champagne

1 cup chicken stock
1 cup sour cream
1½ cups seedless green grapes
Cayenne pepper (optional)
½ cup grated Swiss cheese

Preheat the oven to 300°.

Season the chicken pieces lightly with salt and pepper. In a heavy frying pan, heat the butter until foaming, and sauté the chicken for 3 to 4 minutes, turning to brown on all sides. Remove to an oven-proof serving dish and keep warm. Add the wine and stock to the pan and reduce the liquid by about half. Beat in the sour cream and pour the sauce over the chicken pieces. Bake for 35 to 45 minutes, until the chicken is tender but not at all dry. Add the grapes and adjust the seasonings, adding cayenne pepper if desired. Sprinkle the cheese over all and brown lightly under the broiler. *Do not overcook:* the grapes should be hot but still crisp. Serve immediately with steamed rice and a crisp, bright green vegetable.

Frederica von Stade, mezzo-soprano

CHICKEN IN LEMON CREAM

Serves 6

6 small chicken breasts, boned,
  skinned, and split
Salt
Freshly ground white pepper
Flour
1/4 pound butter
3 tablespoons dry vermouth
2 tablespoons lemon juice

3 teaspoons grated lemon peel
1 cup all-purpose cream at room
  temperature
1 5-ounce can water chestnuts,
  drained and sliced
1/4 to 1/2 cup freshly grated Parmesan
  cheese

Preheat the oven to 350°.

Season the chicken with salt and pepper and dust lightly with flour. Heat the butter in a heavy frying pan and sauté the chicken pieces for about 5 minutes on each side. Remove to a buttered casserole. Deglaze the pan with the vermouth and add the lemon juice and peel. Beat in the cream slowly and bring to a boil. Add the water chestnuts and pour the sauce over the chicken, covering each piece completely. Cool quickly; then cover and refrigerate overnight.

About 1 hour before serving, place the casserole in a cold oven and set the control at 350°.

Bake, covered, for 35 to 45 minutes, basting occasionally. When the chicken is almost done, remove the cover, sprinkle with the Parmesan cheese, and bake for 10 to 15 minutes more. The chicken should be tender and juicy, and the topping lightly browned. Allow to stand for 5 to 10 minutes, and serve with rice and a crisp green vegetable.

Mrs. Charles L. Terry III
Council of the BSO

CHICKEN JORGE MESTER

Serves 6

Conductor Jorge Mester has led the Boston Symphony in a number of highly acclaimed performances. His marvelous chicken dish had no name when he submitted it for this book, so the Cookbook Committee christened it appropriately.

6 small chicken breasts, boned,
  skinned, and halved
Dry white wine
½ pound butter, softened
2 tablespoons chopped parsley
2 tablespoons chopped chives
1 teaspoon fresh thyme, or ½ teaspoon
  dried

1 clove garlic, minced
¼ teaspoon Hungarian paprika, or
  ⅛ teaspoon cayenne pepper
Salt
1½ cups dry bread crumbs

Pound the chicken breasts until they are flat and fairly thin, and place them close together in a shallow dish. Cover with wine and marinate in the refrigerator while preparing the butter "fingers." Form ¼ pound butter into a long thin roll, about ¼ to ½ inch thick. Wrap the roll in waxed paper and freeze until firm. Meanwhile, place the herbs and seasonings in a flat dish. Cut the butter into twelve fingers and roll each one in the herbs. Reserve any leftover herbs. Melt the remaining butter, and set it aside.

Drain the chicken and reserve the marinade. Place a butter finger in the center of each piece of chicken and wrap it into a neat cylindrical package. Pat the outsides dry; then brush them very generously with the melted butter. Roll in the bread crumbs and refrigerate, seam side down, for at least 1 hour, or overnight.

Preheat the broiler.

Set the chicken rolls, seam side down, on a buttered broiler pan, and broil for 6 to 8 minutes, until the coating is golden. Turn and brown the underside for about 5 to 6 minutes more. Place on a heated serving platter and set in a warm oven for several minutes.

Deglaze the broiling pan with the marinade and add any reserved herbs. Boil vigorously for several minutes and pour the mixture around, not over, the chicken. Serve immediately, with rice, creamed mushrooms, and steamed broccoli or another bright green vegetable.

Variation

Use brandy for part of the marinade, or Grand Marnier or crème de cassis, and add a little of the liqueur to the final sauce.

Jorge Mester, conductor

CHICKEN PATTIES

Serves 10

Pianist Myron Romanul is a familiar figure in Symphony Hall, having performed regularly with the Boston Symphony and the Boston Pops for many years. His chicken recipe, he says, "of Lithuanian inspiration, is a most personal Romanul specialty."

2 large onions, sliced
1 very large clove garlic, minced
2 tablespoons olive oil
1 pound fresh mushrooms, sliced
5 to 6 ounces stale French rolls or bread
4½ pounds boneless chicken breast, poached and cooled
1 egg, beaten
1 cup chicken stock
½ cup sour cream
1 tablespoon salt
Flour
Rendered chicken fat, unsalted butter, oil, or a combination, for frying
2 cups light cream sauce, flavored with dill (optional)

Sauté the onions and garlic in the olive oil over medium-low heat until they are transparent but not brown, and set aside. Drain off the excess oil. Add the mushrooms and stir over fairly high heat until their moisture is almost evaporated; set aside. Soak the rolls or bread in cold water for several minutes and squeeze out the extra liquid.

Grind the chicken, onions, mushrooms, and bread·using a meat grinder or food processor, and combine in a large mixing bowl. Stir in the egg, stock, sour cream, and salt, and mix thoroughly. Refrigerate for 24 hours.

Form the mixture into ½-inch-thick patties using ⅓ cup for each. Coat the patties with flour and set aside to dry. Heat 1 inch of the cooking fat in a deep, heavy frying pan over medium-high heat. Fry the patties in the order in which they were floured for about 8 to 10 minutes a side, until they are crisp and delicately browned, adding additional fat as required. Drain on paper towels and serve immediately with the cream sauce.

Variation
Substitute turkey meat and a curry sauce for a post-Thanksgiving treat.
Myron Romanul, piano

CHICKEN, MUSHROOMS, AND CHEESE
Serves 6

This recipe for chicken breasts may be multiplied to serve a crowd.

6 small whole chicken breasts, skinned and boned
Flour
6 tablespoons butter
2 tablespoons olive oil
½ pound mushrooms, thinly sliced
2 tablespoons red wine
1 tablespoon dry white wine
Salt
Freshly ground black pepper
½ pound Muenster cheese, cut into six slices

Pound the chicken breasts flat between two sheets of waxed paper. Dredge with flour and sauté in 2 tablespoons of butter and the olive oil until tender and well browned, approximately 5 minutes on each side. Place the cooked breasts in one layer in an oven-proof dish and keep them warm.

In a separate pan, sauté the mushrooms lightly in 2 tablespoons of butter and set aside.

Preheat the broiler.

Deglaze the chicken pan with the wines and cook until the scrapings are loosened, stirring constantly. Add the remaining butter and beat until the sauce thickens slightly. Add salt and pepper to taste. Cover each breast with sautéed mushrooms and top with a slice of the cheese. Pour the sauce over the chicken breasts and broil until the cheese is melted. Serve immediately.

Mrs. R. Douglas Hall III, Overseer
Council of the BSO
Founding co-chairman, Junior Council of the BSO

CHICKEN WILLIAM

Serves 2

2 small chicken breasts, skinned, boned, and split
Flour
1 egg, lightly beaten with 1 tablespoon water
¼ cup vegetable oil
3 tablespoons butter
¼ teaspoon chopped shallots

2 teaspoons lemon juice
½ cup sliced mushrooms
Tabasco and Worcestershire sauce
3 tablespoons sweet Marsala, warmed slightly
¼ cup chicken or veal stock, thickened with a little cornstarch
4 slices mozzarella cheese

Dredge the chicken breasts in flour and dip them in the egg mixture. Heat the oil in a frying pan until almost smoking. Add the chicken and turn when browned. Reduce the heat to medium and cook for 5 minutes. Drain the oil from the pan and add the butter, shallots, lemon juice, mushrooms, and Tabasco and Worcestershire sauce to taste. Carefully pour the Marsala over all, and flame. Add the stock and place a slice of the mozzarella on each chicken breast. Simmer till the chicken is tender and the cheese has melted.

Place the chicken on heated serving plates and pour the sauce around the chicken.

Lily's and Cricket's Restaurants, Boston
Michael DiGravio, chef

MORG POLO (Middle Eastern Rendition of Marco Polo)

Serves 6

This exotically named chicken dish may be multiplied to serve a large number.

⅓ cup flour
2 teaspoons salt
2 teaspoons freshly ground black pepper
½ teaspoon cinnamon
3 large boned chicken breasts, halved
¾ cup butter
1 cup golden raisins

1 cup chopped dried apricots
2 cups boiling water
1 cup chopped onion
4 cups cooked rice, slightly underdone
¼ cup chopped salted peanuts
½ cup shredded coconut
1½ teaspoons curry powder
¼ cup pine nuts (optional)

Combine the flour, salt, pepper, and cinnamon, and dredge the chicken thoroughly. Dust off the excess. Heat ½ cup butter until foaming in a large frying pan, and brown the chicken over medium heat. Remove from the pan and set aside.

Place the raisins and apricots in a bowl and pour the boiling water over them. Soak the fruit for about 10 minutes♦, drain, and set aside.

Preheat the oven to 300°.

Meanwhile, add the remaining butter to the frying pan and sauté the onions until they are limp but not browned. Remove with a slotted spoon and set aside in a large bowl.

Add the drained fruit to the butter left in the frying pan, and stir until the raisins puff up, adding more butter if necessary. Add to the onions. Stir the rice, peanuts, coconut, and curry powder into the onion-fruit mixture. Toss lightly, and adjust the seasonings if necessary.

Spread the rice mixture in an ungreased 12-by-8-inch baking dish. Top with the chicken, skin side up. Cover tightly and bake for 45 minutes, or until the chicken is tender. Top with the pine nuts, and serve immediately.

Mrs. Michael H. Davis
Council of the BSO
Past chairman, Junior Council of the BSO

CHINESE CHICKEN WITH WALNUTS

Serves 4 to 6

Soprano Evelyn Lear and her husband, baritone Thomas Stewart, have been popular guests with the Boston Symphony on a number of occasions. Mr. Stewart's Chinese rice (see Chen Fan♦) is an excellent accompaniment to this dish.

1 egg white
2 tablespoons cornstarch
½ teaspoon sugar
½ teaspoon salt
½ teaspoon ground ginger
2 medium-sized cloves of garlic,
  minced
1 pound boneless chicken breasts, cut
  into bite-size pieces

2 tablespoons soy sauce
2 tablespoons dry sherry
A pinch of red pepper flakes
4 tablespoons peanut oil
1 cup walnut halves
¼ pound snow peas, trimmed
2 medium-sized tomatoes, peeled and
  cut into wedges

Beat the egg white in a small bowl and add the cornstarch, sugar, and half of the salt, ginger, and garlic. Mix well. Add the chicken and turn to coat thoroughly. Cover and refrigerate for at least 30 minutes, or overnight.

Combine the soy sauce, sherry, red pepper flakes, and the remaining salt, ginger, and garlic. Set aside.

Heat 3 tablespoons of the peanut oil in a wok or a large frying pan until almost smoking. Add the walnuts, and stir-fry over high heat for 1 minute, or until golden. Remove with a slotted spoon and set aside in a warm oven. Add the snow peas, stir-fry until crisp-tender, and set aside with the walnuts. Add the tomatoes, stir-fry for about 45 seconds (until barely heated), and set aside with the snow peas and walnuts.

Add the remaining oil and the chicken. Stir-fry until the chicken is golden and cooked through; remove and set aside as above.

Deglaze the pan with the soy sauce mixture. Return everything to the pan and stir over high heat for about 1 minute.

Serve with Chen Fan♦ or plain boiled white rice.

Evelyn Lear, soprano

POLLO ALLA STRADIVARI

Serves 4 to 6

Violinist Gerald Elias was twenty-three when he joined the BSO, and he was the first player to submit a recipe to the Cookbook Committee. Despite a very active professional life, his hobbies are many and varied — fortunately for us, they include cooking.

4 chicken breasts, boned, skinned, and
  halved
Flour
Salt
Freshly ground black pepper
2 eggs, beaten
1 cup white or yellow cornmeal
¼ cup butter

¼ cup olive oil
1 clove garlic, minced
2 whole cloves
1 small jar Tuscan peppers
½ cup dry white wine or chicken stock
1 tablespoon minced oregano, or
  1 teaspoon dried
½ pound mozzarella cheese, sliced

Dust the chicken pieces with flour seasoned to taste with salt and pepper. Dip in the beaten eggs and roll in the cornmeal. Refrigerate for several hours or overnight, so that the coating is firm and dry.

Preheat the oven to 350°.

Heat the butter and olive oil in a large frying pan over medium heat until foaming, and add the garlic and cloves. Cook for 1 minute; then add the chicken and sauté until golden brown on all sides. Arrange the pieces in a buttered shallow baking dish. Slice as many peppers as desired into the frying pan and toss to coat with the oil. Place them around the chicken pieces. Discard the surplus fat, deglaze the pan with the wine or chicken stock, and pour this mixture over the peppers, but not the chicken.

Sprinkle the oregano over all and bake for 20 to 30 minutes. When the chicken is almost tender, top the pieces with slices of cheese, and return to the oven until the cheese is lightly browned. Serve immediately with a creamy pasta to balance the pungency of the peppers.

Gerald Elias, violin

Pollo alla Cacciatore: *Substitute chicken legs (one per person) or quartered broilers for the veal in Clara Stagliano Benson's Vitello alla Cacciatore.*◆

SCHROCK'S CHICKEN BOSOMS

Serves 4 to 6

Carol Procter joined the cello section of the Boston Symphony in 1965, rejecting a Fulbright scholarship to do so. A latter-day Renaissance woman, her interests and talents are wide-ranging and catholic. She has been a part of the cultural exchange with the Japan Philharmonic and a member of the Players' Committee for a number of years. She plays the viola da gamba, is a member of the Curtisville Consortium and the New England Harp Trio, both composed of members of the BSO and their families, and, obviously, likes to cook.

4 large chicken breasts, boned, skinned, and split	2 teaspoons tarragon
2 medium-sized onions, chopped	Salt
¼ pound butter	Freshly ground black pepper
¾ cup dry white wine	1 pint sour cream
	Boiled rice (white or brown)

In a large covered frying pan, sauté the chicken and onions in the butter until the onions are limp. Add the wine and tarragon. Season to taste with salt and pepper. Spread half the sour cream over the chicken. Cover the pan and simmer for 30 to 40 minutes, until the chicken is tender but not dry. Top with additional sour cream, reheat, and serve over rice.

Serve with Avocado-Grapefruit Salad.◆

Carol Procter, cello

CHICKEN LIVERS IN WINE SAUCE

Serves 3 or 4

Violinist William Waterhouse, who has retired to Winnipeg, Manitoba, was one of the first pilots in the BSO to offer flying premiums for the Orchestra's annual Musical Marathon. His chicken liver dish is an inexpensive luxury that is quick and easy to prepare.

½ cup orange juice
1 cup port wine
1 chicken bouillon cube
⅓ cup flour
¾ teaspoon salt
Freshly ground black pepper
Paprika

½ teaspoon oregano
1 pound fresh chicken livers, cut in
   half
4 tablespoons butter
⅓ cup cream
2 cups hot cooked rice

Combine the orange juice, port, and bouillon cube in a saucepan, stir to dissolve the cube, and reduce over medium heat by about half.

Place the flour in a plastic bag and add the salt, pepper, paprika, and oregano. Shake the chicken livers in the flour until well coated, and dust off any excess. Heat 2 tablespoons of the butter until foaming and sauté the livers for about 5 minutes. Remove them from the pan and keep hot. Deglaze the pan with the reduced port mixture, and add the remaining butter. Reduce or add liquid to make about ⅔ cup. Whisk in the cream. Heat but do not boil, and pour over the chicken livers.

Place the cooked rice in the center of a heated serving platter. Arrange the livers and sauce around the rice and serve immediately.

William Waterhouse, violin

SIMPLIFIED CHICKEN KIEV

Serves 6 to 8

Russian-born violin virtuoso Emanuel Borok has many talents, chief among them his enormous and contagious zest for life. The Boroks have simplified one of the great dishes of their native land, which they serve with Rice Israeli Style.◆

4 large chicken breasts, boned,
   skinned, and halved
Dijon mustard
Salt
Freshly ground white pepper
½ pound cream cheese, softened
¼ pound domestic blue cheese,
   softened

¼ pound unsalted butter, softened
Nutmeg
1 cup grated Swiss cheese
Flour
2 eggs, beaten
1 cup dry bread crumbs
4 tablespoons butter

Cut a pocket in each of the chicken breast halves, making the opening as small as possible and being careful not to cut through. Spread lightly with mustard inside the pockets, and dust with salt and pepper.

Combine the cream cheese, blue cheese, softened butter, and nutmeg to taste; form this mixture into eight small balls. Roll the balls in the Swiss cheese and insert them in the pockets, adjusting the size of the balls to the size of the pockets. Fasten securely with toothpicks, or tie with coarse cotton thread, leaving a long tail to facilitate handling.

Coat each chicken piece carefully with flour, then egg, then bread crumbs. Place in a single layer on paper towels and refrigerate for at least 2 hours, but preferably overnight: the coating should be dry and the filling very cold.

Preheat the oven to 400°.

Brown the chicken quickly in the butter. Transfer it to an oven-proof dish and bake for 15 to 20 minutes, or until just tender. *Do not overcook.* Remove fastenings before serving.

Bonus
Mix any leftover stuffing with leftover Swiss cheese to make a marvelous cheese spread for crackers, filling for grilled cheese sandwiches, or garnish for broiled lamb or steak.

Emanuel Borok, violin
BSO assistant concertmaster
Boston Pops concertmaster

PROKOFIEV CHICKEN LIVERS

Serves 4

Most New Englanders who love classical music cannot begin their day without the familiar voice of "Robert J." His characteristic delivery on the Public Radio Cooperative's *Morning pro musica* is so well known that the unveiling of his culinary accomplishments can only add to the urbane legend.

2 tablespoons olive oil
1 large clove garlic, minced
1/3 pound beef kidneys, cut into
   bite-size pieces
1 pound chicken livers, cut into
   bite-size pieces
3/4 pound small button mushrooms

1/2 teaspoon ground ginger
1 tablespoon Schlichte or kirschwasser
1/4 cup Curaçao
Salt
Freshly ground black pepper
Seeded tangerine segments (optional)

Heat the olive oil in a large frying pan and sauté the garlic until golden. Add the kidneys, chicken livers, and mushrooms, and toss well to coat with the oil. Sprinkle with the ginger and liqueurs. Stir until the livers and kidneys are cooked through. *Do not overcook.* Season to taste with salt and pepper. Serve immediately, garnished with cold tangerine segments if desired.

Robert J. Lurtsema
Morning pro musica

DUCK WITH ORANGE SAUCE

Serves 4

Mme. Voisin, the mother of Roger Voisin, former principal trumpet of the Boston Symphony and the Boston Pops, is a legendary chef de cuisine in the BSO world.

2 4-pound ducks

3 large or 4 medium-sized cloves of garlic, pressed

Sauce
4 large oranges
4 tablespoons butter
2 large shallots, chopped
2 tablespoons flour
1 tablespoon sugar
2 tablespoons white wine vinegar

1 cup jellied beef consommé
3 tablespoons lemon juice
3 tablespoons currant jelly
¼ cup Cointreau

Parsley or watercress sprigs (optional)

Remove any loose fat from the ducks and wash and dry them thoroughly. Prick the skin all over with a sharp fork. Rub the birds thoroughly with the garlic, wrap them tightly in plastic wrap or foil, and refrigerate them for 24 hours.

Preheat the oven to 425°.

Set the ducks on a rack in a deep-sided baking dish. Bake them for 20 minutes, drain off the fat, and lower the heat to 350°. Cook the birds for 1½ hours longer. Cut into halves, through the breast bone, and set aside but keep hot.

Cut the zest of three of the oranges into thin strips, using a martini "twist" tool, a zester, or a sharp paring knife. Remove as much of the white pith as possible. Cover the strips with cold water, bring to a boil, and drain. Repeat this process, but cook the peel for 5 minutes over medium heat. Drain the peel and set it aside. Squeeze the juice from the three oranges, strain, and measure 1 cup. Set it aside. Cut the remaining orange into thin slices and set it aside for the garnish.

Heat 2 tablespoons of the butter till foaming in a medium-sized frying pan, and sauté the shallots until wilted. Add the flour and stir for 3 to 4 minutes, until medium brown, and set aside. In another pan, combine the sugar and vinegar and reduce by half. Add the consommé, orange and lemon juices, and jelly; heat; then beat slowly into the shallot mixture over low heat. Cook for 10 minutes, stirring frequently. Add the strips of orange zest and cook for 10 minutes more, stirring often. Set aside until just before serving.

Place the hot duck halves on a heated serving platter. Bring the sauce to a boil, remove from the heat, and add the remaining butter and the Cointreau. Stir briskly until the butter is melted and pour over the ducks. Garnish with the orange slices and parsley or watercress sprigs, and serve immediately.

Marie Voisin

CANETON RÔTI MONTMORENCY

Serves 8

4 ducklings, 4 to 4½ pounds each,
  washed and dried
2 onions, diced
Thyme
Bay leaves
2 cups poultry stock

1 cup cider or apple juice
Salt
Freshly ground black pepper
Calvados
4 apples, peeled and thinly sliced
¼ cup sugar

Preheat the oven to 350°.

Place the ducklings on their backs on a rack in a metal roasting pan, and bake them, uncovered, for 2 hours. Remove the birds and cool slightly. Discard all the fat from the pan, but leave the drippings. Cut the ducklings in half and remove all the bones from the inside, without breaking the outer skin. Set the ducklings in a warm oven.

Add the bones to the drippings in the pan, and set it over medium heat. Add the onions and the herbs to taste, and stir for about 10 minutes; then pour in the stock and the cider or apple juice. Bring to a fast boil and reduce the sauce by about half. Remove the bay leaves and season with salt and pepper. Strain the sauce into a bowl and add Calvados to taste.

Preheat the broiler.

Arrange the apples in a pie plate, sprinkle them with the sugar, and broil until lightly caramelized. Arrange the ducklings on a heated platter and garnish with the caramelized apples. Pour the sauce over the birds and serve immediately. Wild rice is the obvious accompaniment, with crisp-tender Brussels sprouts or another bright green seasonal vegetable.

Ritz-Carlton Hotel, Boston

OVEN-BARBECUED DUCKLING, CHINESE STYLE

Serves 2 to 4

Mimi Sheraton, well-known food writer for the *New York Times*, is a subscriber to the Boston Symphony's New York Series of concerts. We are grateful to her for sharing her recipes with us.

1 5-pound duckling, quartered

Barbecue Sauce

1 small onion, minced
2 large cloves garlic, minced
2 tablespoons olive oil
½ cup honey
1 cup tomato chili sauce
½ cup red wine vinegar
¼ cup Worcestershire sauce
2 teaspoons Japanese soy sauce (see Note)

1 tablespoon hoisin *sauce (see Note)*
1½ teaspoons dry mustard
¼ teaspoon oregano
Pinch rosemary
½ teaspoon freshly ground black pepper
Salt

Preheat the oven to 325°.

Place the duckling, skin side down, on a rack in an open pan, and roast for 20 minutes. Turn and roast 1 hour longer, draining the fat from the pan during the cooking process. While the duckling is cooking, make the barbecue sauce.

Sauté the onion and garlic in the olive oil until they are soft but not brown. Add the remaining ingredients and bring to a boil, stirring constantly. Lower the heat, simmer for 5 minutes, and set aside.

Baste the duckling with the sauce after the hour is up, reserving half the sauce for later. Cook the duckling for 20 to 30 minutes more, basting two or three times. It should be thickly glazed, but not black, and the meat should be tender but not dry. Remove to a heated serving platter.

Reheat the remaining sauce, and pour it into a heated gravy boat. Serve the duckling with Wild Rice with Mushrooms and Chives♦ or steamed white rice, and pass the extra sauce.

Note

Japanese soy sauce and other Oriental specialties are increasingly available in supermarkets, as well as gourmet food shops.

© *Mimi Sheraton*
Food and restaurant critic
The New York Times

ROAST DUCKLING CANTONESE

Serves 2 to 4

1½ quarts strong beef stock
1½ cups firmly packed dark brown
  sugar
2 teaspoons ground ginger
6 cloves garlic, crushed
1 cup soy sauce

1 cup rice wine or white wine
1 teaspoon monosodium glutamate
  (optional)
1 4- to 5-pound duckling, cleaned,
  trimmed, and securely trussed

Combine all the ingredients except the duckling in a saucepan just large enough to hold the bird. Bring to a boil, cover, and simmer for about 20 minutes.

Meanwhile, prick the duckling's skin all over with a large darning needle, making the holes about ½ to ¾ inch apart. Immerse the duckling in the stock and simmer gently for about 1 hour. Remove it from the pot and set it aside but keep it hot. Boil and skim the stock over medium-high heat until it is reduced to about 2 cups. Strain and degrease the sauce, and reduce to 1½ cups — it should be quite thick and dark.

Preheat the oven to 450° to 500°.

Place the duckling on a rack in a shallow oven-proof dish and baste thoroughly with the sauce. Roast until the skin is dark brown and very crisp, about 35 to 45 minutes. Do not baste again, but reserve the remaining sauce to pass with the duckling. Serve with rice and vegetables.

The Restaurant
Lenox, Massachusetts

ROAST PHEASANT

Serves 3 or 4

1 pheasant
Salt
Freshly ground black pepper
2 small apples, peeled and chopped
2 ribs celery, chopped

1 medium-sized onion, chopped
3 bacon strips
Red or white wine
Parsley or watercress sprigs (for
  garnish)

Preheat the oven to 450°.

Wash and dry the pheasant. Sprinkle the cavity lightly with salt and pepper.

Combine the apples, celery, and onion and stuff the bird fairly firmly. Truss it securely and set it on a rack in a small baking dish. Sprinkle it with salt and pepper, baste thoroughly with a little wine, cover with the bacon strips and roast for 10 minutes. Baste again; then skim off any excess fat and reduce the heat to 325°. Cook for about 45 minutes, or until the skin is crisp and the bones move a little in the flesh. Do not overcook the bird, and do not burn the bacon. Remove the cooked pheasant to a heated platter and keep it hot. Discard the accumulated fat and deglaze the pan with a little more wine. Pour the sauce over the bird, garnish with parsley or watercress sprigs, and serve immediately with wild rice and a crisp green vegetable such as Brussels sprouts.

Mrs. William D. Manice, Jr.
Council of the BSO

ROCK CORNISH HENS WITH OYSTER STUFFING

Serves 6

1 pint shucked oysters
6 tablespoons melted butter
3 tablespoons chopped green pepper
2 tablespoons chopped celery
2 tablespoons chopped onion
3 tablespoons chopped parsley
1½ cups coarse dry bread crumbs or packaged stuffing mix
⅛ teaspoon cayenne pepper

1 teaspoon salt
Freshly ground black pepper
6 Rock Cornish hens, approximately 1¼ pounds each
2 cups dry white wine
½ cup boiling water
Watercress or parsley sprigs (for garnish)

Preheat the oven to 400°.

Drain the oysters thoroughly and reserve the liquor. Heat 4 tablespoons of the butter over medium heat and sauté the vegetables and parsley until limp but not brown. Add the oysters and stir gently until the edges just begin to curl. Remove from the heat immediately, and add the bread crumbs and enough oyster liquor to bind the mixture together — do not make it too wet. Season to taste with cayenne, salt, and pepper.

Stuff the birds: Use all the stuffing, as the oysters shrink slightly when they cook. Brush the birds with the remaining 2 tablespoons of butter. Pour the wine into a large baking pan and add the boiling water. Set a rack above the liquid, and place the birds on their sides on the rack. Bake for about 15 minutes, baste with the pan juices, and turn to the other side. Baste again, and bake for 15 minutes longer. Baste and turn the birds on their backs. Continue to cook, basting frequently, until the birds are tender but not dry. *Do not overcook.* Allow the birds to stand for about 10 minutes, but keep them hot. Serve garnished with parsley or watercress and accompanied by currant jelly or Brandied Cranberries.◆

Mrs. Wilbert R. Sanger
Council of the BSO

SQUAB PRINCE CHARLES

Serves 4

¼ pound chopped chicken breast
⅛ pound chopped veal
4 tablespoons Madeira
3 shallots, chopped
¼ pound butter
2 eggs, beaten
Salt
Freshly ground black pepper
Nutmeg
Paprika
12 squabs

¼ cup soy sauce
¼ cup honey
1 large carrot, chopped
2 leeks, white part only, chopped
1 medium-sized onion, chopped
2 tablespoons kirschwasser
12 lean bacon strips
½ cup Dry Sack or other sweet sherry
½ tablespoon cornstarch
1 tablespoon water

Marinate the chopped meats in the Madeira for 1 hour. Sauté the shallots in 1 tablespoon of butter until soft, and set aside. Mix the marinated meats with the eggs, add the shallots, and season to taste with salt, pepper, nutmeg, and paprika. Cut out the breastbones of the squabs, stuff the cavities with the meat mixture, and tie each bird to hold the wings close to the body. Mix the soy sauce and honey and brush the birds with the glaze. Heat 4 tablespoons of butter in a large frying pan, add the squabs four at a time, and brown lightly on all sides, turning carefully. Remove the birds to a generously buttered baking dish and brush again with the soy-honey mixture.

Preheat the oven to 375°.

In the same frying pan, sauté the carrots, leeks, and onions for 5 minutes, adding more butter if necessary, and arrange around the birds. Drizzle the kirschwasser over the vegetables, top each bird with a strip of bacon, and bake, uncovered, for 12 minutes. Remove from the oven, pour the sherry over the squabs, transfer to a heated serving platter, and remove the strings. Strain the pan juices into a saucepan, and thicken with the cornstarch mixed with the water. Simmer for 2 to 3 minutes. Adjust the seasonings, and pour the sauce over the birds. Serve with red cabbage or Brussels sprouts, glazed chestnuts, and turnips.

The Bay Tower Room, Boston
Chef Blanken

Turkey Mozzarella: *Substitute fillets of breast of turkey for the veal in Joseph Silverstein's Veal Mozzarella.*♦

HARVEST TURKEY SUPREME

Serves 8 to 10

2 medium-sized onions, chopped
2 green peppers, chopped
2 cloves garlic, minced
4 apples, peeled, cored, and cut into
    1-inch slices
6 fresh tomatoes, peeled and coarsely
    chopped
¼ cup corn oil
1 cup cooked butternut squash or
    pumpkin

2 tablespoons chutney
2 teaspoons basil
2 teaspoons thyme
1 cup cider
6 cups bite-size pieces roasted turkey
    breast
½ cup slivered almonds
Boiled rice or baked yams

Preheat the oven to 350°.

In a large frying pan, sauté the onions, peppers, garlic, apples, and tomatoes in the oil for about 3 minutes. Add the squash, chutney, herbs, and cider. Mix thoroughly. Add more cider if the sauce is too thick, and set it aside.

Pour a thin layer of sauce into a lightly buttered shallow baking dish. Cover with half the turkey and pour on more of the sauce. Arrange the remaining turkey in a second layer and cover with the sauce. Top with the almonds and bake for 10 to 15 minutes, until the sauce is bubbling. Serve with rice or baked yams.

Mrs. Richard E. Schroeder

MUSHROOMS STUFFED WITH BREAST OF TURKEY

Serves 8 to 10

3 pounds medium-sized mushrooms

Stuffing
3 pounds cooked turkey breast meat
2 small onions
2 large cloves garlic, minced
½ loaf stale French bread, soaked in
    water and squeezed dry

6 eggs, beaten
½ cup melted chicken fat
2 tablespoons freshly ground black
    pepper
Salt

Sauce
1 medium-sized onion, diced
½ pound butter
Mushroom stems, sliced
1 cup chopped parsley, loosely packed
2½ cups water

3 tablespoons lemon juice
Salt
Freshly ground black pepper
2 tablespoons flour
2 cups all-purpose cream

Clean the mushrooms, remove the stems, and set the caps and stems aside separately.

To make the stuffing, grind together the turkey, onions, garlic, and bread, using a meat grinder or a food processor. Combine this mixture with the other stuffing ingredients, adding salt to taste, and knead well. Fill the mushroom caps with this stuffing, pressing it firmly into place.

To make the sauce, sauté the onion in the butter until golden. Add the mushroom stems and half the parsley, and cook for about 2 minutes. Add the water and lemon juice, and bring to a boil; then add the remaining parsley, and season with salt and pepper to taste.

Drop in the stuffed mushroom caps, cover, and simmer until the stuffing is firm. Remove the mushrooms and set aside but keep hot.

Make a smooth paste of the flour and ½ cup of the cream. Off the heat, pour the remaining cream into the hot sauce and beat in the flour paste. Return to the heat and stir until the flour taste is gone. Return the mushrooms to the sauce and serve immediately.

The Café Budapest serves these mushrooms with *rizi-bizi* (two parts boiled white rice to one part cooked green peas) and a cranberry orange relish flavored with cinnamon.

The Café Budapest, Boston
Edith Ban, proprietor

TURKEY CRÊPES

Serves 6 to 8

Crêpes

3 eggs, beaten	*1 cup milk*
⅔ cup flour	
½ teaspoon salt	*Cooking oil for crêpe pan*

Filling

2 cups sliced mushrooms	*½ teaspoon freshly ground white*
¼ cup sliced green onions	*pepper*
¼ cup butter	*2 cups chopped cooked turkey*
3 tablespoons flour	*1½ cups shredded Cheddar or Swiss*
1 cup milk	*cheese*
½ teaspoon salt	

Combine the ingredients for the crêpes. Beat the batter until smooth and set aside for 30 minutes or more.

Briefly heat and oil a crêpe pan. For each crêpe, pour ¼ cup or less of the batter into the pan, swirl it around, and cook over high heat until the top is almost dry and the bottom is brown. Do not flip. The crêpes should be paper-thin. Reverse the crêpes onto a clean dishtowel and set aside, covered with another towel.

To make the filling, sauté the mushrooms and green onion in 1 tablespoon butter until the mushrooms render their juice; set aside. Make a white sauce with the remaining butter and the flour, milk, and seasonings. Add the mushroom mixture, turkey, and 1 cup cheese. Mix well and set aside.

Preheat the oven to 350°.

Place the crêpes on a flat surface, brown side down, and divide the filling among them. Roll up and place in a buttered, shallow oven-proof dish, seam side down. Sprinkle with the remaining cheese,* and bake for 20 minutes, until the cheese is brown and bubbly. Serve immediately.

*May be prepared ahead to this stage. Pour 2 tablespoons melted butter carefully over the crêpes before setting them aside, to keep the tops from drying out. Cover, refrigerate until about 1 hour before serving, and finish as above.

Laura Breau

BEASTS

Music, like all the arts, relies on a special relationship between teacher and pupil that allows for the transmission of the indefinable from one generation to the next. The Berkshire Music Center at Tanglewood, established under the leadership of Serge Koussevitzky in 1940 and maintained by the Boston Symphony Orchestra, has become one of the most influential centers in the United States for advanced musical study. Each summer, eager and talented young composers, conductors, instrumentalists, and singers from all over the world come to Tanglewood for eight grueling and enthralling weeks of living and working in music, in close contact with some of the world's greatest musicians. Here *(overleaf)* Seiji Ozawa continues in the Koussevitzky tradition as he works with a young conductor in the living room of "Seranak," Koussevitzky's home in Lenox.

STUFFED TENDERLOIN OF BEEF

Serves 8

Elizabeth Dunton presides over the Subscription Office at Symphony Hall with awesome and unflappable efficiency, somehow managing to satisfy almost everyone.

4 pounds beef tenderloin strip
½ cup butter
¾ pound mushrooms, chopped fine, stems included
½ cup chopped scallions
1 cup finely diced lean cooked ham
½ teaspoon salt

⅛ teaspoon freshly ground black pepper
3 cups toasted white bread cubes
2 tablespoons water
Chopped parsley, parsley and/or watercress sprigs (for garnish)

Sauce
4 tablespoons butter
2 tablespoons flour
1 cup strong beef stock
2 cups peeled chopped tomatoes, with juice
½ teaspoon meat extract (optional)

¼ teaspoon salt
⅛ teaspoon freshly ground black pepper
Sugar (optional)
Brandy

Cut a pocket in the tenderloin, being careful not to cut all the way through, and set the meat aside at room temperature while making the stuffing.

Reserve 2 tablespoons of the butter for later use.

Sauté the mushrooms and scallions in the remaining butter until the scallions are limp. Add the ham, salt, and pepper, and simmer for about 5 minutes. Remove from the heat and add the bread cubes and water; cool the stuffing slightly.

Preheat the broiler.

Fill the pocket in the meat with the stuffing, lightly packed, and tie the roll with kitchen string in at least four places. Place the roll on a buttered broiler pan, and arrange the extra stuffing beside it on a sheet of buttered foil. Cover the stuffing loosely with the foil, and spread the meat with the reserved butter. Broil for 10 minutes per side for rare meat, 15 minutes for medium. Remove both the meat and the stuffing to a heated serving platter. Remove the strings, garnish as desired, and allow the meat to stand for 10 minutes in a warm place.

Meanwhile, make the sauce. Stir the butter and flour over low heat until the flour is golden. Beat in the stock, and bring to a boil. Add the tomatoes and seasonings, and simmer over low heat until the meat is ready. Adjust the seasonings if necessary, and remove the sauce from the heat. Stir in brandy to taste, a little at a time. Spoon a little of the sauce over the meat. Pour the remaining sauce into a heated sauceboat and serve the tenderloin immediately.

Notes
Both the meat and the sauce may be prepared ahead and refrigerated for later finishing.

Refrigerated meat will take a little longer to cook.

Elizabeth G. Dunton
BSO Director of Sales

POT ROAST MY STYLE

Serves 7 or 8

An easy, quick-to-prepare, and unusual version of the old standard — this can be prepared ahead for later cooking.

4- to 5-pound chuck roast *1½ or 2 cans beer*
2 packages onion soup mix *1 to 2 boxes pitted prunes*

Preheat the oven to 325°.

Rub the roast with the onion soup mix and place it in a large shallow pan or casserole. Pour the beer around the meat. Cover the roast with prunes stuck with toothpicks, and place the remaining prunes in the beer. Cover the pan with aluminum foil and seal it tightly to keep in the juices. Bake for 2½ to 3 hours, or until the meat is tender.

Allow the roast to cool for 15 minutes before slicing, but keep the prunes and sauce very hot.

Variation
Cook over very low heat on top of the stove.

Mrs. Nat King Cole
Tanglewood Council of the BSO

CHOLENT MIRYAM

Serves 10

An alumnus of the Berkshire Music Center, currently on the faculty of the Eastman School, violinist Zvi Zeitlin performed Gunther Schuller's Violin Concerto with the Boston Symphony at Tanglewood in 1977. His recipe, he says, "demonstrates how inspiration is born of necessity: forbidden to light a fire on the Sabbath, the Jews created a dish that could be started the day before and consumed on the Sabbath."

1 cup dried lima beans
1 cup navy or pea beans
4 tablespoons chicken fat
2 pounds onions, sliced
2½ pounds small potatoes, quartered
5 pounds beef brisket
Salt

Freshly ground black pepper
1 cup medium barley
4 tablespoons flour
4 teaspoons paprika
1 bottle rosé wine
Boiling water

Soak the beans overnight, or cover them with cold water, bring to a boil, and set aside for 1 hour.

Preheat the oven to 200°.

Melt the chicken fat in a large casserole. Add the sliced onions and potatoes and sauté until slightly golden. Remove from the heat and place the brisket on the bed of onions and potatoes. Arrange the drained beans over and around the meat. Sprinkle salt and pepper liberally over and between the layers, and add the barley. Mix the flour and paprika and sprinkle over the barley and beans. Pour in the wine and just enough boiling water to cover. Bring to a boil on top of the stove; then cover and cook *very slowly* for 8 to 10 hours in the oven.

Zvi Zeitlin, violin

NEW ENGLAND BOILED DINNER

Serves 6 to 8

There are many versions of New England boiled dinner, which should never be boiled but rather simmered very gently. The basic ingredients are corned beef, potatoes, onions, carrots, turnips, and cabbage. Traditionally, the dinner is accompanied by a horseradish or mustard sauce, and beets, either hot and lightly buttered, or cold and pickled. Some contemporary cooks prefer to reverse the cooking procedure, cooking the vegetables separately until they are barely tender, then using the vegetable liquid to cook the meat. This imparts additional flavor to the beef and allows the vegetables to retain their identity, but it takes a little extra time.

4 pounds corned brisket of beef,
    trimmed of all excess fat
1 large bay leaf
1 large clove garlic
Freshly ground black pepper
6 to 8 carrots, whole or halved
2 or 3 parsnips, halved or quartered
2 or 3 cups yellow turnips, in large
    cubes, or 3 or 4 white turnips,
    halved

16 small white boiling onions
3 or 4 medium-sized boiling potatoes,
    halved
1 medium-sized head green cabbage,
    cored and cut into wedges
Chopped parsley (for garnish)

Cover the beef with cold water in a large stockpot. Cover the pot, bring the liquid to a boil, and immediately remove from the heat and drain. Cover again with cold water, add the seasonings, and return to a boil. Reduce the heat immediately, and simmer, covered, over verý low heat, for 3 to 4 hours, or until the meat is just tender. It should be turned several times to ensure even cooking. Remove the meat and add the carrots, parsnips, and turnips. Simmer for 10 minutes; then add the onions and simmer for 10 minutes more. Add the potatoes and cook for about 15 minutes more; then stir in the cabbage. Cook gently, covered, until the cabbage is tender. Replace the meat in the pot and heat thoroughly; then remove it to a heated platter. Surround the meat with the vegetables, sprinkle with parsley, and serve immediately with horseradish sauce or mustard and beets.

Encore
The liquid left in the pot makes an excellent base for pea or lentil soup, and should be strained and frozen for future use.

The Cookbook Committee

DOWNING STREET BEEF AND KIDNEY PIE

Serves 4 to 6

This savory English specialty is particularly good for a dinner when the seating time is uncertain.

2 pounds stewing beef, cut in 1-inch
    cubes
3 lamb kidneys, quartered
4 tablespoons flour
1 teaspoon salt
1/8 teaspoon freshly ground black
    pepper
2 tablespoons bacon fat
1 medium-sized onion, sliced

1/4 pound mushrooms, sliced
1 cup beef stock
2 tablespoons chopped parsley
1 clove garlic, pressed
1/4 cup broken walnuts
Puff pastry to cover a 3-quart casserole
    (about 2 cups)
1 egg, beaten

Shake the beef and kidneys in a plastic bag with the flour, salt, and pepper. Discard the excess flour mixture. Heat the bacon fat in a heavy saucepan, and brown the beef, kidneys, onions, and mushrooms. Pour off any surplus fat and add the stock, parsley, and garlic. Bring to a boil, cover, and simmer over low heat for 2 to 2½ hours, or until the beef is barely tender. Add more stock or water if the sauce becomes too thick. Add the walnuts, adjust the seasonings, and turn into a buttered 3-quart casserole.

Preheat the oven to 400°.

Place an egg cup or other small glass or china object in the center of the dish to support the pastry, and dampen the edges of the casserole. Top with the pastry, and trim with a sharp knife, pressing the edges firmly to seal. Decorate the crust with leftover pastry, and cut several slits to allow steam to escape. Brush with the beaten egg and bake for 25 to 30 minutes, until the crust is puffed and golden brown. The pie will hold in a warm oven for about half an hour.

Ann Hobbs

GROUND NUT STEW

Serves 6

Conductor Niklaus Wyss worked closely with Boston Symphony music director Seiji Ozawa and served on the faculty of the Berkshire Music Center for several years. As evidence of his worldwide interests, he submitted this improvisation on a theme of Nigerian ground nut stew immediately after his return from a tour of Australia and the South Pacific.

¼ cup flour
1 teaspoon salt
1 tablespoon paprika
1 teaspoon Italian herb mix (or other preferred herbs)
2 pounds lean beef, cut into 1½-inch cubes
4 tablespoons olive oil
1 large onion, sliced

2 cups peeled and chopped tomatoes
1 cup beef stock or bouillon
1 cup dry white wine or vermouth
Chunk-style peanut butter
Lemon juice
Freshly ground black pepper
Dry roasted peanuts (for garnish)
Chopped parsley (for garnish)

Mix the flour, salt, paprika, and herbs. Toss the beef in the seasoned flour until thoroughly coated, and shake off the excess. Heat 3 tablespoons of the olive oil over medium-high heat, brown the meat very thoroughly, and set it aside. Add the remaining oil and sauté the onions until transparent. Pour off any surplus fat, stir in the tomatoes, and bring to a boil. Add the meat, stock, and wine and stir until the sauce boils again. Reduce the heat, add peanut butter, and stir until dissolved. Cover and simmer over very low heat until the meat is tender, about 1 hour.

Add lemon juice and more peanut butter to taste. If the sauce becomes too thick, it may be thinned with additional white wine, beef stock, or water. If it is too thin, add more peanut butter. Continue to simmer until the beef is tender, and correct the seasonings. Garnish with a sprinkling of dry roasted peanuts and chopped parsley, and serve with a simple brown rice pilaf and very crisp steamed or stir-fried vegetables.

Niklaus Wyss, conductor

SALMIS OF BEEF

Serves 4

A quick way to dramatize leftover beef . . .

2 tablespoons butter	*½ cup red Burgundy*
2 tablespoons flour	*1 teaspoon Worcestershire sauce*
1 cup beef stock	*4 generous slices of tender cold roast*
1 teaspoon lemon juice	*beef, the rarer the better*

Heat the butter in a chafing dish over direct heat. Stir in the flour and cook until it is lightly browned. Add the stock and stir until the sauce is thick and bubbling; then add the lemon juice, Burgundy, and Worcestershire sauce. Mix well and adjust the seasonings to taste. Place the meat in the sauce and heat through, but do not cook. Serve immediately with pasta, risotto, or spoon bread.

Mrs. Henry E. Foley
Council of the BSO

FILET MIGNON AU POIVRE VERT

Serves 4

1 small can (approximately 2 ounces)	*2 tablespoons cognac*
green peppercorns, drained	*Salt*
4 filets mignons	*2 tablespoons dry white wine*
1 tablespoon butter	*4 tablespoons heavy cream*
2 tablespoons olive oil	

Chop the peppercorns and press them into the steak. In a heavy frying pan, heat the butter and olive oil over medium heat until foaming. Add the filets and cook quickly, rare or medium-rare as preferred. Remove from the heat, add the cognac, and flame. Salt to taste as the flames die down. Remove the meat from the pan, arrange it on a heated serving platter, and set it in a warm oven. Add the wine to the pan and boil hard for 2 minutes.

Pour in the cream and stir for 4 to 5 minutes, until the sauce thickens slightly. Adjust the seasonings, pour the hot sauce over the meat, and serve immediately on heated plates.

Mrs. James C. Curran
Council of the BSO

BARBECUED "TOURNEDOS" WITH BÉARNAISE

Serves 6 to 8

3 pounds flank steak
1 pound sliced bacon
Meat tenderizer
2 cloves garlic, split in half
2 tablespoons chopped parsley

Freshly ground pepper
Béarnaise sauce
Watercress sprigs and/or sautéed
  mushroom caps (for garnish)

Pound the steak into pieces ¼ inch thick. Sauté the bacon until crisp and drain well.*

One hour before serving, sprinkle both sides of the steak with meat tenderizer, rub with garlic, and season with parsley and pepper. Arrange the bacon in a sideways single layer on top of the steak, across the grain. Roll up the steak lengthwise and secure it with toothpicks. Cut the roll into 1-inch "tournedos" and secure with additional toothpicks, if necessary.

Grill over hot coals for 5 minutes on each side. Serve with béarnaise sauce, and garnish with watercress and sautéed mushroom caps or any other fancy trimmings.

*May be prepared ahead to this point and refrigerated.

Mrs. Frank H. Healey, Jr.
Council of the BSO

STEAK ABRUZZESE

Serves 4

½ cup olive oil
4 1-inch-thick top-grade sirloin steaks
2 cloves garlic, chopped
2 cups full-bodied red wine
2 cups beef stock
4 anchovy fillets
3 tablespoons lemon juice
2 tablespoons capers

2 tablespoons whole green peppercorns
Freshly ground black pepper
Cayenne pepper (optional)
½ teaspoon rosemary (fresh, if
  possible)
¼ teaspoon chopped fresh sage (do not
  use dried)
4 tablespoons unsalted butter

In a heavy frying pan, heat the olive oil until sizzling but not smoking, and sear the steaks for about 3 minutes per side. Set aside and keep warm.

Discard the excess fat. Stir in the garlic, and deglaze the pan with the wine. Add the stock and reduce by one third. Stir in the remaining ingredients except the butter and reduce to about 1 cup. Correct the seasonings if necessary.

Replace the steaks in the pan, turn to coat with the sauce, and place them on a heated serving platter. Whisk the butter into the sauce, pour over the steaks, and serve immediately.

Davio's serves this dish accompanied by lyonnaise potatoes seasoned with garlic and rosemary, and cauliflower and broccoli flowerets seared in oil and seasoned with salt, pepper, and lemon juice.

Davio's Ristorante, Boston
Thomas Golden, chef

SUKIYAKI

Serves 8

Soprano Beverly Sills, who needs no introduction, was a frequent guest of the Boston Symphony during Erich Leinsdorf's years as music director. Her approach to entertaining is implicit in what she says about her recipe — "If everything is prepared ahead of time, and arranged attractively in baskets and small individual dishes, the host or hostess may prepare sukiyaki in full view of the guests without missing a thing."

2 tablespoons chopped beef suet
3 cups thinly sliced onions
1 bunch scallions, chopped
3 cups diagonally sliced celery
1 pound spinach, picked over and
stems removed
1 package fresh bean sprouts
1 can bamboo shoots, drained
1 can water chestnuts, drained and
sliced
1 cup sliced mushrooms

⅓ cup slivered almonds
2 pounds London broil steak, cut into
⅛-inch slices
1 pound tofu (bean curd), thoroughly
drained and cut into 1-inch cubes
⅓ cup tomato juice
¼ cup soy sauce
2 tablespoons Worcestershire sauce
⅓ cup sugar
¾ cup chicken stock

Heat the suet in a wok. When it is lightly browned, stir in all the vegetables except the mushrooms, and cook for about 5 minutes. Add the mushrooms and almonds and stir for about 5 minutes more. Stir in the meat, bean curd, tomato juice, soy and Worcestershire sauces, and sugar. Cook for about 15 minutes, stirring frequently. Pour in the chicken stock, and simmer for another 10 minutes. Serve in individual bowls with rice and additional soy sauce. Hot *sake* and cold beer add to the Japanese atmosphere that this nourishing and low-calorie dish evokes.

Beverly Sills, soprano

AUNT MARIE'S TAMALE PIE

Serves 10 to 12

"Tiny" Martin is a familiar figure: he plays jazz and classical bass with equal skill. He is a member of Wuz, a jazz quartet of BSO colleagues. He teaches at the New England Conservatory and Boston University, ties flies, catches trout, tells tall and amusing stories, and likes to cook. His aunt Marie was a contemporary and friend of Fanny Brice, Mary Pickford, Clara Bow, and a whole generation of movie greats, who, according to Tiny, "ate enormous quantities of this pie to keep their energy levels high."

3 cups yellow cornmeal
1½ teaspoons salt
3 cups cold water
6 to 8 cups boiling water
4 tablespoons olive oil
2 large onions, minced
1 large scallion, chopped
2 or 3 medium-sized cloves of garlic, pressed
2 pounds ground beef
4 tablespoons chopped parsley
2 tablespoons chili powder, dissolved in a little water

2 dozen pitted ripe olives
4 dozen seedless raisins
4 cans kidney beans
1 1-pound can whole kernel corn
4 cups tomatoes, peeled, chopped, and drained
½ pound Monterey jack or mild Cheddar cheese, grated
Salt
Freshly ground black pepper
Paprika
Cayenne pepper

In the top of a large double boiler, combine the cornmeal, salt, and cold water. Slowly beat in 6 cups of boiling water until the mixture is smooth and somewhat stiff. Cover and cook over boiling water for about 45 minutes, stirring frequently to avoid lumps. Add more boiling water if the mixture appears too dry.

Preheat the oven to 350°.

Heat the olive oil in a large frying pan. Add the onions, scallion, garlic, ground beef, and parsley. Cook until the beef is lightly browned. Stir in all the other ingredients except the cheese, salt, pepper, paprika, and cayenne. Bring to a boil. Reduce the heat and simmer, stirring often, for 45 minutes.

Line a large buttered baking dish with half the cooked cornmeal. Add the meat mixture and top with the rest of the cornmeal. Sprinkle with the cheese, salt, pepper, plenty of paprika, and cayenne, and bake for 35 to 45 minutes. Serve at once.

Leslie Martin, double bass

GOLABKI (Stuffed Cabbage)

Serves 4

Metropolitan Opera concertmaster Raymond Gniewek, who is also the husband of soprano Judith Blegen, demonstrates that he is a virtuoso of Polish cuisine as well as the violin with this recipe (pronounced go-WUMBki), which begs for black bread and sweet butter as a "juice blotter."

1 3- to 3½-pound cabbage (see Note)
1 1½- to 2-pound cabbage
1 tablespoon vegetable oil
⅓ cup diced salt pork (¼-inch dice)
½ cup chopped onion
1 clove garlic, minced
2 cups slightly underdone cooked rice
⅔ pound ground round steak

⅓ pound ground pork
2 cups canned whole tomatoes, chopped and drained, the liquid reserved
½ teaspoon salt
¼ teaspoon freshly ground black pepper

Remove the core of the larger cabbage carefully so the leaves do not fall off. Remove the eight outer leaves of the small cabbage, and reserve. Shred 1 to 2 cups of the inner part, and set aside. Place the larger cabbage in a soup pot filled with water, bring to a boil, and simmer, covered, for 10 to 20 minutes, or until the leaves are flexible but not too tender to roll. Drain well and set aside to cool.

Meanwhile, heat the vegetable oil and salt pork in a large frying pan and cook for 2 or 3 minutes. Add the onion and garlic, and sauté over low heat for 15 or 20 minutes, until the mixture is golden brown. Remove from the heat, add the rice, and set aside to cool slightly. Combine the meats in a large mixing bowl, add the onion-rice mixture, 1½ cups of tomatoes, and the salt and pepper.

Preheat the oven to 350°.

Line a large casserole or Dutch oven with the eight outer leaves from the small cabbage. Remove the leaves from the larger cabbage and place about a tablespoonful of the meat mixture in the center of each. Fold over the core edge, fold in both sides, and roll up the remainder of the leaf. Pack the rolls into the casserole close together, seam side down, and alternating directions with each layer. Cover the rolls with the shredded cabbage and the remaining tomatoes and tomato liquid. Bake, covered, for 1 to 1¼ hours, until the rice is tender and the flavors are well blended. Serve immediately.

Note

Savoy cabbage, when available, is easier to roll than flat-leaved cabbage.

Raymond Gniewek, concertmaster
Metropolitan Opera Orchestra

KIDNEY BEAN BARBECUE

Serves 6

2 tablespoons bacon fat
1 pound ground beef
1 medium-sized onion, chopped
1 cup diced celery
1 green pepper, chopped
2 tablespoons flour
½ cup ketchup
½ cup red wine
1 tablespoon red wine vinegar

1 tablespoon brown sugar
2 tablespoons Worcestershire sauce
2 teaspoons chili powder
Salt
2 1-pound cans kidney beans,
    drained, liquid reserved
Shredded lettuce and grated Monterey
    jack cheese (for garnish)

Heat the bacon fat in a large heavy frying pan, and sauté the beef, onion, celery, and pepper until lightly browned. Blend in the flour and add the remaining ingredients, except the beans and garnishes. Cover and simmer for 1 hour. Add the beans, and simmer 10 minutes longer. Add ½ cup or more of the reserved bean liquid if the mixture becomes too thick. Serve in a bowl garnished with lettuce and cheese, or on a bun like a Sloppy Joe.

Ruth B. Ripley
Tanglewood Council of the BSO

CAVATERZONE (Hamburger Pie)

Serves 6

Mezzo-soprano Rose Taylor has performed frequently with the Boston Symphony. She has sung the music of Bach, Haydn, Mahler, Monteverdi, Tchaikovsky, and Verdi. She says about her contribution, "A show stealer at any potluck supper, this recipe creates a special dish from readily available ingredients."

1½ pounds extra-lean ground beef
½ cup chopped onion
1 egg, lightly beaten
¼ teaspoon Tabasco
1 teaspoon salt
2 tablespoons chopped parsley

2 cups packaged biscuit mix
½ cup milk
¼ cup mayonnaise
¼ cup grated Parmesan cheese
⅔ cup grated Swiss cheese
1 egg yolk, beaten

Preheat the oven to 400°.

Sauté the ground beef and onion together until the onion is transparent; remove from the heat and drain off any excess fat. Add the egg, Tabasco, salt, and parsley, and set aside. Combine the biscuit mix, milk, and mayonnaise. Pat half the dough into the bottom of a buttered 8-inch square or 9-inch round baking pan. Cover with the beef mixture; then spread the cheeses over the beef. Top with the reserved half of the biscuit mixture, and paint that with the beaten egg yolk. Bake for 25 to 30 minutes, until the topping is crisp and golden, and serve immediately or keep warm for later serving. It holds well.

Rose A. Taylor, mezzo-soprano

CHILI CON GIN

Serves 4

Sherman Walt, the Boston Symphony's principal bassoon, held the same position with the Chicago Symphony before coming to Boston in 1953. A protégé of Dmitri Mitropoulos, he is now on the faculty of Boston University. He likes to cook, which is fortunate for this book. Guacamole or a green salad with sliced avocados makes a cool and soothing contrast to the spicy chili.

1½ pounds lean ground beef
2 tablespoons chili powder (see Note)
1 teaspoon cumin seed
1½ cups chopped onions
3 medium-sized cloves of garlic,
*   minced*
2 tablespoons butter
1 green pepper, chopped
2 cups tomatoes, peeled and chopped
*   (or canned Italian-style tomatoes,*
*   drained)*

¼ cup gin
½ teaspoon salt
Freshly ground black pepper
1 can kidney beans, drained
Sour cream and chopped scallions or
*   red onions (for garnish)*

Combine the beef with the chili powder and cumin seed and set aside. Sauté the onions and garlic in the butter until transparent. Stir in the seasoned beef and brown thoroughly, breaking up the meat into small lumps. Pour off any excess fat and add all the remaining ingredients except the beans and garnishes. Cover and simmer for 30 minutes, stirring occasionally. Add more chili powder if a hotter sauce is desired.

Add the beans and cook for 15 to 30 minutes longer, or until the beans are tender but not mushy, and correct the seasonings. Serve with tacos or corn chips, and pass small bowls of sour cream and chopped onions to be spooned on to taste.

Note

Chili powders vary enormously in intensity, and may be augmented by cayenne pepper or Tabasco or other red or green pepper sauce. Tex-Mex chili powders are available at gourmet and specialty shops. Like curry powders, they must be kept tightly sealed or they will lose their authority.

Sherman A. Walt
Principal bassoon

MARIAN'S MYSTERIOUS MEAT LOAF

Serves 6 to 8

This is a strange-sounding combination of ingredients, which may account for the inability of those eating it to identify the flavoring. It is a moist, tender loaf that is equally good hot or cold.

½ pound sausage meat
2 tablespoons butter
1 medium-sized onion, chopped
1 medium-sized green pepper, chopped
1 cup chopped celery
2 large or 3 small very ripe bananas, mashed
1 cup coarse dry bread crumbs or prepared stuffing mix
½ teaspoon each of oregano, thyme, and rosemary
¼ teaspoon ground nutmeg
1 teaspoon salt
Freshly ground black pepper
2 pounds lean ground beef
¾ cup grated mozzarella or Monterey jack cheese
1 egg, beaten
1 large or 2 small bay leaves
Flour or cornstarch

Preheat the oven to 275° to 300°.

Brown the sausage meat in the butter, and remove to a large bowl. Add the chopped vegetables, and sauté until the onion is golden. Drain off the excess fat and add the vegetables to the sausage meat. Mix in all the other ingredients except the bay leaf and flour or cornstarch, and combine thoroughly but gently. Place the bay leaf in the bottom of a buttered 9-by-5-by-3-inch loaf pan, and pat in the meat mixture. Bake for 1 to 1¼ hours, or until the loaf has pulled away from the sides of the pan. Pour off and reserve the juices, and allow the loaf to stand for 5 to 10 minutes before unmolding onto a heated serving platter. Meanwhile, degrease the pan juices and thicken with a little flour or cornstarch. Remove the bay leaf and serve the loaf, sliced, with a little of the sauce on each serving.

Variation

Add sufficient orange juice to the pan juices to make 1 cup, and thicken with 1½ teaspoons cornstarch dissolved in 1 tablespoon orange juice. When the sauce is thick, stir in 1 teaspoon freshly grated orange peel, and serve as above.

Mrs. Robert W. Palm
Council of the BSO

MEAT LOAF SOUFFLÉ

Serves 8

Award-winning composer Barbara Kolb studied for several summers at Tanglewood with Lukas Foss and Gunther Schuller, and composed *Soundings* on commission from the Koussevitzky Music Foundation. She accompanied the Boston Symphony on its 1978 Japanese tour. Her contribution to the cookbook is also a notable composition, because, she says, "though some soufflés never fail to fall, this one will never fail or fall."

1½ pounds ground beef
1 egg, beaten
½ cup dry bread crumbs
½ cup chopped onion
½ cup milk
1½ teaspoons salt
⅛ teaspoon freshly ground black
   pepper

2 tomatoes, peeled and sliced
4 ounces Cheddar cheese, grated
3 eggs, separated
1 cup sour cream
¾ cup presifted granular flour
   ("instant")
½ teaspoon salt
Freshly ground black pepper

Preheat the oven to 350°.

Combine the first seven ingredients. Press lightly into a lightly buttered 9-inch square baking pan or a 10-inch round springform with 2-inch sides and bake for 25 minutes. Drain off any excess fat, and top with the tomato slices and cheese.

Meanwhile, beat the egg whites and salt until stiff, and set aside. Beat the remaining ingredients together until creamy and fold them in to the egg whites, blending well. Spread this topping over the cheese and return the meat loaf to the oven. Bake until the topping is golden brown and well puffed, and serve immediately, with confidence.

Barbara Kolb, composer

SICILIAN MEAT ROLL (via Montreal)

Serves 8

2 eggs, beaten
¾ cup soft bread crumbs
½ cup tomato juice
2 tablespoons chopped parsley
½ teaspoon oregano
¼ teaspoon salt
¼ teaspoon freshly ground black
   pepper

1 small clove garlic, crushed
2 pounds lean ground beef
8 thin slices cooked ham
1½ cups shredded mozzarella cheese
1 or 2 triangular slices mozzarella
   cheese

Preheat the oven to 350°.

Combine the first eight ingredients, and add them to the ground beef, mixing well. On foil or waxed paper pat the mixture into a 12-by-10-inch rectangle ¼ inch thick. Arrange the ham slices on top of the meat mixture, leaving a 1-inch margin around the edge. Sprinkle the shredded cheese over the ham. Starting with a 10-inch side, carefully roll up the meat, using the foil or paper to lift. Seal the ends and edges very carefully.

Place the roll, seam side down, in a buttered 13-by-9-by-2-inch pan and bake for 1 to 1¼ hours, or until well browned. Pour off any excess fat. Place the cheese triangles on top of the roll and return it to the oven for a few minutes until the cheese melts.

Transfer the roll to a heated platter and serve immediately. Tomato Coulis♦ makes a good accompaniment.

Caroline Dwight Bain
Former BSO staff

PICADILLO WITH PITA

Serves 6 to 8

2 pounds ground chuck
6 tablespoons olive oil
3 medium-sized onions, sliced
4 tablespoons tomato paste
4 cloves garlic, crushed
¼ cup capers
½ cup seedless raisins

½ cup pitted green olives
½ cup red wine
1 teaspoon cumin powder, or ½
   teaspoon crushed cumin seed
Salt
Freshly ground black pepper
6 to 8 ''loaves'' pita bread

In a large heavy frying pan, brown the beef in the olive oil over high heat. Remove the meat and set it aside. Add the onions to the pan drippings and fry until lightly browned. Pour off any excess fat. Return the meat to the pan and add all the remaining ingredients. Stir well, cover, and simmer for about 30 minutes over very low heat. Adjust the seasonings if necessary and serve in pita bread ''pockets.''

Variation
Use this *picadillo* as a stuffing for peppers, tomatoes, or zucchini.

Mrs. Eugene Schnell
Tanglewood Council of the BSO

BARBECUED LAMB

Serves 10

Barbecued lamb is good hot or cold. Prepared without the vegetables, it is a surprising and delicious addition to a summer buffet or picnic. This recipe looks complicated, but it is well worth the effort involved.

1 6- to 8-pound leg of lamb
10 medium-sized potatoes
Seasoned salt
Flour

1 large onion, thinly sliced
8 carrots, peeled and cut into 1½-inch
   pieces

Sauce 1

⅔ cup ketchup
½ cup water
¾ teaspoon A-1 Sauce

1 teaspoon Worcestershire sauce
¼ teaspoon freshly ground black
   pepper

Sauce 2

½ cup ketchup
¾ cup water

1 teaspoon Worcestershire sauce
¾ teaspoon steak sauce

Preheat the oven to 450°.

Wipe the lamb with a damp cloth. Place it, skin side up, in a V-shaped rack in a large pan and brown it for 15 to 20 minutes; then reduce the heat to 325°.

While the lamb is browning, parboil the potatoes; then cool, peel, and halve them, and set aside.

Remove the meat from the oven and pour off the surplus fat. Dust the lamb with seasoned salt, and dredge with flour. Arrange the onion slices on top of the lamb.

Mix Sauce 1, stir well, and pour over the lamb. Cover and bake for 1 hour longer. Skim off any accumulated fat, and add the potatoes and carrots.

Mix Sauce 2 and pour it over the vegetables. Cover and return to the oven. Bake, basting frequently, for about 30 to 45 minutes, or until the vegetables are tender. Place the lamb on a heated platter, surround it with the vegetables, and keep it hot. Pour off the sauce and degrease it. Spoon a little over the lamb, and serve the rest in a heated gravy boat.

Mrs. Samuel A. Levine
Council of the BSO

LEG OF LAMB, SAUCE SURPRISE

Serves 4

Closely associated with London's Royal Ballet and a frequent conductor of ballet companies throughout the world, John Lanchbery also appears regularly as guest conductor of the Boston Pops. This recipe, he says, was "learned in Australia, where lamb is appreciated."

6 or 7 small cloves garlic
1 tablespoon salt
1 tablespoon dry mustard
1 small leg of young lamb, 2½ or 3
   pounds

2 teaspoons sugar
1 tablespoon heavy cream
1 cup strong black coffee

Preheat the oven to 500°.

Pound the garlic in a mortar with the salt and mustard to make a paste, adding a few drops of water if necessary. Spread this paste all over the lamb. Place the lamb in a roasting pan and roast for 15 minutes. Remove it from the oven and carefully pour off any fat that has accumulated. Mix the sugar and cream with the coffee and pour it over the lamb. Reduce the oven temperature to 350° and return the lamb to the oven. Roast, basting every 7 minutes or so, for another 30 minutes or until done. The liquid will have reduced to a thick, dark, piquant sauce that combines very well with the crusty remnants of the paste. Serve with fresh peas and small new potatoes.

John Lanchbery, conductor

ROAST LAMB "LADY CAROL FROM BELMONT"

Serves 8 to 10

1 pound fresh spinach, washed, picked over, stems removed
10 tablespoons clarified butter
1 cup chopped onion
1½ teaspoons minced garlic
½ cup chopped green pepper
¼ cup chopped celery

2 teaspoons salt
½ teaspoon freshly ground black pepper
3 cups croutons
½ teaspoon nutmeg
1 7- to 8-pound leg of lamb, boned

Cook the spinach quickly. Drain, squeeze dry, and chop very fine.

In 4 tablespoons of the butter, sauté the onion and garlic until the onion is transparent; add the green pepper and celery. Sauté for 2 to 3 minutes, add the spinach, and simmer until most of the liquid has been absorbed, stirring frequently. Transfer to a mixing bowl and stir in 1 teaspoon salt, ¼ teaspoon pepper, and the croutons, nutmeg, and remaining butter.

Preheat the oven to 325°.

Lay the lamb flat, cut side up, season with the remaining salt and pepper, and spread evenly with the stuffing. Roll it up into a tight cylinder and tie it securely. Place it, seam side down, on a rack in a baking dish and bake for 1½ hours, or until it is thoroughly browned, turning several times. Allow it to stand for about 15 minutes, and serve, cut into ¼- to ½-inch slices.

Serve with grilled tomatoes, creamed corn, and a seasonal green vegetable.

Zachary's at The Colonnade, Boston

KIDNEY SAUCE FOR LAMB

Makes 2 to 2½ cups

Singer Dennis Helmrich, an indispensable part of the Berkshire Music Center, also performs outstandingly in the kitchen. Cold lamb reheated in this sauce could never be regarded as a leftover.

6 small lamb kidneys
1 tablespoon olive oil
2 tablespoons butter
1 tablespoon Dijon mustard

½ pint heavy cream
Lemon juice (optional)
Tabasco (optional)

Trim the kidneys carefully.

Heat the oil and butter in a small frying pan until foaming. Sauté the kidneys until crusty and brown outside but still pink inside. Remove from the pan and set aside.

Mix the mustard and cream, pour into the frying pan, and bring quickly to a boil. Stir to loosen the scrapings and cook rapidly until the sauce is thick and smooth. Chop the kidneys to the size of peas. Add lemon juice and Tabasco to the sauce and boil rapidly until it thickens again.

Add the kidneys, adjust the seasonings, and heat thoroughly.

Serve with roast lamb or broiled lamb chops.

Dennis Helmrich, chief vocal coach
Berkshire Music Center

SHISH KEBAB AVGOLEMONO

Serves 4

One of today's great mezzo-sopranos, Tatiana Troyanos has performed the music of Schoenberg, Schumann, Stravinsky, and Verdi with the Boston Symphony. She generously shares her version of a classic Middle Eastern dish, which, as she says, "is easy to prepare and all my friends love it."

1 cup lemon juice
½ cup olive oil
1 teaspoon salt
¼ teaspoon freshly ground black
  pepper
1 medium-sized clove of garlic, minced
¼ cup chopped parsley

1 pound lean lamb, cut into 1-inch
  cubes
2 strips thick bacon, cut into 1-inch
  pieces
Onions, cut into 1-inch pieces
Cherry tomatoes

Combine the lemon juice, olive oil, and seasonings, and pour over the pieces of lamb. Cover, and marinate in the refrigerator for two or three days, turning twice a day.

When you are ready to cook, preheat the broiler.

Partially cook the bacon pieces, drain, and set them aside. Drain the lamb and reserve the marinade. Place lamb, onion, bacon, and tomato alternately on two or three skewers. Brush with the reserved marinade and broil for about 10 minutes on each side. Brush again with the marinade if desired, and serve the kebabs with pilaf and salad.

Variations
Other vegetables, such as green peppers, mushrooms, or slices of partly cooked carrot, may be added to the above.

The kebabs may be cooked over an indoor or outdoor grill, in which case slices of eggplant brushed with the marinade may also be grilled.

Bonus
This marinade is equally good on chicken or strong-tasting fish.

Tatiana Troyanos, mezzo-soprano
Metropolitan Opera

SOSATIES (Lamb Kebabs)

Serves 6

This recipe from South Africa shows the Malayan influence on the cuisine of Cape Town. The kebabs go well with saffron rice and cold beer.

6 medium-sized onions — 2 chopped, 4 cut into wedges	½ cup lemon juice
2 tablespoons olive oil	½ cup water
1 tablespoon curry powder	3 pounds boneless leg of lamb cut into 1½-inch cubes
1 tablespoon ground coriander	1 cup dried apricots or peaches
1 teaspoon ground ginger	1 small fresh chili, cored, seeded, and minced
1 teaspoon allspice	2 cloves garlic, minced
1 teaspoon cinnamon	6 bay leaves, quartered
1 teaspoon salt	

Sauté the chopped onions in the oil until soft but not browned. Remove from the heat and stir in the curry, spices, salt, lemon juice, and water. Arrange the lamb cubes in layers in a glass or enamel bowl, moistening each layer with a little of the curry mixture. Cover and allow to stand in the refrigerator for 24 to 48 hours, turning occasionally.

Cover the apricots or peaches with boiling water, and soak them for 1 to 2 hours before draining. Mix the chili with the garlic and set aside.

Remove the lamb from the marinade and thread on skewers alternately with wedges of onion, pieces of fruit, and bits of bay leaf. Roll the kebabs in the chili mixture and grill them over a medium-hot fire until they are brown on all sides but remain pink inside. Serve with pilaf and cold beer.

Mrs. James C. Curran
Council of the BSO

LAMB KIDNEYS IN MUSTARD SAUCE

Serves 4

14 lamb kidneys
3 shallots, minced
¾ pound butter
½ cup red wine
1 tablespoon Dijon mustard
½ cup chopped parsley
1 teaspoon lemon juice

¾ pound mushrooms, quartered
1½ cups strong brown lamb stock
1 tablespoon cornstarch
2 tablespoons cold water
Salt
Freshly ground black pepper

Clean the lamb kidneys and cut them into ½-inch-thick slices. Set aside.

Sauté the shallots in 2 tablespoons of butter over medium heat for 2 to 3 minutes. Add the red wine and boil rapidly to reduce by half. Stir in the mustard, ¼ cup parsley, and the lemon juice, mixing well after each addition. Set aside. In another small pan, sauté the mushrooms in 4 tablespoons of butter over high heat for 2 to 3 minutes.

Bring the lamb stock to a boil. Make a smooth paste of the cornstarch and cold water, and whisk it into the boiling stock. Simmer for 5 minutes, until the sauce is slightly thickened. Add the wine mixture, mushrooms, and salt and pepper to taste.

Heat 6 tablespoons of butter in a large pan and quickly sauté the kidneys over medium-high heat. While they are still pink in the center, add the sauce and mix well.

Serve immediately, garnished with the remaining parsley.

Piaf's Bistro, Boston
Richard L. Pilla, proprietor

STUFFED GRAPE LEAVES

Serves 25 to 30 as an hors d'oeuvre,
15 to 20 as a main course

Mezzo-soprano Rosalind Elias has been a leading singer with the Metropolitan Opera, the Opera Company of Boston, and other companies around the world. She has been a guest artist with the Boston Symphony on several occasions, and she has generously shared her culinary talents as well as her musical ones.

2 cups rice
2 pounds chopped lamb
1 teaspoon cinnamon
½ cup chopped mint (optional)
Salt
Freshly ground black pepper

1 pound fresh or canned grape leaves,
  rinsed and drained
Boiling water
6 tablespoons lemon juice
Lemon wedges (for garnish)

Boil the rice for about 5 minutes, drain, and rinse under cold water. Drain very thoroughly. Mix the lamb, cinnamon, mint, and salt and pepper to taste with the rice. Line a large saucepan with grape leaves and set it aside.

Place about 1 tablespoon of the filling on a grape leaf, with the light side up. Fold over the stem end, then the sides, and roll up into a neat package. Pack the rolls, fold side down, close together in the leaf-lined pan, alternating directions with each layer. Sprinkle about 1 teaspoon salt over the top, cover with additional grape leaves, and place a weighted plate on top of the rolls so they will stay submerged. Pour in boiling water to about ½ inch over the rolls. Bring to a boil, reduce the heat to low, and simmer, covered, for 30 to 40 minutes, until the rice and the meat are tender. Add the lemon juice, swirl the liquid around, and simmer for 5 to 10 minutes longer. Serve hot or cold, garnished with lemon wedges, as an hors d'oeuvre or a main course.

Note
Grape leaves may be picked fresh early in the spring, or bought bottled in brine in Near Eastern specialty stores.

Rosalind Elias, mezzo-soprano

FRENCH ROAST PORK

Serves 8

4 to 5 pounds boned and rolled pork
Olive oil
¼ teaspoon thyme
¼ teaspoon oregano
¼ teaspoon fennel seed

1½ teaspoons salt
6 black peppercorns
Flour
1 medium-sized onion, sliced
   paper-thin

Sauce
1 cup chicken broth
1 cup dry white wine
1 clove garlic, minced
⅛ teaspoon nutmeg
Additional chicken stock and dry
   white wine

2 tablespoons butter
1½ tablespoons flour
½ cup sour cream

Coat the pork lightly with olive oil. Grind the herbs, salt, and pepper together in a mortar. Rub the herb mixture into the pork and dust lightly with flour. Fasten onion slices all over the meat with toothpicks at an angle close to the meat. Seal carefully in plastic wrap and refrigerate for 12 to 24 hours. One hour before cooking, remove the roast from the refrigerator, discard the plastic wrap, and place the meat in a roasting pan with all its juices.

Preheat the oven to 375°.

Before cooking the meat, mix the first four sauce ingredients together and boil for 5 minutes. Set aside.

Cook the roast in the preheated oven for 20 minutes, then pour the warm basting sauce over it. Reduce the temperature to 325°, and cook the pork for 2 hours more, basting occasionally. If you wish, continue cooking for another 20 to 30 minutes, basting every 10 minutes. Remove the roast from the pan and remove the toothpicks, leaving the onions adhering to the meat. Set the roast on a serving platter and keep hot.

Remove the juices from the pan and degrease. Add stock and wine to make 2 cups of liquid. Melt the butter in the roasting pan, stir in the flour, and brown lightly. Beat in the liquid and stir constantly for about 5 minutes. Remove from the heat, beat in the sour cream, and strain the sauce if necessary. Pour it into a heated gravy boat and serve with the meat.

Anonyme de Paris

PORC À L'ORANGE

Serves 6 to 8

This pretty pork dish needs bright green vegetables such as steamed broccoli or Brussels sprouts to set it off.

1 4- to 5-pound center-cut pork loin roast	Freshly ground black pepper
	½ teaspoon thyme
Salt	2 tablespoons flour

Sauce

3 navel oranges	½ teaspoon salt
2 cups fresh orange juice	Freshly ground black pepper
1 tablespoon cornstarch	½ cup water
1 tablespoon cognac	

Preheat the oven to 450°.

Rub the pork with the seasonings and flour. Place it on a rack in a shallow roasting pan and set it in the oven. Immediately reduce the oven temperature to 350° and cook for 35 minutes per pound.

Meanwhile, prepare the sauce. Cut the zest from two of the oranges into fine julienne. Cover the zest with cold water and bring to a boil. Cook for 10 minutes and drain. Peel all three oranges so no pith remains. Cut the flesh into ½- to ¾-inch-thick circles and set aside. Mix the orange juice and cornstarch in a small saucepan, and cook over low heat until thickened, about 5 minutes. Remove from the heat and stir in the cognac, salt, pepper, and zest strips.

When the roast is done, set it on a heated platter and let it rest for 10 minutes. Pour off the accumulated fat in the pan and deglaze the pan with the water. Scrape the brown bits into the sauce and pour it into the orange juice mixture. Bring it to a boil, stirring vigorously. Strain if necessary and add the orange slices. Heat thoroughly, but do not cook the oranges.

Arrange the orange slices around the pork and pour some sauce over all. Serve the rest of the sauce in a heated gravy boat.

Mrs. Alva Cuddeback
Council of the BSO

CALVADOS COUNTY PORK OR BACK-COUNTRY APPLEJACK PORK

Serves 6

The name changes according to the liquor used.

3 pork loin fillets (approximately 1 pound each), cut into diagonal, slanting medallions ½ inch thick
Salt
Freshly ground black pepper
Flour
1 tablespoon vegetable oil

½ cup butter
Paprika
¼ to ½ cup Calvados or applejack
1 cup heavy cream
1 tablespoon Dijon mustard
2 tablespoons chopped parsley (for garnish)

Flatten the medallions slightly with a mallet, season with salt and pepper, and sprinkle with flour.

In a large heavy frying pan, heat the vegetable oil and ¼ cup of butter and sauté the medallions gently, a few at a time: do not allow them to touch. Dust them with paprika before turning; then dust again. As the medallions are cooked through, remove them from the pan and keep them hot. Add more butter as needed during the sautéing process.

When all the medallions are done, return the pork to the frying pan and flame with slightly warmed Calvados or applejack. Put out the flame before it dies, to retain the flavor of the liquor. Remove the meat and keep it hot.

Whisk the cream and mustard into the juices in the pan and simmer until slightly thickened, stirring gently. Add more paprika for color, and adjust the seasonings.*

Place the medallions on a heated platter and cover with the sauce. Sprinkle with parsley, and serve immediately with brown rice pilaf and a green vegetable.

*May be prepared ahead to this point. Set the meat and the sauce aside separately. Reheat both and proceed as above.

Marianne and Karl Lipsky
Tanglewood Council of the BSO

PUERCO EN SALSA VERDE
(Pork in Green Sauce)

Serves 6

2 pounds pork tenderloin, cut into
    medallions ½ inch thick
Flour
½ cup olive oil
¾ cup minced onion
¾ cup finely chopped coriander
2 4-ounce cans mild roasted and
    peeled green chilies (jalapeños)

1 cup white wine
1 teaspoon thyme
2 teaspoons oregano
1½ teaspoons cumin seed
Salt
Freshly ground black pepper
¼ cup sour cream

Dredge the pork medallions lightly in flour, and brown them well in the olive oil in a heavy frying pan. As they are browned, remove the medallions to a heated plate; keep them warm. In the same pan, sauté the onions until translucent. Add all the remaining ingredients except the sour cream, and mix well. Return the pork to the pan, and cook over low heat for about 15 minutes. Arrange on a heated serving platter, garnish each medallion with a dollop of sour cream, and serve with warm tortillas.

José L. Romero, Jr.

GINGER PORK WITH GREEN BEANS

Serves 4

There has long been a particular rapport between the Boston Symphony and Japanese musicians, even before Seiji Ozawa's arrival on the Boston scene. Yuka Kikkawa, the daughter of a Japanese exchange player, collected, translated, and adapted most of the Japanese recipes in this book. Japanese food should be eaten with chopsticks and accompanied by warm *sake* (readily available in the United States) and/or cold beer.

1 pound pork tenderloin, thinly sliced
½ cup cornstarch
1 inch-long piece of gingerroot, grated
4½ tablespoons soy sauce
2 tablespoons sugar
3 tablespoons dry white wine or sweet
    sherry

3 tablespoons peanut oil
1 pound green beans, trimmed, sliced
    lengthwise, and cut in half
Salt
1 tablespoon prepared mustard
2 cups hot cooked white rice

Coat the pork with the cornstarch, shake off the excess, and set the meat aside. Mix the grated ginger with 3 tablespoons soy sauce, the sugar, and 2 tablespoons wine; set aside. Heat the peanut oil in a heavy frying pan, and brown the pork thoroughly. Remove the meat, and pour off any surplus fat. Deglaze the pan with the ginger mixture, and stir briskly for several minutes. Remove from the heat, stir in the meat, and set aside but keep warm.

Cook the beans in boiling salted water for 2 to 4 minutes, until barely tender, and drain thoroughly. Combine the mustard, 1½ tablespoons soy sauce, and 1 tablespoon wine in a bowl large enough to hold the beans. Add the beans and toss to coat thoroughly.

Mound the rice in the center of a heated serving dish, surround it with the beans, and pour the hot pork mixture over the rice. Serve immediately.

Hiromi Ono

PORK CHOPS VINTNER'S STYLE

Serves 6 to 8

This is a very fashionably wine-colored dish. Serve it with white and bright green vegetables to emphasize its color.

2 tablespoons olive oil	12 black Greek olives
2 cloves garlic, minced	Salt
8 thick pork chops	Freshly ground black pepper
2 cups dry red wine	1 tablespoon cornstarch dissolved in 1
2 tablespoons tomato paste	tablespoon water
4 anchovy fillets	1 tablespoon capers

Heat the oil in a heavy frying pan and cook the garlic until golden. Raise the temperature and briefly sear the chops, three at a time, until barely grey on both sides. Remove from the pan and set aside.

Deglaze the pan with the wine, add the tomato paste, and mix well. Stir in the anchovies and olives, and season to taste. Return the meat to the pan and cook very slowly, loosely covered, for about 45 minutes, or until the meat is tender. Remove from the heat, and place the chops on a heated serving dish.

Stir a little of the sauce into the cornstarch paste; then beat this mixture back into the sauce. Stir the sauce over low heat for several minutes, until it has thickened and the cornstarch taste is gone. Correct the seasonings and strain the sauce if it is lumpy.* Add the capers, pour the sauce over the chops, and serve immediately.

*May be prepared ahead to this stage and refrigerated separately. Reheat the sauce and finish as above.

Alberto Fabbri, M.D.

THE SINGER'S PORK CHOPS

Serves 4

John Oliver, in addition to his talents as conductor of the Tanglewood Festival Chorus, enjoys working in his greenhouse and his fully equipped kitchen. He grows some of the herbs for this recipe himself.

4 loin pork chops, about 1½ inches
  thick
½ teaspoon dry mustard
½ teaspoon paprika
Salt
Freshly ground black pepper
2 medium-sized cloves of garlic, halved
6 tablespoons finely chopped fresh basil
Flour

2 tablespoons peanut oil
2 tablespoons rice wine vinegar
½ to 1 cup dry white wine
1 pound mushrooms, chopped
6 tablespoons unsalted butter
1 teaspoon Worcestershire sauce
Tabasco
¾ cup sour cream
Parsley sprigs (for garnish)

"Butterfly" the chops by cutting a horizontal pocket through the eye of each chop to the bone, making as small an incision in the edging fat as possible. Rub both the inside and outside surfaces with the mustard, paprika, and salt and pepper to taste. Crush the garlic into the cavities and fill them with basil. Secure with toothpicks or sew with coarse thread. Dredge the chops with flour and brown them thoroughly in peanut oil over medium-high heat. Remove from the pan.

Pour all but 1 tablespoon of oil from the pan and deglaze it with the vinegar and ½ cup wine. Return the meat to the pan and simmer gently for about 40 minutes, turning several times and adding more wine if necessary. When the chops are tender, remove them to a heated platter and keep them hot. Set the pan and contents aside.

Using another frying pan, sauté the mushrooms in the butter until the liquid evaporates. Season with Worcestershire sauce, a few drops of Tabasco, and salt and pepper to taste. Reduce the liquid in the chop pan to ⅓ cup (or add wine if necessary) and beat in the sour cream. Heat thoroughly, but *do not boil*. Add the mushrooms, stir, and pour the sauce over the chops. Garnish with parsley and serve with homemade noodles or boiled new potatoes.

John Oliver, conductor and singer
Director, Tanglewood Festival Chorus

SPICY ITALIAN SAUSAGES

Serves 4

8 hot Italian sausages, at room
  temperature
Water
2 medium-sized onions, sliced
2 green peppers, seeded and sliced

4½ cups ground peeled tomatoes
  (1 28-ounce can)
½ teaspoon oregano (optional)
½ teaspoon basil (optional)

Prick the sausages several times with a fork. Place in a large frying pan and add a small amount of water. Cover and steam gently for 15 minutes, pricking again while cooking.

Cut each sausage into three or four pieces, add the onions, and cook over medium heat, uncovered, until the water evaporates and the sausage browns. Add the peppers, cover, and cook for 2 or 3 minutes. Add the tomatoes, cover, and simmer for 10 minutes, or until the vegetables are tender. Serve immediately with noodles or boiled or mashed potatoes.

Mrs. Frank Remick
Council of the BSO

BIGOS (Polish Casserole)

Serves 6 to 8

This is a simplified version of a traditional Polish dish that used to be served in country houses after a cold day of hunting. It goes very well with Boston baked beans.

*1 medium-sized red cabbage, cored
  and thinly sliced*
½ cup water
3 tablespoons lemon juice
Salt

Sugar
1 large onion, chopped
2 tablespoons butter
*1½ pounds kielbasa (Polish sausage),
  cut into ½-inch pieces*

Place the cabbage in a deep pan, add the water, cover, and cook over high heat for 10 to 12 minutes, stirring occasionally. Add the lemon juice, and salt and sugar to taste. Sauté the onion in the butter until transparent but not brown. Add it to the cabbage, stir, and allow the mixture to stand for several hours or overnight.

Preheat the oven to 350°.

Combine the sausage with the cabbage in a covered casserole. Bake, covered, for 30 to 40 minutes, or until heated through but not overcooked. Adjust the seasonings, and serve immediately as a main course or a side dish.

Leftovers may be heated in a double boiler.

Mrs. E. Anthony Kutten
Council of the BSO

VEAL AND PORK TERRINE

Serves 8 to 10

This terrine is perfect for summer picnics, or for a cold buffet table. Elaine Rosenfeld was co-chairman of the Council of the Boston Symphony when this cookbook was first discussed. She was given this recipe by Mme. Jacques Massenet, wife of the former French consul in Boston.

⅔ cup dry white wine or vermouth
1 teaspoon Worcestershire sauce
1 teaspoon tamari (Japanese soy
  sauce)
4 tablespoons unsalted butter
1 large bay leaf
1 tablespoon chopped parsley
1 teaspoon dried tarragon
1 teaspoon dried thyme

1 teaspoon salt
¼ teaspoon freshly ground black
  pepper
2 pounds veal scallops, pounded very
  thin
2 pounds boneless pork, sliced very
  thin
2 to 3 ounces liver or goose pâté

Mix the wine with the sauces and set aside. Melt the butter in the bottom of a 9-by-5-by-3-inch loaf pan, an equivalent-sized covered earthenware terrine, or a long baking dish of suitable dimensions, and spread it carefully up the sides. Place the bay leaf in the bottom of the pan and sprinkle with half the parsley. Pound the tarragon, thyme, salt, and pepper in a mortar.

Assemble the terrine as follows:

A layer of one fourth of the veal, sprinkled with one eighth of the seasonings.

A layer of one fourth of the pork, sprinkled with one eighth of the seasonings.

Veal as above.

Pork as above.

Pour in half the wine mixture.

Spoon in all the pâté.

Pork as above.

Veal as above.

Pork as above.

Veal as above.

Sprinkle with the remaining parsley, and pour in the rest of the wine.

Cover the terrine tightly and refrigerate for 24 to 48 hours.

Preheat the oven to 350°.

Bake the terrine, uncovered, for 15 minutes; then cover tightly and bake for 1¾ hours more. Remove from the oven and stand the terrine in a large baking dish. Cover it with a sheet of foil or parchment paper, and place a weight of about 3 or 4 pounds on top of the meat mixture: a brick, a large rock, or a loaf pan filled with stones will serve this purpose. The pan juices will overflow into the baking dish. Allow the meat to cool, and then refrigerate it, still weighted, for at least 24 hours. If the juice does not jell, drain it off and add a little gelatin. Pour it back into the terrine and allow it to set firmly.

Unmold the terrine, remove any accumulated fat, and serve sliced thin with cornichons and/or pickled onions.

Mrs. Jerome Rosenfeld, Overseer
Past co-chairman, Council of the BSO

VEAL CLAUDE RAINS

Serves 6 to 8

Dr. Gotlieb says that his old and dear friend, the actor Claude Rains, was a "literary" cook who knew what the characters he portrayed would have eaten. "On my visits to him, he would supervise the preparation of this dish."

3 pounds veal steak, cut into thin
  strips
2 to 3 tablespoons butter
2 tablespoons vegetable oil
3 large white onions, roughly chopped
4 strips bacon, cut into small pieces
1 pound fresh mushrooms, sliced
2 tablespoons paprika

1½ pints sour cream
½ cup cognac or brandy
5 tablespoons tomato sauce
3 to 4 cups steamed rice, buttered and
  lightly seasoned with salt, pepper,
  and nutmeg
Chopped fresh parsley (for garnish)

Quickly brown the veal in the butter and set aside. *Do not overcook.*

Heat the vegetable oil in a large heavy frying pan and sauté the onions until limp but not brown. Drain off the oil. Add the bacon and stir for about 5 minutes. Drain off all but 1 tablespoon of the pan drippings and add the mushrooms. Sprinkle with the paprika, and stir for about 10 minutes; then remove the pan from the heat, and add the veal.

In a bowl, beat the sour cream, cognac, and tomato sauce until smooth. Return the veal to the heat and pour in the sour cream mixture. Stir over low heat for 5 to 10 minutes, until the sauce almost boils. Mound the rice in the center of a heated platter and surround with the veal. Sprinkle chopped parsley over both and serve immediately.

Dr. Howard B. Gotlieb
Director of twentieth-century archives
Boston University

TOURNEDOS OF VEAL COPLEY'S

Serves 4

4 tournedos of veal, 6 ounces each
¼ cup flour
6 tablespoons clarified unsalted butter
¾ cup dry Marsala
5 medium-sized shallots, minced
1 medium-sized clove of garlic, minced
¼ cup chopped smoked ham
½ pound mushrooms, chopped
2 cups heavy cream

1 to 2 tablespoons beurre manié for
  thickening (see Note)
Salt
Freshly ground black pepper
4 large whole mushrooms
4 croutons (¼-inch-thick bread
  rounds, lightly toasted)
4 thin slices Virginia ham

Dredge the tournedos in the flour and sauté them quickly in 2 tablespoons of butter until lightly browned and medium-rare. Remove them from the pan and keep warm. Deglaze the pan with half the Marsala and reserve the liquid.

Sauté the shallots in 2 tablespoons of butter until transparent. Add the garlic, chopped ham, and chopped mushrooms and cook gently until soft. Add the remaining wine and reserved liquid. Reduce by about half and add the cream. Thicken by beating in small amounts of *beurre manié* (see Note). Reduce again until the sauce reaches the desired consistency. Correct the seasonings, if necessary. Set aside and keep warm.

Sauté the whole mushrooms lightly in the remaining butter, set aside, and keep warm.

Place the hot croutons on a heated platter; top with the ham slices and then the veal. Pour the sauce over all, garnish with the whole mushrooms, and serve immediately. Creamed spinach, "touched" with garlic, goes well with this dish.

Note

Beurre manié is a smooth paste used to thicken soups and sauces. It is made of equal parts of flour and softened butter.

Copley's Restaurant, Boston

DELIZIE IMBOTTITE (Stuffed Veal Scallops)

Serves 2 or 3

Matthew Ruggiero, principal bassoon for the Boston Pops, was the Orchestra's representative on the Cookbook Committee. He played for the National Symphony before joining the BSO in 1961, and in 1967 he toured the Soviet Union with the Boston Symphony Chamber Players. He is a creator of beautiful things in exotic woods, a lover of stringed instruments, and a very, very funny man who confesses that he stole this recipe.

1 pound veal cutlets, pounded thin
Salt
Freshly ground black pepper
2 tablespoons cream cheese
¼ cup minced ham
1 tablespoon chopped truffles or
  mushrooms

2 tablespoons minced celery
5 tablespoons butter
⅓ cup port wine
Flour

Sprinkle the meat lightly with salt and pepper. Mix the cream cheese, ham, truffles or mushrooms, and celery. Place some of this stuffing in the center of each veal slice; fold over the top and bottom, then the sides, to make a neat bundle. Tie each with strong thread, leaving a long tail to facilitate handling.

Heat 4 tablespoons of the butter in a heavy frying pan; add the bundles of veal, seam side down, and ¼ cup of the wine. Cook over medium heat for 8 to 10 minutes, turning occasionally. Remove the threads, and place the bundles on a heated serving dish, or set aside to be reheated later.

Add the remaining butter and wine to the frying pan and whisk in a little flour. Cook until the sauce thickens and does not taste of flour. Adjust the seasonings, if necessary. Just before serving, strain the hot sauce over the meat. Serve with pasta or new potatoes.

Variation
Imbottite can be prepared ahead, and heated with the sauce in a chafing dish at the table.

Matthew Ruggiero
Boston Pops principal bassoon

FAUSTIAN VEAL

Serves 4 to 6

Equally at home on the great concert and opera stages of the world, tenor Kenneth Riegel has performed annually with the Boston Symphony since 1971. He commemorates one of these performances with this quick and easy veal recipe, which, he says, "was invented after a performance of *The Damnation of Faust* I had just sung with the BSO."

2 pounds veal cutlets pounded thin, then cut into even strips	3 tablespoons chopped parsley
Salt	1 teaspoon thyme
Freshly ground black pepper	1 teaspoon oregano
2 tablespoons flour	2 tablespoons tomato purée
3 tablespoons butter	1 teaspoon Dijon mustard
3 tablespoons olive oil	½ teaspoon lemon juice
4 shallots or 1 medium-sized onion, minced	½ cup dry white wine
	¼ cup water
	½ cup grated Parmesan cheese

Season the veal with salt and pepper and dredge lightly with the flour. Heat the butter and olive oil until foaming in a large shallow frying pan and sauté the veal over medium heat until golden brown. Remove the veal and keep it hot. Sauté the shallots or onion in the same pan until translucent but not browned; pour off any excess fat. Stir in the herbs and cook briefly. Mix together the tomato purée, mustard, lemon juice, wine, and water and stir into the pan. Boil the sauce until it is fairly thick, and correct the seasonings.* Replace the veal in the sauce and heat for a few moments; then sprinkle generously with the cheese. Turn off the heat, cover, and let stand for 5 minutes, until the cheese melts. Serve immediately with green noodles and a salad.

*May be prepared ahead to this stage and refrigerated for a later finishing.

Kenneth Riegel, tenor

VEAL ORVIETO

Serves 8

½ pound butter
24 veal medallions (3 per serving)
1 rib celery, minced
2 medium-sized onions, minced
6 cloves garlic, minced

½ bottle Orvieto wine
16 artichoke hearts, cooked and
    drained
8 whole pimientos, drained

Melt the butter in a heavy frying pan. Sauté the veal lightly, remove, and set aside. Add the celery, onions, and garlic and sauté gently until soft but not brown. Stir in the wine and reduce the mixture to the consistency of heavy cream. Add the artichoke hearts and pimientos to the sauce, and heat.* Then add the veal and heat thoroughly.

Place three medallions on each heated serving plate with one pimiento and two artichoke hearts. Spoon sauce over all and serve immediately. The Charles serves this dish with linguini marinara and a simple green salad.

*May be prepared ahead to this stage and reheated when ready to serve. Do not add the veal until just before serving, as above.

The Charles Restaurant, Boston
Edmund Sportini, chef

VEAL MOZZARELLA

Serves 6

Violin virtuoso Joseph Silverstein, whose chair onstage bears the name of Charles Munch, is the product of a musical family. His first teacher was his father, to whom those privileged to listen to the son's elegant playing must be eternally grateful. Despite a professional schedule of enormous complexity, "Joey" finds time to play good golf and mean tennis, to take excellent photographs, and to place cooking high on his list of interests.

2 pounds veal scallops
2 eggs, lightly beaten
Seasoned bread crumbs
¼ pound butter or 4 tablespoons butter
    and 4 tablespoons olive oil

1 12-ounce jar sweet Italian fried
    peppers
1 8-ounce can tomato sauce
1 cup dry red wine
8 thin slices mozzarella cheese

Dip the veal in the beaten eggs and coat with crumbs. Refrigerate for at least 1 hour, or as long as overnight, to dry the coating.

Heat the butter in a large frying pan until foaming. Brown the veal on both sides and remove it to a large baking dish. Keep hot in a warm oven. Add the peppers, tomato sauce, and wine to the butter in the pan, and simmer for about 5 minutes. Arrange the cheese slices on top of the veal and surround it with the pepper mixture. Broil until the cheese is melted and lightly browned, and serve immediately with pasta and salad.

Joseph Silverstein, violin
Boston Symphony concertmaster
Boston Symphony assistant conductor

VEAL SCALOPPINE ALLA MARSALA

Serves 4

One of the world's greatest violin virtuosos, as well as an educator, diplomat, and humanitarian, Henryk Szeryng has performed the music of Brahms, Chausson, Lees, Schumann, and Tchaikovsky with the Boston Symphony Orchestra. His elegantly simple veal dish can be prepared in no time at all.

1 pound veal scallops
Flour
Salt
Freshly ground black pepper

3 tablespoons butter
¼ to ½ cup Marsala
2 tablespoons concentrated chicken
  stock

Pound the veal lightly until very thin. Dredge with flour seasoned to taste with salt and pepper. Heat the butter in a heavy frying pan until it starts to brown, add the veal, and brown on both sides over medium heat. Turn up the heat to moderately high, add the Marsala, and cook for 1 minute longer, shaking the pan. Transfer the meat to a warm platter.

Add the chicken stock to the pan drippings. Scrape loose all the brown particles and bring to a boil. Pour over the veal and serve with creamed spinach and new potatoes boiled in their jackets.

Ambassador Henryk Szeryng, violin

VEAL SCALLOPS IN GOAT CHEESE SAUCE

Serves 4

The music director of the St. Louis Symphony Orchestra, Leonard Slatkin was a guest conductor with the Boston Symphony during the 1979–80 season. His contribution to this cookbook is his version of a famous Scandinavian dish with a very unusual sauce.

3 tablespoons unsalted butter
3 tablespoons vegetable oil
1/4 cup finely chopped onion
4 large veal scallops, sliced 3/8 inch
  thick and pounded to 1/4 inch thick
1 cup sour cream

1 cup shredded gjetöst (Norwegian
  goat cheese)
Salt
Freshly ground white pepper
Parsley or watercress sprigs (for
  garnish)

Heat 1 tablespoon of butter and 1 tablespoon of oil in a heavy frying pan over medium heat. Add the onions and sauté for about 4 minutes, until transparent. Remove to a small bowl. Add the remaining butter and oil, and sauté the veal over medium heat until it is golden brown, about 4 or 5 minutes on each side. Remove the veal to a heated platter and keep warm.

Pour off all but 1 tablespoon of fat and add the cooked onions to the frying pan. Cook over high heat, stirring constantly, for 3 minutes. Remove from the heat, and stir in the sour cream and cheese. Stir over very low heat until the cheese is melted and the sauce is smooth. *Do not boil.* Season to taste, and return the veal to the frying pan. Coat thoroughly with the sauce, and arrange on a heated serving platter. Garnish with parsley or watercress and serve immediately.

Variation
This recipe works well with thin slices of raw turkey substituted for the veal — an economy that is all but unnoticeable because of the unique flavor of the sauce.

Leonard Slatkin, conductor
St. Louis Symphony Orchestra music director

VEAL SCALLOPS IN MUSTARD SAUCE

Serves 4

3/4 pound veal scallops
Salt
Freshly ground white pepper
1/2 cup flour
4 tablespoons butter

3 tablespoons finely chopped shallots
1/2 cup or more dry white wine or
  vermouth
1/2 cup heavy cream
3/4 tablespoon Dijon mustard

Pound the veal with a mallet until thin. Dredge the meat with a mixture of salt, pepper, and flour, shaking off the excess. Melt 2 tablespoons of the butter until foamy; quickly sauté the veal until golden, no more than 2 minutes on a side. Transfer the veal to a heated serving platter and keep warm.

In the same pan, briefly cook the shallots in the remaining butter; stir in the wine and cook until thickened. Add the cream and boil for about 30 seconds. Remove from the heat and beat in the mustard.

Spoon the sauce over the veal. Serve with noodles.

SZEKELY GULYAS

Serves 6

Gulyas is reliably reported to have been the favorite food of the late great Arthur Fiedler. There are many versions of this famous dish, all of which are good. This one is superior.

4 tablespoons lard
1 large onion, chopped
2 tablespoons paprika
2 pounds veal or pork, cubed
1 tablespoon tomato paste
2 pounds sauerkraut, drained and
  rinsed

2 teaspoons caraway seeds
½ teaspoon salt
½ pound kolbacz, *sliced (see Note)*
Sour cream

In a large saucepan, heat the lard and sauté the onion until soft. Remove from the heat, add the paprika, and stir until the onion is coated. Add the meat, tomato paste, and water to cover; bring to a boil. Cover, reduce the heat, and simmer for 20 minutes.

Add the sauerkraut, caraway seeds, salt, and *kolbacz*. Cover and simmer for 1 hour, or until the meat is tender. If necessary, add more water so that the *gulyas* does not dry out. Serve immediately, topped with sour cream, or set aside for reheating the following day. Cucumber salad is a traditional accompaniment.

Note

Kolbacz, a Hungarian smoked sausage, contributes a unique quality to *gulyas*. Westphalian ham or any other smoked meat or sausage may be substituted.

VITELLO ALLA CACCIATORE

Serves 6

Mrs. Benson is doubly a member of the Boston Symphony family. Her husband, Stanley Benson, was a long-time member of the violin section, and her brother, James Stagliano (also a superb cook), was a horn player for many years. The interest in Italian cooking may have been inherited, but the expertise is hers alone.

2 tablespoons butter
4 tablespoons olive oil
1½ pounds veal rump cut into
  1½-inch cubes
1 large onion, sliced
¼ cup chopped celery
1 large clove garlic, minced
4 large green peppers, seeded and cut
  into 1-inch strips

½ pound mushrooms, sliced
3 tablespoons tomato paste
½ cup Marsala or sweet vermouth
¼ cup chopped fresh parsley
Salt
Freshly ground black pepper
Water

Heat half the butter and olive oil together in a large heavy frying pan, and brown the veal cubes on all sides for about 10 minutes. Remove the veal and keep warm. Heat the remaining butter and oil and sauté the onions, celery, and garlic for 2 to 3 minutes over low heat. Add the peppers and mushrooms and cook for about 5 minutes more. Mix the tomato paste with the wine, parsley, and salt and pepper to taste; add to the vegetable mixture. Cover and simmer slowly for 10 to 15 minutes.

Stir the veal and any accumulated juice into the sauce and add about ¼ cup water. Simmer over low heat for 20 minutes or so, stirring occasionally to prevent sticking. It may be necessary to add a little more water if the sauce becomes too thick. Serve immediately with hot pasta or plain rice, or set aside for later reheating.

Clara Stagliano Benson

VEAL WITH RAISINS IN SOUR CREAM

Serves 6

A delicately colored and flavored dish, this will hold for some time.

3 pounds veal, cut into 1-inch cubes
½ teaspoon salt
⅛ teaspoon freshly ground black
  pepper
4 tablespoons butter
3 tablespoons dry sherry, warmed
½ cup golden raisins

¼ cup sliced mushrooms
1 teaspoon tomato paste
2 tablespoons flour
2 cups chicken stock
1 tablespoon currant jelly
1 cup sour cream

Season the meat with salt and pepper, and brown it quickly in the butter in a heavy frying pan. Stir in the sherry, and remove the veal.

Add the raisins to the pan and cook over high heat for several minutes. Stir in the mushrooms and tomato paste. Beat the flour into 1 cup chicken stock, and stir this into the mushroom mixture. When the sauce is smooth and thick, add the remaining stock and bring to a boil. Add the jelly and stir until it is dissolved. Return the veal to the sauce and simmer gently for about 30 minutes, or until the meat is very tender, turning once. Remove the meat, place it on a heated serving dish, and keep hot. Reduce the liquid by half, and add the sour cream. Stir and heat, but do not boil. Pour the sauce over the hot meat and serve with spinach noodles and poppy seeds, or plain noodles garnished with slivered almonds and chopped parsley.

Mrs. William Beautyman
Tanglewood Council of the BSO

ITALIAN VEAL BALLS

Serves 4 to 6

This excellent veal dish will hold well on a hot tray for a buffet dinner.

1 pound ground veal (hip, shoulder, or rump)
½ to ¾ cup dry bread crumbs
1 egg, beaten
1 clove garlic, minced
⅛ teaspoon dried basil
⅛ teaspoon dried oregano
⅛ teaspoon dried rosemary
Salt

Freshly ground black pepper
1 to 2 tablespoons olive oil
1 medium-sized onion, finely chopped
½ cup tomato sauce
1 20-ounce can cannellini (white kidney beans), with juice
1 to 2 tablespoons chopped parsley (for garnish)

Place the veal in a large bowl with ¼ cup bread crumbs. Add the egg, garlic, herbs, and salt and pepper to taste. Mix well. Form the mixture into balls the size of walnuts, and roll them in the remaining bread crumbs.

Heat 1 tablespoon olive oil in a 10-inch frying pan and brown the meatballs on all sides. Remove from the pan and set aside but keep warm. Using the same pan, with more oil if necessary, sauté the onion until wilted. Add the tomato sauce and cannellini, and mix well.

Return the veal balls to the sauce, cover, and cook at a low temperature until tender, approximately 20 to 30 minutes. Adjust the seasonings, pour into a heated shallow serving dish, and garnish with parsley.

Eleanor Gelfond

SAUTÉED SWEETBREADS

Serves 2

This elegant yet simple recipe is a specialty of the famous Red Lion Inn in Stockbridge, Massachusetts.

1 pair veal sweetbreads
¼ cup chopped onion
3 ribs celery, chopped
4 or 5 black peppercorns
2 bay leaves
Flour

Salt
Freshly ground white pepper
2 tablespoons butter
¼ cup dry sherry
2 tablespoons lemon juice
2 tablespoons chopped parsley

Soak the sweetbreads in water to cover for several hours. Drain, place in a small saucepan, and cover with boiling water. Add the onion, celery, peppercorns, and bay leaves, and simmer until the sweetbreads are firm, about 15 to 20 minutes.

Discard the vegetables. Drain the sweetbreads and refrigerate until just before ready to serve.

Slice the sweetbreads about ⅜ inch thick and dredge in flour seasoned with salt and pepper. Shake off the excess. Heat the butter in a small frying pan until the foam subsides. Brown the slices lightly on each side. Pour in the sherry, shaking to loosen any brown bits on the bottom of the pan. Add the lemon juice and 1 tablespoon parsley and heat through.

Serve over toast points or buttered rice. Garnish with the remaining parsley. Serve with brightly colored vegetables — such as grilled tomatoes, steamed broccoli, or buttered peas.

Mrs. John Fitzpatrick, Trustee
Tanglewood Council of the BSO

SWEETBREADS IN LEMON CREAM

Serves 4

1 pound sweetbreads
3 tablespoons lemon juice
5 tablespoons butter
3 small white onions, thinly sliced
Salt

Freshly ground white pepper
½ pound mushrooms, sliced
1 cup heavy cream
3 egg yolks, lightly beaten
Watercress sprigs (for garnish)

Place the sweetbreads in a saucepan and pour 1½ tablespoons of lemon juice over them. Add cold water to cover and soak for 1 hour. Drain thoroughly. Cover again with cold water, bring to a boil, and simmer gently for 15 minutes. Drain and rinse under cold water. Peel off the thin membrane around the sweetbreads and discard the connecting tubes. Cut into ¼-inch slices.

Heat 3 tablespoons of butter in a saucepan just large enough to hold the sweetbreads comfortably. Stir in the onions and simmer, covered, for 10 minutes. Add the sweetbread slices, stir, and continue to simmer, covered, for about 20 minutes. Season with salt and pepper to taste.

Sauté the mushrooms quickly in a large pan in the remaining butter, stirring constantly until the liquid has evaporated. Add the sweetbreads. Beat the cream and egg yolks together. Pour this over the sweetbreads and cook slowly, stirring constantly, until the sauce is slightly thickened. *Do not boil.* Add lemon juice to taste and adjust the seasonings. Pour onto a heated platter and serve with steamed rice or couscous, garnished with watercress.

Laura G. Blau

VENISON CUTLETS

Serves 6 to 8

Dr. Clowes, a long-time Trustee, is also an ardent sailor. He and his wife found this recipe for venison in Charleston, South Carolina, probably ashore and not afloat.

2 pounds venison steaks
Flour
Celery salt
Freshly ground black pepper

2 tablespoons butter
½ cup sour cream
Worcestershire sauce
1 bay leaf

Cut the venison into individual cutlets and roll them in flour seasoned with celery salt and pepper. Heat the butter in a large frying pan over medium heat, and brown the cutlets thoroughly on both sides. Pour the sour cream over the meat and season the sauce to taste with Worcestershire sauce, celery salt, and pepper. Add the bay leaf, cover, and cook for about 1 hour, until the cutlets are tender. Remove the cutlets to a heated serving platter. Adjust the seasonings and pour the sauce over the meat. Serve immediately with a well-seasoned Rice Pilaf.◆

Mrs. George H. A. Clowes, Jr.

VENISON RIB CHOPS

Serves 4

Frozen venison should be thawed very slowly and completely in the refrigerator.

3 tablespoons butter
4 venison rib chops
¼ cup chopped onion

¼ cup chopped celery
½ cup dry red wine
Watercress sprigs (for garnish)

Heat the butter in a heavy frying pan and brown the chops thoroughly on both sides. Add the onion and celery and cook for a few minutes in the butter and juices. Pour in the wine, cover, and simmer over very low heat for 25 minutes, or until the venison is very tender. Remove the meat to a heated serving dish. Adjust the seasonings in the sauce, if necessary, and pour over the venison. Garnish with watercress and serve immediately with wild rice or a brown rice pilaf.

Mrs. James T. Mountz
Council of the BSO

VEGETABLES

Most professional orchestra musicians passionately enjoy play-ing chamber music. This fact, coupled with the realization that there is a great deal of fine music for unusual groups of instru-ments and that the principal players of the Boston Symphony are free in May and June (they do not play with the Boston Pops), led to the creation in 1964 of the Boston Symphony Chamber Players as a regular part of the BSO organization. Since then, they have toured the country and the world and have made many diverse recordings for RCA, Deutsche Grammophon, and Nonesuch; they are an important part of the burgeoning cham-ber music scene in America. Many other members of the Boston Symphony are active chamber musicians. They have organized themselves into a number of ensembles that play a rich and seldom-heard repertory, displaying their virtuosity and versatil-ity. Performing in Boston's Jordan Hall *(overleaf)* are members of the Boston Symphony Chamber Players' wind section: Doriot Anthony Dwyer, principal flute; Harold Wright, principal clarinet; Sherman Walt, principal bassoon; Charles Kavalovski, principal horn; and Ralph Gomberg, principal oboe. Gilbert Kalish, director of keyboard activities at the Berkshire Music Center, is at the piano.

LIMA BEAN CASSEROLE

Serves 6 to 8

3 10-ounce packages frozen Fordhook
    lima beans
1 teaspoon salt
1½ cups sour cream
¼ cup melted butter

2 tablespoons maple sugar or syrup
2 teaspoons dry mustard
¼ cup grated mild Cheddar cheese
Freshly ground black pepper

Cover the beans with water, add the salt, and bring to a boil. Cook for 1 minute, drain, and rinse under cold running water. Combine the sour cream with the remaining ingredients and beat well. Add the beans, and adjust the seasonings if necessary. Turn into a buttered oven-proof serving dish, and bake for 1 hour, or until the beans are tender and the top is very lightly browned. Serve hot or cold.

Mrs. Stephen Heartt
Council of the BSO

SESAME BROCCOLI

Serves 6 to 8

2 pounds fresh broccoli cut into 2-inch
    pieces
2½ tablespoons sugar
2 tablespoons sesame seeds

2 tablespoons oil
2 tablespoons vinegar
2 tablespoons soy sauce

To cook the broccoli, bring a saucepan of lightly salted water to a rolling boil, put in the broccoli, and cook for only 1 or 2 minutes after the water returns to a boil. Drain.

While the broccoli is cooking, combine the remaining ingredients in a small saucepan and bring to a boil over medium heat. Pour over the broccoli, turning to coat well. Serve immediately.

Nancy Reynolds

BAKED CARROTS

Serves 6

Composer John Cage's music has sparked considerable controversy at Boston Symphony concerts, but there can be no dispute about his culinary masterwork for carrots.

12 medium-sized or 6 large carrots, scraped
3 tablespoons sesame oil
Salt

Freshly ground black pepper
2 tablespoons chopped parsley or toasted sesame seeds (for garnish)

Soak a covered clay baking dish for ½ hour. Place the carrots in the bottom and sprinkle with the sesame oil. Dust with a little salt and pepper, cover, and place the dish in a cold oven. Set the thermostat at 400° and bake for about 1 hour, or until the carrots are lightly caramelized, turning occasionally. Serve immediately, sprinkled with parsley or sesame seeds.

John Cage, composer

CARROT SOUFFLÉ RING

Serves 6 to 8

2 tablespoons butter
2 tablespoons flour
½ cup milk
4 egg yolks, beaten
2 cups mashed cooked carrots

½ teaspoon salt
Freshly ground white pepper (optional)
Cinnamon and/or nutmeg (optional)
4 egg whites, whipped until stiff

Preheat the oven to 375°.

Make a very thick white sauce using the butter, flour, and milk. Remove it from the heat and beat in the egg yolks. Stir in the mashed carrots and season to taste. Gently fold in the egg whites and pour into a buttered 1¼- to 2-quart ring mold. Set it in the oven in a pan of boiling water and bake for 40 minutes, or until the soufflé is puffed and firm to the touch.

Allow the ring to stand for a few minutes before you turn it out onto a hot platter. Fill the center with green peas, broccoli flowerets, chopped spinach, or another green vegetable. Serve immediately.

Mrs. George R. Rowland, Trustee
Council of the BSO

CARROTS AND PARSNIPS IN CREAM

Serves 6 to 8

1 pound parsnips, peeled and trimmed
2 pounds carrots, peeled and trimmed
2 tablespoons butter
½ cup dry sherry
1 tablespoon sugar

Salt
Freshly ground black pepper
1 cup medium or heavy cream
Grated Parmesan cheese

Grate the parsnips by hand or in a food processor fitted with the grating disk. Clean the equipment; then repeat the process with the carrots. Keep the two vegetables separate. Heat the butter in a large frying pan. Add the parsnips, sherry, sugar, and salt and pepper to taste. Stir well, cover, and steam over low heat until the parsnips are almost tender. Drain and set aside.

Steam the carrots until almost tender. Drain thoroughly.

Preheat the oven to 350°.

Arrange half the cooked carrots in a buttered shallow casserole. Cover with the parsnips and top with the remaining carrots. Pour the cream carefully over all and top with Parmesan cheese. Bake uncovered for 30 to 45 minutes, until the vegetables are tender and the topping is crisp and browned. Serve immediately.

Mrs. Bruce P. Shaw

CAULIFLOWER SAN JUAN

Serves 4 to 6

1 large white onion, quartered
½ cup dry white wine
1 large cauliflower, broken in pieces

Salt
Freshly ground white pepper

Sauce
4 tablespoons butter
4 ounces Longhorn, Monterey jack, or
   Swiss cheese

¼ cup milk

Purée the onion and wine in a blender. Place in a deep saucepan, add the cauliflower, cover, and simmer for about 10 minutes, or until the cauliflower is tender but still crisp. Drain thoroughly and season to taste with salt and pepper.

While the cauliflower is cooking, prepare the sauce. Melt the butter in a double boiler, add the cheese and milk, and stir until smooth. Remove from the heat but keep hot.

Place the drained, seasoned cauliflower on a heated serving dish, dress with the sauce, and serve immediately.

Alberto Fabbri, M.D.

NEW BEDFORD CORN PUDDING

Serves 6 as a luncheon dish,
8 to 10 as a vegetable

BSO Trustee Albert L. Nickerson is fortunate indeed: his wife has invented a delicious way to use corn of uncertain age.

12 ears of mature corn
5 tablespoons melted butter

½ teaspoon salt
1 tablespoon sugar

Preheat the oven to 400°.

   Scrape the corn from the cobs, using the back of a blunt knife. Reserve 2 tablespoons butter, combine the corn with the remaining ingredients, and pour the mixture into a well-buttered pie plate.* Bake for 15 minutes; then reduce the heat to 350° and continue to cook for about 45 minutes more. Brush with melted butter during the last 15 minutes of baking. The pudding should be brownish on top and of a sticky-solid texture when done. Serve with a salad for luncheon, or as a vegetable with dinner.

*May be prepared ahead to this stage.

Variation

Use one 10-ounce package frozen cream-style corn and two 10-ounce packages frozen whole kernel corn instead of the fresh corn.

Mrs. Albert L. Nickerson

It is not necessary to peel eggplant. To remove the bitterness, winter eggplant should be salted on the cut sides and set aside for about half an hour. Rinse off the salt and dry well before cooking.

EGGPLANT À LA MODE

Serves 8 to 10

Vera Ozawa's mother, Maki Irie, has written a Western cookbook for Japanese who have a taste for French food. Here she contributes a dish that lends itself to microwave cooking.

6 small eggplants, 6 to 8 inches long
1 tablespoon salt
1 quart water
¼ cup flour
Salt
Freshly ground black pepper

½ cup olive oil
2 medium-sized onions
2 cloves garlic, minced
4 large tomatoes, peeled and sliced
   ¼ to ½ inch thick

Partially peel the eggplant, making lengthwise stripes, and cut it into ½-inch slices. Mix the salt and water and soak the eggplant in the liquid for about 20 minutes, turning occasionally. Drain, rinse in clear water, and dry thoroughly. Dust the slices with flour, salt, and pepper.

Preheat the oven to 350°.

Heat 3 tablespoons of olive oil in a large frying pan, and sauté the eggplant slices until well browned on both sides. Add more oil as needed. Remove the eggplant and set aside. Add another 2 tablespoons of oil to the pan, and sauté the onion and garlic until soft and transparent. Set aside.

Cover the bottom of a shallow oven-proof dish with half the partly cooked eggplant, followed by half the onion mixture and half the sliced tomatoes. Salt and pepper lightly. Repeat the layers. Drizzle the remaining oil over the top.* Cover and bake for 30 to 40 minutes, or until the eggplant is tender. Serve immediately.

In a microwave oven, cook for about 12 minutes on the high setting, turning every 3 to 4 minutes.

*May be prepared ahead to this stage and refrigerated for later reheating.

Maki Irie

EGGPLANT KATHLEEN

Serves 3 or 4 as a main course,
6 as a side dish

1 small eggplant cut into ¼-inch slices
(see Note)
4 medium-sized tomatoes, peeled and
sliced fairly thick
2 medium-sized green peppers,
chopped
1 medium-sized onion, chopped
1½ teaspoons sugar

¾ teaspoon garlic salt
⅛ teaspoon monosodium glutamate
(optional)
Salt
¾ pound sharp Cheddar cheese in
⅛-inch slices
Freshly ground black pepper

Preheat the oven to 400°.

Parboil the eggplant until almost tender in salted water to cover. Drain thoroughly. Arrange the eggplant in a buttered shallow casserole, and cover with the tomatoes. Combine the peppers and onions and fill the spaces with this mixture. Sprinkle lightly with the sugar, garlic salt, MSG, and salt; top with the cheese and a dusting of pepper. Cover and bake for 20 to 30 minutes, or until steaming.

Remove the cover, and reduce the oven temperature to 350°. Cook for 20 to 30 minutes more, until the eggplant is tender and the sauce is thick and golden. Keep warm in the oven until ready to serve as a vegetable with chicken or as a luncheon dish with rice or pasta and a salad.

Barbara Ann Quill

EGGPLANT WITH MISO AND EGGS

Serves 4

The *miso*-wine mixture adds a piquant flavor to the eggplant.

1 large or 2 medium-sized eggplants,
*   unpeeled (see Note at Eggplant*
*   Kathleen♦)*
Peanut oil
¼ cup miso (bean paste)
1 tablespoon brown sugar

1 tablespoon dry white wine
1 tablespoon mirin (Japanese wine)
*   or sweet sherry*
1 tablespoon poppy seeds
2 to 4 hard-boiled eggs, quartered (for
*   garnish)*

Cut the eggplants into ¾-inch-thick slices and brush them with peanut oil. Brown the slices quickly on a hot griddle, or over an indoor or outdoor grill. *Do not overcook.* Place the slices on an oiled cookie sheet.

Preheat the oven to 350°.

Combine the *miso,* sugar, and wines and spread on the partially cooked eggplant slices. Bake for 15 minutes, or until soft, and remove to a heated serving dish. Sprinkle with the poppy seeds and garnish with the hard-boiled eggs.

Mrs. Konnaske Ono

STUFFED ENDIVES WITH WINE SAUCE

Serves 6

6 large Belgian endives
3 tablespoons olive oil
1 cup dry bread crumbs
¾ cup chopped walnuts
½ cup chopped parsley
3 tablespoons tomato purée, or 1
*   tablespoon tomato paste thinned*
*   with 2 tablespoons water*

¼ cup raisins
Salt
Freshly ground black pepper
½ to 1 cup dry white wine
Parsley sprigs (for garnish)

Drop the endives into 1½ inches boiling salted water and cook for 5 minutes. Reserve the cooking water and plunge the endives into cold water. Drain and dry them thoroughly, and set aside.

Heat the olive oil in a small frying pan and add the bread crumbs, walnuts, parsley, and half the tomato purée. Stir over medium heat for 2 to 3 minutes; then add the raisins and salt and pepper to taste. Mix well and remove from the heat.

Preheat the oven to 350°.

Carefully pull open the endive stalks and stuff them with the walnut mixture. Restore each endive to its original shape, and tie with strong thread. Place the endives in a lightly oiled baking dish, add the wine, and cover with the remaining tomato purée. Cover the dish and bake the endives for 45 minutes; remove them to a heated serving dish. Deglaze the baking pan with a little of the reserved cooking water, and pour the resultant sauce over the endives. Garnish with the parsley and serve hot.

Velia N. Tosi
Council of the BSO

BAKED MUSHROOMS

Serves 6

2 pounds fresh mushrooms
½ cup butter
1 clove garlic, pressed
½ cup chopped onion
¾ cup fresh bread crumbs
2 teaspoons salt

2 teaspoons lemon juice
½ teaspoon tarragon, or other
   preferred herb
½ cup chopped parsley
¼ cup olive oil
½ cup white wine

Clean the mushrooms and separate the stems from the caps. Chop the stems. Heat half the butter in a heavy frying pan and add the garlic, onions, and chopped stems. Sauté until the onions are tender: *do not overcook.* Remove from the heat and stir in the bread crumbs, salt, lemon juice, tarragon, and all but 1 tablespoon of the parsley.

Preheat the oven to 325°.

Pour the oil into a flat oven-proof dish, and swirl to coat well. Place half the mushroom caps, hollow sides up, in an even layer on the bottom. Cover with the bread-crumb mixture and top with the remaining mushroom caps, rounded sides up. Dot with the remaining butter and pour the wine over all. Bake for about 30 minutes, until the mushrooms are brown and tender. Garnish with the remaining parsley before serving.

Mrs. Worthing L. West
Council of the BSO

MUSHROOM CASSEROLE SUPREME

Serves 6

1½ pounds mushrooms, sliced
Salt
4 tablespoons plus ¼ pound butter,
   melted
3 tablespoons flour
2 tablespoons chopped parsley
1 egg yolk

1 cup light cream
1½ tablespoons lemon juice
½ large box loose-pack Ritz crackers,
   crushed
¼ pound butter, melted
Freshly ground black pepper

Preheat the oven to 350°.

Lightly salt the mushrooms and sauté them in 4 tablespoons butter for about 5 minutes. Add the flour and parsley, cover, and simmer for 10 minutes, stirring frequently. Beat the egg yolk with 1 tablespoon of the cream and set aside. Add the remaining cream and lemon juice to the mushroom mixture and stir until bubbling. Remove from the heat and add the egg yolk mixture. Pour the mushroom mixture into a shallow baking dish or large pie plate. Combine the Ritz crackers and the remaining melted butter and sprinkle over the casserole. Bake for 30 minutes, or until the crumbs are brown and the sauce is bubbling.

This dish may be assembled up to a day ahead and refrigerated. Remove it from the refrigerator half an hour before baking.

Lindsey Humes
Former BSO staff

GREAT-GRANDMOTHER ST. CLAIR'S ONION SOUFFLÉ

Serves 4

For Thanksgiving or any other festive meal . . .

2 to 2½ pounds white boiling onions, peeled (enough for 1½ to 2 cups cooked onion pulp)	3 egg yolks, beaten
	3 egg whites, whipped to stiff peaks
	Nutmeg
4 tablespoons butter	Salt
4 tablespoons flour	Freshly ground white pepper
⅓ cup heavy cream	

Boil the onions, which shrink rather alarmingly when mashed. Drain very thoroughly, reserving the onion water. Mash the onions and drain again. Reduce the onion liquid to about ⅓ cup.

Melt the butter and stir in the flour. Beat in the cream and the onion liquid; then quickly add the onion pulp. Bring to a boil, stirring constantly. Remove from the heat, add the beaten egg yolks, and season to taste. Set aside to cool.*

Preheat the oven to 350°.

Fold the whipped egg whites into the onion mixture. Pour into a greased 6-cup soufflé dish or straight-sided casserole and bake for about 30 minutes, until the center is firm and puffed and the top is delicately browned. Serve immediately.

*May be prepared ahead and refrigerated at this stage.

Betty Parker
Council of the BSO

Boiling and Baking Potatoes: *Always boil potatoes in their jackets and peel after cooking to preserve their nutritional value and enhance their flavor.*

Potatoes baked in aluminum foil are not baked but steamed. Try cooking them unwrapped. Also, try eating them without either butter or sour cream. The taste is remarkable and the calorie count is surprisingly low.

Crisp-Skinned Baked Potatoes: *Prick the skins of well-scrubbed, uniformly sized baking potatoes in several places with a thin skewer. Rub them with ¼ to ½ teaspoon coarse salt and a little freshly ground black pepper. Bake at 425° for 1 to 1½ hours, turning at least once. Dust off the surplus salt and serve immediately with butter and/or sour cream or yogurt.*

Dennis Helmrich's Blue Potatoes: *Add about 1 tablespooon crumbled Roquefort cheese or a blue cheese of comparable quality to baked potatoes, instead of, or in addition to, butter.*

SWEET POTATO CASSEROLE WITH HERBS

Serves 5 or 6

3 to 4 cups mashed sweet potatoes
¼ cup brandy or sherry
½ teaspoon oregano
½ teaspoon marjoram
1 teaspoon crushed coriander
  (optional)

Salt
1 cup applesauce
Cinnamon and/or nutmeg
½ cup brown sugar
1 tablespoon butter

Preheat the oven to 350°.

Combine the sweet potatoes with the brandy, herbs, and salt to taste. Place the mixture in a buttered casserole. Flavor the applesauce with cinnamon and/or nutmeg and spread it over the potato mixture. Sprinkle lightly with brown sugar, dot with butter,* and bake for 20 to 30 minutes, until the top is crisp and browned.

*May be prepared ahead to this stage and set aside for baking later.

Jean M. King

SWEET POTATO AND CORN CASSEROLE

Serves 6

Albert Yves Bernard was a long-time member of the viola section of the BSO. His wife says of her recipe from the chef at the Detroit Club, "It has stood the test of time — it's a simple 'peasant' dish which goes well with pork, ham, or any strongly flavored meat or fish."

2 cups rich cream sauce
Nutmeg
Salt
Freshly ground white pepper
3 cups fresh or frozen cooked corn

3 cups diced cooked sweet potatoes (not yams)
½ cup coarse bread crumbs, or commercial stuffing mix
¼ cup melted butter

Preheat the oven to 350°.

Season the cream sauce to taste, and pour a little into a lightly buttered 1½-quart casserole. Add the corn and dust it with salt and pepper. Add the sweet potatoes and pour the sauce over all. Mix the bread crumbs and butter and sprinkle the mixture over the sauce. Bake for about 30 minutes, until heated through. Brown the top under the broiler, if necessary, and serve immediately, although it will hold well for a buffet.

Mrs. Albert Yves Bernard

INTERMISSION SNACK (Microwave Miracle)

Serves 1 or 2

Richard Plaster, who plays the contrabassoon for the Boston Symphony, joined the Orchestra in 1952. He is a member of the faculties of Boston University, the Boston Conservatory, and the New England Conservatory, and he finds the microwave oven in the players' lounge a useful device. "Here's a hot potato for you!"

1 large sweet potato, washed

"Prick the potato skin with any handy musical tool. Place the potato in a microwave oven for about 6 minutes, until it is soft. Remove it and cut it into pieces, which can be handled and eaten without plates, utensils, or mess."

Richard E. Plaster, contrabassoon

SPINACH CASSEROLE

Serves 4

The flour in Mrs. Whitney's hollandaise apparently prevents it from separating when this casserole is cooked.

2 10-ounce packages frozen chopped spinach, completely thawed
1 cup Flornie's Blender Hollandaise Sauce◆

½ cup buttered bread crumbs (optional)

Preheat the oven to 350°.

Squeeze the spinach in cheesecloth or paper towels to remove all the moisture. Stir in the hollandaise, and transfer the mixture to a small buttered casserole. Top with the buttered crumbs if desired, and bake for 30 to 35 minutes, until the spinach is thoroughly heated and the top is crisp and lightly browned. *Do not overcook.* Serve immediately.

Flornie Whitney
Council of the BSO

SUSIE'S SUMMER SQUASH

Serves 8

4 pounds yellow squash, peeled, if
   necessary, and sliced ½ inch thick
½ cup minced onion
1 cup grated sharp Cheddar cheese
1 teaspoon salt

4 eggs, beaten
Freshly ground white pepper
1 cup coarse cracker crumbs
4 tablespoons melted butter
Paprika

Preheat the oven to 350°.

Steam the squash until it is almost tender, and drain well. Place it in a buttered 3-quart shallow baking dish, and layer the onions and cheese over it. Add the salt to the eggs and pour them over the vegetable mixture. Sprinkle with pepper. Mix the crumbs and the butter and spread over the casserole. Dust the top with paprika,* and bake for about 1 hour, until the eggs are set and the topping is lightly browned. Serve immediately.

* May be prepared ahead to this point and refrigerated for later finishing.

Mrs. Jeffrey Wellington

CHRISTINE'S SQUASH SOUFFLÉ

Serves 8

Despite the egg whites, this dish works well in a microwave oven.

2 tablespoons butter
1½ cups cooked winter squash
½ cup flour
4 eggs, separated
2 cups light cream
¼ to ⅓ cup sugar

½ teaspoon cinnamon
½ teaspoon nutmeg
Salt
Freshly ground black pepper
1 teaspoon vanilla extract (optional)

Preheat the oven to 350°.

Melt the butter in a glass or ceramic 1½- to 2-quart soufflé dish and swirl it around until thoroughly coated.

Place the squash, flour, egg yolks, cream, ¼ cup sugar, and spices in a blender, and blend until frothy. This may have to be done in batches. Add salt and pepper to taste, and the additional sugar; add the vanilla if desired.* Whip the egg whites until stiff but not dry and fold gently into the squash mixture.

Pour the mixture into the soufflé dish. Bake for about 1 hour, until the center is firm and the top is browned. Serve immediately.

* May be prepared ahead to this stage, but beat the squash mixture again before adding the egg whites.

Variation

Add ¼ cup brown sugar and the vanilla, double the spices, but omit the pepper. The result is a different and delicious dessert soufflé, to be served with whipped cream or vanilla ice cream.

Mrs. F. Corning Kenly, Jr., Overseer
Council of the BSO

VENERABLE SQUASH

Serves 6 to 8

This recipe was developed to salvage the harvest of an overenthusiastic planting of squash and zucchini, a problem familiar to all gardeners. It can be made quickly using a conventional oven — even more quickly with a microwave.

4 tablespoons butter
1 cup coarse dry bread crumbs
¼ cup grated Parmesan cheese
¼ cup grated Swiss or mild Cheddar cheese
½ cup coarsely chopped scallions
3 cups summer squash or zucchini, peeled, seeded, and cut into 2-inch cubes

1 teaspoon chopped fresh dill, or ¼ teaspoon dried dill weed
Mace or nutmeg
Salt
Freshly ground black pepper

Preheat the oven to 350°, if using the conventional baking method.

Melt 2 tablespoons butter in a small saucepan, add the bread crumbs and cheese, toss lightly until well mixed, and set aside.

Heat the remaining butter in a large frying pan, add the scallions, and stir until wilted. Add the squash and stir-fry over high heat until the squash is transparent: it should still be very crisp. Sprinkle with dill, a dash of mace or nutmeg, and salt and pepper to taste. Transfer to a buttered shallow baking dish. Spread the bread crumbs over the squash* and bake for 30 minutes, or until the squash is barely tender and the topping is lightly browned. Allow to stand for 5 to 10 minutes before serving.

To cook in a microwave, use a glass or ceramic dish. Cook at the high setting for 10 to 12 minutes, turning the dish several times. When the squash is almost tender, brown the topping under the broiler, and serve as above.

*May be prepared ahead to this stage and set aside for baking later.

Mrs. Thomas Gardiner, Overseer
Council of the BSO

ROMAN-STYLE BAKED STUFFED TOMATOES

Serves 20

Cooked tomatoes will hold well, up to several days, but once the tomatoes are assembled, they must be cooked immediately.

40 fairly small tomatoes, evenly sized
Salt
1½ pounds rice (about 9 or 10 cups
when cooked)
2 cups olive oil
1 cup chopped fresh basil

2 large or 4 small cloves garlic, minced
3 large onions, slivered
5 large carrots, sliced thin lengthwise
Basil leaves or Italian parsley sprigs
(for garnish)

Cut ½-inch slices off the bottoms of the tomatoes and set aside. Hollow out the insides, sprinkle them with salt, and turn upside down to drain. Chop the pulp and set it aside, including the juice.

Boil the rice for 8 minutes and drain it. Rinse it with cold water, drain it again, and place it in a large bowl. Add ½ cup olive oil, the tomato pulp and juice, basil, garlic, and salt to taste. Mix well and fill the tomatoes three quarters full. Cover the rice mixture with the sliced-off bottoms, skin side up.

Preheat the oven to 400°.

Pour a little oil into several large baking pans. Spread the onions and carrots evenly over the bottom, and arrange the tomatoes on top. Drizzle the remaining oil over all. Cover the pans with foil and bake for 20 minutes, or until the rice is barely tender. Do not allow the tomatoes to disintegrate. Remove the foil and cool the tomatoes to room temperature before serving, garnished with basil leaves or parsley sprigs.

The Romagnoli's Table, Boston
Margaret and Franco Romagnoli

LECSO ("Letshko")

Makes 3 to 4 cups

Hungarian composer Sándor Balassa's *Cries and Calls*, one of the Boston Symphony's centennial commissions, was first performed in Symphony Hall in October 1982. The composer's version of one of the great paprika-flavored sauces typical of his native cuisine is quick, easy, and remarkably versatile. In addition to being a sauce for meat, poultry, seafood, or noodles, it may be served hot or cold as an appetizer, hot as a vegetable, or cold as a salad. The recipe we received was written in Hungarian in Mr. Balassa's own hand.

2 medium-sized red onions, chopped
2 tablespoons lard
1 pound green peppers, seeded and
 thinly sliced
2 medium-sized tomatoes, peeled and
 sliced or chopped

1 teaspoon Hungarian paprika, or 1
 tablespoon ''regular'' paprika and
 cayenne pepper to taste
Salt

Sauté the onions in the lard until golden. Add the peppers and tomatoes, cover, and cook slowly for about 20 minutes, stirring occasionally. Add the paprika and salt to taste. When the vegetables are soft, the dish is ready to serve, with noodles or as suggested above.

Variations
For breakfast or luncheon, serve scrambled eggs with hot *lecso*.

Add ½ pound *kolbacz* (Hungarian sausage), kielbasa (Polish sausage), or other smoked sausage or meat, sliced ½ inch thick, and cook with the peppers and tomatoes. Serve with a green salad for luncheon or supper.

Sándor Balassa, composer

CHINESE-STYLE VEGETABLES WITH TOFU

Serves 4

This Oriental recipe provides a perfectly balanced meal in one dish.

1 to 2 tablespoons sesame oil
1 onion, diced
1 carrot, sliced diagonally
1 rib celery, sliced diagonally
1½ cups Chinese cabbage, sliced
 diagonally
1 cup bean sprouts
⅔ cup fresh snow peas, or ½ package
 frozen (optional)

¼ cup sliced water chestnuts (optional)
½ pound tofu (bean curd), rinsed and
 pressed to remove excess moisture
1½ cups water
2 tablespoons arrowroot dissolved in 2
 tablespoons water
Tamari (Japanese soy sauce)
Dry sherry

Heat the sesame oil in a large frying pan over moderate heat and sauté the onions until transparent, about 2 to 3 minutes. Add the carrots and celery and cook for 3 to 4 minutes more. Add the remaining vegetables, the tofu, and the water. Bring to a boil, then reduce the heat to low and stir in the arrowroot mixture. Stir until the sauce is smooth; season to taste with tamari and/or sherry. Cover and cook for 2 to 3 minutes: the vegetables should be very crisp. Serve immediately, alone or with freshly cooked whole-wheat spaghetti or noodles.

Luc Bodin

PLESION TOURLOU (Greek Vegetable Casserole)

Serves 10 to 12

Tourlou may be made with all fresh vegetables, in which case it may be frozen very successfully. It is perfect for a large buffet, and, because it does not have to be served either very hot or very cold, it makes an excellent picnic dish. To quote Mrs. Drapos, whose daughter worked for the Berkshire Music Center for several years, *"Kali epetichia!"*

½ cup olive oil (or half olive oil, half corn oil)

1 medium-sized eggplant, peeled and cut into bite-size pieces

2 medium-sized zucchini, cut into bite-size pieces

3 ribs celery, cut into bite-size pieces

½ 10-ounce package frozen artichoke hearts, whole or halved

½ 10-ounce package frozen Fordhook lima beans

½ 10-ounce package frozen okra

½ 10-ounce package frozen Italian green beans

1 16-ounce can stewed tomatoes, mashed

1 bunch scallions, cut into 1-inch pieces

½ cup chopped parsley

4 small cloves garlic

Salt

Freshly ground black pepper

½ teaspoon fines herbes

2 cups water

Preheat the oven to 375°.

Pour 2 tablespoons of oil into a 15-by-10-by-2-inch oven-proof serving dish and arrange the vegetables and parsley in the pan in the order given. Pour the remainder of the oil over all. Push toothpicks into the garlic cloves and place one in each corner of the baking dish. Sprinkle the seasonings over the vegetables, season to taste, and pour the water over everything.* Bake for 1 to 1½ hours, stirring occasionally, until the vegetables are tender but not mushy. After cooking, remove the garlic cloves, or mash them and add to the juice in the dish. Serve hot, at room temperature, or cold, as an appetizer, a vegetable, or a main course.

*May be prepared ahead to this point.

Mrs. James E. Drapos

PERSIAN VEGETABLE PIE

Serves 4 to 6 as a main course,
6 to 8 as a vegetable

1 pound spinach, washed, picked
over, stems removed, and chopped;
or 1 10-ounce package frozen
chopped spinach, thawed and well
drained
2½ cups chopped scallions
1 cup chopped lettuce (iceberg is fine)
1 cup chopped parsley
½ cup chopped walnuts

2 tablespoons flour
1½ teaspoons salt
¼ teaspoon freshly ground black
pepper
⅛ teaspoon nutmeg
4 tablespoons butter
8 eggs, beaten
Yogurt

Preheat the oven to 325°.

Toss vegetables, parsley, walnuts, flour, and seasonings in a large bowl.

Melt the butter in a large pie plate or deep quiche dish and coat thoroughly. Pat the vegetable mixture evenly into the pan and pour the beaten eggs over it. Bake for 35 to 50 minutes, or until the eggs are set and the top is brown and crisp. Serve hot, warm, or cold, with a dollop of yogurt.

Lindsey Humes
Former BSO staff

SALADS

One of the legendary figures of American music was Arthur Fiedler *(overleaf)*, who joined the Boston Symphony as a twenty-year-old violinist in 1915. In 1930 he was named conductor of the Boston Pops, the post he held until his death in 1979. Fiedler was early determined to provide a series of outdoor public orchestral concerts and, in 1929, beginning a Boston tradition, he conducted the first Esplanade Concert on the east bank of the Charles River. These concerts have attracted a multitude of visitors over the years, but no evening was quite as memorable as the Fourth of July celebration for the nation's bicentennial in 1976. Nearly half a million people crowded every inch of space on the Esplanade itself, the windows and roofs of surrounding buildings, and, by boat, the Charles River itself to hear the concert and to see the fireworks.

PENNSYLVANIA DUTCH HOT GREEN BEAN SALAD

Serves 4

This traditional recipe came to Jean Koch from her mother, Florence Fassnacht Emery, who received it from *her* mother.

1 pound green beans, trimmed
4 strips bacon
1 small onion, thinly sliced

2 tablespoons vinegar
Salt
Freshly ground black pepper

Leave small beans whole; cut large beans in half. Steam or simmer the beans in water until barely crisp-tender and drain. Fry the bacon until crisp, drain it thoroughly, and crumble it when cool. Pour off all but 2 tablespoons of bacon fat from the pan; add the sliced onion and toss quickly over high heat. Remove from the heat; add the vinegar and salt and pepper to taste. Add the beans and crumbled bacon and mix well. Reheat thoroughly and serve immediately, or set aside for later reheating.

Mrs. Carl Koch, Overseer
Council of the BSO

BEET AND ANCHOVY SALAD

Serves 4 or 5

Mrs. Conley's is a good winter salad.

1 1-pound can tiny whole beets,
  drained and halved
1 cup diced celery
18 small stuffed green olives
1 2½-ounce tin rolled anchovies,
  drained, the oil reserved

2 tablespoons red wine vinegar
⅓ to ½ cup olive oil
Freshly ground black pepper
1 tablespoon chopped chives (optional)
Lettuce (romaine, escarole, or chicory),
  washed and chilled

Marinate the beets, celery, olives, and anchovies in the vinegar for several hours.

When ready to serve the salad, drain the beet mixture and set it aside. Pour the marinade into a covered jar. Add enough olive oil to the reserved anchovy oil to make ½ cup, and add to the jar. Shake vigorously, and season to taste with pepper and chives. Place the marinated beet mixture in a lettuce-lined bowl. Pour the dressing over all and serve.

Variation
Use shoestring beets and thinly sliced red onion instead of halved beets and celery.

Mrs. Thomas W. Conley

MARINATED BROCCOLI

Serves 6 to 8

This is an excellent picnic food, and the marinade may be used again.

1 cup cider vinegar
1 tablespoon sugar
1 tablespoon dill weed
1 cup vegetable oil
½ cup olive oil

1 teaspoon salt
1 teaspoon freshly ground black pepper
1 clove garlic, pressed
3 bunches broccoli, flowerets only

Mix all the ingredients except the broccoli in a blender, or beat thoroughly by hand. Pour this marinade over the broccoli and refrigerate for 24 hours, turning occasionally.

Pour off the marinade, and serve the broccoli as a salad. It looks very pretty in the center of a tomato aspic ring.

Variation
Serve as an hors d'oeuvre.

Polly Wilbert

EGGPLANT SALAD

Serves 6 to 8

Music director of the Baltimore Symphony, Sergiu Comissiona has been a guest conductor with the Boston Symphony, interpreting music ranging from Haydn to Shostakovich. His wife, Robinne, frequently serves this unusual salad. It goes well with any meat or chicken, and it can make an elegant luncheon main course with crisped whole-wheat pita bread.

4 medium-sized eggplants
6 to 8 large ripe tomatoes, hollowed
  out and drained, the pulp reserved
½ cup olive oil
1 large or 2 small cloves garlic, pressed
Lemon juice

Salt
Freshly ground black pepper
6 to 8 teaspoons chopped chives or
  scallions
Black olives (for garnish)
Parsley sprigs (for garnish)

Broil the eggplants for about 30 minutes, turning frequently. Do not allow them to burn, but be sure they are evenly cooked. When the skin slips off easily, remove the eggplants from the oven and set aside to cool. When the eggplants are cool enough to handle, peel and drain them thoroughly. Chop the pulp by hand or in a food processor, but do not purée it; the firm texture is important. Chop the pulp from the drained tomatoes, and add to the eggplant. Add the oil and garlic, and season to taste with lemon juice, salt, and pepper. Fold in the chives and fill the tomato cases with the mixture. Refrigerate until ready to serve, garnished with black olives and parsley sprigs.

Mrs. Sergiu Comissiona

Avocado-Grapefruit Salad: Slice a large avocado, and add the sections from one large or two small grapefruit and ¼ to ½ cup slivered red onion. Nest on a bed of Bibb, romaine, or other crisp, mild lettuce and toss with a parslied vinaigrette. Serve with hot or cold meats, poultry, or fish.

Place the avocado seed on top of an avocado salad or guacamole, and cover tightly with plastic wrap. The avocado will remain green for a long time.

MARINATED ONIONS

*Serves 8 as a salad,
10 as a buffet side dish,
many as an hors d'oeuvre*

This recipe was given to Mrs. Watkins "at cocktails on the SS *Mauretania*, by the ship's physician, Dr. Elder." Malt vinegar, standard in Britain, is hard to find in the United States. However, growing interest in the use of different vinegars has led gourmet shops to increase their inventories, so buy it when possible, if only for this unusual dish.

3 pounds yellow onions, very thinly
  sliced
1 cup malt vinegar
1 cup olive oil
1 teaspoon dry mustard

1 teaspoon salt
1 teaspoon freshly ground black pepper
1 teaspoon sugar
Bright green lettuce leaves or other
  crisp salad greens

Mix all the ingredients except the lettuce in a heavy ceramic crock or wide-mouthed glass jar. Cover tightly and set in the refrigerator for at least three days. Turn the contents regularly; the onions will become limp and delicate. Drain off the marinade, which may be reused, and serve the onions on a bed of lettuce on a large chilled platter or individual plates.

Variation
Serve on small baking powder biscuits or unsalted crackers for an hors d'oeuvre.

Mrs. Joseph R. Watkins
Council of the BSO

POTATO SALAD

Serves 8

BSO personnel manager Bill Moyer and his wife, Betsy, are part of a number of musical aggregations, performing frequently in the Boston and Tanglewood areas.

8 medium-sized boiling potatoes, boiled in their skins	*1 tablespoon chopped parsley*
½ to ¾ cup Vinaigrette◆	*1½ teaspoons salt*
1 medium-sized red onion, chopped or very thinly sliced	*⅛ teaspoon freshly ground black pepper*
¼ cup mayonnaise	*1 small green pepper, chopped (optional)*
1 teaspoon Dijon mustard	*Tomato wedges and/or black olives (for garnish)*
¼ cup sweet pickle relish	

When the potatoes are cool enough to handle, peel them and cut into ½-inch cubes or slices. Toss them with ½ cup of vinaigrette in a large bowl, cover, and refrigerate for about 3 hours. Add the remaining ingredients and toss thoroughly, adding more vinaigrette if necessary. Serve immediately, or keep under refrigeration until needed. Garnish at the last moment.

If this salad is planned for a picnic, the mayonnaise should be kept chilled and served separately.

Mrs. William Moyer

VARIATIONS ON A THEME OF SPINACH SALAD

Serves 4

Good-quality prewashed spinach is available almost year-round in 10-ounce bags, and there are many different ways to prepare it for a change-of-tempo salad. Following are two of the many spinach salads submitted to the Cookbook Committee.

#1: Spinach-Mushroom Salad with Sesame Dressing

1 10-ounce package spinach, washed,
  picked over, stems removed
2 cups crisp salad greens (for texture)
½ cup sliced raw mushrooms

2 thin slices red onion, separated into
  rings
¼ cup sesame seeds
⅓ cup Vinaigrette♦

Combine the spinach, salad greens, mushrooms, and onion in a bowl and refrigerate until ready to serve.

Toast the sesame seeds in a small frying pan over medium heat until they begin to pop. Remove from the heat, cool slightly, and pour over the salad. Add the vinaigrette, toss thoroughly, and serve immediately.

To enhance the sesame flavor, substitute 1 tablespoon sesame oil for 1 tablespoon of the olive oil in the vinaigrette.

Geraldine J. Hill

#2: Spinach Salad with Chutney Dressing

⅓ to ½ cup Vinaigrette♦
1 tablespoon chopped Major Grey's or
  other mango or peach chutney
1 teaspoon curry powder
1 10-ounce package spinach, washed,
  picked over, stems removed

2 cups sliced unpeeled red Delicious
  apples
¼ cup very thinly sliced red onion
¼ cup dry-roasted peanuts
¼ cup golden raisins

Combine the vinaigrette, chutney, and curry powder in a covered jar. Shake well and store at room temperature until ready to serve. Assemble the salad in the order given, and toss with the dressing just before serving.

Mrs. Michael H. Davis
Council of the BSO
Past chairman, Junior Council of the BSO

TOMATOES OLÉ

Serves 8

This unusual presentation of good companions goes particularly well with a Mexican or Tex-Mex entrée.

8 large firm ripe tomatoes, peeled
3 or more ripe avocados (enough to fill
  the tomatoes)
3 tablespoons lemon juice
1 clove garlic, minced
4 to 6 tablespoons minced green pepper
  and/or celery

1 tablespoon chopped parsley
Mexican chili powder
Salt
Freshly ground black pepper
Parsley sprigs (for garnish)

Cut the tops off the tomatoes, and carefully scoop out the pulp. Turn the tomatoes upside down, cover, and refrigerate.

Peel and mash the avocados, using a wooden spoon or stainless steel fork. Do not purée. Add the lemon juice and stir thoroughly. Fold in all the other ingredients and season to taste. Place this guacamole in a small glass bowl, sprinkle with a little additional lemon juice, set one or two avocado seeds on top, and cover tightly. Refrigerate until serving time.

Just before serving, fill the tomato cases with the guacamole, and top with a sprig of parsley.

Mrs. Frank Remick
Council of the BSO

Tips for Tomatoes: *Tomatoes ripen best in a brown paper bag: setting them on the windowsill in the sun will not hasten the ripening process, only speed their decay. For the best flavor, do not refrigerate tomatoes, but once they have been chilled they must stay chilled or they will quickly go bad.*

CUCUMBER JADE

Serves 6

1 cup seeded, chopped, and drained
  cucumber
1 tablespoon gelatin
3 tablespoons lime juice
Hot water
3 to 4 tablespoons sugar
1 teaspoon salt
1 tablespoon vinegar
1 teaspoon grated onion
1 teaspoon horseradish
1 cup sour cream
¼ cup mayonnaise
Salad greens
Chopped fresh dill and/or sliced
  radishes (for garnish)

Squeeze the cucumber in paper towels to extract all the liquid and set aside.

Soften the gelatin in the lime juice. Pour in very hot (not boiling) water to equal 1 cup. Add sugar to taste and stir until the gelatin is completely dissolved. Stir in the salt, vinegar, onion, and horseradish, and refrigerate until the mixture is syrupy. Add the sour cream and mayonnaise, beat until smooth, and fold in the cucumbers. Pour into a lightly oiled mold and chill until firm. Unmold onto a bed of greens and garnish with dill and/or radishes.

Variation
Substitute 1 3-ounce package lime-flavored gelatin for the gelatin, lime juice, and sugar. Use 1 cup hot water to dissolve the gelatin.

Mrs. Folke Lidbeck

TOMATO ASPIC ALINE

Serves 6

This takes about as long to make as it does to read about!

1 30-ounce can whole tomatoes
1 3-ounce package lemon-flavored
  gelatin
2 tablespoons chopped fresh basil, or 1
  tablespoon dried basil

½ to 1 teaspoon horseradish, drained
⅛ to ¼ teaspoon Tabasco
Salad greens

Heat the tomatoes and gelatin over low heat until the gelatin is dissolved. Remove from the heat and add the remaining ingredients except the salad greens. Mix thoroughly and adjust the seasonings if necessary. Pour into a small oiled mold and refrigerate until the aspic is set, at least 2 hours but as long as overnight. Unmold on a bed of greens, and serve with a delicate lemon mayonnaise, a cucumber sauce, or a dill-flavored sour cream or yogurt dressing.

Variation
Fill the center of the mold with chicken, shrimp, or rice salad.

Coda
Any leftover aspic may be melted and remolded into individual servings.

Mrs. Geoffrey C. Farnum
Council of the BSO

TOMATO CHEESE RING

Serves 6 to 8 as a salad,
4 to 6 as a luncheon main course

To serve this ring as a luncheon main course, add the optional chopped chicken or seafood; or fill the center with a chicken or seafood salad, or any brightly colored vegetable salad.

½ pound cream cheese, softened
1 10-ounce can condensed tomato soup
1 tablespoon gelatin
¼ cup tomato or orange juice
¾ cup mayonnaise
½ cup chopped celery
½ cup chopped red onion or scallions

¼ cup chopped green pepper
1 tablespoon chopped parsley
1 cup chopped chicken, shrimp, or
  crab meat (optional)
Salad greens or watercress (for
  garnish)

Stir the cream cheese and soup over very low heat until well blended. Soften the gelatin in the juice, add to the soup mixture, and stir until dissolved. Remove this mixture from the heat and cool, but do not allow it to set. When it begins to thicken, stir in the mayonnaise, vegetables, and parsley. Correct the seasonings if necessary, and add any of the optional ingredients if desired. Pour into an oiled 1½-quart ring mold and refrigerate for several hours or overnight.

Turn out onto a chilled platter and garnish with greens. Fill the center with salad such as Pea Salad,✦ mayonnaise, or a yogurt or sour cream dressing.

Linda Abegglen
Council of the BSO

SALAD AL FRESCO

Serves 6

This pretty salad travels well to picnics at Tanglewood.

1 cup raw rice
2 cups chicken stock
1 cup cooked green peas, fresh if
*   possible*
1 green pepper, seeded and cut into
*   julienne*
½ red onion, thinly sliced
½ cup sliced black olives

3 tablespoons pine nuts or slivered
*   blanched almonds*
2 tablespoons chopped parsley
2 tablespoons salad oil
2 tablespoons lemon juice
Salt
Freshly ground black pepper
Salad greens
12 cherry tomatoes (for garnish)

Cook the rice in the chicken stock according to the package directions. Rinse quickly with cold water to stop cooking, and drain well. Combine the rice with all the other ingredients while it is still warm. Chill for several hours or overnight. Serve on a bed of bright greens and garnish with the cherry tomatoes.

Mrs. Thomas S. Morse
Tanglewood Council of the BSO

THREE-GREEN SALAD WITH WARM BRIE

Serves 8

½ cup olive oil
¼ cup freshly squeezed lemon juice
Salt
Freshly ground black pepper
Dijon mustard (optional)
8 wedges Brie cheese, 4 inches long
*   and 1 inch wide at base, or 1 small*
*   wheel, divided into eighths*

Any three complementary salad bowl
*   lettuces, washed, dried, and torn*
*   into suitably sized pieces*
Chopped chives or parsley (for
*   garnish)*

Combine the oil and lemon juice in a covered jar, and season to taste. Shake well, and set aside at room temperature for at least 1 hour.

Preheat the oven to 350°.

Place the Brie wedges on a lightly buttered baking sheet and bake for several minutes, until the cheese is slightly warmed and soft but not too runny. Meanwhile, dress the salad and arrange it on chilled individual salad plates. Top each serving with a wedge of warm cheese, sprinkle with chopped chives or parsley, and serve immediately.

Ann Hobbs

PEA SALAD

Serves 2 or 3

A good winter or emergency salad, this should be prepared ahead to allow the flavors to blend.

1 10-ounce package tiny frozen peas, thawed but not cooked
4 strips bacon, cooked until crisp, crumbled
¼ to ⅓ cup chopped scallions, or 2 tablespoons slivered red onion

2 teaspoons lemon juice
Sour cream
Salt
Freshly ground black pepper

Mix the peas with the bacon, scallions, and lemon juice. Add just enough sour cream to hold the mixture together, and season to taste. Refrigerate until ready to serve on a bed of crisp greens such as escarole, chicory, or romaine, or in the center of a tomato aspic ring.

Mrs. Harry Sweitzer
Council of the BSO

WINTER SALAD

Serves 4

Dennis Helmrich's talents extend from the vocal program at Tanglewood to innovative production in the kitchen. His recipe using fennel displays a too often neglected vegetable in all its finery.

1 bulb fennel, well trimmed
1 small red sweet pepper, seeded
Escarole, chicory, watercress, and/or romaine, washed and torn into suitably sized pieces
¼ cup olive oil

2 tablespoons lime juice, or 1 tablespoon red wine vinegar
1 tablespoon Dijon mustard
1 medium-sized clove of garlic, pressed
1 medium-sized ripe avocado

Slice the fennel into rings about ⅓ inch thick and place in a salad bowl. Cut the pepper into thin lengthwise strips and add to the fennel. Wrap the greens in paper towels and set in the bowl. Refrigerate until ready to serve.

Meanwhile, combine the olive oil, lime juice, mustard, and garlic in a small covered jar, shake well, and allow to stand at room temperature.

At serving time, mix the greens, fennel, and pepper. Shake the dressing well, pour it over the salad, and toss thoroughly. Scoop out teaspoonfuls of avocado, place them on top of the salad, and serve immediately without further tossing.

Do-Ahead Tip
Slice the avocado, if preferred, dip in lemon juice, and seal with the seed in plastic wrap. It will stay green for a long time.

Dennis Helmrich, chief vocal coach
Berkshire Music Center

Salad Presto: Place 2 or 3 teaspoons salad dressing in the bottom of a plastic container. Add mixed salad (meat, chicken, pasta, vegetable, and so on). Top with whole lettuce leaves, and cover. Take the salad and a paper plate to a lunch meeting, instead of the usual sandwich. Up-end the container and, presto, the perfect salad is neatly served.

MERCY'S SUMMER SPECIAL

Serves 4

A quick, easy, and unusual luncheon or supper dish for hot summer days.

2 hard-boiled eggs	*1 pound crab meat or lobster meat, or*
Lettuce (Boston, romaine, or other)	*1½ pounds cooked shrimp*
4 Holland rusks	*1 cup Russian dressing*
Softened butter	*4 sprigs parsley or watercress (for*
Anchovy paste	*garnish)*
4 thick slices peeled tomato	

Chop the egg whites and yolks separately and set them aside.

Arrange beds of salad greens on individual luncheon plates.

Spread the rusks generously with butter and lightly with anchovy paste. Place the rusks on the lettuce with a slice of tomato on each. Mix the shellfish with enough Russian dressing to hold it together and divide this mixture evenly on top of the tomatoes. Spoon the remaining Russian dressing over all. Sprinkle with the egg whites and then with the yolks. Top with parsley or watercress and serve immediately.

Mrs. Richard K. Thorndike
Council of the BSO

LOBSTER IN MELON

Serves 6

With its unusual combination of flavors, this salad is a reputation maker.

1¼ to 1½ *pounds lobster meat, cut*   ½ *cup mayonnaise, preferably made*
  into bite-size pieces   *with lemon juice*
1 *large ripe honeydew melon*   2 *tablespoons gin*
                                  Salt

Determine the cup measure of the lobster; then place it in a large bowl. Cut
the top off the melon carefully so that it can be used as a cover. Scoop out
the melon meat and cut it into bite-size pieces or use a ball cutter. Measure
¾ cup of melon pieces for each cup of lobster meat and add it to the bowl.
Beat the gin into the mayonnaise and pour it over the lobster mixture. Toss
well and add salt to taste. Spoon the mixture into the melon shell, replace
the cover, and refrigerate for at least 1 hour before serving.

Mrs. C. Russell Eddy
Council of the BSO

MOULES AU RIZ

Serves 10 to 12 as a first course,
8 as a luncheon main course

4 *quarts mussels (see Preparing*   1 *large onion, sliced*
  Mussels♦)   2 *medium-sized cloves of garlic,*
¼ *cup dry white wine*   *minced*
1 *teaspoon Dijon mustard*   2 *tablespoons olive oil*
1 *tablespoon chopped chives*   3 *cups cooked white rice*
1 *cup Vinaigrette♦*   3 *tablespoons chopped parsley*
2 *cups sliced carrots*   *Crisp salad greens*
¾ *cup chopped celery*

Steam the mussels in the wine. Cool and shuck them. Add the mustard
and chives to the vinaigrette and marinate the mussels in ½ cup of the
mixture. Set the remainder of the vinaigrette mixture aside at room temperature.

Sauté the vegetables and garlic in the olive oil until they are almost
tender, and place in a large bowl. Add the rice and the marinated mussels
and toss to coat thoroughly, adding more vinaigrette if necessary. Cover
and refrigerate until serving time. Mound the rice mixture on a bed of
greens and serve for luncheon, or arrange on individual plates as a first
course at dinner.

Julia Booth Myers

SHRIMP SALAD CHINOISE

Serves 4

1 pound (26 to 30) shrimp, shelled,
  deveined, and cooked until just firm
1 small red onion, very thinly sliced
2 ribs celery, thinly sliced on the
  diagonal
½ cup sliced water chestnuts
½ cup toasted slivered almonds
½ cup mayonnaise

2½ tablespoons lemon juice
2 tablespoons horseradish
¼ cup tomato purée
Salt
Freshly ground black pepper
Bibb or other bright green lettuce
  leaves
Watercress sprigs (for garnish)

Combine all the ingredients except the greens and chill thoroughly. Arrange on a bed of lettuce leaves, topped with a sprig of watercress, and serve with French bread and sweet butter.

St. Botolph Restaurant, Boston
John Harris, proprietor
David Joyce, chef

ORIENTAL CHICKEN SALAD

Serves 4 for dinner,
6 for luncheon

1 whole frying chicken
1 small head iceberg lettuce, shredded
  and chilled

1 cup fresh bean sprouts, chilled
¼ cup slivered almonds, toasted

Dressing

4 tablespoons sugar
2 teaspoons salt
¼ teaspoon freshly ground black
  pepper
½ teaspoon monosodium glutamate
  (optional)

4 tablespoons rice vinegar
¼ cup salad oil
2 tablespoons sesame oil
1 teaspoon soy sauce

Poach the chicken in lightly salted water to cover and set aside in the poaching liquid until cool enough to handle. Remove the meat, cut it into thin strips or dice, and refrigerate.

Mix all the ingredients for the dressing and heat until the sugar dissolves. Set aside to cool; then refrigerate.

When ready to serve, toss the chicken, lettuce, and bean sprouts with the dressing; sprinkle with the toasted almonds.

Mrs. Kenneth A. Steiner
Junior Council of the BSO

RICE SALAD WITH GARLIC-SOY DRESSING

Serves 6 to 8

½ cup olive oil
2 tablespoons rice or white wine
  vinegar
2 cloves garlic, pressed
1 tablespoon soy sauce
½ teaspoon freshly ground black
  pepper
3 cups hot cooked white rice
¼ pound fresh spinach leaves cut into
  julienne

4 scallions, chopped
1 small zucchini, cut into julienne
½ cup julienne of celery
¾ cup pine nuts, chopped walnuts, or
  slivered almonds
Brightly colored salad greens
2 tablespoons chopped parsley (for
  garnish)

Shake the first five ingredients in a covered jar. Pour this dressing over the hot rice, toss thoroughly, and cool; then cover and chill until just before serving time. Prepare the vegetables and refrigerate them.

At serving time, combine the rice and vegetables. Add the nuts and adjust the seasonings. Pile the rice on a bed of crisp greens, sprinkle with parsley, and serve immediately.

Teddie Preston
Council of the BSO

HIGH-PROTEIN VEGETABLE SALAD

Serves 12

Pianist Byron Janis has performed the music of Beethoven, Liszt, Prokofiev, and Rachmaninoff during his many appearances with the Boston Symphony. His wife submitted this original, nutritious, and delectable dish that has and needs no added salt.

1 pound lentils, soaked overnight (see
  Notes)
1 pound pretreated soybeans, soaked
  overnight (see Notes)
1 small red cabbage, shredded, rinsed
  in cold water
2 cups grated carrots
2 cups broccoli flowerets, blanched
½ cup raisins (optional)

½ cup coarsely chopped walnuts
  (optional)
2 tablespoons chopped fresh dill
½ cup chopped fresh parsley
1 bunch watercress, carefully picked
  over
1 to 1½ cups Dijon Dressing♦
Bright green lettuce leaves (optional)

Drain the lentils and soybeans. In separate pans, cover with cold water, and bring to a boil. Cover and simmer until they are barely tender. Drain and cool; then refrigerate for several hours or overnight. Meanwhile, prepare and chill the vegetables.

When ready to serve, place the lentils, soybeans, and chilled vegetables in a large bowl, add the raisins, nuts, and herbs, and toss with the dressing. Serve on whole lettuce leaves as an accompaniment to cold meat or chicken, or as a main course for luncheon or supper with cheese and crisp whole-wheat pita bread.

Notes
Quick-cooking lentils need no soaking.

We suggest that pretreated soybeans be used in this recipe, or that navy, pinto, California pea, Mexican red, Swedish brown, or other beans be substituted. Regular soybeans require very long cooking — at least 4 hours in the oven or on top of the stove, or 20 minutes in a pressure cooker at 15 pounds pressure.

Mrs. Byron Janis

BLENDER MAYONNAISE

Makes about 1½ cups

Retired double bass player Gaston Dufresne is an excellent cook, and he and his wife work together as a team. Their recipe for mayonnaise never fails.

2 *"extra large" egg yolks, or 1 whole "extra large" egg*	*½ teaspoon salt*
	½ cup olive oil
1 *teaspoon Dijon mustard, or ½ teaspoon dry mustard*	*½ cup corn or other tasteless oil*
	Lemon juice (optional)
2 *teaspoons tarragon wine vinegar*	*White or cayenne pepper (optional)*

Using a blender, process the first four ingredients until thick and lemon colored. Add the oils in a very slow stream, blending continuously, until the mixture begins to thicken. Add the remaining oil more quickly and stop processing as soon as the oil is incorporated. Add lemon juice, pepper, and additional salt to taste. If the sauce is not to be used immediately, add 1½ tablespoons boiling water with the blender running. Refrigerate until ready to serve.

Gaston and Martha C. Dufresne

TOFU "EGG" SALAD OR SPREAD

Serves 4 to 6

Little known in American kitchens, tofu is the perfect food: it contains no cholesterol, it is nutritious and low in calories, and its blandness lends itself to an infinite variety of flavorings. This salad travels well to meetings and picnics.

1 cake tofu (bean curd), rinsed and
    thoroughly drained
½ cup mayonnaise, preferably made
    with lemon juice
½ cup celery, chopped

1 tablespoon minced onion or scallion
1 tablespoon chopped dill pickle
    (optional)
Salt
Freshly ground black pepper

Mash or chop the tofu as if preparing eggs for a salad. Add mayonnaise and
the other ingredients, seasoning to taste. Serve as a filling for hollowed out
and drained ripe tomatoes, or as a sandwich spread with dark or light rye
bread.

Variation
Flavor the salad with 1 to 3 tablespoons curry powder and 1 to 2 tablespoons chopped chutney.

Geraldine J. Hill

BLUE CHEESE DRESSING

Makes 4 cups

1 cup mayonnaise
2 cups sour cream
¾ cup buttermilk
½ teaspoon salt

¼ teaspoon sugar
1 teaspoon freshly ground white
    pepper
4 ounces crumbled blue cheese

Process all the ingredients in a blender until smooth, and place in a tightly
sealed jar. Refrigerate for at least four days. This dressing will keep for up to
two weeks.

Mrs. J. P. Barger
Council of the BSO

COUNTRY GARDEN HERB DRESSING

Makes about 1½ cups

¼ cup white wine vinegar
½ cup light olive oil
½ cup corn or safflower oil
1 teaspoon Dijon mustard
1 teaspoon salt
⅛ teaspoon freshly ground black
    pepper

1 tablespoon chopped parsley
1½ teaspoons chopped chives
1 teaspoon each chopped fresh
    tarragon, basil, chervil, and mint,
    or any preferred combination of
    fresh herbs
½ teaspoon celery seed

Combine all the ingredients in a covered jar and shake well. Allow to stand for 30 minutes to 1 hour to blend flavors. Refrigerate any surplus dressing, which will keep for several days.

The Cookbook Committee

DIJON DRESSING

Makes 1¼ cups

2 to 3 tablespoons lemon juice, or 1 to
   2 tablespoons red wine vinegar
1 cup olive oil, or ½ cup olive oil and
   ½ cup corn, peanut, or safflower oil
Salt

Freshly ground black pepper
2 tablespoons Dijon mustard (see Note)
1 tablespoon chopped chives (optional)
1 medium-sized clove of garlic
   (optional)

Place the smaller amount of lemon juice or vinegar in a covered jar with the oil and salt and pepper to taste. Shake well, add the flavorings, and set aside at room temperature to blend the flavors. Just before serving, remove the garlic, shake well, and add more lemon juice or vinegar if necessary. Refrigerate any surplus dressing, but bring it to room temperature before using.

Note

Smooth or whole-seed Dijon mustards may be used, including those flavored with tarragon, fennel, or green peppercorns.

The Cookbook Committee

MR. CHICKEN'S SALAD DRESSING

Makes about ½ cup

A good dressing for vegetable or chicken salads, this recipe borrows the nickname of the distinguished Polish diplomat who invented it.

2 tablespoons light cream
2 teaspoons white wine vinegar
1 teaspoon chopped fresh basil, or ⅓
   teaspoon dried basil

1 teaspoon chopped fresh dill, or ⅓
   teaspoon dried dill
1 small clove garlic (optional)
Curry powder (optional)

Shake all the ingredients together in a covered glass jar and adjust the seasonings to taste. Store in the refrigerator, but bring the dressing to room temperature before serving. Shake well, discard the garlic, and pour over the salad.

Constance V. R. White
Council of the BSO

DRESSY DRESSING

Makes 2½ cups

1 large clove garlic, minced, or 2
    tablespoons chopped scallions
1 cup grated Cheddar cheese

1 cup mayonnaise
½ cup Vinaigrette◆

Mix all the ingredients in a covered glass jar and shake well. Allow to stand for 24 hours or longer to blend the flavors.

Marie Haffenreffer Fox
Council of the BSO

MUSTARD DRESSING

Makes about 1 cup

Use this dressing with strongly flavored salads of greens, beans, or pasta.

2 egg yolks
2 tablespoons red wine vinegar
½ teaspoon sugar
Freshly ground black pepper
Cayenne pepper

1 tablespoon dry mustard
1½ tablespoons Dijon mustard
¾ cup oil (olive, peanut, safflower, or
    a combination)
Salt (optional)

Place the first seven ingredients in a blender or a food processor fitted with the steel blade, and start the machine. Very gradually add the oil — in droplets at first, then in a thin steady stream. Process until the sauce thickens. Adjust the seasonings, and store in a covered jar. Coat the top of the dressing with a little oil unless it is to be used almost immediately. Refrigerate, but bring to room temperature before serving. Shake vigorously or whisk lightly and pour over the salad.

Elisabeth B. Alsberg

ZACHARY'S DRESSING

Makes about 1½ cups

1 cup walnut oil
⅓ cup cider vinegar
½ teaspoon chopped garlic
1 teaspoon fresh basil, or ¼ teaspoon
    dried basil

½ teaspoon mustard
1 teaspoon freshly ground black pepper
Salt

Mix all the ingredients together in a jar and shake well. Set aside for an hour to blend the flavors, and pour over salad as needed.

Zachary's at The Colonnade, Boston

VINAIGRETTE (Basic French Dressing)

Makes about 1¼ cups

A good salad dressing is so easy, quick, and inexpensive to make that it is a wonder our supermarkets are filled with bottles of exotically colored concoctions apparently designed to cover the taste of salad ingredients. What follows is a basic framework: it may be varied by changing the vinegars and/or the oils. Use only the finest quality ingredients, bought in small quantities, and experiment with herbs and other flavorings.

¼ cup wine vinegar (white for delicately flavored foods, red for more robust ones)
½ cup olive oil
½ cup salad oil (corn, sunflower, safflower, or peanut)

1 teaspoon salt
1 teaspoon dry mustard
⅛ teaspoon freshly ground pepper
⅛ teaspoon monosodium glutamate (optional)
Dash of cayenne pepper (optional)

Shake all the ingredients together in a covered glass jar, and allow to stand until ready to serve. The remaining dressing may be refrigerated, but it should be returned to room temperature before using.

Add chopped fresh herbs directly to the salad. Dried herbs may be pounded in a mortar with the dry ingredients and added to the salad dressing. Parsley and chives are basic, tarragon complements most greens, and dill should be used sparingly and, generally, alone.

The Cookbook Committee

EGGS, CHEESE, PASTA,
BEANS, AND GRAINS

When the Boston Symphony Orchestra was founded, only those music lovers who were able to be physically present in the concert hall could hear the ensemble. Today, through recordings on tape or disc and broadcasts via radio or television, the performers can reach audiences numbering in the millions all over the world. As long ago as 1917, under conductor Karl Muck, the Boston Symphony made one of the first recordings by any orchestra of a portion of the symphonic repertory, the Prelude to Act III of Wagner's *Lohengrin.* Today, a large catalogue of BSO recordings, live concert broadcasts on public radio, and taped concerts played on more than one hundred radio stations through the Boston Symphony Transcription Trust reach an ever-larger audience. The repertory for broadcasts and recordings ranges from the earliest orchestral music of the eighteenth century to compositions so new that the ink is still wet. Here (*overleaf*) composer Andrzej Panufnik (seated at far left) leafs through the score while the producer oversees the recording of his *Sinfonia Votiva,* one of the BSO's centennial commissions.

SWEDISH OMELET

One of the world's most highly regarded dramatic tenors, James Mc-Cracken has sung Beethoven's *Fidelio* and Schoenberg's *Gurrelieder* with the Boston Symphony. He says that his wife, Sandra Warfield, discovered this low-calorie and unusual omelet while she was traveling in Europe. It was a favorite of Alfred Lunt and Lynn Fontanne in the late hours after a performance.

1½ cups milk
1 teaspoon sugar
4 eggs
2 teaspoons butter

1 cup crushed fruit (berries,
*   pineapple, or other)*
Kirschwasser

Preheat the oven to 400°.

Scald the milk with the sugar; cool.

Beat the eggs until light, add the milk and sugar, and beat until the sugar is dissolved. Melt the butter in a 1½- to 2-quart soufflé dish or casserole and swirl it around to butter the dish. Pour in the egg mixture and bake for 15 to 20 minutes, or until the center is set and the top is puffed and browned. Serve immediately with the crushed fruit to which kirsch has been added to taste.

James McCracken, tenor

Storing Eggs: *If possible, buy eggs that have never been refrigerated and store them at room temperature. They will keep much longer and much better than eggs that have been chilled. Once chilled, however, they must be kept cold.*

CUAUHTEMOC (Baked Eggs in Black Beans)

Serves 6

Eggs in chocolate sauce?

1 pound black beans
1½ tablespoons oil or butter
1 large onion, chopped
2 cloves garlic, minced
1 large tomato, peeled and chopped
2 teaspoons salt

1 or 2 eggs per serving
Salt
Freshly ground black pepper
½ cup grated Parmesan or Gruyère
  cheese
1 tablespoon butter

Soak the beans for 6 to 7 hours, or overnight, in cold water to cover. Then drain and discard the soaking water. Cover the beans with fresh water and bring to a boil. Cover and simmer for 2 to 2½ hours, until the beans are very tender; then drain and cool them. Purée the cooled beans and set the purée aside.

Preheat the oven to 375°.

Heat the oil in a large frying pan and sauté the onions and garlic until golden. Add the tomato and salt and cook, covered, for 8 to 10 minutes. Stir the bean purée into this mixture and put it all through a food mill or strainer. Adjust the seasonings, and pour the purée into a large buttered baking dish. Make small indentations in the purée and break the eggs individually into the depressions. Season them lightly with salt and black pepper. Sprinkle the cheese over all, dot with butter, and bake until the eggs are not quite set. Do not overcook, as the eggs keep right on cooking after leaving the oven. Serve immediately with salad and warm crusty bread.

Mrs. Howard M. Turner, Jr.
Council of the BSO

Poached Eggs: Eggs may be poached hours or even days ahead and refrigerated, tightly covered. Always add a little tarragon vinegar to the poaching water. To reheat, drop the eggs into a large pan of boiling water, about 1 cup per egg, cover, and immediately remove from the heat. It will take about 2 minutes for all the eggs to be heated through without any further cooking. Drain and proceed.

CHEESE SOUFFLÉ

Serves 4 to 6

This soufflé *will not fall.* The tapioca, which disappears entirely in the cooking, keeps it upright.

3 tablespoons tapioca
1 teaspoon salt
1½ cups milk

½ pound sharp Cheddar cheese, grated
6 eggs, separated

Preheat the oven to 300°.

Combine the tapioca, salt, and milk and bring to a boil over low heat, stirring constantly. Add the cheese and stir until melted. Beat the egg yolks and stir slowly into tapioca mixture. Remove from the heat and set aside to cool.*

Whip the egg whites until stiff but not dry; fold them into the cheese mixture. Pour into an ungreased 2-quart soufflé dish or casserole. With a spoon handle, draw a circle in the batter 1 inch from the outer edge. Bake for about 1 hour, until the soufflé is puffed and golden. Cook for another 15 minutes if a firmer center is preferred. Serve immediately.

*May be prepared ahead to this stage.

Mrs. Roger Wellington
Council of the BSO

EGG IN A NEST

Serves 1

Easy — and fun for a child.

Cut a 3-inch circle in a slice of bread — preferably heavy textured — and place in a frying pan with 1 tablespoon melted butter. Break an egg into the center of the bread and cook until the egg sets. Flip it over and cook until done.

Cheryl Long
Junior Council of the BSO

POACHED EGGS IN GREEN SAUCE

Serves 4

This pretty dish is perfect for brunch, luncheon, or Sunday supper.

1 pound spinach, washed, picked over, and stems removed
½ teaspoon salt
2 tablespoons butter
2 tablespoons flour
2 tablespoons sour cream, at room temperature

1 cup firm yogurt, at room temperature
Nutmeg
Freshly ground black pepper
4 English muffins, split and toasted
8 eggs, poached (see Poached Eggs♦)

Toss the spinach with the salt in a large pan and steam until it is wilted but not soft. Cool slightly and purée with its accumulated liquid.

Make a roux with the butter and flour over low heat. Slowly stir in the spinach purée, and continue to stir for 5 minutes, or until the taste of flour has disappeared. Add the sour cream and yogurt, and season to taste with nutmeg and pepper. Heat the sauce thoroughly, but do not boil: it will curdle!

Place the hot muffins on a heated platter. Top each with a hot poached egg, pour the sauce over all, and serve immediately.

Mrs. Jerrold Mitchell
Junior Council of the BSO

BERKELEY CHILIES RELLENOS

Serves 6

Trustee Jane Bradley was chairman of BSO–100, the highly successful multimillion-dollar capital fund drive that celebrated the Orchestra's hundredth birthday. She reports that her version of chilies rellenos "was brought back from California by my daughter, who makes it in a Dutch oven over the campfire on wilderness river trips. I make it, prosaically, in a casserole in a suburban kitchen."

2 3½-ounce cans green chilies, rinsed
*   and seeded*
1 pound cheese (medium-sharp
*   Cheddar, Tillamook, or California*
*   jack), sliced*

1 cup prepared biscuit mix
1 teaspoon salt
3 eggs, lightly beaten
3 cups milk
1 tablespoon melted butter

Preheat the oven to 350°.

Arrange the peppers and cheese in layers in a generously buttered flat-bottomed casserole. Beat the other ingredients together and pour over all. Bake uncovered for 45 minutes, or until the center is set and the top is browned. Serve immediately.

Microwave Method
Cook at high setting for 15 to 20 minutes. Turn two or three times, and brown when almost done.

Variation
Mushrooms, chopped bell peppers, or other vegetables may be used instead of the green chilies.

Jane Bradley, Trustee
Past chairman, Council of the BSO

QUICHE CLARINET

Serves 6

Felix Viscuglia, who retired from the Boston Symphony in 1979, wields an artist's brush as well as a clarinet. Before he joined the Orchestra in 1966, he played in a number of the "big bands," and in the early 1970s he became one of the founding members of Wuz, a group of BSO colleagues who specialize in jazz.

Pastry for a 9-inch pie crust (see
   Never-Fail Pie Crust♦)
½ pound bacon
2 medium-sized onions, thinly sliced
2 tablespoons butter
1¼ pounds Jarlsberg, Gruyère, or
   Emmenthaler cheese

4 eggs
1 tablespoon flour
½ tablespoon salt
2 cups light cream
⅛ teaspoon nutmeg
Cayenne pepper

Prepare and partially cook a 9-inch pie or quiche shell, and refrigerate when cool. Fry the bacon until slightly crisp; drain, crumble, and set aside. Sauté the onions in 1 tablespoon of butter until golden and add to the bacon.

Preheat the oven to 375°.

Arrange the cheese, onions, and bacon in the chilled pie crust and return to the refrigerator. Beat together the eggs, flour, salt, and cream. Melt the remaining butter and add it to the egg mixture along with the nutmeg and a dash of cayenne. Mix thoroughly and pour over the cheese mixture. Bake for 45 to 60 minutes, or until the center is set and the top is a golden brown. Cool slightly before serving.

Felix Viscuglia, clarinet

MUSHROOM FONDUE

Serves 4 to 6

2 pounds mushrooms, thinly sliced
4 tablespoons butter
1 teaspoon salt
¼ teaspoon freshly ground white
   pepper

2 tablespoons flour
1 cup light cream
1 cup grated Gruyère cheese

Sauté the mushrooms in 2 tablespoons of the butter over medium-high heat until tender. Season with salt and pepper and set aside.

Preheat the oven to 450°.

Melt the remaining butter in a large saucepan, blend in the flour, and stir for 2 or 3 minutes, being careful the butter does not brown. Add the cream and stir rapidly until the sauce thickens. Add the mushrooms and cook over low heat for 10 minutes. Remove from the heat, and stir in the cheese. Turn into a lightly buttered shallow baking dish,* and bake for about 5 minutes, until the top is delicately browned. Serve immediately as a main course for luncheon or as a vegetable for dinner.

*May be prepared ahead to this stage.

Elizabeth H. Valentine
Council of the BSO

QUICHE DE WAART

Serves 8

Edo de Waart, music director of the San Francisco Symphony, has been a welcome guest with the Boston Symphony Orchestra at both Symphony Hall and Tanglewood. He and his wife, Sheri Greenwald, are a very talented kitchen duo. Their quiche is delicious hot or cold.

1 10-ounce package frozen chopped spinach, cooked, drained, and squeezed dry
5 tablespoons sour cream
1 teaspoon horseradish
Salt
Freshly ground black pepper
1 partially baked 9-inch pie or quiche shell (cooked at 350° for 10 to 12 minutes)

1 cup grated aged Gouda cheese
4 eggs
1½ cups heavy cream
¼ cup dry white wine or vermouth
1 tablespoon all-purpose flour
Cayenne pepper
Nutmeg

Preheat the oven to 375°.

Combine the spinach, sour cream, horseradish, ¼ teaspoon salt, and pepper to taste, and spoon into the prepared crust. Spread the cheese evenly over the spinach. Beat the eggs, cream, wine, and flour until smooth and season to taste with salt, pepper, cayenne, and nutmeg. Pour the custard mixture gently over the spinach-cheese filling. Bake for 45 to 60 minutes, until the custard is puffed and golden. Cool for 5 minutes before serving.

Edo de Waart
Music director, San Francisco Symphony Orchestra

MUSHROOM CRUST QUICHE

Serves 4

A light, unusually low calorie quiche, with a very different "crust."

½ pound mushrooms, chopped
5 tablespoons butter
½ cup coarse cracker crumbs
½ cup minced onion
1 cup finely shredded Cheddar cheese
1 cup cottage cheese

3 eggs
Salt
Cayenne pepper
Paprika
Chopped parsley or chives (for garnish)

Preheat the oven to 250°.

Sauté the mushrooms in 3 tablespoons butter for 5 minutes and stir in the cracker crumbs. Pat the mixture into a buttered 8-inch quiche pan, and set it aside.

Sauté the onions in 2 tablespoons butter until transparent. Spread the onions over the crust, and sprinkle the Cheddar cheese on top. Process the cottage cheese and eggs in a blender until smooth; season to taste with salt and cayenne. Fill the crust with the egg mixture and dust the top with paprika. Bake for 1 to 1¼ hours, until a knife inserted in the center comes out clean. The top will be pale. Allow the quiche to stand for 15 minutes before serving, but keep it hot. Sprinkle with chives or parsley for color, and serve with salad for luncheon or supper.

Mrs. Samuel A. Levine
Council of the BSO

HAM AND LEEK GOUGÈRE

Serves 6

Sir Michael Tippett is one of the world's most highly regarded composers, and his music has been featured many times by the Boston Symphony, particularly under the baton of Sir Colin Davis, the Orchestra's principal guest conductor. Sir Michael's most recent work is an oratorio for soloists, chorus, and orchestra which was commissioned by the Boston Symphony as part of its centennial celebration. His elegant *gougère,* which follows, was received written in his own hand: it has been adapted slightly to suit American ingredients and measurements. It appears complicated, but, as with his music, once the challenge is accepted, the rewards are enormous.

1½ cups milk
4 medium-sized leeks, white part only,
  sliced or chopped
2 whole cloves
1 bay leaf
1½ teaspoons salt
Freshly ground black pepper
Freshly grated nutmeg

1 cup water
5 tablespoons butter
7 tablespoons flour
4 eggs
¼ pound grated Cheddar cheese
½ to ¾ cup all-purpose cream
¾ cup diced cooked ham
⅛ teaspoon dry mustard

Heat the milk in a large saucepan over medium heat and add the leeks, cloves, bay leaf, 1 teaspoon salt, and a good pinch each of pepper and nutmeg. Bring to a boil, cover, and simmer for 15 to 20 minutes, until the leeks are tender. Discard the cloves and bay leaf; drain the leeks and set aside, reserving the liquid.

To make the "crust," heat the water over medium heat, add the remaining salt and 3 tablespoons of butter, and increase the heat until the mixture boils. Add 5 tablespoons of the flour all at once and stir vigorously until the mixture forms a ball. Remove from the heat and add the eggs one at a time, beating thoroughly after each addition. Add 2 tablespoons of grated cheese and continue to beat until the mixture is smooth and glossy.

Preheat the oven to 425°.

Make a sauce using the remaining butter and flour, as well as sufficient cream added to the reserved leek liquid to make 2 cups. When the sauce is smooth and bubbling, remove from the heat and add the ham and the leeks. Season to taste with salt, pepper, and nutmeg.

Arrange the "crust" around the edges of a buttered shallow round baking dish. Spoon the ham and leek mixture into the center and sprinkle the remaining cheese over all. Bake for approximately 30 to 40 minutes, until the *gougère* is puffed, crisp, and golden brown. Serve immediately.

Sir Michael Tippett, composer

NO-CRUST CHEESE AND SPINACH "PIE"

Serves 6 to 8

1 10-ounce package frozen chopped spinach
2 pounds ricotta cheese
1 cup grated cheese (mozzarella, feta, Cheddar, or a combination)
4 eggs, lightly beaten
2 tablespoons olive oil
1 teaspoon onion or garlic salt, or dill
1 teaspoon salt
½ teaspoon freshly ground black pepper

½ medium-sized zucchini, sliced and sautéed (optional)
¼ pound fresh mushrooms, sliced and sautéed (optional)
½ green pepper, diced and sautéed (optional)
½ cup chopped ham or cooked sausage (optional)
2 tablespoons melted butter

Preheat the oven to 350°.

Cook the spinach in ¾ cup boiling water, covered, for 5 minutes; then drain very thoroughly.

Combine the remaining ingredients except the butter. Use as many or as few of the options as you like, in whatever combination appeals. Pour into a buttered deep-sided quiche pan or deep pie plate. Drizzle the butter or oil over the top, and bake for 40 to 45 minutes, until the center is firm and the top is delicately browned.

Serve hot or warm as a main course for brunch, luncheon, or supper, as a side dish at a buffet, or as a first course for dinner.

Rosalie's Restaurant
Marblehead, Massachusetts
Rosalie Harrington, proprietor

GRILLED CHEESE PIE

*Serves 3 or 4 for luncheon,
6 to 8 for hors d'oeuvres*

¼ pound Muenster cheese, grated
1 egg, beaten
¾ cup flour
½ teaspoon salt
*⅛ teaspoon freshly ground black
  pepper*

1 cup milk
*½ teaspoon oregano or Italian
  seasoning*
*¼ pound chopped salami, pepperoni,
  or ham*

Preheat the oven to 325°.

Reserve ⅓ cup cheese for the top. Mix all the other ingredients together, and pour into a buttered 8-inch pie plate. Bake for 30 minutes. Sprinkle the reserved cheese on top and bake several minutes longer, until the topping is lightly browned. Serve immediately, cut into wedges.

Variation

For hors d'oeuvres, use an 8-inch square pan and cut into 1-inch squares. Serve hot or warm.

*Mrs. Robert B. Newman
Council of the BSO*

SPANAKOPITA (Spinach Pie)

Serves 12

Chauffeur Paul Kehayias has driven most of the great, near-great, to-be-great, and would-be-great conductors, singers, and performing musicians of the world. His wife, Connie, has sustained many of them with her justifiably famous version of a great Greek delicacy.

1 pound phyllo dough, fresh or frozen
*3 pounds spinach, washed, picked
  over, and stems removed*
1 medium-sized onion, chopped
2 bunches scallions, chopped
3 tablespoons butter
½ cup chopped parsley

¼ cup chopped mint (optional)
1 pound feta cheese, crumbled
4 eggs, beaten
¾ cup pine nuts (optional)
1 tablespoon salt
¾ cup olive oil

Defrost frozen dough in the refrigerator for several hours or overnight. Frozen phyllo leaves are thinner than fresh, so the smaller number given below is for fresh leaves, the larger for frozen.

Squeeze the spinach completely dry; chop it and place in a large bowl. Sauté the onion and scallions in the butter until the onion is transparent. Stir in the parsley and mint and add this mixture to the spinach. Combine the cheese, eggs, pine nuts, and salt, and stir into the spinach mixture, mixing thoroughly.

Preheat the oven to 350°.

Cover the phyllo dough with a damp cloth to keep it from drying out. Brush each leaf with olive oil as you use it. Line a buttered 13-by-16-inch rectangular pan with four or six phyllo leaves, extending the pastry several inches over the edges of the pan all around. Spoon one third of the spinach mixture into the pastry shell, and cover with three or four leaves fitted inside the pan. Repeat this process once, and add the remaining filling. Fold the overlapped dough back over the filling and cover all with four or six leaves.

With a sharp knife, cut the pie into diamond-shaped serving pieces. Brush or spray the top lightly with warm water and bake for 20 to 30 minutes, until the crust is crisp and brown and the filling is set. Remove from the oven and allow to stand for about 30 minutes before serving.

Mrs. Paul Kehayias

POLENTA GORGONZOLA

Serves 4 to 6

6 tablespoons butter
1 cup yellow cornmeal
½ teaspoon salt
2 cups boiling water
3 eggs, beaten

1 cup milk
2 teaspoons baking powder
8 to 10 ounces Gorgonzola, cut into
    1-inch pieces

Preheat the oven to 400°.

Melt the butter in a 9-by-12-inch baking dish in the oven while it is heating, and allow it to brown slightly. Mix the cornmeal and salt together in a saucepan, and stir in the melted butter. Beat the boiling water into the mixture and stir for a few minutes over low heat. Beat the eggs, milk, and baking powder together and stir into the cooked polenta. Pour the mixture into the baking dish and arrange the cheese pieces evenly over the top. Push them into the polenta and bake for about 35 minutes, until the mixture is puffed and golden and the cheese is melted. Cut into squares and serve with salad as a luncheon dish, or as a side dish for dinner.

Coda

The leftovers are delicious sliced and fried quickly in a little butter.

Stephen R. Parks
Curator of the Osborne Collection
Beinecke Rare Book and Manuscript Library
Yale University

CHEESE-STUFFED TOMATOES

Serves 4

Naomi Perahia is the wife of the distinguished award-winning pianist Murray Perahia, who has appeared in Symphony Hall on a number of occasions including during the Orchestra's centennial season. Mrs. Perahia's unusual tomato and cheese dish is, she says, "a traditional Sephardic dish, which can be prepared several days in advance and refrigerated until it is time to cook it."

*4 large ripe tomatoes with the pulp
  removed, drained*
Salt
*1 pound ricotta, cottage cheese, or pot
  cheese*

½ pound cream cheese, softened
4 eggs, beaten
1 tablespoon matzo meal or cornmeal

Arrange the tomatoes in a buttered baking dish and sprinkle with a little salt. Beat all the other ingredients together until creamy and pour the mixture into, around, and over the tomatoes.

Preheat the oven to 325°.

Cook for 40 to 50 minutes, until the tomatoes are cooked but not soft and the cheese is puffed and delicately browned.

Serve as a main course for luncheon, or as a side dish for dinner.

Naomi Perahia

SWISS CHEESE FONDUE

Serves 2 (see Note)

This classic fondue is perfect for Sunday supper, accompanied by more of the same wine that is used in the fondue. Each guest spears a cube of bread and dips it in the fondue. Traditionally, if a woman loses her bread in the pot, she must kiss the man at her right: if a man loses, he must buy the next bottle of wine. It all leads to considerable good fellowship.

1 clove garlic, split
1 cup medium-dry white wine
*8 ounces well-aged Swiss cheese
  (Gruyère, Emmenthaler, Jarlsberg,
  or domestic), cubed or grated*
2 tablespoons kirschwasser
1 tablespoon cornstarch

Nutmeg
Salt
Freshly ground white pepper
Cayenne pepper (optional)
*8 ounces unsliced day-old French or
  Italian bread, cubed*

Rub the inside of a fondue pot with the garlic, leaving the pieces in the pot. Pour in the wine and heat slowly to just below the boiling point. Do not allow to boil; the wine must *not* bubble. Add the cheese a handful at a time, stirring constantly. Mix the kirsch and cornstarch to a paste and stir it slowly into the cheese; this will produce the perfect creamy texture. Add nutmeg and the other seasonings to taste.

Place the fondue pot on its stand over the flame. The fondue may now boil safely. If it becomes too thick, thin it with more wine and/or kirsch. Serve the fondue with the bread and a simple salad, followed by a fruit dessert.

Note
This recipe may be multiplied by four (to serve eight), but be sure that the pot is large enough, or make it in two pots.

Mrs. Peter P. Papesch
Council of the BSO

DEEP-FRIED CAMEMBERT

Serves 4 to 6 as an hors d'oeuvre,
2 as a first course,
2 to 4 as a salad

2 1-inch triangles firm Camembert
* cheese, chilled*
¼ cup flour
¼ teaspoon salt
Freshly ground black pepper

1 egg beaten with 2 tablespoons water
½ cup dry bread crumbs
Oil for deep-frying, approximately 2 to
* 3 inches deep*

Dust the cheese with the flour seasoned with salt and pepper, dip it in the egg wash, and roll it in the bread crumbs. Heat the oil to 375° and fry the cheese over medium heat until the crumbs are golden. The inside should be soft and runny, the outside crisp and chewy.

As an hors d'oeuvre, serve with Melba toast or warm French bread, and sprigs of French-fried parsley.

As a first course, serve on lettuce garnished with a cherry tomato, and a sprig of parsley or watercress.

As a salad, serve on salad greens with Vinaigrette♦ and a garnish of thinly sliced red onions.

Mrs. Richard McAdoo

MOZZARELLA IN CARROZZA
(Fried Cheese Sandwiches)

Makes 16 tiny "sandwiches"

Bass baritone Ezio Flagello has performed many times with the Boston Symphony, singing music ranging from Mozart and Beethoven to Wagner and Stravinsky. Now he shares another of his talents, with this version of a famous Italian specialty.

*8 slices white sandwich bread, crusts
 removed*
*¾ pound mozzarella cheese, thinly
 sliced*
¼ pound cooked ham, thinly sliced
2 eggs, lightly beaten

¼ teaspoon salt
*¼ teaspoon freshly ground white
 pepper*
1 cup lard
*Freshly grated Parmesan or Romano
 cheese*

Make four sandwiches, using two slices unbuttered bread and a slice of cheese and ham for each. Trim the filling carefully to fit the bread. Add the salt and pepper to the egg, and dip each sandwich carefully in the egg bath.

Heat the lard over medium heat, and fry the sandwiches quickly but gently until golden and crisp on both sides. Remove, drain on paper towels, and dust with grated cheese. Cut each into four squares or triangles, and serve immediately, as hors d'oeuvres or for luncheon with a salad.

Ezio Flagello, bass baritone

FRENCH THEME ON A CLAM SAUCE, WITH VARIATIONS

Serves 4

Born in Paris into a musical family, violinist Roger Shermont lists cooking and clam digging as among his special pursuits. Chasing the elusive clam to produce such an end result as this excellent recipe is a relaxing activity for a very distinguished musician.

*1 dozen quahaugs or 2 dozen
 cherrystones, shucked*
⅓ cup olive oil
3 cloves garlic, minced
2 shallots, minced
2 or 3 bay leaves
½ teaspoon dried oregano

½ teaspoon dried tarragon
½ teaspoon dried sweet basil
½ cup dry white wine
*⅛ teaspoon freshly ground black
 pepper*
¼ teaspoon cayenne pepper
¼ teaspoon sugar

Drain the shucked clams, and reserve the liquid. Cut the meat into small pieces, or chop coarsely in a food processor, and set aside.

In a 1½-quart saucepan, combine the oil, garlic, shallots, and herbs. Heat until foamy over low heat, but do not allow the garlic to brown. Pour in the wine, "sizzle" to evaporate the alcohol, and set aside.

Carefully strain the clam liquid several times through four layers of cheesecloth in a fine sieve to remove any sand. If it is excessively salty, it should be diluted with a little water. Add the clam liquid, peppers, and sugar to the herb mixture and simmer, uncovered, over low heat for 20 to 25 minutes. *Do not boil.* Remove the sauce from the heat, cover, and set aside for 10 to 15 minutes to steep. Strain through a fine sieve once or twice to remove all traces of the herbs and spices.

Reheat the sauce without boiling it and add the clams. Heat only enough to warm them completely. Be extremely careful not to overcook clams, as they quickly become rubbery. Serve immediately over cooked and drained pasta (linguine or spaghetti) that has been tossed with chopped fresh parsley.

Variations
If pasta is not desired, this sauce may be served with a combination of cooked seafood; 2 to 3 cups total of any or all of the following ingredients may be added: medium-sized shrimp, lobster meat, crab meat, langostinos, cubed haddock or other firm white fish. Serve in heated soup bowls with French bread and sweet butter, salad, and more of the same white wine used in the sauce.

Roger Shermont, violin

BASIC TOMATO SAUCE FOR PASTA

Makes 6 to 7 cups

World-renowned soprano Eileen Farrell has sung the music of Beethoven and Wagner under the batons of three Boston Symphony music directors — Charles Munch, Erich Leinsdorf, and William Steinberg. Here is her recipe for a fragrant pasta sauce.

1 large onion, chopped
3 medium-sized cloves of garlic,
* minced*
3 tablespoons olive oil
1 28-ounce can ground peeled Italian
* tomatoes*
1 6-ounce can tomato paste
½ teaspoon fresh rosemary (or ¼
* teaspoon dried)*
1 tablespoon chopped fresh basil (or
* 1½ teaspoons dried)*

1 teaspoon chopped fresh oregano (or
* ½ teaspoon dried)*
½ teaspoon salt
⅛ teaspoon freshly ground black
* pepper*
1 tablespoon sugar
¼ cup chopped Italian parsley
1 cup hot water
1 cup red wine (optional)
1 large bay leaf

Sauté the onions and garlic in the olive oil until the onions are transparent. Transfer to a large saucepan and add the remaining ingredients. If dried herbs are being used, grind them in a mortar with the salt, pepper, and sugar. If the wine is not used, an additional cup of hot water will be required. Bring the mixture to a boil, stirring constantly. Cover and simmer over very low heat for several hours, stirring occasionally. When the sauce has reached the desired consistency, remove it from the heat and set it aside until serving time. Reheat the sauce and serve it over pasta with freshly grated cheese, or in any other situation calling for tomato sauce.

Variation
For a meat sauce, brown ½ pound lean ground beef and ½ pound ground pork, or hot and/or sweet Italian sausage; pour off the excess fat, and add to the sauce for the final hour of cooking. A little more salt may be required.

Eileen Farrell, soprano

PASTA WITH CANNELLINI

Serves 2 to 4

To celebrate the Boston Symphony's hundredth birthday, composer John Corigliano wrote his *Promenade Overture* for the Boston Pops. His lovely blond blend is the *pasta e fagioli* of song and story: it is quick to cook and delicious to eat.

⅓ pound tubular pasta (such as ziti or macaroni)
4 cups boiling water
2 teaspoons salt
2 tablespoons olive oil
1 medium-sized clove of garlic, crushed or minced

1 20-ounce can cannellini (white kidney beans)
2 to 3 tablespoons unsalted butter
Freshly ground white pepper
Freshly grated Romano cheese

Boil the pasta in the salted water for 10 to 12 minutes, until it is *al dente*. Meanwhile, heat the olive oil in a large frying pan and sauté the garlic until it is soft but not browned. Add the cannellini, including the liquid, and simmer until the sauce is slightly thickened and the beans are soft but not mushy. Remove from the heat and season to taste with salt and pepper. Set aside but keep hot.

Drain the pasta thoroughly. Melt the butter in the pasta pan, and add the hot pasta. Toss to coat thoroughly with the butter and add the pepper and cheese to taste. Add the bean mixture to the pasta, stir lightly, adjust the seasonings, and serve immediately.

John Corigliano, composer

FETTUCCINE WITH FRESH TOMATOES

Serves 8 to 10 as a first course,
6 as a side dish,
4 as a luncheon main dish

Famous composer of film scores John Williams, who succeeded the legendary Arthur Fiedler as conductor of the Boston Pops, has brought new ideas to enhance a successful tradition. His wife, Samantha, an excellent cook who served on the Testing Committee, invented this wonderful dish for the late summer, when the garden is full of fragrant red tomatoes.

2 pounds ripe tomatoes, peeled	*Freshly ground black pepper*
1 cup olive oil	*1 pound fresh mozzarella cheese*
1 cup fresh basil leaves, chopped	*2 pounds homemade fettuccine or*
3 teaspoons oregano	*linguine*
Salt	*½ cup freshly grated Parmesan cheese*

Cut the tomatoes into thin wedges and drain. Add the olive oil, herbs, and a little salt and pepper. Refrigerate until ready to toss with the pasta.

Cut the mozzarella into small chunks (½ inch or less), and set aside.

Cook the pasta until *al dente* and drain. Place in a serving bowl and toss quickly with the mozzarella and tomatoes. Sprinkle with the Parmesan and serve immediately.

Note

This pasta is *not* served piping hot. It is supposed to be warm only. Serve it with veal or other meat for dinner, with a green salad for luncheon, or "as is" for a first course.

Samantha Williams
John Williams, composer
Boston Pops conductor

MARIA'S QUICK SPAGHETTI SAUCE

Serves 5 or 6

2 medium-sized cloves of garlic,	*1 teaspoon sugar*
crushed or minced	*1 teaspoon salt*
½ cup olive oil	*Freshly ground black pepper*
4 cups skinned and coarsely chopped	*Cayenne pepper (optional)*
ripe tomatoes, or 1 2-pound can	*1 tablespoon chopped fresh basil, or 1*
imported Italian plum tomatoes	*teaspoon dried basil*
½ cup water	*Pinch of powdered cloves (optional)*
½ cup red wine	*1 tablespoon tomato paste*

In a large frying pan, sauté the garlic in the oil until golden, and add the tomatoes, water, and wine. Bring to a boil, stirring often, and add the sugar and seasonings. Reduce the heat and simmer, covered, for about 20 minutes, stirring occasionally. Add the tomato paste and simmer for about 20 minutes more. Adjust the seasonings and serve immediately over hot buttered spaghetti, or set aside for later reheating.

Mrs. Joseph Pellegrino
Council of the BSO

LINGUINE ALL' UOVA

Serves 6

1 pound linguine
2 tablespoons olive oil
5 eggs, beaten
½ pound freshly grated Parmesan
   cheese
Butter

1 large onion, coarsely chopped
2 medium-sized cloves of garlic,
   minced
Salt
Freshly ground black pepper

Cook the linguine until *al dente* in lightly salted boiling water with 1 tablespoon of olive oil added. Drain thoroughly, set aside, and keep hot. Mix the eggs and the cheese and set aside.

In a large frying pan, heat 1 tablespoon each of oil and butter. Sauté the onion until transparent and add the garlic. Cook gently for 2 minutes, reduce the heat, and add the linguine. Toss the pasta quickly to coat with the oil mixture, adding more butter if necessary. Remove from the heat and add the egg and cheese mixture. Stir quickly and thoroughly, until the cheese begins to melt. The eggs should not cook, but the mixture should be hot. Season to taste with salt and pepper, and arrange on a heated platter. Serve immediately with additional butter and grated Parmesan cheese.

Matthew P. Curran

PASTA AL PESTO

Serves 5 or 6

Applauded in both concert and opera, tenor John Aler has sung many times with the Boston Symphony since his first appearance in 1974, always to great critical and audience acclaim. As he says, "There is nothing like the taste of fresh basil, especially after a long winter of waiting. When it is in season, make a few extra batches, as this pesto keeps for months in the freezer."

2 cups fresh basil leaves, lightly packed
½ cup olive oil
2 tablespoons pine nuts
2 cloves garlic, peeled and lightly
   crushed
1 teaspoon salt

½ cup freshly grated Parmesan cheese
2 tablespoons freshly grated Romano
   cheese
3 tablespoons unsalted butter, softened
Hot cooked pasta

Mix the first five ingredients at high speed in a blender, stopping occasionally to scrape the sides of the container with a spatula. Pour the mixture into a bowl and beat in the cheeses and the softened butter. Serve by spooning a few dollops over any variety of hot cooked pasta.

John Aler, tenor

PASTA AND ZUCCHINI WITH BASIL SAUCE

Serves 4

Violist Joseph Pietropaolo is one of the few Boston Symphony players who is a Boston native. He studied the viola d'amore in Italy while on a Fulbright grant, and possibly honed his culinary talents there as well. He is reputed to be one of the best cooks in the Orchestra.

7 tablespoons olive oil
3 medium-sized zucchini, halved
  lengthwise and sliced thin
4 cloves garlic, chopped
8 fresh basil leaves, coarsely chopped

Salt
Freshly ground black pepper
1 pound spaghetti
¼ cup freshly grated Parmesan or
  Romano cheese

In a heavy frying pan, heat 3 tablespoons of the olive oil and sauté the zucchini until golden brown. Drain, set aside, and keep hot.

Place the remaining olive oil, as well as the garlic, basil, and salt and pepper to taste in a small saucepan and heat carefully, but do not cook.

Cook the spaghetti until *al dente,* drain thoroughly, and place in a warmed bowl. Pour the hot zucchini and the garlic mixture over the pasta, and sprinkle with the cheese. Toss to coat thoroughly and serve immediately on warm plates.

Joseph Pietropaolo, viola

SPINACH LASAGNA

Serves 10 to 12

Lasagna made with uncooked noodles is a novelty not to be overlooked.

Sauce

3 cups coarsely chopped tomatoes
½ cup water
1 tablespoon chopped fresh basil (or 1
  teaspoon dried)

1 teaspoon salt
1 teaspoon sugar
1 clove garlic, minced
¼ cup chopped parsley

Filling

1 pound ricotta cheese
½ cup freshly grated Parmesan cheese
1 10-ounce package frozen chopped
  spinach, thawed and thoroughly
  drained

1 egg, slightly beaten
Salt
Freshly ground black pepper
Nutmeg (optional)

1 tablespoon olive oil
1 pound lasagna noodles, flat or frilly
½ pound mozzarella cheese, grated or
  thinly sliced

Tomato sauce (optional)

Combine the sauce ingredients and simmer over low heat for about 20 minutes, stirring occasionally. Set aside to cool slightly.

Preheat the oven to 375°.

Meanwhile, mix the filling, seasoning to taste with salt, pepper, and nutmeg.

Pour the olive oil into a large lasagna dish, and cover the sides and bottom thoroughly. Assemble the lasagna in layers as follows: one fourth of the sauce, one third of the noodles, half the filling, one fourth of the sauce, one third of the noodles, half the filling, one fourth of the sauce, one third of the noodles, and one fourth of the sauce. Cover tightly with aluminum foil and bake for 45 minutes. Reduce the oven temperature to 350°, and remove the foil. Arrange the mozzarella on top of the mixture, and bake the lasagna, uncovered, for 20 minutes or until the cheese is golden.

Remove the dish from the oven and allow it to stand for 10 to 15 minutes. Cut it into squares and serve with additional tomato sauce if desired (see Tomato Coulis✦).

Abby Sue Nathan

SPAGHETTI ALLA CARBONARA

Serves 4 to 6

Award-winning pianist Emanuel Ax has performed the music of Beethoven, Liszt, and Mozart with the Boston Symphony. Equally acclaimed will be his cookbook contribution, which is, as he says, "easy and quick." Mr. Ax's spaghetti takes about 15 minutes from boiling the water to unfolding the napkin.

12 ounces number-9 spaghetti	*1 tablespoon unsalted butter*
2 quarts boiling water	*⅓ pound freshly grated Parmesan*
2 teaspoons salt	*cheese*
½ pound sliced bacon, cut into 1-inch	*⅓ pound freshly grated Cheddar*
strips	*cheese*
4 eggs	*Freshly ground black pepper*
1 cup heavy cream	

Cook the spaghetti in the boiling salted water until *al dente* and drain thoroughly. Fry the bacon until crisp; drain and set aside. Combine the eggs and cream and beat lightly.

Melt the butter in a large frying pan over low heat. Add the spaghetti and all the other ingredients except the pepper. Stir until the eggs are just cooked and the cheese is melted, about 4 or 5 minutes. Sprinkle with pepper and serve immediately with a chilled green salad, warmed Italian bread, and an Italian red wine such as Chianti Classico.

Emanuel Ax, piano

SPAGHETTI WITH HERBS AND WINE

Serves 6

1/4 cup olive oil
1/4 cup butter
1/4 cup chopped onion
1/4 cup chopped green pepper
1 cup sliced fresh mushrooms
1 medium-sized clove of garlic, minced
1/4 cup chopped parsley
1 teaspoon rosemary
1 teaspoon marjoram

2 cups diced ham
1 cup dry red wine
2 cups chopped peeled tomatoes
1/2 pound semolina or whole-wheat
    spaghetti
Salt
Freshly ground black pepper
1/2 cup freshly grated Parmesan cheese

Heat the olive oil and butter in a frying pan and sauté the vegetables and herbs until lightly browned. Add the ham, wine, and tomatoes, and bring to a boil. Reduce the heat, cover, and simmer for about 30 minutes.

Preheat the oven to 400°.

While the sauce is cooking, boil the spaghetti in salted water until it is not quite *al dente* — still a little crunchy. Drain, rinse it under cold water, drain thoroughly, and set aside.

When the sauce is done, add salt and pepper to taste. Toss the spaghetti and sauce together and place in an oiled 2-quart casserole. Sprinkle with cheese, and bake for about 25 minutes, or until the cheese is lightly browned. Serve immediately.

Mrs. Robert Mansfield Flint
Junior Council of the BSO

SPAGHETTI WITH CHICKEN LIVERS AND MUSHROOMS

Serves 6

James Stagliano, master of the French horn, has had more time to devote to cooking since his retirement from the Boston Symphony. The following recipe makes it clear that his reputation as a chef par excellence is well deserved.

1/2 pound chicken livers
1 onion, finely chopped
2 small garlic cloves or 1 large, minced
4 tablespoons butter
2 cups Italian plum tomatoes, chopped
1/2 teaspoon sugar
1/2 bay leaf
1/4 teaspoon dried thyme

Cayenne pepper
Salt
Freshly ground black pepper
1 cup mushrooms, sliced thin
2 tablespoons all-purpose flour
3/4 cup beef stock
1/4 cup red wine
1 pound spaghetti or fettuccine

Pick over the chicken livers and cut them into quarters.

Sauté the onion and garlic in 2 tablespoons of butter until soft but not brown. Add the tomatoes, sugar, bay leaf, thyme, and salt, pepper, and cayenne to taste. Simmer for about 30 minutes, stirring occasionally.

Melt the remaining butter in a separate pan, and sauté the chicken livers and mushrooms, stirring until the livers are lightly browned. Sprinkle with the flour and stir in the stock and wine. Bring to a boil, stirring constantly until the sauce is thick and smooth.

Add the liver mixture to the tomato sauce, and simmer for about 5 minutes longer. Adjust the seasonings if necessary.

Meanwhile, cook the pasta in lightly salted water until *al dente*. Drain, rinse under hot water, and drain again. Pour the sauce over the pasta, toss lightly, and serve immediately.

James Stagliano, horn

PASTITSIO

Serves 8 to 10

Despite the recipe's formidable length, pastitsio is easy to make. It is a perfect buffet supper dish; it keeps well, and it is inexpensive, hearty, and unusually delicious. It may be served hot, warm, or cold.

1 pound ziti or other tubular pasta
2 tablespoons butter
Salt

Freshly ground white pepper
1 egg, beaten

Filling
2 tablespoons butter
1 large onion, chopped
1 pound ground beef and ½ pound ground lamb, or 1½ pounds ground beef

4 tablespoons tomato paste
½ cup red wine
¼ cup finely chopped parsley
½ teaspoon cinnamon

Béchamel Sauce
8 tablespoons butter
6 tablespoons flour
4 cups scalded milk
1½ cups freshly grated Parmesan cheese

3 eggs, beaten
¼ teaspoon freshly grated nutmeg
Salt
Freshly ground white pepper

Cook the ziti until *al dente* in boiling water to which 2 teaspoons salt have been added. Drain thoroughly, toss with the butter, and add salt and white pepper to taste. Cool, toss with the beaten egg to coat, and set aside.

Filling

Heat the butter in a heavy pan and sauté the onion until transparent. Add the meat and cook and stir for about 10 minutes. Stir in the remaining filling ingredients and simmer until most of the liquid is absorbed. Season to taste and set aside.

Béchamel Sauce

Melt the butter, blend in the flour, and add the hot milk, whisking constantly. When the sauce is bubbling, remove from the heat. Stir in 1 cup cheese, the eggs, the nutmeg, and salt and pepper to taste. Blend thoroughly and set aside.

Assembly

Each layer must be leveled before the next is added. Place half of the pasta in a buttered 13-by-11-by-1½-inch lasagna pan or equivalent-sized casserole. Pour in the filling and cover with the remaining pasta. Pour the béchamel over all, top with remaining cheese, and bake in a preheated 350° oven for 30 to 40 minutes, or until puffed and golden. Cool for 10 to 15 minutes, cut into squares, and serve plain or with tomato sauce (see Tomato Coulis♦).

Joan Pernice Sherman
Tanglewood Festival Chorus

APRICOT NOODLE PUDDING

Serves 12 or more

This tart-sweet and creamy pudding goes well with ham or pork, and is an excellent addition to a buffet table. It is substantial enough for a luncheon or supper dish accompanied by a simple green salad.

1 pound dried apricots, whole or coarsely chopped	¾ pound cream cheese, softened
Boiling water	½ cup sugar
1 pound broad noodles	½ to 1 cup light brown sugar
½ pound butter, melted	3 tablespoons lemon juice
12 eggs	Cinnamon

Cover the apricots with boiling water and allow to stand for about 10 minutes. Drain and set aside to cool.

Meanwhile, cook the noodles in lightly salted boiling water until almost tender: *do not overcook!* Drain, rinse under cold running water, and drain again.

Preheat the oven to 325°.

Use some of the butter to grease a 13-by-15-inch baking pan; then beat together the remaining butter, the eggs, the cream cheese, sugar in the desired amount, and the lemon juice. When the mixture is smooth and creamy, pour one fourth of it into the baking dish. Cover with one third of the noodles, and top with half the apricots. Add another fourth of the egg mixture, another third of the noodles, and the remaining apricots. Cover with a fourth of the egg mixture, the remaining noodles, and lastly the remaining egg mixture. Make sure the apricots are thoroughly covered, as they tend to burn. Dust with cinnamon and bake for 1 hour, or until the pudding is puffed and golden and the center is firm but not dry. Serve immediately.

Janet Wohlberg

MACARONI PUFF

Serves 6

A very dressed up version of an old standby, macaroni and cheese, this dish can be a main course for luncheon or a side dish for dinner.

1 cup ziti or elbow macaroni
½ cup fresh bread crumbs
2 tablespoons melted butter
1 teaspoon salt
½ teaspoon dry mustard

Cayenne pepper (optional)
3 eggs, separated
1½ cups scalded milk, cooled slightly
1½ cups grated sharp Cheddar cheese

Preheat the oven to 350°.

Cook the pasta in salted water until *al dente,* rinse in cold water, and drain well. Add the bread crumbs, butter, and seasonings. Beat the egg yolks and milk together, add the cheese, and fold into the pasta. Whip the egg whites until stiff and fold into the pasta mixture. Pour into a buttered 2-quart casserole and set it in the oven in a pan of boiling water. Bake for 40 to 45 minutes, until well puffed and browned. Serve immediately.

Elizabeth H. Valentine
Council of the BSO

MOCK SOU-BOREG (Noodle Casserole)

Serves 4 to 6

8 ounces medium-wide egg noodles
4 tablespoons melted butter
½ pound Muenster or Monterey jack
  cheese, grated
6 ounces feta cheese, crumbled, or 1
  cup large-curd cottage cheese

½ teaspoon salt
2 eggs, beaten
¼ cup chopped parsley

Preheat the oven to 375°.

Cook the noodles until *al dente* in salted water according to the package directions. Drain well and rinse with cold water. Return to the pot in which they were cooked and toss, gently but thoroughly, with 2 tablespoons of melted butter.

Add the cheeses and salt to the eggs and beat thoroughly. Set half the mixture aside, and mix the parsley with the remainder.

Arrange half the noodles in a layer in a buttered 9-inch square baking pan, and spread evenly with the parsley mixture. Cover with the remaining noodles and top with the plain cheese mixture. Drizzle the remaining butter over the cheese, and bake for about 30 minutes, until the filling is set and the top is delicately browned. Cut into squares and serve hot, as a side dish for dinner, or as a main course for luncheon.

Mrs. Lillian Jingozian

Quick Method of Preparing Beans: Cover beans or other dried legumes (chick peas, lentils, and such) with water and bring to a full rolling boil. Remove from the heat and allow to stand, uncovered, until cool. This takes about an hour, and saves overnight soaking.

BOSTON BAKED BEANS

Serves 4 to 6

Traditional Boston beans are baked slowly with molasses, onion, and various seasonings: the proportions vary according to individual family preferences. They should be served with Codfish Balls,♦ coleslaw or a green tossed salad, brown bread or Corn Bread,♦ and pickles and/or ketchup. Experiment with varieties of beans: Jacob's cattle, Swedish brown, Mexican red, pinto, and yellow-eye all bake well, as does even the lowly soybean.

2 cups California pea beans
¼ pound lean salt pork
1 small yellow onion, peeled
¼ to ⅓ cup unsulphured molasses
1 teaspoon dry mustard

⅛ teaspoon freshly ground black
  pepper
¼ teaspoon fresh or dried savory
  (optional)
1 tablespoon brown sugar (optional)

Soak the beans overnight in cold water to cover; or cover with cold water, bring to a boil, and set aside for about 1 hour. Drain, cover with cold water, and bring to a boil. Simmer for about 5 minutes, or until the bean skins split when blown upon. Drain, reserving the cooking water.

Preheat the oven to 250°.

Meanwhile, cut the pork into four pieces, cover with cold water, and bring to a boil. Simmer for 5 minutes; then drain and discard the water. Place the pork in a small frying pan and "try it out" (render it) over low heat, turning often. When it is lightly browned, place it in the bottom of a bean pot with the onion, discarding the rendered fat. Add the hot beans. Mix together ¼ cup molasses, the seasonings, and 1 cup of bean water; pour this over the beans. Add sufficient bean water to cover the beans, cover the pot, and place it in the oven for 6 to 8 hours, or until the beans are tender. Add more bean water if the level falls.

When the beans are almost done, take off the cover and pull the pork to the surface to brown a little. Adjust the seasonings, adding more molasses and the sugar if necessary. Serve with the traditional accompaniments listed above, or as a side dish with pork or ham.

The Cookbook Committee

JOSEPHINE'S BEANS

Serves 6 to 8

Here follows another splendid recipe from Felix Viscuglia in addition to his Quiche Clarinet.◆

1 pound dried lima beans (or other dried beans)
1 pound bacon strips, cut into 1-inch pieces
1 large onion, chopped
2 or 3 cloves garlic, chopped
1 28-ounce can tomato sauce

½ teaspoon dried basil
1 bay leaf
Oregano
Salt
Freshly ground black pepper

Soak the beans for 2 hours, or overnight if more convenient. Drain well and discard the water.

Cook the bacon until it is not quite crisp, and remove the pieces to a large saucepan. Sauté the onion and garlic in the bacon drippings until transparent. Drain off any surplus fat and add the onion to the bacon, along with the tomato sauce and the beans. Add the basil and bay leaf, and oregano, salt, and pepper to taste. Bring to a boil; then lower the heat and simmer, covered, for 2 to 3 hours, until the mixture thickens and the beans are soft. Add a little water and adjust the seasonings if necessary. Serve as a side dish with meats or chicken, or as a main course with salad.

Felix Viscuglia, clarinet

LENTILS AND SAUSAGE

Serves 6

Actress Lee Remick particularly enjoys cooking when she is vacationing on Cape Cod. She and her husband, Kip Gowans, joined the Friends of the BSO during one of the Orchestra's European tours.

1 cup brown lentils, rinsed and
   drained
1 teaspoon salt
2 tablespoons oil
2 medium-sized onions, chopped
3 cloves garlic, minced
1 1-pound can tomatoes, drained and
   chopped

2 pounds kielbasa, chorizo, or other
   firm spicy sausage, sliced
1 tablespoon sugar
1 bay leaf
Freshly ground black pepper

Place the lentils and 1 teaspoon of salt in a large saucepan and cover with cold water. Bring to a boil, reduce the heat, cover, and simmer for 20 minutes. Drain and set aside, reserving the cooking liquid.

Preheat the oven to 350°.

Heat the oil in a heavy flame-proof casserole. Sauté the onions and garlic until soft. Add the tomatoes and cook, stirring frequently, until all the liquid has evaporated. Combine the sausage with the tomato mixture and stir in the lentils and seasonings, including more salt if necessary. Moisten with about ½ cup of the reserved cooking liquid, and bake for 30 minutes, adding more liquid if the mixture becomes too dry. The lentils should be soft but must remain whole. Serve with Brussels sprouts or broccoli.

Note

This dish may be prepared ahead and reheated, but be careful not to overcook the lentils.

Lee Remick Gowans

IRI TOFU (Parched Bean Curd)

Serves 4 to 6

The music of Japanese composer Toru Takemitsu has been heard frequently in Symphony Hall during Seiji Ozawa's years as the Boston Symphony's music director. Mr. Takemitsu's variation on a traditional Japanese theme is, as he says, "easy to cook, a fit food to be eaten with rice and *sake*, healthful, and with a Zen flavor." Japanese cuisine calls for many small and exquisitely prepared and presented courses that are eaten with chopsticks. Both *sake* (served warm) and Japanese beer (served chilled) are readily available in the United States. Either is a perfect accompaniment for this dish.

2 cakes tofu (bean curd), rinsed
3 large dried black mushrooms
1½ cups warm water
2 tablespoons tamari (Japanese soy
   sauce)
2 tablespoons sake
1 teaspoon sugar

1 medium-sized carrot, sliced thin
   diagonally
½ pound string beans, sliced
   diagonally, or ½ pound snow peas
   (fresh or frozen)
Peanut oil

Wrap the tofu in a cloth and set it on a rack with a weight on top to drain thoroughly. This will take 20 minutes or so. Cover the mushrooms with the warm water, and set aside to soak for about 20 minutes.

Drain the mushrooms and reserve the liquid. Slice them very thin and set them aside. Add sufficient water to the mushroom liquid to make 2 cups and bring it to a boil. Reduce the heat, add the tamari, *sake*, and sugar, and continue to simmer while preparing the vegetables.

Sauté the mushrooms in 2 tablespoons peanut oil until they are limp but not brown. Add the carrots and beans (or snow peas) and stir-fry over medium heat until the vegetables are almost tender. Remove from the pan and set aside.

Press the tofu firmly to remove as much liquid as possible, and chop it very fine. Add the tofu to the frying pan with 1 or 2 more tablespoons oil. Stir over medium heat until the mixture is quite dry, and pour off any excess oil. Deglaze the pan with the mushroom liquid and add the vegetables. Cook for about 15 to 20 minutes over low heat, until most of the liquid has evaporated. Serve as a main course with boiled rice, or serve as a side dish with broiled chicken or fish.

Toru Takemitsu, composer

BARLEY PILAF

*Serves 10 as a side dish,
6 as a luncheon dish*

½ cup butter
½ pound chopped mushrooms
½ cup chopped onions
1 small bunch scallions, chopped
1⅓ cups pearl barley

1 5¼-ounce can water chestnuts,
    drained and sliced
5 cups chicken stock
Chopped parsley (for garnish)

Preheat the oven to 350°.

Heat the butter until foaming and sauté the vegetables until the onions are transparent. Add the barley and water chestnuts and stir until the barley begins to brown. Remove from the heat and pour into a buttered 2-quart casserole. Stir in 2 cups of chicken stock and bake uncovered for 30 minutes. Add 2 more cups of chicken stock, cover, and cook 30 minutes longer.*

Remove the cover, stir in the remaining chicken stock, and cook uncovered for 20 minutes more, or until the liquid is absorbed. Sprinkle with chopped parsley and serve immediately as a side dish with meats or chicken, or as a main luncheon dish with a green salad.

* May be prepared ahead to this stage and refrigerated or frozen for later finishing. Defrost and reheat for 15 minutes before adding the last cup of stock.

*Mrs. Robert Kraft
Council of the BSO*

MIM'S BULGUR

Serves 8

Bulgur is good with any meat, and especially delicious with lamb.

¾ cup olive oil
6 large onions, chopped
6 cloves garlic, minced
1 medium-sized eggplant, peeled and
  cubed
1 medium-sized zucchini, cubed

3 cups cooked bulgur wheat (see Basic
  Bulgur♦)
½ cup chopped fresh mint
½ cup chopped parsley
Salt
Freshly ground black pepper

Heat ½ cup of the oil in a large frying pan, and sauté the onions, garlic, and eggplant for about 10 minutes. Add the zucchini and extra oil, if needed, and cook until the vegetables are tender, stirring frequently.* Add the cooked bulgur and the herbs, and season to taste. Toss the mixture lightly over low heat until warmed through, and serve immediately.

*May be prepared ahead to this point.

Mrs. Ames Stevens, Jr.

Basic Bulgur (Cracked Wheat): *To each cup of cracked wheat, add 2 cups water. Bring to a boil, add salt, and simmer until the water is absorbed. Remove from the heat and cool before proceeding.*

TEXAS CORN PUDDING

Serves 6 to 8 as a vegetable,
4 as a main course

This recipe was given to Mrs. Alsberg by Paul Zinc, a friend from New Mexico who is an extensive traveler and a gourmet cook.

¼ pound butter
2 eggs
1 cup stone-ground cornmeal
1 teaspoon baking soda
1 teaspoon salt
2 cups freshly grated corn (see Note)

⅓ cup all-purpose cream (see Note)
1½ cups milk
1 pound very sharp Cheddar cheese,
  grated
2 4-ounce cans green chili peppers,
  chopped

Preheat the oven to 350°.

Melt the butter in a 1½- to 2-quart earthenware casserole in the oven as it heats. Set aside to cool slightly. Beat the eggs and add the cornmeal, baking soda, and salt. Add the corn, cream, and milk and beat well. Pour one third of the batter into the casserole. Spread a layer of one third of the cheese and peppers over the batter. Repeat these layers twice, ending with the cheese and peppers. Cover the casserole loosely so the dish gets a little air, and bake for 35 to 45 minutes, until the top is golden brown.

Serve immediately as a side dish or, with a salad, as a simple luncheon main course.

Note

A 17-ounce can of cream-style corn may be substituted for the fresh corn and cream.

Elisabeth B. Alsberg

GRITS SOUFFLÉ

Serves 8

Sure doesn't taste like *grits!*

1 cup grits	*½ pound Boursin cheese, softened (or*
4 cups boiling water	*Cheddar cheese, grated)*
1 teaspoon salt	*1 teaspoon Worcestershire sauce*
¼ pound butter, softened	*2 eggs, beaten until thick and lemon*
½ to 1 teaspoon dill weed	*colored*

Cook the grits in the boiling salted water until tender but not dry (the cooking time depends on the type of grits used).

Preheat the oven to 350°.

Add the remaining ingredients and mix thoroughly. Pour into a buttered shallow oven-proof dish and bake for ½ hour, or until the soufflé is puffed and golden brown. Serve immediately in place of potatoes or pasta.

Mrs. Geoffrey C. Farnum
Council of the BSO

ACCIUGHE E CECI (Anchovies and Chick Peas)

Serves 2 to 4

1 2-ounce can flat anchovy fillets, in	*1 20-ounce can chick peas*
olive oil	*(garbanzos), drained*
Olive oil	*1 cup chopped parsley*
1 medium-sized clove of garlic, minced	*Freshly ground black pepper*

Drain the anchovies, reserving the oil, and chop or mash them. Add enough olive oil to the anchovy oil to make 1 tablespoon, and heat it in a medium-sized frying pan. Sauté the garlic over low heat until soft; stir in the anchovies and the chick peas. Heat thoroughly, stirring gently so as not to mash the peas. Add the parsley, and more oil and pepper to taste. Serve immediately as a side dish, with hot or cold meats or fish.

As an hors d'oeuvre, serve with crackers or Melba toast. As a salad, serve on lettuce, garnished with tomatoes and black olives. As a main course, serve with a green salad and toast or crisp hot bread.

Variation
Add more olive oil, to taste, and use as a sauce over homemade pasta. Dust with freshly grated Parmesan or Asiago cheese.

Mrs. Howard M. Turner, Jr.
Council of the BSO

Couscous (Quick-Cooking or Regular): Cook couscous according to the package directions. Sauté 1 cup chopped onion in 3 tablespoons butter, add salt and freshly ground black pepper to taste, and stir into the couscous. Serve instead of rice, potatoes, or pasta with any dish that needs something to absorb a sauce. Add a little chopped parsley for color.

BUFFET RICE

Serves 6

When increasing this recipe to serve a large crowd, bake it in several 2-quart dishes rather than one large one.

1 cup white rice
8 ounces Monterey jack cheese,
  shredded
1 4-ounce can green chilies,
  (jalapeños), drained, seeded, and
  chopped

2 cups sour cream
Paprika (optional)

Cook the rice according to the package directions, until it is still slightly crunchy — *do not overcook.* Drain, rinse in cold water, drain again, and set aside.

Reserve several tablespoons of the cheese. In a buttered 2-quart casserole layer half the rice, chilies, cheese, and sour cream. Repeat the layers. Sprinkle the top with the reserved cheese and dust with paprika.*

Preheat the oven to 350°.

Bake for 30 minutes, until the center is set and the top is golden brown.

*May be prepared ahead to this point and refrigerated, but allow the casserole to come to room temperature before baking.

Mrs. Thomas Morse
Tanglewood Council of the BSO

CHEN FAN

Serves 6

The on-stage harmony of Thomas Stewart and his wife, Evelyn Lear, extends to the kitchen. Miss Lear's Chinese Chicken with Walnuts♦ is admirably accompanied by Mr. Stewart's Chinese rice.

½ cup chopped onion
3 tablespoons butter
2 teaspoons grated orange peel
½ teaspoon ground ginger
½ teaspoon poultry seasoning
⅛ teaspoon freshly ground black
  pepper

½ cup orange juice
2 cups chicken stock
1 cup rice
Salt

Heat the butter in a large frying pan, and sauté the onion until golden. Stir in the orange peel, ginger, poultry seasoning, and pepper. Add the orange juice and stock and bring to a boil. Stir in the rice, cover, and simmer over low heat until the rice is tender and all the liquid is absorbed, about 20 to 25 minutes. Fluff with a fork before serving and add a little salt if necessary.

Thomas Stewart, baritone

RICE ISRAELI STYLE

Serves 4 to 6

When Emanuel Borok successfully auditioned in 1974 for the position of assistant concertmaster with the Boston Symphony (which means concertmaster of the Boston Pops), his enormous array of talents and interests was as yet unknown in his new country. Formerly assistant concertmaster of the Moscow Philharmonic, he became the concertmaster of the Israel Chamber Orchestra before coming to the United States. He and his wife also contributed a simplified Chicken Kiev♦ as well as the rice dish that follows.

2 tablespoons olive oil
1 medium-sized onion, chopped
1 cup long-grain white rice (see Note)
2 cups hot beef stock

1 to 2 teaspoons curry powder
1 teaspoon salt
½ cup raisins
¼ cup pine nuts

Heat 1 tablespoon of the olive oil in a large frying pan and sauté the onion until golden. Stir in the rice, stock, curry powder, and salt, and simmer, covered, for 20 minutes. Remove from the heat and add the raisins. Sauté the pine nuts in the remaining olive oil until they are golden, and add to the rice. Cover and place over low heat for several minutes. Toss with a fork and serve immediately with any chicken or meat entrée.

Note
Brown rice adds a nutty flavor to this useful and delicious dish, but it takes about 30 to 40 minutes to cook. Add a little more stock if the rice becomes too dry.

Emanuel Borok, violin
BSO assistant concertmaster
Boston Pops concertmaster

PARTY RICE

Serves 6 to 8

This rice will wait happily in a warm oven until tardy guests arrive.

3 cups slightly undercooked white or brown rice
1 medium-sized onion, chopped
1 medium-sized green pepper, seeded and chopped
1 teaspoon salt
Freshly ground black pepper

2 to 3 tablespoons curry powder (see Note)
½ cup melted butter
Tomatoes, peeled and sliced fairly thick, to cover the dish
8 strips bacon, partially cooked

Preheat the oven to 350°.

Add the onion and green pepper to the rice and season to taste. Spread the mixture in a buttered shallow baking dish. Stir the curry powder into the butter and pour it evenly over the rice. Cover with a layer of tomatoes, and top with the bacon. Bake for 30 to 40 minutes, until the vegetables are tender and the bacon is crisp.

Note
Curry powder varies so much in strength that it is dangerous to be dogmatic about amounts.

Mrs. Garrett D. Bowne III
Council of the BSO

RISOTTO PRONTO

Serves 6

Sister and wife of Boston Symphony players, Mrs. Benson is truly a family member. Her recipe for quick risotto (a contradiction in terms!) is a variation on a traditional theme for a cook who is pressed for time.

1½ cups chicken stock
Powdered saffron (see Note)
3 tablespoons butter
¼ cup minced onion

1 cup white rice
⅓ cup dry white wine or vermouth
Freshly grated Parmesan cheese
Freshly ground black pepper

Heat the chicken stock in a small saucepan with a pinch of saffron until the saffron has dissolved, and set it aside. Melt the butter in a 3-quart saucepan over medium heat and sauté the onions until they are transparent. Add the rice and stir until the grains are opaque. Pour in the stock and wine, and bring to a boil, stirring frequently. Reduce the heat, cover, and simmer for about 15 minutes, until the rice is tender. Sprinkle with Parmesan cheese and black pepper to taste, and serve immediately.

Note

If powdered saffron is not available, pound a few threads of whole saffron in a mortar.

Clara Stagliano Benson

RICE PILAF

Serves 6

3 tablespoons butter
1 onion, coarsely chopped
1 cup converted long-grain white rice
¼ cup medium bulgur (cracked wheat)
½ cup fine noodles, crushed or broken
  into 1-inch pieces

½ cup pine nuts
2¼ cups chicken stock
2 tablespoons chopped parsley
Salt
½ teaspoon freshly ground white
  pepper

Melt the butter in a heavy saucepan and sauté the onion until transparent. Add the rice, noodles, bulgur, and nuts, and cook until the rice is opaque. Add 2 cups of stock and bring to a boil. Reduce the heat, cover and steam for 14 minutes. *Do not stir.*

Uncover and test; if the rice is still hard in the center and the liquid is absorbed, add ¼ cup more stock, cover, and steam for 4 or 5 minutes. *Do not overcook.* Toss in the parsley, season to taste, and serve immediately; or set aside for later reheating.

Variation

Slivered almonds are an acceptable substitute for pine nuts.

Mrs. Robert Kraft
Council of the BSO

WILD RICE WITH MUSHROOMS AND CHIVES

Serves 3 or 4

New York Times food and restaurant critic Mimi Sheraton, who has also written numerous books and articles, is one of the Boston Symphony's fans who live outside the Boston area.

*1 cup wild rice, washed in 5 or 6
   changes of water
2 cups boiling water
½ teaspoon salt
6 tablespoons butter*

*½ pound mushroom caps, sliced
1 tablespoon minced chives
Salt
Freshly ground black pepper
Freshly ground nutmeg*

Cover the washed rice with the boiling water and add the salt. Cover and simmer over low heat for 20 to 25 minutes, without stirring. Check occasionally toward the end of the cooking time, because the rice must be tender but not mushy. Drain thoroughly, and keep warm.

Heat the butter over medium-high heat and brown the mushrooms quickly. Do not burn the butter, but the mushrooms should squeak as they cook so that they do not become soggy. Add the rice and chives, toss to mix, and season to taste. Serve immediately, or keep hot in a double boiler over simmering water.

© *Mimi Sheraton*
Food and restaurant critic
The New York Times

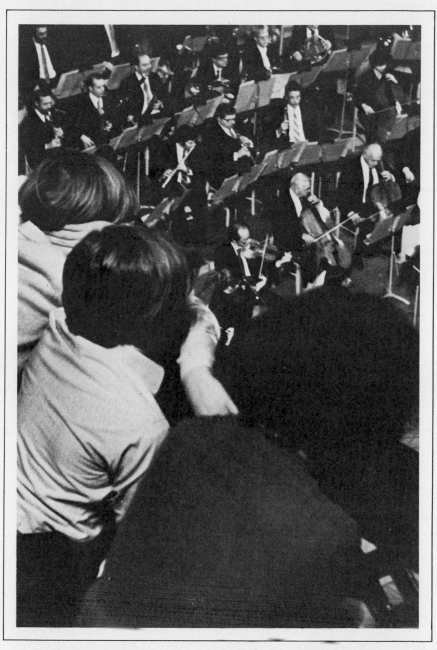

BREADS, MUFFINS, ROLLS, AND PANCAKES

No art can exist without an audience, nor can it have a future without a potential audience among the younger generation. Many performing artists have the urge to share their skills and knowledge with the young, and the Boston Symphony is no exception. Since 1959, Youth Concerts at Symphony Hall have brought thousands of children from their schools for an introduction to great orchestral music under the baton of Harry Ellis Dickson, a violinist of the Boston Symphony and associate conductor of the Pops. During the summer, a program called Days in the Arts (DARTS) brings more than a hundred sixth-graders from urban and suburban Boston to spend a week at Tanglewood, immersed in music, dance, drama, and the visual arts. Through these programs, each child learns how the arts can enrich his or her life.

A# BREAD

Introduction
This bread is regularly made in the five-hour span of *Morning pro musica*.

Score and Instrumentation

1 tablespoon active dry yeast	*1 egg, beaten*
4 tablespoons honey	*6 to 7 cups unbleached flour*
2 cups warm water (100°)	*1 tablespoon salt*
2 tablespoons softened butter	*Cornmeal*

Adagio, Allegro (30 minutes)
In a large mixer bowl combine the yeast, honey, water, and butter. Beat and set aside for 5 minutes. Add the egg and 2 cups of flour and beat at medium speed for 5 minutes. Using a dough hook, add the salt and 3 cups of flour ½ cup at a time, mixing thoroughly after each addition. Knead with the hook until the dough forms a large ball, and add flour slowly until the dough is smooth and resilient but still moist. Knead for 5 minutes by hook or by hand.

Intermission (2 hours)
Place the dough in a deep buttered bowl, turning to coat all sides. Cover with plastic wrap or a damp towel, and place in a warm spot until doubled in bulk, about 2 hours.

Andante (90 minutes)
Punch down the dough and turn out onto a floured surface. Knead briefly, divide the dough into thirds, and shape the loaves carefully. Place the loaves in three buttered 9-by-5-by-3-inch loaf pans that have been thoroughly dusted with cornmeal. Cover and allow to rise for about 45 minutes, until the dough nearly fills the pans. Preheat the oven to 350°. (See Note.)

Finale (35 minutes)

Place the bread on the lower middle shelf of the oven and bake for 35 to 45 minutes, or until the bread sounds hollow when tapped. Cool on a rack, right side up.

Variations

One half cup raisins, stone-ground uncooked oats, bran, whole-wheat flour, sesame seeds, whatever, may be added. One quarter teaspoon cinnamon is also good. Good composition!

Note

If the loaves are started in a cold oven with the thermostat set at 350°, the A# may rise to B# or even higher.

Nathaniel Pulsifer

FITZ-ANADAMA BREAD

Makes 2 large loaves

There are many versions of Anadama bread, which legend attributes to New England. This unorthodox descendant bears a strong family resemblance and is well worth the time it takes: it is moist, keeps well, and makes excellent toast.

2 cups stone-ground cornmeal
2½ cups boiling water
2½ tablespoons active dry yeast (see Note)
½ cup warm water
⅓ to ¾ cup unsulphured molasses

1 cup powdered milk
2 cups whole-wheat flour
2 to 4 cups unbleached flour
1 tablespoon salt
6 tablespoons butter, melted and cooled

Pour the boiling water over the cornmeal, stirring vigorously, and set it aside for 20 to 30 minutes to cool to no more than lukewarm. Dissolve the yeast in the warm water, adding 1 teaspoon of the molasses. When this mixture is foaming, add it to the cornmeal mixture with the molasses and powdered milk. Stir to blend well; then add the whole-wheat flour and 1 cup unbleached flour. Beat at least 100 strokes — a dough hook helps! Cover and set aside for 20 to 30 minutes, until it is doubled in bulk. Stir down and add the salt and 4 tablespoons butter. Knead in more unbleached flour, until the dough is smooth and elastic but not at all dry. Cover, and allow to rise again (each rising takes slightly less time). Punch down, and allow to rise again. Divide the dough into two equal parts. Roll each part into a rectangle approximately 8 by 4 by 1 inches, and roll up like a jellyroll, starting at a wide side. Place each loaf seam side down in a well-buttered 9-by-5-by-3-inch loaf pan. Brush the tops with the remaining butter, using it all and allowing it to run down the sides of the loaves. Allow to rise until doubled.

Preheat the oven to 350°. Bake for approximately 1 hour, until the loaves are well browned and sound hollow when tapped on the bottom. Turn out onto a rack to cool completely.

Note
Imported French yeast works faster than regular yeast. Use about three fourths as much.

Julie Bradley

DANISH RYE BREAD

Makes 2 loaves

4 cups buttermilk
1½ packages active dry yeast
½ teaspoon salt

4 cups rye flour
4 to 4½ cups unbleached flour

Heat half the buttermilk to lukewarm and pour into a large bowl. Dissolve the yeast in the warm milk; add the salt, and then beat in the rye flour, alternating with the remaining buttermilk. Stir in the white flour and knead well, adding more if necessary. The dough should hold its shape, and not be too sticky. Place the dough in an oiled bowl and turn it to grease the top. Cover with a towel and set in a warm place for 1 hour, or until doubled in bulk.

On a floured surface, shape the dough into two loaves; place them in buttered 9-by-5-by-3-inch bread pans. Allow to rise again for half an hour. Bake in a preheated 400° oven for 50 minutes, or until the bread sounds hollow when tapped on the bottom. Lower the heat to 350° if the top gets too dark. Allow to stand in the pans for 5 minutes, and turn out onto a rack. Cool right side up, covered for a tender crust or uncovered for a crisp one.

Mrs. John H. Brooks
Tanglewood Council of the BSO

OATMEAL BREAD

Makes 2 3-pound loaves,
3 2-pound loaves

Violinist Marylou Speaker Churchill has been playing in orchestras since she was ten and joined the BSO in 1970. She has many varied interests, chief among them the sponsoring of students from the People's Republic of

China, where the Orchestra toured in 1979. In addition, Marylou is an excellent cook: she was the first player to donate dinners to the Orchestra's annual Musical Marathon. Of her recipe, she says, "It was given me by the grandmother of one of my students."

2 cups old-fashioned oatmeal (not
   quick-cooking)
1 tablespoon salt
4 cups boiling water
2 tablespoons butter
1/4 cup sugar

3/4 cup molasses
1 tablespoon active dry yeast, or 1 cake
   compressed yeast
1/4 cup warm water
8 to 9 cups all-purpose flour
Oil or melted butter

Place the oatmeal and salt in a large bowl, and stir in the boiling water. Add the butter, sugar, and molasses, and allow to cool to lukewarm. Dissolve the yeast in the warm water and beat it into the oatmeal mixture. Add the flour, 2 cups at a time, and beat well after each addition. (See Method 2.) Place the dough in an oiled or buttered very large bowl, and turn to coat thoroughly. Cover the bowl with plastic wrap, making a pleat each way in the wrapping to allow room for the dough to expand. Refrigerate overnight.

In the morning, remove the dough from the bowl, knead lightly, and form into two or three loaves. Fit the loaves into well-buttered two 11-by-5-by-3-inch or three 9-by-5-by-3-inch loaf pans and brush the tops with oil or melted butter. Cover loosely and set aside in a warm place until the loaves have doubled in bulk.

Preheat the oven to 350°.

Bake the bread for 30 to 50 minutes, or until the loaves sound hollow when tapped on the bottom (the larger loaves, obviously, take longer). Turn out onto a rack, and cool, covered. This bread likes to be eaten warm.

Method 2

When the flour is added, knead the bread by hand or with a dough hook until it is shiny and elastic, adding 1/2 to 1 cup more flour if necessary. Set it aside in a buttered or oiled bowl for 30 minutes to 1 hour; then punch it down and shape it into three loaves. Fit the loaves into buttered 9-by-5-by-3-inch pans, and cover with plastic wrap. Leave a large pleat each way in the wrapping to allow the bread to rise, and set it in the bottom of the refrigerator overnight.

In the morning, place the loaves in a cold oven, set the thermostat for 375° and bake the bread for 30 minutes. Lower the heat to 325° and continue to cook until the loaves are done (see above), and proceed as above.

Variation

For muffins, or small individual loaves, preheat the oven to 400° and cook for 15 to 20 minutes. If using Method 2, allow approximately 20 to 25 minutes' cooking time.

Marylou Speaker Churchill
Principal second violin

OATMEAL BREAD WITH SUNFLOWER SEEDS

Makes 2 loaves

This crunchy bread is good hot, and it makes excellent toast.

2 cups scalded milk
2 tablespoons butter
2 teaspoons salt
½ cup molasses
1 teaspoon sugar
1½ tablespoons active dry yeast
½ cup lukewarm water

2 cups old-fashioned rolled oats
4 to 4½ cups sifted all-purpose flour
1 cup whole-wheat flour
½ cup sunflower seeds, toasted and
  cooled
Cooking oil

Combine the milk, butter, salt, and molasses in a large bowl, and cool to lukewarm. Mix the sugar and yeast with the lukewarm water and when it foams add to the milk mixture. Stir in the oats, 2 cups all-purpose flour, and the whole-wheat flour. Beat until smooth. Add the sunflower seeds and gradually stir in more all-purpose flour until the dough does not cling to the sides of the bowl.

Turn the dough out on a lightly floured board, and knead for 10 minutes, adding flour little by little. It should be smooth and elastic, but not too firm. Place the dough in an oiled bowl, and turn it to oil all surfaces. Cover and allow to rise in a warm place until doubled in bulk, about 2 hours. Punch the dough down, divide it in half, and let it rest for about 10 minutes. Shape the loaves and place them in lightly buttered 9-by-5-by-3-inch bread pans. Brush with oil, cover, and let rise again until double in bulk, about 1½ to 2 hours.

Preheat the oven to 375°.

Bake the bread for 40 to 45 minutes, or until the tops are browned and the loaves sound hollow when tapped on the bottom. Turn out onto a rack to cool, covered with a cloth for a tender crust or uncovered for a crisp one.

Variation

One half cup gluten flour may be substituted for ½ cup of the all-purpose flour.

Mrs. Thomas R. Carrington
Tanglewood Council of the BSO

GRANDMA MALCOLM'S DILL BREAD

Makes 2 large or 3 medium-sized loaves

1 pint cottage cheese, at room
   temperature
¼ cup melted butter
2 eggs
2 packages active dry yeast
½ cup warm water
¼ cup sugar
¾ cup chopped onion

5 cups flour
½ teaspoon baking soda
4 teaspoons dill weed
1½ teaspoons salt
2 tablespoons freshly grated Parmesan
   cheese
Vegetable shortening

Beat together the cottage cheese, butter, and eggs. Meanwhile, dissolve the yeast in the warm water with 2 teaspoons of the sugar. When it foams up, add it to the cottage cheese mixture with the remaining ingredients (except the shortening). Mix thoroughly — a dough hook helps — and knead for about 10 minutes, or until the dough feels silky. Place the dough in a greased bowl, cover, and set in a warm place to rise until doubled in bulk.

Punch down and shape the dough into two large loaves or three medium-sized ones; place in loaf pans thoroughly greased with vegetable shortening. Allow the loaves to rise again until doubled.

Preheat the oven to 350°. Bake for 40 to 45 minutes, or until the loaves are well browned and sound hollow when tapped on the bottom. The larger loaves may require an additional 5 to 10 minutes' cooking time. Turn out onto a rack and cool, covered with a light cloth for a tender crust, or uncovered for a crisp crust.

Mrs. Louis W. Mead
Council of the BSO

RALPH'S ITALIAN COUNTRY BREAD

Makes 2 loaves

1 package plus 1 teaspoon active dry
   yeast
2¼ cups lukewarm water
1 tablespoon sugar

2 tablespoons butter, softened
6 cups unbleached all-purpose flour
½ cup cornmeal, white or yellow
1½ tablespoons salt

Dissolve the yeast in the warm water and add the sugar. Cool for 5 minutes and add the butter. Mix the flour, cornmeal, and salt in a food processor, and add the liquid mixture through the small feed tube. Mix until the dough forms a ball and pulls away from the sides of the processor. Remove the dough to a lightly floured board and knead it for about 1 minute. Place the dough in an oiled bowl and turn to coat it thoroughly. Cover and set in a warm place for about 1½ hours, or until doubled in bulk.

Punch the dough down, divide it in half, and form two tapered loaves 12 to 14 inches long. Place them on a baking sheet sprinkled generously with cornmeal. Cover the loaves and let them rise for 7 to 8 minutes. Slash the tops with a very sharp knife, or razor blade, dipped in flour before each cut.

Set a pan of boiling water on the bottom shelf of a cold oven. Place the loaves in the top third of the oven. Set the oven control at 400° and bake until the tops are brown, and the loaves sound hollow when tapped on the bottom. Cool the bread on wire racks, right side up.

Ralph Dinunzio

BERKSHIRE BRIOCHE

Makes 2 large or 3 medium-sized loaves

Colonel Adams's version of the classic brioche is remarkably easy and comparatively quick to make. It produces a tender, delicate, and versatile bread.

1 cup milk
1 tablespoon salt
½ cup sugar
2 tablespoons active dry yeast
¾ cup lukewarm water

9 to 10 cups all-purpose flour
1 pound butter
6 eggs, beaten
Melted butter

Heat the milk almost to the boiling point and remove from the heat. Stir in the salt and sugar until dissolved, and set aside to cool. Combine the yeast, water, and 1 cup of flour and set aside to proof for 15 to 20 minutes. Stir the mixture down occasionally if it threatens to overflow the bowl.

Place 8 cups of flour in the bowl of an electric mixer. Cut the butter into small pieces and add to the flour. Using low to medium speed, beat the butter and flour together until it resembles coarse meal. Gently add the beaten eggs, and then the milk mixture. When the batter is thoroughly but lightly blended, pour the yeast mixture over it. By hand, mix and knead the dough in the bowl until the yeast is completely incorporated. Do not bruise the dough! Sprinkle with a little extra flour, cover the bowl with plastic wrap, and set it aside until the dough has doubled in bulk. This may take anywhere from 1 to 2½ hours.

Turn the dough out onto a floured board and knead it gently, adding a little more flour if necessary. The dough should be very soft, but not too sticky. Place it in a buttered bowl, turn to coat it completely, cover, and allow it to rise again: the second rising will be shorter. Turn it out onto the floured board and divide it into two or three parts (or nine parts if three braided loaves are desired). Shape the dough into loaves, place them in buttered pans and allow them to rise again until doubled in bulk. (See Note.)

Preheat the oven to 350°.

Bake the loaves for 30 to 40 minutes, depending upon their size: they should be well browned and sound hollow when tapped on the bottom. Turn out onto a rack to cool, and brush the tops of the loaves with melted butter. Serve with unsalted butter and honey or preserves, or just "as is." When several days old, this bread makes excellent toast.

Note

This dough looks very pretty baked in a decorative mold or Bundt pan, as well as in traditional flared-sided brioche pans. It may be baked in muffin tins for individual brioches.

Colonel William M. Adams
Tanglewood Council of the BSO

SHREDDED WHEAT BREAD

Makes 2 large loaves

John Dickson Murray, for many years a violinist with the BSO, was Margaret Murray Bennett's father.

1 cup water	⅓ cup molasses
1 cup milk	⅓ cup sugar
2 shredded wheat biscuits	1 tablespoon yeast
3 tablespoons butter	½ cup lukewarm water
1 teaspoon salt	5 to 6 cups all-purpose flour

Scald the water and milk, pour this liquid over the next five ingredients, and set the mixture aside to cool until lukewarm. Dissolve the yeast in the lukewarm water and add it to the wheat mixture. Mix well, and then add flour 1 cup at a time until the dough can be handled.

Knead the dough for 5 to 8 minutes on a floured board, adding more flour if necessary, until it is smooth and silky. Place it in a buttered bowl and turn it to butter all sides. Cover with a clean cloth, and let the dough rise in a warm place until it doubles in bulk. Punch the dough down, and shape it into two loaves. Place the loaves in buttered 9-by-5-by-3-inch pans and let rise again until the dough is level with the tops of the pans.

Preheat the oven to 400°.

Set the loaves in the oven, and immediately lower the temperature to 350°. Bake for 25 to 35 minutes, until the tops are crisp and brown and the bread sounds hollow when tapped on the bottom. Cool in the pan for 10 minutes; then turn out onto a rack and brush the tops of the loaves with butter.

Margaret Murray Bennett

SWISS TWIST BREAD

Makes 2 loaves

2 cups all-purpose flour
2 cups whole-wheat flour
¼ cup sugar
1½ teaspoons salt
2 tablespoons active dry yeast

1½ cups milk (may be made from
 powdered milk)
¼ cup butter
1 egg white, slightly beaten
Sesame seeds (optional)

Combine the flours in a bowl and set aside. In an electric mixer bowl, mix together ¾ cup of the combined flours, the sugar, salt, and undissolved yeast. Heat the milk and butter until lukewarm, and add to the dry ingredients. Beat for 2 minutes at medium speed, scraping the bowl frequently. Add ½ cup flour and beat for 2 more minutes; then stir in enough of the remaining flour to make a soft but not too sticky dough.

On a floured board, or with a dough hook, knead until the dough is smooth and elastic, about 10 minutes. Place it in an oiled bowl, turning to grease all sides. Cover with a damp cloth and set in a warm place until the dough is doubled in bulk, about 1 hour.

Punch down the dough and divide into six pieces for each loaf. Roll each piece into a 12-inch rope. Braid three ropes together and place on a buttered cookie sheet. Repeat with remaining ropes. Place the second braid on top of the first braid and seal by pinching the ends together. Brush with egg white, and sprinkle with sesame seeds, if desired. Allow to rise uncovered for about 1 hour, or until doubled in bulk.

Preheat the oven to 350°.

Bake until golden brown, remove from the cookie sheet, and cool on a rack.

Moira Suter

BABCIA'S EASTER BREAD

Makes 1 very large loaf

John Barwicki was a player in the first Esplanade concert under the baton of Arthur Fiedler in 1929, and he was also a member of the first Berkshire Festival Orchestra under Serge Koussevitzky in 1936. His recipe produces a truly beautiful and delicious bread. Let him speak for himself: "The word *baba* is the colloquial Polish term for woman, of which *babcia* is the diminutive. This sweet bread, traditionally baked in a tube pan, resembles the full gathered skirts worn by the farm women. The farms of my memory always had dozens of hens clucking around the yard, clannish gossips who squabbled briefly over the fabulously huge roses that housed their favorite beetles. The extravagant number of egg yolks in the baba was a lovely way to use up surplus eggs."

15 egg yolks
1 teaspoon salt
3 tablespoons active dry yeast
1 cup milk, scalded and cooled to
   lukewarm

1 cup sugar
4 cups all-purpose flour
¾ pound butter
1 teaspoon vanilla extract
¾ cup golden raisins

Beat the egg yolks and salt in a large mixing bowl until very thick and lemon colored. Dissolve the yeast in the lukewarm milk with 2 tablespoons sugar, and allow the mixture to stand for 5 minutes. Stir it into the egg yolks, and add 2 cups flour. Beat until the batter is smooth, and set it in a warm place, covered, until it has doubled in bulk.

Melt 1 cup butter, cool it slightly, and beat it into the raised dough. Add the remaining flour and sugar, the vanilla, and the raisins. "Butter your hands, sit down with the bowl in your lap, and squish, poke, punch, and knead the very loose dough until it is shiny and elastic." (Or use a dough hook!) Place the dough in a buttered bowl, cover, and let it rise until doubled again. Punch it down and let it rise a third time. Fit the dough into a generously buttered 10- or 12-inch tube pan and let it rest for 1 hour. Meanwhile, melt the remaining butter, pour off the milky residue, and set it aside but do not allow it to harden.

Preheat the oven to 350°.

Bake the loaf for 50 to 60 minutes, until it is golden and sounds hollow when tapped. Lower the heat if it appears to be browning too fast. Remove it from the oven and spread the top with the soft butter, which will sink into the crust. Cool for an hour or so; then remove the bread from the pan and cool completely on a rack, covered with a cloth. Serve with or without sweet butter and jam.

John Barwicki, double bass

BREAK-AWAY COFFEE CAKE

Serves 8

Children of all ages love this bread, which requires lots of napkins for sticky fingers. Homemade bread, of course, responds magnificently to this treatment.

2 loaves frozen bread dough, defrosted
¾ cup melted butter

1½ cups sugar mixed with 2 teaspoons
   cinnamon
1 cup chopped walnuts or pecans

Preheat the oven to 200°. Then turn it off with the door closed.

Pull off pieces of the dough and form them into balls the size of cherry tomatoes. Roll each ball first in butter, then in the cinnamon-sugar mixture, and finally in the nuts. Place the balls in a buttered 10-inch tube pan, leaving space for the dough to rise. Set the pan in the oven for 1 hour. Turn the oven control to 350° and bake the coffee cake until it is crisp and well browned. Turn it out and serve immediately, with or without more butter, or cool for later reheating.

Mrs. James T. Jensen
Council of the BSO

THREE-GENERATION SQUASH ROLLS

Makes 24 rolls

Chairman of the Board of the Boston Symphony, Abram Collier is unfailingly supportive of volunteer efforts. This is Mrs. Collier's mother's treasured recipe.

½ cup butter
½ cup milk, scalded and cooled to
    lukewarm
½ teaspoon salt
1 cup cooked, drained, and puréed
    Hubbard squash

1 tablespoon active dry yeast
½ cup sugar
¼ cup lukewarm water
3 cups sifted flour

Melt the butter in the scalded milk as it cools, and add the salt and squash. Dissolve the yeast and sugar in the water in a large, warmed mixing bowl and add the milk mixture and flour alternately. Mix well, adding more flour if necessary, until the dough is soft but not sticky. Cover the bowl and set it aside until the dough has doubled in bulk. Punch it down and form it into balls or ovals to make twenty-four rolls. Arrange them on a buttered cookie sheet, and allow to rise for 15 to 20 minutes.

Preheat the oven to 425°.

Bake the rolls for 15 to 20 minutes, until they are crisp and lightly browned. Cool on a rack and serve warm, with butter.

Mrs. Abram T. Collier
Council of the BSO

PARKER HOUSE ROLLS

Makes 4 dozen rolls

This is a contemporary version of the famous roll recipe, which has more to do with the shape than the precise ingredients.

2 tablespoons active dry yeast
3 cups lukewarm water
½ cup sugar
⅓ cup powdered milk

2 teaspoons salt
9 cups all-purpose flour
¾ cup melted butter, slightly cooled

Mix the yeast with about ½ cup of the lukewarm water and add about ½ teaspoon of the sugar. Set the mixture aside for several minutes to proof. In the bowl of an electric mixer, combine the remaining sugar and water with the powdered milk, salt, and about half the flour. Beat in the yeast mixture and ½ cup butter, reserving the remaining butter for later use. When the batter is smooth, add the remaining flour a little at a time, beating by hand or with a dough hook. The dough should be smooth, satiny, and soft, but firm enough to handle easily. Place it in an oiled bowl and set aside, covered, for about 1½ hours, or until double in bulk.

Punch the dough down, turn it out onto a lightly floured board, and knead gently for several minutes. Divide the dough into four equal parts. Working quickly, cut one part into twelve pieces and roll each piece into an oval or circle about ½ inch thick. Crease each piece firmly across the middle, and fold it over along the crease. Arrange the rolls on a buttered cookie sheet and repeat the process until all the dough is shaped. Set the rolls aside to rise, covered lightly, for about 45 minutes, or until double in bulk.

Preheat the oven to 400°.

Bake the rolls for 10 minutes, until golden brown. Brush the hot rolls with melted butter, and cool on a rack. Serve hot, warm, or at room temperature.

The Parker House, Boston

PIZZA CRUST

Makes 1 thick or 2 thin 14- or 15-inch pizzas

1 tablespoon active dry yeast
1 teaspoon sugar
1⅓ cups lukewarm water
2 tablespoons olive oil

1 medium-sized clove of garlic, pressed
  (optional)
1½ teaspoons salt
4 cups sifted all-purpose flour

Dissolve the yeast and sugar in ⅓ cup lukewarm water, and set aside for 5 minutes. In a large bowl, mix the remaining water, and the oil, garlic, and salt; stir in the yeast mixture. Sift in the flour, and mix well. Turn out onto a floured board and knead for about 10 minutes (or use a dough hook), until the dough is smooth and elastic. Place it in a well-oiled bowl, and turn to coat thoroughly. Cover, and allow the dough to rise for at least 1 hour or until it has doubled in bulk. (This may be achieved overnight in the refrigerator.)

Punch down the dough, roll it out into one or two circles, and place it on a hot, oiled pizza plate. Cover it with one of the following fillings (see Pizza

Sauces Italiano◆) or a filling of your choice, and allow the pizza to stand in a warm place for 15 to 20 minutes, until the crust starts to rise.

Preheat the oven to 450°.

Set the pizza on the bottom rack in the oven and bake for 10 minutes. Reduce the heat to 400° and bake for 5 to 10 minutes longer, until the crust is crisp and the filling is bubbling and lightly browned. Serve immediately.

Note

Pizza dough may be frozen either before or after cooking, with or without the filling. Do not heat pizza in a microwave oven, as it makes the crust soggy.

The Cookbook Committee

PIZZA SAUCES ITALIANO

For one pizza

Peppino Natale presides over the stage door at Symphony Hall. His traditional sauces prove that pizza is quick and easy to make at home. Pizza was first served in 1847 at a party given in Naples for King Umberto I and his wife, Margherita di Savoie. She liked pizza so much, the Neapolitans gave the dish her name: when in Naples, one asks for a Margherita, not a pizza.

Margherita (Neapolitan Pizza)

1 Pizza Crust◆

2 cups canned Italian-style tomatoes, drained and seeded

1 tablespoon chopped fresh basil, or 1 teaspoon dried basil

½ teaspoon salt

1½ cups grated mozzarella cheese

Freshly ground black pepper

1 to 2 tablespoons peanut oil

Preheat the oven to 400°.

Arrange the tomatoes over the pizza crust and sprinkle with the remaining ingredients in the order given. Bake in the lower third of the oven for 15 to 20 minutes, or until the crust is crisp on the bottom and the cheese is melted and slightly browned. Serve immediately.

Pizza Pizzaiola (Sicilian Pizza)

Substitute 1 clove garlic, minced, and 1 teaspoon dried or chopped fresh oregano for the basil in the preceding recipe. Follow the directions given above.

Pizza Paesano (Villager's Pizza)

Substitute 3 large ripe tomatoes for the canned Italian tomatoes. Slice them about ½ inch thick, and spread over the pizza crust. Season as above, and cook according to the preceding directions.

Note

All of these pizzas may be frozen before cooking, but they are so quick to make that it is seldom necessary. Do not reheat pizza in a microwave: it makes the crust soggy.

Peppino Natale
Symphony Hall staff

CORN DOILIES

Serves 6 or more

Amsterdam-born percussionist Frank Epstein joined the Boston Symphony in 1968. He was one of the founders of Collage, a contemporary music ensemble, and he is on the faculty of the New England Conservatory. Mrs. Epstein's crunchy traditional Southern corn bread goes well with food from all regions. There is a knack involved: sacrifice a few to the kitchen gods in order to perfect the knack, for the result is well worth it.

1 cup yellow cornmeal
1 teaspoon kosher salt
*¼ teaspoon freshly ground black
  pepper*

½ to 1 cup cold water
Corn oil

Mix all the ingredients except the corn oil, using only ½ cup water.

Pour corn oil into a heavy frying pan to a depth of about ½ inch, and heat the oil to 375° to 400°. The fat must be very hot but not smoking.

Pour 1 to 2 tablespoons of the mixture into the hot oil and use a wooden spoon to help it spread into the shape of a paper doily. It will splatter, so be careful. Fry very quickly on both sides until just slightly browned. Drain on paper towels. Repeat the process, adding water as needed to the cornmeal mixture. The batter must be thin to allow the lacy pattern to appear, but thick enough to hold together.

Serve wherever a crisp bread is indicated, with or without butter.

Mrs. Frank B. Epstein

CHEESE BANNOCKS

Serves 12

¼ cup butter, softened
1 cup oatmeal flour (see Note)
1 cup oatmeal
⅛ teaspoon salt

½ cup hot water
Cayenne pepper (optional)
*1 cup very sharp grated Cheddar
  cheese*

Rub the butter quickly into the oatmeal flour until it resembles coarse bread crumbs. Add the remaining ingredients, and knead until the mixture can be gathered into a ball.

Preheat the oven to 400°.

Divide the dough in half and set on a buttered cookie sheet. Pat into two circles about ¼ inch thick. Score the top of each circle lightly with crisscrossed slashes to mark six wedges. Bake for 20 minutes, until the tops are brown and the bannocks are crisp. Serve hot or warm, with or without butter or cream cheese.

Bannocks may be served for hors d'oeuvres, with soup for lunch, at picnics, or wherever crisp bread or crackers are indicated.

Note

To make oatmeal flour, process rolled oats in a blender until they have the consistency of coarse flour. Measure after blending.

Jocelyne St. Pierre Schanzle

BANANA BREAD BEN MARCATO

Makes 1 loaf

Nelson Darling, the Boston Symphony's indefatigable President, has long been active in all areas of the Orchestra's life. His wife's delicious and useful bread keeps indefinitely in the freezer for emergency tea or breakfast use.

½ cup butter
⅔ cup sugar
2 large ripe bananas, mashed
2 eggs
2 tablespoons molasses
1¾ cups all-purpose flour

¾ teaspoon baking soda
1¼ teaspoons cream of tartar
¼ teaspoon ground coriander
¼ teaspoon salt
1 cup date crystals or chopped sugared dates (optional)

Preheat the oven to 350°.

Cream the butter and sugar together, and add the bananas. Beat in the eggs one at a time, and then add the molasses. Sift the dry ingredients together and stir into the banana mixture; then fold in the dates. Pour into a buttered 9-by-5-by-2-inch loaf pan, and bake for 50 to 60 minutes, until the bread is firm to the touch and the center is dry when tested. Turn out and cool on a rack, right side up.

Serve thinly sliced with cream cheese or sweet butter, or in thick slices, toasted.

Mrs. Nelson J. Darling, Jr,
Council of the BSO

CORN BREAD

Serves 4 to 6

Everyone has his favorite recipe for this typically American bread. The following is an amalgam of recipes, allowing considerable leeway for individual preferences. All stone-ground meal will result in a soft, slightly sweet bread, and all white or yellow degerminated meal will make a very crunchy bread. Begin with equal amounts and experiment with the proportions until the desired consistency is obtained.

¼ cup butter (see Note)
1 cup cornmeal
¼ cup flour
2 teaspoons Symphony Baking
  Powder◆ or 1½ teaspoons
  double-acting baking powder
1 tablespoon sugar and/or 1
  tablespoon brown sugar

½ teaspoon salt
Cayenne pepper, nutmeg, and/or
  allspice (optional)
1 egg
½ cup buttermilk or yogurt, or ½ cup
  sweet milk and ½ teaspoon lemon
  juice

Preheat the oven to 400°.

Melt the butter in an 8- or 9-inch square pan, and coat the bottom and sides thoroughly. Pour the remaining butter into a small bowl.

In another bowl, combine the dry ingredients, including a dash of each of the optional spices. Add the egg and buttermilk to the melted butter, and beat well. Pour the egg mixture into the dry ingredients, and mix quickly and lightly. Spoon the batter into the hot pan, and bake for 20 to 25 minutes, or until the bread is crisp and lightly browned. Cut into squares in the pan, and serve immediately.

Note
When serving corn bread with Boston Baked Beans◆ or other strong-tasting dishes, bacon fat may be substituted for all or part of the butter.

The Cookbook Committee

BERT'S BEER BREAD

Makes 1 loaf

This is a very quick, chewy, sweet bread for breakfast or coffee break. It does not keep, but it does not need to! The original recipe calls for self-rising flour.

3 tablespoons butter
3 cups all-purpose flour
4½ teaspoons Symphony Baking
  Powder◆ or 3 teaspoons
  double-acting baking powder

4 tablespoons sugar
12 ounces beer at room temperature
½ teaspoon salt (optional)

Preheat the oven to 350°, or 325° for a glass pan.

Melt the butter in a 9-by-5-by-3-inch loaf pan, and grease the pan thoroughly. Pour out and reserve the excess butter.

Mix the flour, baking powder, sugar, beer, and salt until the dough is fairly smooth. Pour it into the loaf pan and brush the reserved butter over the top. Set aside to rise for 5 minutes. Bake for 40 to 50 minutes, until the top is crusty and brown and the loaf has pulled away from the sides of the pan. Turn out and cool on a rack. Serve warm or cool in thick slices: it toasts well.

Variation
For whole-wheat beer bread, use 3 tablespoons honey and 3 cups whole-wheat flour in place of the sugar and all-purpose flour.

Mrs. Peter W. Holland

DATE NUT BREAD

Makes 1 loaf

½ pound dates, cut into small pieces
½ cup raisins
¾ cup hot water
2 cups sifted flour
1 teaspoon baking soda
1 teaspoon salt

1 egg
1 cup sugar
1 teaspoon melted butter
1 teaspoon vanilla extract
1 cup walnuts, chopped

Pour the water over the dates and raisins and allow to stand overnight.
Preheat the oven to 350°.
Sift together the dry ingredients. Beat the egg, sugar, and butter. Stir in the dry ingredients, and add the date mixture, vanilla, and nuts.
Pour into a large greased 9-by-5-by-3-inch loaf pan and bake for 1 hour, or until the center is dry when tested. Remove from the pan and cool on a rack.

Peg Hurley

CRANBERRY BREAD

Makes 2 loaves

Not too sweet, this bread is excellent with sweet butter or cream cheese for tea or lunch. It toasts well.

3 cups cranberries
4 tablespoons unsalted butter
2 cups light brown sugar
2 eggs, beaten
4 cups flour
1 teaspoon baking soda

3 teaspoons baking powder
4 tablespoons hot water
1 cup orange juice
½ cup chopped nuts
Granulated sugar

Preheat the oven to 350°.

Chop the berries, using the largest blade of a food grinder; or "pulsate" in a food processor for 2 to 5 seconds. Set aside.

Cream the butter and brown sugar; add the eggs and beat until light. Combine the dry ingredients and sift into the eggs, adding alternately with the combined hot water and orange juice. Beat well, and stir in the berries and nuts. Pour the mixture into two buttered and sugared 9-by-5-by-3-inch bread pans. Sprinkle a little granulated sugar over the tops and bake for 50 to 60 minutes, until the center is firm and the crust is crisp and brown.

Mina Ellis Otis
Council of the BSO

LEMON BREAD

Makes 3 large loaves

Almost a tea cake, this lemon bread may be served buttered or plain.

4½ cups sugar
½ cup lemon juice
½ pound plus 2 tablespoons butter,
  softened
6 eggs
4½ cups flour

1½ tablespoons double-acting baking
  powder
1½ teaspoons salt
1½ cups milk
¼ cup grated lemon peel

Combine 1½ cups sugar with the lemon juice, mix well, and set the glaze aside so the sugar can dissolve.

Preheat the oven to 350°.

Cream the remaining sugar with the butter and eggs. Combine the dry ingredients and beat into the butter mixture alternately with the milk. Beat until the batter is smooth; then add the lemon peel. Pour the batter into three buttered and floured 8½-by-4½-by-3-inch loaf pans and bake for 1 hour, until the top is brown and the center of it is firm to the touch. Allow to stand in the pans for 5 minutes, and turn out onto a rack. Pour the glaze over the loaves while still hot and cool completely before slicing.

Variation

If this mixture is to be used as a cake, cook it in a Bundt pan.

The Williamsville Inn
West Stockbridge, Massachusetts

ORANGE BREAD

Makes 1 loaf

This unusual quick bread comes from a very old Cape Cod cookbook. It has an interesting texture, makes marvelous toast, and puts surplus orange peels to excellent use.

Peel from two oranges, ground or
finely chopped
2 cups cold water
⅓ cup boiling water
1 cup sugar
2¼ cups flour

2 teaspoons cream of tartar
1 teaspoon baking soda
1 teaspoon salt
1 egg, beaten
1 cup milk

Combine the orange peel and cold water in a saucepan, bring to a boil, and simmer for about 15 minutes, or until tender. Drain, add the boiling water and sugar, and cook until the syrup is slightly thickened. Set aside to cool.

Preheat the oven to 350°.

Mix the dry ingredients and beat in the egg, milk, and orange peel mixture. Pour into a buttered and sugared 9-by-5-by-3-inch loaf pan, or two small pans. Bake for 30 to 40 minutes, until the top is just firm to the touch and lightly browned. Cool on a rack.

Mina Ellis Otis
Council of the BSO

QUICK PUMPKIN BREAD

Makes 2 loaves

This bread is especially good served warm.

3½ cups flour
2¼ cups sugar
2 teaspoons baking soda
2 teaspoons salt
2 teaspoons cinnamon
2 teaspoons nutmeg
4 eggs, lightly beaten

1 cup salad oil
⅔ cup orange juice
2 cups mashed fresh pumpkin (or 1
1-pound can)
⅔ cup chopped walnuts or pecans
⅔ cup raisins

Preheat the oven to 350°.

Combine the ingredients in the order given, and mix until well blended. Spoon the batter into two buttered 9-by-5-by-3-inch loaf pans. Bake for 1 to 1¼ hours, or until the center is dry when tested and the bread pulls away from the sides of the pans.

Cool for 5 minutes in the pans; then turn out onto a rack and cool, right side up.

Mrs. Morton S. Baum
Council of the BSO

ZUCCHINI BREAD

Makes 2 loaves

3 eggs, beaten
2 cups sugar
1 cup vegetable oil
1 8½-ounce can crushed pineapple,
   drained
2 cups shredded small zucchini
3 cups flour

2 teaspoons baking soda
½ teaspoon baking powder
1 teaspoon salt
1½ teaspoons cinnamon
¾ teaspoon nutmeg
1 cup raisins
1 cup chopped nuts

Preheat the oven to 350°.

Cream the eggs and sugar until light and beat in the oil, pineapple, and zucchini. Combine the dry ingredients, raisins, and nuts, and add to the zucchini-egg mixture. Pour the dough into two buttered and sugared 9-by-5-by-3-inch loaf pans. Bake for 45 to 60 minutes, or until the center of the top is firm to the touch and the edges have pulled away from the sides of the pans. Cool for 10 minutes in the pans; then turn out onto a rack to cool completely.

Mina Ellis Otis
Council of the BSO

NEVER-FAIL POPOVERS

Makes 6 large or 12 small popovers

The quickest and most spectacular popovers ever . . . *Do not preheat the oven!*

3 "extra large" eggs, beaten
1½ cups flour

¾ teaspoon salt
1½ cups milk

Combine the eggs with the dry ingredients. Add the milk. Mix well with a spoon, but do not beat, and disregard the lumps. Divide the batter among six thoroughly buttered 3-inch deep-sided custard cups. Do not fill them more than three quarters full, or the popovers will not pop.

Place in a *cold* oven with the rack set low (sometimes the popovers hit the ceiling). Set the thermostat to 450°. Do not open the oven door for 45 minutes. *Then only*, check to see if the popovers need 5 to 10 minutes' more cooking. When they are done, remove them from the cups, turn off the heat, and leave them to dry in the oven for about 5 minutes more.

Serve with unsalted butter and honey, marmalade, or jam.

Variation

Twelve smaller popovers may be made in a well-buttered muffin tin. Cook for 35 minutes, and then proceed as above.

Mrs. Arnold D. Jenkins
Council of the BSO

PICAU AR Y MAEN (Welsh Cakes)

Makes about 2 dozen 2-inch cakes

Equally at home in concert or opera, British bass baritone Robert Lloyd has sung Beethoven's music with the Boston Symphony. His grandmother's cakes, "which she made over an open grate in her miner's cottage," are a cross between scones and biscuits. They are equally at home at breakfast, coffee break, teatime, or supper — anytime, in fact.

3½ cups flour
⅛ teaspoon salt
3½ teaspoons double-acting baking
  powder or 5 teaspoons Symphony
  Baking Powder◆
¼ teaspoon mace
¼ teaspoon nutmeg

¼ pound butter
¼ pound lard
⅔ cup sugar
¾ cup dried currants
1 egg
3 tablespoons milk

Sift the flour, salt, baking powder, and spices together into a large bowl. Rub the butter and lard into the flour until the mixture resembles coarse meal; add the sugar and currants. Beat the egg lightly with the milk and pour it over the flour mixture, tossing lightly with a fork until the dough holds together. Add a little more milk if necessary, but do not make the dough too sticky. Turn out onto a floured board and knead briefly. Roll out about ½ inch thick and cut into rounds 2 to 3 inches in diameter (larger are hard to handle). Heat a griddle or heavy iron frying pan over medium heat, and grease lightly with a little butter or lard. Cook the cakes for 5 to 6 minutes on each side, or until they are golden brown and crisp on the outside. Remove from the heat and serve hot, warm, or cold, either plain or with butter and jam or honey.

Robert Lloyd, bass baritone

BLUEBERRY MUFFINS

Makes 14 to 15 large muffins

This unusual method produces very fruity, slightly chewy muffins, perfect for picnics.

½ cup butter, softened
1¼ cups sugar, plus extra for
  sprinkling on muffins
2 eggs
2 cups all-purpose flour

2 teaspoons baking powder
½ teaspoon salt
½ cup milk
1 pound frozen blueberries

Preheat the oven to 375°.

Cream the butter and sugar until light and fluffy. Beat in the eggs, one at a time. Sift together the flour, baking powder, and salt, and add to the butter mixture alternately with the milk. Beat well after each addition; then fold in the frozen blueberries.

Set paper liners in the muffin tins and spoon the batter into the liners, filling to the top. Sprinkle generously with sugar and bake for 25 to 30 minutes, until the tops are browned.

Serve warm or cold with sweet butter.

Anita Ruthling Klaussen
Council of the BSO

GINGER MUFFINS

Makes 12

½ cup sugar
2 cups flour
1 teaspoon baking soda
½ teaspoon allspice
½ teaspoon cinnamon
1 teaspoon ground ginger
¼ teaspoon salt

½ cup butter
2 eggs, beaten lightly
½ cup molasses
½ cup buttermilk
½ cup raisins
½ cup chopped walnuts or pecans

Preheat the oven to 350°.

Sift the dry ingredients together. Cut the butter into small pieces and rub into this mixture until it resembles coarse meal. Combine the liquids and add, stirring just enough to moisten the flour. Add the raisins and nuts and spoon into twelve buttered or paper-lined muffin cups. Bake for about 30 minutes, until the muffins are brown and crusty. Serve hot or warm, with butter or cream cheese.

Mrs. Stephen Stone

WHOLE-WHEAT BLUEBERRY MUFFINS

Makes 12 to 14 muffins

The combination of whole-wheat and oat flours gives these muffins a unique nutty flavor.

¾ cup oat flour (see Note)
¾ cup all-purpose flour
¾ cup whole-wheat flour
⅔ cup sugar
2 teaspoons baking powder
1 teaspoon salt

¼ pound cold butter
1½ tablespoons grated lemon rind
2 cups blueberries (more if very moist
  muffins are desired)
⅔ cup milk
1 egg, lightly beaten

Preheat the oven to 375°.

Sift together the flours, sugar, baking powder, and salt. Cut the butter into small pieces and work it into the dry ingredients. Add the lemon rind and blend the mixture until it resembles coarse meal. Add the blueberries. Mix the milk and egg; immediately add to the flour mixture. Stir until just combined. Spoon into greased muffin tins. Sprinkle a little sugar on top of each muffin, if desired. Bake for 20 to 25 minutes, until the tops are browned and the muffins pull away from the sides. Cool slightly before removing from the tins, and serve hot or warm.

Note

One cup of rolled oats blended in a food processor or blender will make approximately ¾ cup oat flour.

Mrs. Albert E. Pratley
Council of the BSO

HANCOCK CORN FRITTERS

Serves 12

James Persip invented these fritters for the Shakers' "Dinners for the World's People." A versatile recipe, it has been used at Hancock Village for more than fifty years.

3 eggs
1½ cups milk
3 cups commercial pancake mix

2 cups cream-style corn
2 cups crushed pineapple, drained
Oil or lard for frying

Beat the eggs and milk, add the pancake mix, and stir until smooth. Fold in the corn and pineapple. Heat ½ inch of fat in a large deep-sided saucepan, and drop the batter by tablespoons into the hot fat. Fry for about 3 minutes, turn, and brown the other side. Drain on paper towels and keep the fritters in a warm oven. Serve hot with butter and maple syrup for breakfast, or plain as an accompaniment for ham or any other meat.

Hancock Shaker Village, Inc.
Pittsfield, Massachusetts

OKONOMI-YAKI (Japanese Pancakes)

Serves 2

There has long been a particular rapport between the Boston Symphony and the Japan Philharmonic Symphony Orchestra, with considerable exchange of musicians. Violinist Toshiyuki Kikkawa was one of these, and his daughter, Yuka, collected, translated, and adapted most of the Japanese recipes in this book.

A handful of dried seaweed (optional)
  (see Note)
1 tablespoon mayonnaise
1 tablespoon ketchup or chili sauce
5 tablespoons water
2 eggs
½ cup flour
Peanut oil
¼ pound pork tenderloin, very thinly
  sliced

1 large scallion, quartered lengthwise
1 cup shredded cabbage
1 tablespoon chopped red pickled
  ginger or preserved ginger, rinsed
¼ pound cooked shrimp, halved
  lengthwise
2 teaspoons toasted sesame seeds
1 to 1½ cups hot cooked white rice
Tamari (Japanese soy sauce)

Cook the seaweed according to the package directions, and drain well. Mix the seaweed with the mayonnaise, ketchup, and 1 tablespoon water. Set this dipping sauce aside. Beat the eggs with the flour and the remaining water until very smooth; set aside the pancake mixture.

Preheat a medium-sized frying pan and pour in a very thin film of peanut oil. Quickly stir-fry the pork until grey, over medium-high heat; add the scallion and cabbage, and stir-fry for about 2 minutes. Add the ginger, and remove half the mixture from the pan. Add a little more oil; then pour half the pancake mixture in a thin layer over the contents of the pan. Add half the shrimp, and turn the pancake when the bottom begins to brown and the top is firm. Press down and brown the second side. Slide the pancake onto a heated plate, and repeat the process.

Sprinkle the pancakes with sesame seeds and serve immediately, accompanied by the rice and dipping dishes of tamari and the mayonnaise mixture. Chopsticks and warm *sake* or cold beer add to the atmosphere and the taste.

Note
Japanese cuisine uses many seaweeds, which are obtainable at Oriental specialty and health food stores, as are the pickled ginger and tamari.

Yuka Kikkawa

PARSNIP PANCAKES

Serves 4 to 6

2 medium-sized parsnips, peeled and
  cut into ¼-inch sticks about 3 inches
  long
2 eggs
2 tablespoons melted butter
½ to ¾ cup milk

1 cup flour
2 tablespoons sugar
½ teaspoon salt
2 teaspoons baking powder
Butter for the griddle

Cook the parsnips in lightly salted water until tender, and drain.

Preheat the griddle.

Beat the eggs, butter, and ½ cup milk. Combine the dry ingredients, and add to the egg mixture. Stir gently, just enough to moisten the flour. Add more milk if thin pancakes are desired.

Lightly butter the hot griddle. Ladle the batter onto the griddle, making 4- to 6-inch pancakes. Add three or four parsnip sticks to each one, and cook quickly until lightly browned on both sides. Serve with melted butter and syrup or preserves.

Lovett's
Franconia, New Hampshire
Charles Lovett, proprietor

SWEDISH PANCAKES

Serves 5

This recipe produces forty to fifty thin, tender, delicate pancakes.

3 eggs
1 teaspoon sugar
Salt
1 cup flour

2 cups milk
¼ pound butter, melted and cooled
Cooking oil
Warmed maple syrup

Preheat a griddle to 425°.

Lightly beat the eggs, sugar, and a pinch of salt; add the flour and ½ cup of milk. Mix until smooth, add the remaining milk, and pour in the butter gradually, beating constantly.

Oil the griddle lightly for the first batch of pancakes only. Spoon the batter onto the griddle and cook each pancake until the top is barely set, 1 to 2 minutes; flip and brown the other side. *Do not overcook.*

Serve immediately on warmed plates with warm maple syrup and melted butter.

Bonus

Leftover pancake batter may be cooked over lower heat until completely crisp. The result is good with soups, salads, or even as a "dipper" at cocktails.

John B. Newhall

COOKIES AND CAKES

The Boston Symphony Orchestra has always toured outside its mother city — at first on short trips to neighboring Providence and Worcester, then farther afield to New York, Philadelphia, and Washington. The first long tour, in 1915, took the Orchestra to San Francisco for the Panama-Pacific Exposition. Tours abroad began after World War II — to Europe, the Soviet Union, Australia, and Asia. One of the most memorable of these was the one-week visit to China in 1979, with concerts in Shanghai and Peking. The stay in China also included a great deal of communication between Orchestra members and Chinese musicians, as in this demonstration *(overleaf)* by concertmaster Joseph Silverstein.

LUMBERJACKS

Makes 6 dozen

Each of the shortenings gives a different flavor to the finished product. These cookies keep well and may be formed and frozen for weeks.

1 cup sugar
1 cup butter, lard, or vegetable
*   shortening*
1 cup molasses
2 eggs

4 cups sifted flour
1 teaspoon baking soda
1 teaspoon salt
2 teaspoons cinnamon
1 teaspoon ground ginger

Cream the sugar and shortening, and beat in the molasses and eggs. Sift the dry ingredients together and beat into the egg mixture. Cover and refrigerate for at least 1 hour.

Preheat the oven to 350°.

Form the dough into walnut-sized balls and roll in granulated sugar. Arrange on a buttered cookie sheet and bake for 12 to 15 minutes, until crisp and browned.

Variations

Divide the dough into three parts. Form and bake the first part as described above. To the second part add ½ cup chocolate morsels and ½ cup chopped walnuts or pecans. To the third part add ¼ cup raisins and ½ teaspoon grated lemon rind. Drop the dough by teaspoonfuls onto a buttered cookie sheet, and bake as described above.

Mrs. Lawrence L. Clampitt
Council of the BSO

GINGER BISCUITS (Cookies)

Makes 2 to 3 dozen

One of the world's foremost mezzo-sopranos, Dame Janet Baker has performed the music of Berlioz and Mahler with the Boston Symphony. Her very English recipe has been adapted to suit American ingredients and measurements.

4½ cups flour	*2 cups lightly packed dark brown*
4 teaspoons double-acting baking	*sugar*
powder	*1 cup golden syrup, slightly warmed*
1 to 2 teaspoons ground ginger	*(see Note)*
½ pound butter	*Sugar*

Sift together the flour, baking powder, and ginger. Rub in the butter until crumbly, add the brown sugar and golden syrup, and mix thoroughly. Gather into a ball, wrap, and refrigerate overnight.

Preheat the oven to 350°.

Using a teaspoonful of the dough at a time, form into balls, and roll them in sugar. Place about 1½ inches apart on a buttered cookie sheet, and bake for 8 minutes, or until browned on the bottom. Cool on a rack and store in a tightly sealed container.

The balls may be flattened slightly and topped with a sliver of almond, a small piece of crystallized ginger, or a piece of preserved orange or citron. The flatter cookies will take a little less time to cook.

Note

English golden syrup is available in specialty food stores. An acceptable substitute may be made by boiling 1½ cups firmly packed light brown sugar with ⅓ cup water for 2 minutes. Honey, not too heavily flavored, may also be used in place of the golden syrup.

Dame Janet Baker, mezzo-soprano

GINGERSNAPS

Makes about 20 dozen

Dr. Dwight, a long-time Friend, is also one of the best cooks in the BSO family. He says, "I form these cookies while watching television or listening to broadcast concerts." Commercial gingersnaps will never taste the same!

1½ cups vegetable shortening	*2 teaspoons baking soda*
2 cups sugar	*2 teaspoons cinnamon*
2 eggs	*2 teaspoons ground cloves*
½ cup molasses	*1 tablespoon ground ginger*
4 cups sifted flour	*1 to 2 cups additional sugar*

Cream the shortening and sugar until light; add the eggs and then the molasses. Resift the flour with the soda and spices and beat into the shortening mixture. When the dough is thoroughly mixed, cover the bowl and chill for at least several hours, but preferably overnight or for 48 hours, to blend the flavors. The dough will keep in the refrigerator, getting better day by day.

Preheat the oven to 375°.

Sift the additional sugar into a flat-bottomed bowl. Form teaspoonfuls of the dough into balls and roll them in the sugar. Place on a lightly buttered cookie sheet about 2 inches apart, and cook until the snaps are the color of a brown paper bag. Cool them until they are firm enough to be lifted without changing shape. If they stick, a minute in the oven will loosen them. Cool completely on a rack and store tightly sealed. Wrap carefully to freeze, and crisp briefly in a hot oven before serving.

Richard W. Dwight, M.D.

ELISA'S SPICE COOKIES

Makes about 6 dozen

1 cup sugar
3½ teaspoons cinnamon
¾ cup butter
¼ cup molasses
1 egg
2 teaspoons grated lemon peel
  (optional)

2 cups flour
2 teaspoons baking soda
¼ teaspoon salt
½ teaspoon ground cloves

Mix ½ cup sugar and 1½ teaspoons cinnamon in a small bowl and set aside. Beat the remaining sugar, and the butter, molasses, egg, and lemon peel until light. Combine the dry ingredients, including the remaining cinnamon, and sift into the egg mixture. Beat until the batter is smooth, cover, and refrigerate for 1 to 2 hours or overnight.

Preheat the oven to 350°.

Form teaspoonfuls of the dough into balls and roll in the cinnamon-sugar mixture. Place on a buttered cookie sheet and bake for 8 to 10 minutes, or until the cookies are lightly browned and crisp. *Do not overcook.* Cool on a rack and store in an airtight container.

Variation

Flatten the balls with the bottom of a glass, buttered and dipped in the sugar-cinnamon mixture. These will cook more quickly than the balls.

Elisa Morris

APRICOT SQUARES

Makes 40 squares

This recipe was requested very early by those with fond memories of refreshments served at early Musical Marathons, the Council's major annual fund-raising event.

*1 pound dried apricots, cut into ¼- to
  ½-inch dice
2⅔ cups flour
1 teaspoon baking powder
¼ teaspoon salt
½ cup sugar*

*½ pound butter
4 eggs
1 teaspoon vanilla extract
2 cups light brown sugar, firmly
  packed
1 cup chopped walnuts
Confectioners' sugar*

Preheat the oven to 350°.

Simmer the diced apricots in water to cover for 10 minutes. Allow them to cool, stirring occasionally. Drain.

Rub 2 cups of flour, and the baking powder, salt, sugar, and butter together until crumbly. Press into a buttered 10-by-14-inch baking pan and bake for 15 to 20 minutes, but do not allow to brown. Remove from the oven and cool.

Beat the eggs and vanilla until thick and creamy. Beat in the brown sugar and ⅔ cup flour; then fold in the walnuts and drained apricots. Spread evenly on the cake and bake for 20 minutes. Cool in the pan. Cut into 1½-inch squares and roll in confectioners' sugar. Dust again with confectioners' sugar just before serving, as the fruit absorbs it immediately.

Helga Newcomb

MATRIMONIAL DATE CAKES

Makes about 36 1½-inch squares

*8 ounces pitted dates, quartered
½ cup water
¾ cup sweet wine (such as Tokay or
  Sauternes) or orange juice
½ cup sugar
1½ cups flour*

*½ teaspoon baking soda
1 cup dark brown sugar
1½ cups old-fashioned rolled oats
1 teaspoon cinnamon (optional)
¾ cup melted butter*

Place the dates, water, wine or orange juice, and sugar in a small saucepan and cook over medium heat until the dates are soft. The mixture should be moist but not watery. Set aside to cool.

Preheat the oven to 375°.

Meanwhile, combine the dry ingredients and pour the melted butter over all. Mix well, and press about two thirds of the crumbly "batter" into the bottom of a buttered 9-inch square baking pan. Smooth the date mixture over the crumb mixture, and top with the remaining crumbs. Pat lightly and bake for 30 minutes. Remove from the oven and cool slightly before cutting into squares or bars. Serve small squares for tea, and top larger squares with ice cream or whipped cream for dessert.

Variation
Substitute pitted prunes for the dates. Add 1 tablespoon lemon juice, 1 tablespoon grated lemon peel, and proceed as above.

Mrs. Gilman W. Conant
Council of the BSO

ANNIE BOOTH'S BUTTERSCOTCH BARS

Makes 1 to 1½ dozen

½ cup unsalted butter
1½ cups light brown sugar
2 eggs, beaten
1¼ cups cake flour
1 teaspoon baking powder

½ teaspoon salt
1 teaspoon vanilla extract
1 cup chopped nuts
Confectioners' sugar

Preheat the oven to 350°.

Melt the butter, add the brown sugar, and stir over low heat until it dissolves. Cool the mixture and beat in the eggs. Sift the dry ingredients together. Add to the egg mixture with the vanilla and nuts. Stir to combine. Bake in a buttered 9-inch square pan for 20 minutes. Test the bars and cook for 5 to 10 minutes more if necessary. They should be very soft and chewy.

Sprinkle the cooked bars with confectioners' sugar, and cool them in the pan before cutting.

Mrs. John C. Coughlin
Council of the BSO

FROSTED SQUASH BARS

Makes 3 dozen

1 cup chopped nuts
1 cup cooked or canned squash
1¾ cups flour
1 cup sugar
1 teaspoon baking soda
1 teaspoon salt

1 teaspoon nutmeg
1 teaspoon cinnamon
¼ teaspoon ground cloves
1 egg
½ cup salad oil

Frosting

1 cup confectioners' sugar   *4 to 6 tablespoons orange juice*
2 teaspoons dark rum

Preheat the oven to 350°.

Chop the nuts in a food processor, using the steel blade and the on-and-off method. Set them aside. Add all the remaining ingredients to the processor and mix thoroughly. Add the chopped nuts and process until well blended. Spread the batter in a buttered 10-by-15-inch pan and bake for 20 to 25 minutes, until the center is firm and the top is lightly browned.

Meanwhile, make the frosting. Mix together the sugar, rum, and enough orange juice to achieve the consistency of smooth heavy cream. Set aside.

Cool the cake on a rack for 5 minutes; then remove from the pan and turn right side up. Spread the frosting on the warm cake, and cool completely. Cut into bars or squares when the cake is cold and the frosting is set.

Note

Pumpkin may also be used. It makes somewhat chewier bars.

Mrs. James T. Mountz
Council of the BSO

LEMON SQUARES

Makes 2 dozen

William Gibson, retired principal trombone for the Boston Symphony, is a specialist in antique wind instruments. His demonstrations for schoolchildren are legendary. Mrs. Gibson's version of one of the most popular bar cookies should become equally popular.

½ pound butter, softened   *2 cups sugar*
½ cup confectioners' sugar   *6 tablespoons lemon juice*
2 cups plus 5 tablespoons flour   *Confectioners' sugar*
4 eggs, beaten

Preheat the oven to 350°.

Thoroughly cream the butter, confectioners' sugar, and 2 cups flour. Pat the dough into a 9-by-14-inch pan and bake it for 20 minutes. Beat together the eggs, sugar, lemon juice, and remaining flour and pour the mixture over the partially baked crust. Bake for 25 minutes more, and cut the cake into squares while it is still warm. Dust with confectioners' sugar, remove from the pan, and cool completely on a rack.

Mrs. William Gibson

CHOCOLATE MERINGUE BARS

Makes about 50 1-inch squares

½ cup butter, softened
¼ cup granulated sugar
¾ cup light brown sugar
1 egg, separated
1 tablespoon water

1 teaspoon vanilla extract
1 cup flour, sifted
Pinch of salt
½ teaspoon baking soda
1 cup semisweet chocolate bits

Preheat the oven to 325°.

Cream together the butter, the granulated sugar, and ¼ cup light brown sugar. Beat in the egg yolk, water, and vanilla. Sift together the dry ingredients and add to the butter mixture. Blend thoroughly and spread in a buttered 8-inch square pan. Cover the batter with the chocolate bits.

Whip the egg white until foamy and add the remaining light brown sugar very gradually, beating constantly until the meringue is firm and glossy. Spread it over the chocolate bits and bake for 25 minutes, or until the meringue is set.

Cool in the pan and cut into small squares when cold.

Mrs. John G. Cornish
Council of the BSO

FUDGE SQUARES

Makes 16 2-inch squares

2½ ounces bitter chocolate
⅓ cup butter
2 eggs
1 cup sugar
1 teaspoon vanilla extract

½ cup flour
½ teaspoon baking powder
⅛ teaspoon salt
1 cup chopped walnuts

Preheat the oven to 350°.

Melt the chocolate and butter together in a double boiler and set aside to cool. Beat the eggs and sugar until light and fluffy. Stir in the chocolate mixture and the vanilla. Sift the dry ingredients into the batter. Mix well and fold in the nuts. Pour into a buttered 8-inch square pan and bake for 30 minutes. *Do not overcook.*

Remove from the oven, cool on a rack, and cut into squares before removing from the pan.

Mrs. Fabian W. Kunzelmann
Tanglewood Council of the BSO

IRRESISTIBLE BROWNIES

Makes 2 dozen

Virtuoso cellist Samuel Mayes was young when he became principal cello for the Boston Symphony, before he moved to the same chair with the Philadelphia Orchestra. He and his wife, Winifred, were supportive during the founding years of the Council, and the Cookbook Committee is delighted to have them once again in our midst.

*4 squares unsweetened baking
    chocolate
¾ cup butter
1 cup flour
2 cups sugar*

*4 eggs
1 teaspoon vanilla extract
1 cup chopped nuts (walnuts, pecans,
    macadamias)*

Preheat the oven to 350°.

Melt the chocolate and butter together in a double boiler or a microwave oven, and set aside to cool slightly. Sift the flour and the sugar together and stir into the warm chocolate mixture. Add the eggs, one at a time, and the vanilla, and continue to beat until the mixture is smooth. Pour the batter into a lightly buttered 13-by-9-inch pan and sprinkle with the nuts. Bake for 15 to 20 minutes, until barely set. *Do not overcook.*

Remove from the oven, cover tightly with foil, and cool in the pan. Cut into small squares, rewrap the pan tightly, and freeze at least overnight. These brownies should be served cold, even slightly frozen.

*Winifred Mayes
Samuel Mayes, cello*

CANADIAN OATMEAL COOKIES

Makes 60 cookies

These rich and easy cookies freeze very well, either before or after baking.

*1 cup butter, softened
2 cups firmly packed brown sugar
2 eggs, lightly beaten
1 teaspoon vanilla extract
1 teaspoon cinnamon*

*1½ cups flour
1 teaspoon salt
1 teaspoon baking soda
3 cups quick-cooking oatmeal
1 cup raisins*

Preheat oven to 350°.

Mix all the ingredients in a large bowl. Beat until smooth, by hand or with an electric mixer. Drop the dough by teaspoonfuls onto a lightly buttered cookie sheet, spacing 2 inches apart. For thinner cookies, flatten with a fork before baking. Bake for 8 to 12 minutes, or until the edges are golden brown. Remove and cool on a rack.

*Margaret Hopkins
Council of the BSO*

FIDDLER'S OVERNIGHT COOKIES

Makes 30 to 36 cookies

BSO violinist Leonard Moss and his wife, Frances, also a musician, are excellent cooks. His annual Musical Marathon premium, oatmeal bread, is still a closely guarded secret, but the Mosses' oatmeal cookies will not be hidden under a bushel.

4 cups quick-cooking oatmeal	*2 eggs, beaten till light*
2 cups brown sugar	*1 teaspoon salt*
1 cup cooking oil	*1 teaspoon almond extract*

Mix together the oatmeal, brown sugar, and oil, and let stand for 12 hours.
   Preheat the oven to 325°.
   When ready to cook, add the remaining ingredients and mix well. Drop from a teaspoon onto a buttered cookie sheet and bake for 10 to 15 minutes, or until lightly browned around the edges. Cool on a rack.

Frances and Leonard Moss

MY FAVORITE COOKIES

Makes 4 to 5 dozen

1 cup butter	*¼ teaspoon baking powder*
½ cup confectioners' sugar	*Raspberry jam*
2 cups flour	*¼ cup finely chopped walnuts*
¼ teaspoon salt	

Preheat the oven to 350°.
   Cream the butter until very light, and gradually beat in the sugar. Sift the flour, salt, and baking powder together and work into the butter mixture. (The dough will be very stiff.)
   Shape into 1-inch balls, and place on a buttered cookie sheet. Make a small depression in the middle of each ball, and fill it with jam. Sprinkle with the walnuts and bake for 12 to 15 minutes, until the edges are lightly browned. *Do not overcook.*

Variation
Use apricot jam and chopped almonds, marmalade and chopped pecans, or any other combination that pleases.

Mrs. Francis Higgins

MARATHON COOKIES

Makes 6 dozen

These are a feature of the Marathon Café, the haven for tired workers on the BSO's annual Musical Marathon.

1 teaspoon salt
1 teaspoon baking soda
1½ cups sifted flour
1 cup butter, softened
¾ cup brown sugar
¾ cup granulated sugar

2 eggs
1 teaspoon vanilla extract
1 cup chopped walnuts
2 cups quick-cooking rolled oats
1 cup raisins

Preheat the oven to 350°.

Add the salt and soda to the sifted flour and sift again. Set aside. Cream the butter, gradually add both sugars, and cream until light. Beat in the eggs and vanilla. Stir in the sifted dry ingredients. Add the nuts, oats, and raisins, and mix thoroughly.

Drop the batter by teaspoonfuls onto a buttered cookie sheet. Bake for 10 to 12 minutes, until lightly browned around the edges. *Do not overcook.* Cool on a rack.

Mrs. Louis W. Mead
Council of the BSO

COLORADO PRALINE COOKIES

Makes 60 to 70

1 box graham crackers
½ pound butter
1 cup firmly packed light brown sugar
1 cup pecans, chopped

1 teaspoon salt
1½ ounces semisweet chocolate, melted
and cooled

Preheat the oven to 350°.

Arrange the graham crackers in one layer in a buttered jellyroll pan approximately 15 by 12 by 1½ inches. They should be close together but not overlapping.

In a small saucepan, melt the butter and brown sugar and boil for 1 minute. Add the chopped pecans and salt and boil for 1 minute more. Pour this mixture over the graham crackers as evenly as possible. Bake for 10 minutes and remove from the oven. Cool slightly and cut into squares or fingers while hot, when the praline is still soft but not too runny. Before removing the squares to cooling racks, drizzle the chocolate evenly over the top.

If making more than one batch, cook them one at a time, as the praline hardens very quickly. If the praline sets too quickly, put the pan back into the oven for a minute to soften it.

Mrs. Richard H. Thompson, Overseer
Council of the BSO

YELLOW HOUSE COOKIES

Makes about 50

These cookies are named for the Yellow House in Gardiner, Maine, which was the home of Laura E. Richards, poet and author.

¾ cup butter, softened
1 cup sugar
1 egg
1 teaspoon vanilla extract

1½ cups flour
½ teaspoon salt
2 cups crushed corn flakes

Cream the butter, sugar, egg, and vanilla, and add the flour and salt. Chill the dough for at least 1 hour.

Preheat the oven to 375°.

Form the dough into 1-inch balls and roll them in the corn flakes. Space far apart on a buttered cookie sheet. Flatten each ball with the bottom of a glass, buttered and dipped in sugar. Bake the cookies for 7 to 10 minutes, until they begin to brown around the edges. *Do not overcook.*

Variation

Stir 2 cups corn flakes (not crushed) into the batter and drop on a buttered cookie sheet. Cook as above.

Mrs. Eliot T. Putnam
Council of the BSO

GINGERBREAD PEOPLE

Makes 4 to 6 dozen

1 teaspoon salt
¼ teaspoon nutmeg
½ teaspoon ground cloves
3 teaspoons cinnamon
1 teaspoon ground ginger
5 cups sifted flour

1 cup butter (see Note)
1¼ cups sugar
1 egg, well beaten
1 cup light molasses, slightly warmed
1⅛ teaspoons baking soda
⅓ cup hot water

Sift the salt and spices with 1 cup of flour. Cream the butter, sugar, and egg until light, and beat in the molasses. Dissolve the baking soda in the hot water and stir it in. *Do not beat.* Add all the flour, a cupful at a time, until the dough is soft but not sticky.

Chill the dough for 6 to 8 hours or overnight.

Preheat the oven to 350°.

Divide the dough into four parts, and refrigerate three. Roll the dough very thin (⅛ to ¼ inch), and cut into people or animal shapes or any other form that appeals. Place on a lightly greased cookie sheet. Decorate with currants, raisins, dates, frosting, nuts, pieces of candy, or chocolate bits —

candied orange peel is especially good. (Plain cookies may be frosted *after* baking, when cool.) Bake for 8 to 10 minutes, until the edges are slightly browned, and cool on a rack. Make the remaining cookies in the same manner.

Note

Unsalted butter, vegetable shortening, and lard add different flavors and textures. Experiment with ¾ butter and ¼ lard or any preferred combination.

Sylvia Gilman
Junior Council of the BSO

PEPPARKAKOR (Swedish Spice Cookies)

Makes 6 to 8 dozen

A native New Englander, Earl Hedberg has been a member of the viola section of the Boston Symphony since 1956. His particular interest is in Americana, especially American Indian artifacts. Mrs. Hedberg shares her version of the traditional Swedish Christmas cookies, which make excellent presents for friends far and near. They keep well if sealed in an airtight container: if left exposed they will soften.

½ cup butter	*1 teaspoon salt*
1 cup sugar	*1½ teaspoons baking soda*
¼ cup orange juice	*1½ teaspoons ground cloves*
2 teaspoons grated orange peel	*1½ teaspoons cinnamon*
½ cup molasses	*1½ teaspoons ground ginger*
¼ cup heavy cream	*¼ teaspoon white pepper*
4 cups sifted flour	*Slivered almonds*

Cream the butter and sugar in a large mixing bowl. Combine the orange juice, orange peel, molasses, and cream. Stir into the butter mixture. Sift the flour with all the dry ingredients and stir into the butter-molasses mixture. Form into a ball and wrap in waxed paper. Refrigerate at least overnight or for up to a week, to allow the flavors to blend.

Preheat the oven to 375°.

Divide the dough into four parts and roll very thin on a well-floured board. Keep the extra dough refrigerated until needed. Cut into fancy shapes, and top each with a sliver of almond. Bake for 8 to 10 minutes, until crisp but not hard, and cool on a rack.

Note

Cookies that have softened may be refreshed by rebaking for 2 to 3 minutes in a 300° oven.

Albertha E. Hedberg

FEATHER CAKE

Serves 6

This light and easy cake was requested by a number of Camille Speyer's fans. Her husband, Louis Speyer, was a popular member of the cello section for many years before his retirement.

3 eggs
1 cup sugar
1½ cups sifted cake flour
2¼ teaspoons Symphony Baking
  Powder, ♦ or 1½ teaspoons
  double-acting baking powder

½ pint heavy cream, whipped
½ teaspoon vanilla extract
1 cup butter frosting, lightly flavored
  with lemon

Preheat the oven to 350°.

Beat the eggs and sugar until lemon colored and very light. Sift the flour and baking powder into a bowl and make a well in the center. Pour in the egg mixture, and beat until all the flour is incorporated. Gently fold in the whipped cream and vanilla and pour the batter into a buttered and floured 8-inch pan. Bake for 50 minutes — *no peeking during baking!* Allow the cake to stand for 5 minutes; then turn it out on a rack to cool, right side up. Frost with lemon frosting when the cake is cool.

Mrs. Louis Speyer

QUICK DESSERT CAKE

Serves 8 to 10

Soprano Jessye Norman has been a regular and welcome guest with the Boston Symphony since her first appearance at Tanglewood in 1972. She has taken part in many memorable performances, and her appearance in these pages will give her fans additional pleasure. Miss Norman recommends that her rich and buttery cake be served with cut-up fresh fruit for dessert. We especially recommend it with Compote of Oranges, ♦ with fruit or wine sorbet, or with ice cream. This cake freezes superbly.

2 cups flour
3 teaspoons baking powder
¾ teaspoon salt
¾ cup milk
3 eggs, well beaten
¾ cup unsalted butter

¾ cup brown sugar
½ cup raisins
1½ teaspoons lemon extract
½ cup Grand Marnier
Confectioners' sugar (optional)

Sift the flour, baking powder, and salt together into a large electric mixer bowl. Add the remaining ingredients except the confectioners' sugar, and beat with the mixer at medium speed for 4 minutes. Set aside to rest for 10 minutes.

Preheat the oven to 350°.

Beat the batter at high speed for 2 to 3 minutes, and pour into a buttered and floured 10-inch Bundt or tube pan. Bake for 45 to 55 minutes, or until the top is firm to the touch and the edges have pulled away from the sides of the pan. Allow the cake to stand for 5 minutes; then turn it out onto a rack to cool completely. Dust with confectioners' sugar, if desired. Serve as described above for dessert, or thinly sliced for tea.

Jessye Norman, soprano

KATE'S CAKE

Serves 8 to 10

½ *pound butter, softened*
2 *cups sugar*
2 *eggs, at room temperature*
2 *cups sifted flour*
1 *teaspoon baking powder*

1 *tablespoon almond extract*
1 *teaspoon vanilla extract*
1 *cup sour cream*
1 *tablespoon confectioners' sugar*

Preheat the oven to 350°.

Cream the butter and sugar until light. Add the eggs, one at a time, and beat until the mixture is again light. Sift the flour and baking powder together and add slowly to the butter mixture. Beat in the flavorings and sour cream, and pour into a buttered and floured 10-inch Bundt or tube pan. Bake for 50 to 60 minutes, until the top is springy and a cake tester comes out clean.

Remove from the oven and place the pan on a wet cloth for about 10 minutes. Turn the cake out onto a rack and cool. Dust with confectioners' sugar before serving for tea or as a dessert with ice cream.

Note

This cake keeps for weeks in a closely covered container in the refrigerator, or indefinitely in the freezer.

Mrs. Frank B. Gunther

OLD-FASHIONED POUND CAKE

Serves 10 to 12

The hand mixing of this traditional cake definitely adds to its mystique. It is a pleasant way to occupy the hands when listening to records or a radio concert.

1 *cup unsalted butter, softened*
1⅔ *cups superfine sugar*
5 *eggs, at room temperature*

2 *cups sifted pastry flour*
½ *teaspoon mace*

This cake *must* be mixed by hand.

Cream the butter until light and slowly add the sugar. Continue beating until the mixture is very light and does not sound scratchy.

Preheat the oven to 375°.

Add the eggs one at a time, beating well after each addition. Resift the flour with the mace, and fold it into the butter mixture. Spoon the batter into a buttered and floured 8- or 9-inch tube pan; bake until the top is lightly browned and the edges have pulled away from the sides of the pan. Let the cake stand for 15 minutes before turning it out onto a rack to cool. Serve in thin slices, unfrosted.

Variations

For seed cake, add 1½ tablespoons caraway seeds. For currant cake, add ½ cup dried currants, plumped in boiling water and drained.

Mrs. Channing Bacall, Jr.
Council of the BSO

CRANBERRY-APPLE-NUT CAKE

Serves 10 to 12

This recipe is full of good, nutritious ingredients: it is perfect for children's snacks.

1¾ cups light brown sugar
½ cup safflower oil
2 eggs
1 teaspoon vanilla extract
1 cup all-purpose flour
1 cup whole-wheat pastry flour
1 teaspoon baking soda
1 teaspoon cinnamon

½ teaspoon nutmeg
1 teaspoon salt
2 cups chopped peeled apples
  (preferably McIntosh)
½ pound fresh cranberries
½ cup large walnut pieces
2 cups chopped walnuts

Preheat the oven to 350°.

Cream the brown sugar and safflower oil and beat in the eggs and vanilla. When the mixture is light and fluffy, sift the dry ingredients together and add to the egg mixture. Beat until smooth and stir in the apples, cranberries, and nuts.

Pour into a buttered and floured 9-by-13-by-2-inch pan, and bake for 45 to 50 minutes, or until the center is firm to the touch and the edges have pulled away from the sides of the pan. Allow to cool for a few minutes in the pan before turning out onto a rack. Cool right side up, and cut into squares.

Mrs. Jerrold Mitchell
Junior Council of the BSO

AUTUMN APPLE CAKE

Serves 10 to 12

Hilde Rotenberg's violinist husband was one of the BSO's representatives during the cultural exchange with the Japan Philharmonic in Tokyo. Avid readers and excellent tennis players, the Rotenbergs enjoy collecting wines — and eating well! The quality of this cake depends on the quality of the apples: add lemon juice and grated lemon peel if the apples lack flavor.

¾ cup butter, softened
¾ cup honey, granulated sugar, or
   light brown sugar
2 eggs
1 teaspoon vanilla extract
1 cup unbleached flour
1 cup whole-wheat flour
1½ teaspoons baking soda
1 teaspoon cinnamon

1 teaspoon nutmeg (optional)
⅛ teaspoon ground cloves (optional)
1 teaspoon salt (optional)
3 to 4 cups chopped peeled apples
1 cup chopped walnuts, pecans, or
   cashews
½ cup raisins (optional)
Confectioners' sugar

Preheat the oven to 350°.

Cream the butter, honey, and eggs until the mixture is light and fluffy; then beat in the vanilla. Sift the dry ingredients together and mix thoroughly with the butter mixture. Fold in the apples, nuts, and raisins, and pour the batter into a buttered and floured 10-inch Bundt or tube pan. Bake for 40 to 50 minutes, or until the cake is firm to the touch and a cake tester comes out clean. Cool in the pan for 10 minutes; then turn out onto a rack to cool completely. Dust with confectioners' sugar. Serve for dessert with whipped cream or ice cream, or serve plain for tea.

Mrs. Sheldon Rotenberg

SOUTH DAKOTA OATMEAL CAKE

Serves 12

This cake from the Bad Lands keeps well; it does not need refrigeration.

1 cup rolled oats
1½ cups boiling water
¾ cup butter
1 cup brown sugar
2 eggs

1½ cups all-purpose flour
1 teaspoon baking soda
1 teaspoon salt
1 teaspoon cinnamon

Frosting

⅓ cup melted butter
1 cup brown sugar
½ cup evaporated milk

1 cup chopped pecans or walnuts
   (optional)
1 cup shredded coconut
1 teaspoon vanilla extract

Mix the oats and boiling water and set aside.

Preheat the oven to 350°.

Cream the butter and brown sugar until light and beat in the eggs one at a time. Add the oatmeal and stir. Combine the dry ingredients and sift into the butter mixture. Stir to incorporate completely. Pour the batter into a lightly buttered 7-by-11-inch pan, and bake for 25 to 30 minutes, until the top is firm and a cake tester comes out clean. Remove from the pan and turn right side up on a rack.

Beat all the frosting ingredients together and spread evenly over the warm cake. Brown the topping under the broiler, watching carefully that it does not burn, and serve warm or at room temperature.

Wendy Walcott Mackey
Tanglewood Council of the BSO

GREAT AUNT CARRIE'S BLUEBERRY CAKE

Serves 8 for dessert,
10 to 12 for tea

2 cups flour
1 cup sugar
1½ teaspoons baking powder
½ teaspoon allspice
½ teaspoon ground cloves
1 egg

½ cup milk
1½ tablespoons melted butter
1 cup blueberries, fresh or frozen
Nutmeg
1 teaspoon grated lemon peel
* (optional)*

Preheat the oven to 350°.

Combine the dry ingredients and sift into a mixing bowl. Beat the egg, milk, and butter together and stir into the flour mixture. Dust the blueberries with nutmeg to taste, sprinkle with the lemon peel, and fold into the batter. Spoon into a buttered 8- or 9-inch square pan and bake for 30 minutes, or until the center is firm to the touch. Cool for 5 to 10 minutes in the pan; then cut into squares while still warm. For dessert, serve warm with whipped cream or ice cream. For tea or coffee, serve warm or cool, unadorned.

Mary Anne Patterson
Council of the BSO

BUBBIE'S PINEAPPLE MERINGUE CAKE

Serves 12

Principal librarian for the Boston Symphony, violist Victor Alpert lists cooking among his hobbies, which also include three kinds of skiing — water, downhill, and cross-country. His musical family is fortunate, indeed, as this opulent cake demonstrates.

Cake

½ cup butter, softened
½ cup sugar
4 egg yolks, lightly beaten
1½ teaspoons vanilla extract
½ cup plus 2 tablespoons cake flour, sifted

¼ cup milk
¼ teaspoon salt
1 teaspoon double-acting baking powder

Meringue

4 egg whites
1 teaspoon vanilla extract
¾ cup sugar

¾ cup chopped macadamias, walnuts, or blanched almonds

Filling

1 cup crushed pineapple, well drained
1 cup whipped cream

1½ tablespoons confectioners' sugar
¼ teaspoon vanilla extract

To make the cake, cream the butter and sugar, add the egg yolks and vanilla, and beat until creamy. Sift in ½ cup of the flour, adding it alternately with the milk. Combine the remaining flour with the salt and baking powder and add to the batter, mixing thoroughly. Pour into two buttered 9-inch springforms and set aside while making the meringue.

Preheat the oven to 325°.

To make the meringue, whip the egg whites and vanilla, using a wire whisk and a copper bowl for best results. Sift in the sugar very gradually, beating constantly until very stiff and glossy.

Spread the meringue on the unbaked cake layers and sprinkle with the nuts. Bake for 20 to 25 minutes, or until the cakes pull away from the sides of the pans. Cool slightly; then remove from the pans and cool completely on a rack, meringue sides up.

Meanwhile, combine the ingredients for the filling. Place one cake layer meringue side down on a serving plate. Spread the filling on this layer. Place the second layer on top of the filling, meringue side up, and refrigerate until ready to serve.

Victor Alpert
Principal librarian of the BSO

ORANGE BLOSSOMS

Makes 12 large, 18 medium-sized, or 24 small cakes

These little cakes may be made almost any size: the cooking time must be adjusted, but the rest of the procedure remains the same.

2½ cups sugar
½ cup orange juice
3 tablespoons lemon juice
2 tablespoons grated orange peel
¼ pound butter, softened
2 eggs, lightly beaten

2¼ cups flour
2 teaspoons baking powder
¼ teaspoon salt
¾ cup milk
1 teaspoon vanilla extract

Preheat the oven to 400°.

Make the frosting first. Mix together 1½ cups sugar, the juices, and the orange peel. Set aside until the cakes are cooked.

Cream the butter, remaining sugar, and eggs. Sift in the dry ingredients, adding them alternately with the milk. Beat well and add the vanilla. Spoon the batter into buttered muffin tins, or paper or foil cake cups. Bake for 15 minutes, or until the cakes are firm to the touch and have pulled slightly away from the sides of the pan. Allow to stand for several minutes; then remove the cakes. Immediately dip each one in the frosting, stirring it well between dippings. Cool the cakes on a rack, and serve for tea or with a fruit dessert.

Elizabeth Simonds Cook

PFLAUMEN KUCHEN (German Plum Cake)

Serves 10 to 12

½ cup butter, softened
1 cup sugar
2 eggs
1 teaspoon vanilla extract
2 cups sifted flour

2 teaspoons baking powder
½ cup milk
2 pounds prune or other dark-skinned
    plums, pitted and halved
Confectioners' sugar

Preheat the oven to 375°.

Cream the butter and sugar together until light and fluffy. Add the eggs, one at a time, beating well after each addition, and stir in the vanilla. Sift the flour and the baking powder together and add to the batter alternately with the milk, beginning and ending with flour. Pour into a buttered 13-by-9-by-2-inch pan. Arrange the plum halves on top and dust lightly with confectioners' sugar.

Bake for 40 to 50 minutes, until the cake pulls away from the sides of the pan. Remove from the oven, sprinkle with more confectioners' sugar, and cool in the pan. Cut the cake into small squares and store in a covered container. Dust again with confectioners' sugar just before serving.

Virginia Kasabian
Council of the BSO

BRANDIED FRUITCAKE

Serves 14 to 18

George Brown, music director of WCRB-FM, which produces the BSO's annual Musical Marathon, has given his unusual fruitcake as a premium to the Marathon for several years.

3 eggs, beaten until foamy
1 14-ounce can sweetened condensed milk
1 28-ounce jar brandied mincemeat
2 cups chopped mixed peels (fruitcake mix)
1 cup chopped pecans, walnuts, or almonds
2 cups plain or honey graham cracker crumbs
1 teaspoon baking soda
Brandy

Preheat the oven to 300°.

Beat together all the ingredients except the brandy, in the order given. When the mixture is too heavy to beat, stir it vigorously. Pour the batter into a buttered 9-inch tube pan that has been lined with buttered paper, and bake for 2 hours or until a cake tester comes out clean. Cool for 15 minutes; then remove from the pan and cool completely. Peel off the paper. Lace the cake with brandy, and wrap in foil. Store in the refrigerator or another cool place, and add more brandy after several days. Serve cold, sliced very thin. This cake will keep for a year in the refrigerator, tightly sealed, or indefinitely if frozen.

Variations

To lower the sugar content, substitute 1 cup evaporated milk and ⅓ cup honey for the condensed milk, and add an additional ⅓ cup of cracker crumbs. If desired, bourbon may be substituted for the brandy.

George C. Brown
Music director, WCRB-FM

TANGLEWOOD CAKE

Serves 12 to 15

This is a very moist cake that keeps for a long time at room temperature and indefinitely if frozen.

1 pound raisins
2 cups water
1 cup orange juice, light rum, sherry, or a combination of all
2 cups sugar
¼ pound butter, softened
4 tablespoons all-purpose flour
1 tablespoon baking soda
1 teaspoon salt
1 teaspoon nutmeg
1 teaspoon cinnamon
1 teaspoon ground cloves
½ pound chopped mixed peels (fruitcake mix)
1 3½-ounce jar maraschino cherries, drained and halved (optional)
½ cup slivered almonds

Preheat the oven to 350°.

In a large covered saucepan, simmer the raisins in 1 cup of water for 15 minutes; transfer the raisins to a large bowl. Add the rest of the water to the hot pan and stir in the sugar and butter until they have melted. Set aside to cool.

When it is cool, add the butter mixture to the raisins and mix well. Combine the flour, soda, and spices and sift into the raisin mixture. Mix well and fold in the fruits and nuts. Pour into a lightly buttered 10-inch tube or angel cake pan, and bake for about 50 minutes. Lower the heat if the cake starts to get too brown. Bake for 30 minutes more, or until a cake tester comes out dry.

Allow to cool for 20 minutes before removing from the pan, and cool completely on a rack, right side up.

Mrs. Kenneth D. Beardsley
Tanglewood Council of the BSO

NUT CAKE WITH SYRUP

Serves 12

This splendid cake is the perfect ending to a Greek dinner.

½ cup honey	6 eggs
3 cups water	1 cup sifted flour
2 cups sugar	2 heaping teaspoons baking powder
1 cinnamon stick	1 teaspoon cinnamon
1 slice lemon	1 cup farina
¼ cup whiskey	1 teaspoon grated orange peel
½ pound butter, softened	1 cup finely chopped walnuts
1 cup sugar	

Mix the honey, water, sugar, cinnamon stick, and lemon in a saucepan and boil over medium heat for 10 minutes. There should be about 2½ cups of syrup. Remove from the heat, stir in the whiskey, and set the syrup aside to cool.

Preheat the oven to 350°.

Cream the butter and sugar until light. Add the eggs one at a time and again beat until light. Combine the dry ingredients and add with the orange peel, then the walnuts, beating thoroughly after each addition. Pour the batter into a buttered 9-by-13-by-2-inch pan, and bake for 25 to 30 minutes, until the cake is firm and well browned. Remove from the oven and cool slightly. Pour the cooled syrup over the hot cake. Cool thoroughly and cut into small diamond shapes to serve.

Mrs. James G. Garivaltis, Overseer
Tanglewood Council of the BSO

TROPICAL CARROT CAKE

Serves 20

Liona Boyd, renowned and much-recorded guitarist, has performed as a guest artist with the Boston Pops. Her magnificent cake is sure to be as popular with musical hosts and hostesses as she is on stage.

2 cups flour
4 teaspoons baking powder
2 teaspoons cinnamon
½ teaspoon nutmeg
½ teaspoon allspice
½ teaspoon salt

1 8-ounce can crushed pineapple,
  drained
4 eggs
1½ cups sugar
1½ cups corn or safflower oil
2 cups grated raw carrot
½ cup flaked coconut or wheat germ

Frosting
1 cup whipping cream
½ cup confectioners' sugar
¼ cup drained crushed pineapple (see
  instructions)

¾ cup flaked coconut
2 teaspoons grated orange peel
1 teaspoon vanilla extract

Preheat the oven to 350°.

Mix the dry ingredients and set aside. Reserve ¼ cup of the drained crushed pineapple for the frosting. Beat the eggs until light; then beat in the sugar and oil. Sift the dry ingredients directly into the egg mixture, and mix well. Then fold in the pineapple, carrots, and coconut or wheat germ. Beat well and spoon the batter into three buttered and floured 9-inch layer cake pans. Bake for 35 to 45 minutes, until the centers are firm to the touch and the edges have come away from the sides of the pans. Remove from the oven and cool in the pans for 10 minutes; then turn out onto racks to cool thoroughly. Frost when cold.

To make the frosting, whip the cream, gradually adding the sugar. Fold in the remaining ingredients, including the reserved pineapple, and spread between the layers and on top of the cake. Do not frost the sides.

Liona Boyd, guitar

CARROT CAKE

Serves 8 to 10

Conductor laureate of the Detroit Symphony, and a highly regarded specialist in the music of Joseph Haydn, Antal Dorati has been a guest with the Boston Symphony on a number of occasions. He and his wife, pianist Ilse von Alpenheim, celebrated Haydn's birthday with a special performance in Symphony Hall in 1982. Maestro Dorati, who contributed his wife's recipe, says that she recommends the use of a food processor, but this flourless cake may be made very successfully by hand.

5 eggs, separated
½ cup honey
1½ tablespoons lemon juice
2 teaspoons grated lemon peel

2 cups very finely grated carrots,
lightly packed
2 cups hazelnuts, chopped very fine

Beat the egg yolks and honey until foamy, and add the lemon juice and peel. Stir in the carrots and hazelnuts and mix thoroughly. Whip the egg whites until soft peaks form and fold gently into the batter. Pour the mixture into a buttered round glass or ceramic baking dish. Place it in a cold oven and set the control at 275°. Bake for about 50 minutes, until the top is firm to the touch and the edges have pulled away from the sides of the pan. Remove the cake from the oven and set it on a rack for several minutes; then turn it out and cool completely, right side up. Cover the cake and allow it to stand for at least two days before serving. It will keep for several weeks, if no one knows it is there.

Ilse von Alpenheim, piano
Antal Dorati, conductor

BERKSHIRE DELIGHT (Maple Pumpkin Roll)

Serves 10

4 eggs, separated
¾ cup sugar
5 tablespoons maple syrup
½ teaspoon cinnamon
¼ teaspoon nutmeg
¼ teaspoon cloves

1 cup mashed cooked pumpkin or
squash
1 teaspoon salt (optional)
1 cup flour
Confectioners' sugar
½ cup cream, whipped

Preheat the oven to 350°.

Beat the egg yolks and sugar; then beat in 4 tablespoons of the syrup and the spices. Slowly add the pumpkin or squash, mix well, and set aside.

Whip the egg whites and salt until soft peaks form. Add 1 tablespoon syrup and beat until stiff and glossy. Sift the flour into the pumpkin mixture, and mix well; then fold in the egg whites. Spread the batter in a buttered 15-by-10-by-1-inch jellyroll pan, and bake for 20 minutes, until the top is springy to the touch. Remove the cake from the oven and allow it to stand on a rack for 5 to 10 minutes.

While it is still slightly warm, turn the cake out onto a dishtowel well dusted with confectioners' sugar. Cover with a second towel for 5 minutes; then remove the top towel. Spread the cake with unsweetened whipped cream and roll it up very carefully, using the towel for support. Set the cake seam side down on a long platter and refrigerate until ready to serve. Dust again with confectioners' sugar just before serving.

Variation
The rolled cake may be frosted with Maple Frosting. ◆

Tjasa Sprague
Tanglewood Council of the BSO

Maple Frosting

1 cup real maple syrup   *2 egg whites, whipped to soft peaks*

Boil the syrup to the soft-ball stage, 238°. Pour in a slow stream into the egg whites, beating continuously. Continue beating until the frosting is cool enough to spread. Use on plain or spice cake.

BLACK FOREST TORTE

Serves 10 to 12

This is not a Black Forest cake but a sinfully rich treat for chocoholics.

Cake
1¾ cups flour, sifted
1¾ cups sugar
1¼ teaspoons baking soda
1 teaspoon salt
¼ teaspoon baking powder
⅔ cup butter, softened

4 1-ounce squares unsweetened chocolate, melted and cooled
1¼ cups water, at room temperature
1 teaspoon vanilla extract
3 eggs

Chocolate Filling
8 ounces sweet dark chocolate
¾ cup butter

½ cup chopped toasted almonds

Cream Filling
2 cups whipping cream
1 tablespoon superfine sugar

1 teaspoon vanilla extract

Cake
Preheat the oven to 350°.

Place all the ingredients except the eggs in a large electric mixer bowl. Beat at low speed to blend, and then beat at medium speed for 2 minutes, scraping the bowl frequently. Add the eggs and beat for 2 minutes longer. Pour the batter into four lightly buttered 9-inch round cake pans: the layers will be thin. Bake for 15 to 18 minutes, in two installments if preferred, until a tester comes out clean. Cool the layers slightly before removing from the pans; then cool thoroughly on a rack.

Chocolate Filling
Melt 1½ bars of chocolate over hot water, reserving the other half bar, and cool. Slowly add the butter, beating until the mixture is light and well blended. Stir in the almonds and set aside, but do not chill.

Cream Filling
Whip the flavored cream until stiff, but do not overbeat.

Assembly
Place one cake layer upside down on a serving plate and spread with half the chocolate filling. Top with a second layer and spread with half the cream filling. Repeat the layers so that the cream filling is on top. Do not frost the sides. Using a vegetable peeler, make curls from the remaining half bar of chocolate, and arrange them on top of the cream. Place in a covered cake container and refrigerate for 24 hours before serving.

Helga Newcomb

CHOCOLATE TRUFFLE CAKE

Serves 8

16 ounces semisweet chocolate
½ cup unsalted butter
1½ teaspoons all-purpose flour
1½ teaspoons sugar

1 teaspoon hot water
4 eggs, separated
1 cup heavy cream, whipped

Preheat the oven to 425°.

Melt the chocolate and butter in the top of a double boiler. Stir in the flour, sugar, and water, and mix thoroughly. Add the egg yolks, one at a time, beating well after each addition. Remove from the heat and cool slightly.

Whip the egg whites until stiff but not dry, and fold into the chocolate mixture. Turn into a buttered 8- or 9-inch springform and bake for 15 minutes. It will look very uncooked in the center. Cool completely on a rack; then refrigerate or freeze the cake: it will sink in the center.

Several hours before serving, spread the whipped cream smoothly on top of the cake. Return it to the refrigerator. Cut the cake while it is cold but bring it to room temperature before serving.

Marcy Prager
Brookline Symphony Orchestra

MISSISSIPPI MUD CAKE

Serves 10 to 12

This cake keeps well, refrigerated or at room temperature.

½ cup cocoa
1 cup unsalted butter, melted and
  slightly cooled
2 cups sugar
4 "large" eggs, lightly beaten
½ teaspoon salt

1 teaspoon vanilla extract
1½ cups sifted flour
1½ cups chopped nuts (pecans,
  walnuts, or cashews)
Small marshmallows (or large ones cut
  in half), enough to cover top of cake

Frosting
1 pound confectioners' sugar
½ cup cocoa
4 tablespoons unsalted butter

½ cup milk, at room temperature
½ teaspoon vanilla extract

Preheat the oven to 350°.

Add the cocoa to the butter, stir well, and allow to cool. Add the sugar to the eggs and beat until light and lemon colored. Stir in the cooled butter mixture, and the salt and vanilla. Add the flour and mix thoroughly but gently. Fold in the nuts and pour into a buttered and floured 12-inch round pan. Bake for 35 to 45 minutes, or until the center is firm and the edges pull away from the pan.

Cool the cake in the pan for about 5 minutes before turning it out to cool on a rack, right side up. Cool for 5 to 10 minutes more; then cover the top of the warm cake with a layer of marshmallows and allow them to melt. When the marshmallows are set, spread the frosting over the whole thing while the cake is still slightly warm. Set it in the refrigerator to cool.

To make the frosting, combine the confectioners' sugar, cocoa, and butter in a small bowl, add the milk and vanilla extract, and beat until smooth enough to spread on the cake.

Variation
Substitute 3 tablespoons, or to taste, of crème de cacao or Tia Maria for an equal amount of the milk.

Bernadette Vitti
Junior Council of the BSO

DESSERTS AND PASTRIES

The Boston Symphony's one hundredth birthday was celebrated with a free outdoor performance of Beethoven's Ninth Symphony before an audience of a hundred thousand on the Boston Common on October 22, 1981, an unusually balmy evening. Four days earlier, five musical greats who had been associated with the Orchestra over the years appeared in a single gala concert at Symphony Hall, which was televised live to Europe and later broadcast within this country. Here *(overleaf)*, left to right, are Leontyne Price, Isaac Stern, Itzhak Perlman, Mstislav Rostropovich, and Rudolf Serkin.

ZAPPLESAUCE

Makes 2 to 3 pints

The microwave oven has revolutionized the manufacture of applesauce, which is a good use for less than perfect apples. As with cider, the more varieties the better the flavor.

8 cups peeled and sliced apples, firmly packed
Antidiscoloration Solution◆
2 thin slices lemon, seeded
⅛ teaspoon each ground cloves, nutmeg, cardamom (optional)

½ teaspoon ground cinnamon (optional)
½ cup Boiled Cider◆
Sugar

Prepare the apples, dropping them immediately into the antidiscoloration solution. When ready to cook the applesauce, measure the apples, rinse under cold running water to remove any lingering taste of the solution, and drain thoroughly. Place the lemon slices and optional spices in the bottom of a very large glass casserole, add the apples, and pour the boiled cider over all. Cover and cook at the high setting, turning and stirring every 5 minutes or so. When the sauce is almost done, stir it vigorously and add sugar to taste. Cook for several minutes more, until it has reached a satisfactory consistency. (Total cooking time will be about 10 to 15 minutes.) Cool; then refrigerate if using within a week.

If preserving, spoon the boiling sauce into hot sterilized jars before it is completely done, leaving about ¼ inch headroom. Seal the jars and process in a boiling water bath for 5 minutes for pints and 10 minutes for quarts (see any standard cookbook for canning and preserving procedures).

Variation

The same process may be followed in a regular oven set at 350°, which takes both more time and less watching.

Thomas Gardiner

Antidiscoloration Solution

2 quarts cold water   1 tablespoon white or cider vinegar
1 tablespoon kosher salt

Mix until the salt is dissolved, and drop in the peeled fruit (apples, peaches, or others). The solution may be reused many times. Immediately before cooking, rinse the fruit thoroughly under cold running water to remove any lingering taste of the solution, and dry thoroughly.

DORIOT'S DELIGHT

Serves 4

Virtuoso flutist Doriot Anthony Dwyer, from a family of mold-breaking women, became the first woman principal with the Boston Symphony, where she sits in the chair bearing Walter Piston's name. In the words of the citation read when she received the honorary Doctor of Music degree from Harvard University in 1982, "her silvery notes gloriously embody the supreme achievement of a great orchestra." Her annual Musical Marathon contribution (also a dessert) is still a secret, but here she shares another favorite.

1 cup dried apricots, firmly packed   1 cup all-purpose cream, whipped
½ cup seeded dates, firmly packed   Freshly grated nutmeg
½ to ¾ cup orange juice   Toasted slivered almonds (optional)
Sugar

Cover the apricots with water and bring to a boil in a small saucepan. Simmer for about 5 minutes, and allow to cool. Drain completely and discard the water. Add the dates and orange juice, mix thoroughly, and refrigerate overnight. Before serving, mash slightly and sweeten to taste. Serve in individual glass dishes. Top with whipped cream, dust lightly with nutmeg, and sprinkle with slivered almonds.

Variation
Serve with Donald McIntyre's Fruit Delight,♦ vanilla ice cream, or Double Yogurt♦ instead of the whipped cream.

Doriot Anthony Dwyer
Principal flute

Mock Crème Fraîche: *An acceptable* crème fraîche *may be achieved by beating together equal parts of heavy cream and either sour cream or Double Yogurt.♦ Do not use this for cooking, as it will separate: it is for dessert use only.*

BLUEBERRY-APPLE COBBLER

Serves 8

1 cup flour
¾ cup sugar
1 teaspoon baking powder
¾ teaspoon salt
1 egg, beaten
2 cups fresh blueberries

3 Granny Smith apples, peeled and
sliced
1 tablespoon brown sugar
⅓ cup melted butter
2 tablespoons sugar mixed with ½
teaspoon cinnamon

Preheat the oven to 375°.

Combine the first four ingredients and stir into the beaten egg. Mix the fruits with the brown sugar and place in a buttered 13-by-9-by-2-inch baking dish. Cover with the batter, and pour the melted butter over all. Sprinkle the top with the cinnamon-sugar mixture and bake for 30 minutes, until the center is firm to the touch and the top is pleasingly browned. Serve hot or warm, with cream or ice cream.

Variation
Four or five large peaches, peeled and sliced, may be substituted for the apples.

Mrs. R. Willis Leith, Jr.
Council of the BSO

CAPE COD BLUEBERRY PUDDING

Serves 6

10 tablespoons butter
1½ cups sugar
1 cup flour
4 teaspoons baking powder

¾ cup milk
4 cups native blueberries
1 cup water

Preheat the oven to 400°.

Cream 8 tablespoons of butter and ½ cup sugar. Sift in the flour and baking powder, adding alternately with the milk. Spread the batter evenly in a buttered 13-by-9-by-2-inch glass baking dish or oven-proof ceramic serving dish. Cover with the blueberries and the remaining sugar. Pour the water over all (it looks messy, but it works!), dot with 2 tablespoons of butter, and bake for 5 to 10 minutes, until the batter begins to rise. Reduce the heat to 350°. Bake for about 20 minutes more, until the batter is set and the top delicately browned.

Serve hot, warm, or cool, topped with whipped cream or ice cream.

Mrs. Frances W. Schaefer
Council of the BSO

CRANBERRY "PIE"

Serves 6 to 8

Cranberries freeze remarkably well, so this "pie" may be enjoyed year round.

2 cups raw cranberries	*¾ cup melted butter*
½ cup chopped walnuts	*2 eggs, beaten*
1½ cups sugar	*2 teaspoons almond extract*
1 cup flour	

Preheat the oven to 325°.

Combine the cranberries, nuts, and ½ cup sugar and place in a buttered 10-inch pie plate. Beat the remaining ingredients into a smooth batter and spread it over the cranberry mixture. Bake for 35 to 45 minutes, until the batter is crisp and golden and a cake tester comes out clean. Serve warm with whipped cream or ice cream.

Gladys M. Dykstra

ROCKEFELLER'S DELIGHT

Serves 4 to 6

1 tablespoon gelatin (see Note)	*1 cup boiling water*
1 cup cold water	*1 cup sugar*
½ cup orange juice	*½ pound chopped pecans*
3 tablespoons lemon juice	*3 tablespoons bourbon*
3 tablespoons grated orange peel	*Whipped cream, slightly*
2 teaspoons grated lemon peel	*sweetened and flavored with*
½ pound dried white figs, cut into	*whiskey (optional)*
small pieces	

Soften the gelatin in the cold water.

Place the juices, peels, and figs in a saucepan with the boiling water and sugar. Simmer it for a few minutes to soften and bring out the flavor of the figs. Add the gelatin and stir until dissolved; then stir in the pecans and bourbon. Cool the mixture slightly and pour into a crystal bowl or oiled decorative mold and refrigerate for 2 to 3 hours or overnight. Serve with whipped cream.

Note

If the dessert is to be unmolded, add ½ tablespoon more gelatin.

Mrs. John Harwood
Council of the BSO

COMPOTE OF ORANGES

Serves 6

6 large navel oranges   Grand Marnier
¾ cup sugar

With a sharp knife, score the orange peels into quarters running from top to bottom. Steep the oranges for 1 to 2 minutes in boiling water to cover. Peel the oranges and slice them into a serving bowl, reserving the peel from four of the oranges. Remove all the white pith from the skins and cut the zest into very fine strips (see Note). Place the strips of peel in a saucepan and cover with cold water. Bring to a boil for 5 minutes; drain, rinse, drain, and cover again with cold water. Bring to a boil, simmer for 20 minutes, and drain. Cover again with water, add the sugar, and simmer until the strips take on a glazed appearance. Cool slightly, add Grand Marnier to taste, and pour the sauce over the orange slices.

Refrigerate for at least two days, stirring occasionally and adding more Grand Marnier if desired. Serve chilled or at room temperature with plain sugar cookies, or Jessye Norman's Quick Dessert Cake. ◆

Note

The bar tool for making martini "twists," wielded carefully, makes this a quick and easy task, which can be done before peeling the oranges.

Bonus

Save the extra orange peels for candied orange peel or for orange shred marmalade.

Mrs. Neil MacKenna
Council of the BSO

ITALIAN PEACHES

Serves 6

In 1980, John Williams succeeded the legendary Arthur Fiedler as conductor of the Boston Pops. His sensitivity to long tradition and his own innovative flair have combined to add a new dimension to one of Boston's best-known institutions. His wife, Samantha, served faithfully and well as a member of the testing team for the cookbook: she is, obviously, as outstanding in the kitchen as he is on the podium.

6 large freestone peaches, peeled   6 teaspoons butter
6 teaspoons sugar   6 tablespoons amaretto liqueur
6 tablespoons chopped almonds   ½ cup heavy cream, whipped
12 amaretti cookies (or 12 small
   almond macaroons), crumbled

Cut the top off each peach. Gently remove the pit and a little surrounding pulp, being careful not to break the outside "shell." Discard the pits, but reserve the pulp.

Preheat the oven to 350°.

Chop the reserved pulp and combine it with the sugar. Place the peaches upright and close together in a small buttered baking dish. Fill each with 1 tablespoon almonds, 2 crumbled cookies, and 1 to 2 teaspoons pulp mixture; top with 1 teaspoon butter.

Add ⅛ inch of water to the pan and bake for 15 minutes. Pour the amaretto over the peaches and bake for 10 minutes more. Remove from the oven and cool, but do not refrigerate. Serve warm or cool, topped with whipped cream flavored with amaretto to taste, or *crème fraîche*.

Samantha Williams
John Williams, composer
Boston Pops conductor

PEACHES PANUFNIK

Serves 6 to 8

Polish composer Andrzej Panufnik's *Sinfonia Votiva* was first performed in Symphony Hall in January 1982, as one of the Boston Symphony's centennial commissions. His composition for peaches is accompanied by several musical instructions: "Test this 'toffee topping' with taps of a tablespoon. When the properly percussive sound is achieved, the dish is ready." (Downbeat!) Despite the composer's stern injunction, our testers report that cooks who live out of the range of fresh peaches for most of the year need not despair. A top grade of home-canned peaches may be used to make a very tasty version of this excellent dish, which is, of course, at its best "live."

6 large, perfectly ripe peaches ("must   1½ cups heavy cream or crème
be fresh"), peeled   fraîche (or a combination)
                                            ½ to ¾ cup soft dark brown sugar

Slice the peaches into a buttered shallow 10-inch pie plate or baking dish, leaving ½ inch room at the top; the peaches should lie as flat as possible. Whip the cream until very thick, and smooth it over the peaches. Place in the freezer for 2 to 3 hours, until the cream is very firm but the peaches are not frozen solid.

Preheat the broiler (or a salamander) about 15 minutes before serving. Let your guests wait — they will be rewarded. Just before serving, sift some of the brown sugar over the semifrozen cream in a layer no more than ⅛ inch thick, covering the cream completely. Broil quickly until the sugar caramelizes. Add another layer and repeat the process, but work fast.

Allow a few moments for the melted sugar to harden, and test with a tablespoon, as described above. When the topping "rings," rush it to the table, and serve immediately.

Andrzej Panufnik, composer

PLETTENSPUDDING

Serves 6

8 egg yolks
2 cups light cream
½ cup sugar
⅛ teaspoon salt
1½ teaspoons gelatin
1 tablespoon water
2 tablespoons vanilla extract

2 tablespoons framboise or
   kirschwasser
1 pint fresh raspberries
1 cup raspberry purée, made from
   fresh or frozen berries
6 to 10 amaretti, crumbled (see Note)
½ cup heavy cream, whipped

Combine the egg yolks, light cream, sugar, and salt in the top of a large double boiler set over moderate heat. Stir until the mixture coats the spoon and has the consistency of extra-heavy cream. Remove from the heat. Meanwhile, soften the gelatin in the tablespoon of water. Whisk the gelatin, vanilla, and liqueur into the custard until the gelatin is dissolved. Set aside to cool to room temperature; then beat until very smooth.

Divide the berries among six individual crystal or clear glass dishes. Spoon half the raspberry purée over the berries, and cover with the cooled beaten custard, filling the dishes three fourths full. Sprinkle the crumbled amaretti over the custard, and chill thoroughly.

Just before serving, spoon the remaining purée over the top of each serving and garnish with whipped cream.

Note
If amaretti cookies are unavailable, macaroons may be substituted.

Felix Krull's Restaurant
Marblehead, Massachusetts
Chris Evans, proprietor/chef

SUMMER PUDDING

Serves 6 to 8

For many years associated with the Academy of St. Martin in the Fields in London and now music director of the Minnesota Orchestra, Neville Marriner has been a popular guest conductor with the Boston Symphony. He grows the fruit for Summer Pudding in his garden.

3 to 4 cups raspberries and red
currants (about 1 pound together)
1 loaf firm white bread, thinly sliced,
with crusts removed

½ to ¾ cup sugar
4 to 6 tablespoons unsalted butter,
softened

Gently simmer the fruits and sugar for about 5 minutes and set aside.

Butter a deep bowl, and line it with overlapping slices of buttered bread, buttered side out. This makes a shell, so be sure the pattern is pretty. Place one fourth of the fruit in the bottom, and cover it with several slices of buttered bread. Using one fourth of the fruit each time, make three more layers, ending with a double layer of bread. Cover with a plate that fits easily into the bowl. Set a heavy weight on the plate, and refrigerate overnight, or for several days.

About an hour before serving time, take the pudding out of the refrigerator and remove the weight. Pour off any surplus juice and set it aside. Just before serving, unmold the pudding, pour the reserved juice over it and serve with heavy cream or *crème fraîche*.

Variations

If red currants are not available, summer pudding can be made with black currants, or all raspberries, but it will require a bit more sugar and will not be quite such a bright color.

If desired, substitute blueberries for the raspberries and ½ cup currant jelly for the sugar. This is a break with the tradition of Olde England, but a delight to New England blueberry lovers.

Neville Marriner, conductor

GORGEOUS STRAWBERRIES

Serves 6

This lily is truly gilded!

1 quart large ripe strawberries,
hulled, washed, and dried
½ cup confectioners' sugar
2 ounces Cointreau

½ cup granulated sugar
2 10-ounce packages frozen
raspberries, thawed
1½ ounces crème de cassis

Arrange a single layer of the strawberries in a large flat glass bowl. Dust with confectioners' sugar and drizzle with Cointreau.

Combine the thawed raspberries and granulated sugar in a blender and whirl briefly. Strain the mixture through a very fine sieve and add the crème de cassis. Pour over the strawberries, cover, and allow to stand at room temperature for a few hours. Do not chill. Serve in small glass dishes, or champagne glasses.

Mrs. Elting E. Morison, Overseer

MINTED FRUIT

World-renowned soprano Eileen Farrell has been a frequent and welcome guest with the Boston Symphony. Her quick and easy dessert is unusually pretty and delicious.

Pour a little crème de menthe over cut-up fresh fruit and allow it to stand in the refrigerator until serving. Top with sprigs of fresh mint.

Eileen Farrell, soprano

FRUIT DELIGHT

Serves 6

Baritone Donald McIntyre, who has sung leading roles with most of the world's great opera companies as well as the Boston Symphony, shares a double-threat dessert: it is equally good in summer or winter.

2 egg whites
2 tablespoons sugar
1 cup yogurt
1 cup heavy cream, whipped

2 cups fresh or frozen fruit (such as raspberries, peaches, or grapes, alone or in combination)

Beat the egg whites until stiff peaks form; then slowly add the sugar and beat until glossy. Fold in the yogurt, cream, and fruit. Pour into a crystal bowl or individual sherbet or parfait glasses, and chill until serving time.

Donald McIntyre, baritone

BAKED BLINTZES

Serves 6

One of the most important aspects of the work of the Boston Symphony is that which brings classical music to the young people of Boston and its environs. Mrs. Kurland has been in the forefront of this activity for a number of years; her hard work and dedication have made her an acknowledged expert in her field. Her recipe for blintzes is easy to follow and delicious to eat.

¼ pound butter
12 Blintzes,♦ with Blueberry Filling♦
  or Cheese Filling♦
4 eggs
½ cup sugar

1 teaspoon vanilla extract
1 pint sour cream
¼ teaspoon salt
Cinnamon

Preheat the oven to 350°.

Melt the butter in a large flat oven-proof serving dish. Arrange the blintzes in it side by side, fold side down.

Combine all the other ingredients except the cinnamon, and beat until smooth. Pour the mixture over the blintzes and sprinkle with cinnamon. Bake for 40 to 45 minutes, until the topping is golden, and serve immediately.

Anita Kurland
BSO administrator of youth activities

BLINTZES

Makes 10 to 12

Fill blintzes with Blueberry Filling◆ or Cheese Filling,◆ apricot or cherry preserves, apple butter, or any filling of your choice.

6 tablespoons unsalted butter	*1 cup sifted flour*
2 eggs	*½ teaspoon salt*
1 cup milk	*2 tablespoons salad oil*

Bring the butter to a boil over high heat, and set it aside to settle. Skim 4 tablespoons of clarified butter off the top and set it aside. Pour the residue into the blender container and add the remaining ingredients except the oil. Process until the mixture is the consistency of thick cream, scraping the sides occasionally to ensure even mixing.

Mix 2 tablespoons of clarified butter with the oil, and pour 1 teaspoon of this mixture into a 10-inch frying pan. Shake the pan over high heat until the fat is almost smoking, and pour in 3 tablespoons of batter. Swirl the batter around with the pan off the heat; then cook over high heat for a few moments, until the bottom of the blintz is brown and the top is set. Stack the cooked blintzes, brown side up, on a dishtowel, until all the batter has been used.

Place a blintz on a board, brown side up, and place 2 to 3 tablespoons of filling in the middle. Fold over the edges into a neat package and set aside, folded side down. Use at this stage for Baked Blintzes,◆ or fry the blintzes a few at a time in the remaining clarified butter, starting with the fold side down. It may be necessary to make more clarified butter. Dust with confectioners' sugar, if desired, and serve with sour cream.

The Cookbook Committee

BLUEBERRY FILLING FOR BLINTZES

For 12 blintzes

2 cups blueberries	*1 tablespoon lemon juice*
1 tablespoon cornstarch	*⅓ to ½ cup sugar*
1 teaspoon grated lemon peel	*Cinnamon*

Stir the first four ingredients and ⅓ cup sugar in a saucepan and bring to a boil over medium heat. When the mixture is thick and smooth, add more sugar, if desired, and a little cinnamon to taste. Cool; then refrigerate until ready to use.

The Cookbook Committee

CHEESE FILLING FOR BLINTZES

For 12 blintzes

3 ounces cream cheese, softened
1½ cups dry cottage cheese, farmer
  cheese, or ricotta
1 egg yolk
2 tablespoons sugar

Nutmeg
½ teaspoon grated lemon peel
1 tablespoon lemon juice, or ½
  teaspoon vanilla extract

Beat the first four ingredients together until smooth. Season with a dash of nutmeg, the lemon peel, and the lemon juice or vanilla. Refrigerate until ready to use.

The Cookbook Committee

PERSIMMON PUDDING

Serves 12

Persimmons have a short season: they may be stored in the freezer if not fully ripe and thawed before puréeing, so that this perfect holiday pudding may be enjoyed at any time. One large persimmon yields about 1 cup of purée.

1 cup melted butter, cooled slightly
2½ cups sugar
2½ cups sifted flour
1 teaspoon cinnamon
½ teaspoon nutmeg
½ teaspoon ground cloves
½ teaspoon allspice
4 cups persimmon purée

5 teaspoons baking soda dissolved in 5
  tablespoons hot water
5 tablespoons brandy
1 tablespoon vanilla extract
1 tablespoon lemon juice
1 cup raisins
¾ cup chopped walnuts
5 eggs, well beaten

Beat the butter and sugar together, and stir in the flour and spices. Add the persimmon purée and the remaining ingredients in the order given, folding in the eggs last. Pour the batter into one or several buttered decorative pudding molds, filling no more than three fourths full. Pleasingly shaped ceramic, glass, or stainless steel bowls with a lip will serve instead of special molds. Cover the batter with a sheet of waxed paper; then seal securely with the mold's own cover or a sheet of foil tightly tied with kitchen string.

Set on a rack in a large covered saucepan or stockpot and pour boiling water halfway up the side of the mold. Cover the pan and simmer for 2 to 2½ hours, depending on the size of the pudding, adding more boiling water as the level drops. Do not allow the pudding to boil dry.

Remove the mold from the pan and set on a rack, right side up, for about 5 minutes. Remove the cover, reverse the mold onto a heated platter, and cover with a dishtowel. Allow it to stand until the pudding drops onto the plate. Serve with hard sauce flavored with rum, or a hot Foamy Sauce.◆

Mrs. F. Brooks Cowgill
Council of the BSO

GRANDMA BARNES'S HOLIDAY PUDDING

Serves 8 to 12

"At least four generations of my family have made this old New England recipe part of our holiday tradition," says Charlotte Priest. It is very rich, and very sweet if the larger amount of sugar is used.

⅓ *cup flour*
5 *cups milk*
1 *cup minus 1 tablespoon yellow*
  cornmeal
¾ *teaspoon salt*
¼ *to* ½ *cup sugar*
⅔ *to 1 cup molasses*

1 *cup butter*
½ *cup finely chopped suet*
1 *teaspoon cinnamon*
½ *teaspoon ground ginger*
1 *cup raisins*
¼ *cup rum, dry sherry, or brandy*
Whipped cream or crème fraîche

Make a smooth paste of the flour and ½ cup of milk and set aside. Mix the cornmeal with another ½ cup of milk. Heat, but do not scald, the remaining milk in the top of a double boiler. Set aside 2 cups of the hot milk. Beat the cornmeal mixture and salt into the hot milk remaining in the double boiler and stir until thickened over simmering water.

Preheat the oven to 350°.

In a large bowl, combine the sugar, molasses, butter, suet, and spices. Beat in the flour mixture, the cooked cornmeal from the double boiler, and the reserved hot milk. Mix very thoroughly and add the raisins and liquor.

Pour the batter into a buttered shallow baking dish and set it in the oven in a pan of simmering water. Bake uncovered for 2½ hours, stirring occasionally to prevent lumping. Serve warm with unsweetened whipped cream, or *crème fraîche.*

Charlotte C. R. Priest
Tanglewood Festival Chorus

FOAMY SAUCE

Variations on a theme: these are the old-fashioned pudding sauces that remind us of our childhood. They go wonderfully with plain cake, as well as with hot steamed puddings. The first one is served hot; it is rich and buttery, and makes 1½ to 2 cups. The second should be served cold; it is light and fluffy, and makes 2½ to 3 cups. Foamy sauces will separate if held too long, but they may be reheated or served "as is."

Allie's Foamy Sauce

½ cup unsalted butter
1 cup confectioners' sugar
1 egg, separated

½ teaspoon salt
Vanilla extract, rum, or brandy

Cream the butter and sugar, and add the egg yolk, beating until light. Place in the top of a double boiler over barely simmering water and stir vigorously and constantly until the sauce is hot and thick. Whip the egg white and salt, fold it gently into the hot egg mixture, and add vanilla, rum, or brandy to taste.

Allie Blodgett
Council of the BSO

Mopey's Foamy Sauce

2 eggs, separated
2 cups sifted confectioners' sugar
1 cup heavy cream, whipped

Vanilla extract, sherry, brandy, or
   other flavoring
Freshly grated nutmeg

Beat the egg yolks with 1 cup confectioners' sugar until light and lemon colored. Whip the egg whites until stiff, and gradually beat in the remaining sugar. Gently combine the egg mixtures and fold in the cream. Flavor to taste and refrigerate until ready to serve. Dust lightly with nutmeg.

Mrs. Helen Vose Carr

Add a pinch of cream of tartar to each egg white before whipping. It will increase the volume and help keep the whites stable.

INDIAN PUDDING

Serves 8

Many old recipes for Indian pudding call for no eggs: some contemporary cooks use as many as four. There are myriad versions of this traditional New England dessert, almost all of them good. Experiment! This is not an extravagant dish.

⅓ cup degerminated yellow cornmeal
  or ½ cup stone-ground
¾ teaspoon salt
4 cups milk (see Note 1)
1 or 2 eggs
2 tablespoons melted butter
½ cup dark molasses (see Note 2)

2 to 4 tablespoons dark brown sugar
½ teaspoon cinnamon
½ teaspoon ground ginger
⅛ teaspoon nutmeg or allspice
  (optional)
Whipped cream or vanilla ice cream
  (for garnish)

Combine the cornmeal, salt, and 2 cups of milk in the top of a double boiler over simmering water, and stir until the mixture is hot and thick. Set aside to cool slightly.

Preheat the oven to 350°.

Beat together the eggs, butter, molasses, brown sugar, and spices until creamy. Beat in 1 cup of milk, and add this mixture to the hot cornmeal. Stir well, and pour into a buttered baking dish or buttered individual serving dishes. Bake for about 1 hour, stirring several times; then pour the remaining milk over the pudding and bake without stirring for another 1½ hours. The heat may be lowered to 250° and the pudding cooked for 2½ hours longer if this timing is more convenient. Allow the pudding to stand for at least 15 to 20 minutes before serving, topped with whipped cream or vanilla ice cream. It may be served hot, warm, or at room temperature, *never* cold.

Note 1

One cup light or medium cream may be substituted for 1 cup of the milk for a richer, creamier pudding.

Note 2

The secret of good Indian pudding is the quality of the molasses. Barbados molasses has a milder flavor than blackstrap, but a stronger taste than the average supermarket molasses.

Variations

Thin slices of seeded unpeeled orange may be buried in the pudding; ½ cup of raisins may be stirred in before cooking, or the top may be sprinkled with a little chopped crystallized ginger when the pudding is removed from the oven.

The Cookbook Committee

Drunken Prunes: *Pour a little bourbon, rum, or red wine over prunes and seal in a covered jar for several days or weeks. Shake occasionally. Serve with ice cream, or as a* confit *with meats or at a buffet. Any dried fruit lends itself to this treatment, although some will need considerable added sugar.*

MARMALADE SOUFFLÉ

Serves 4

4 egg whites
Salt
4 tablespoons sugar

3 tablespoons orange marmalade
1 teaspoon vanilla extract (optional)
Butter

Sauce

2 egg yolks
1 teaspoon sugar

2 tablespoons dry sherry
1 cup heavy cream, whipped

Whip the egg whites and a pinch of salt until stiff peaks form. Gradually add the sugar, 1 tablespoon at a time, and beat until glossy. Beat the marmalade just enough to soften it. Fold it gently into the egg whites and add the vanilla. Generously butter the top and cover of a double boiler and spoon in the soufflé mixture. Place a sheet of waxed paper over the pudding, and cover tightly: do not lift the cover for at least 1 hour. Cook over simmering water for 1½ hours, or until the center is firm to the touch.

Meanwhile, prepare the sauce: beat the egg yolks with the sugar and sherry until light and lemon colored. Fold gently into the whipped cream and refrigerate until ready to serve. Unmold the soufflé onto a heated platter, spoon the cold sauce over the hot soufflé, and serve immediately.

Mrs. Richard S. Jackson
Tanglewood Council of the BSO

CREAMY PANCAKE

Serves 4

Hungarian-born pianist Tamas Vasary gave the first Boston Symphony performance of Mendelssohn's Concerto in D for Piano and Orchestra at Tanglewood in 1977. The word "pancake" may be a translation from the Hungarian, but the resulting omeletlike dish is, as Mr. Vasary says, "a voluptuously light dessert — quick and easy to make — adapted by my wife from a famous Hungarian recipe."

8 tablespoons unsalted butter
4 eggs, separated
4 tablespoons sugar
1 tablespoon flour

⅛ teaspoon baking powder
2 teaspoons milk
Cognac or Grand Marnier (optional)

Set 4 tablespoons of the butter aside for cooking the pancakes, and melt the remaining butter. Whip the egg whites until stiff and glossy, adding half the sugar. Combine the melted butter and egg yolks with the flour, baking powder, milk, and remaining sugar in a blender, and process at medium speed until light and frothy. Fold the yolk mixture into the egg whites.

Heat 1 tablespoon of butter in an omelet pan until it is foaming; then ladle in one fourth of the batter. Shake gently and cook over medium heat until the pancake is golden on the bottom and still creamy on top. Slide it onto a heated plate, creamy side up, and fold it in half. Repeat the process three times, and serve immediately. Sprinkle the pancakes with a little cognac, Grand Marnier, or other fruit brandy if desired.

Variation
Slide the first pancake onto a heated platter, and set each of the succeeding pancakes on top, as in a layer cake. Cut into wedges, and serve as above.

Tamas Vasary, piano

POFFERTJES (Dutch Dessert Pancakes)

Serves 6 to 8

Distinguished Dutch soprano Elly Ameling, a favorite guest artist with the Boston Symphony, shares a traditional Dutch delicacy with her fans. Poffertjes (pronounced POH-fer-chiz) pans are available at better cookware stores, but the little pancakes may also be cooked on a well-buttered griddle, using about a tablespoon of batter for each.

4 cups plus 2 tablespoons flour
1 tablespoon baking powder
1 teaspoon salt
2 eggs, lightly beaten
7 cups milk
8 tablespoons unsalted butter

2 teaspoons grated lemon peel
Cooking oil
Confectioners' sugar
Cointreau or other orange-flavored
* liqueur (optional)*

Sift the dry ingredients together into a large bowl. Stir in the eggs, milk, and 2 tablespoons of melted butter to make a smooth batter. Allow to stand for several minutes; then add the lemon peel. Preheat the poffertjes pan over medium heat.

Lightly oil the indentations in the pan, and almost fill them with the batter. When the bottom is slightly browned, turn and brown the other side. Dot each with a little cold butter, and arrange on a heated serving platter or individual plates, slightly overlapping, like roof tiles. Sprinkle with confectioners' sugar and a few drops of Cointreau and serve immediately.

Elly Ameling, soprano

FRENCH COFFEE BAKED ALASKA

Serves 8 to 10

This is one dessert the guests will wait for happily. It is sinfully rich. "Don't eat it all at once — the coffee will keep you awake!"

*⅓ cup finely ground French roast
    coffee (⅓ pound beans)
1 cup cold water
1 quart milk
12 egg yolks
1¾ cups sugar
2 cups heavy cream
2 tablespoons vanilla extract*

*⅛ teaspoon salt
2 tablespoons butter
2 tablespoons honey
1½ cups graham cracker or gingersnap
    crumbs
6 egg whites
Kahlua or other coffee brandy*

Cover the coffee with the cold water in a large saucepan. Scald the milk and pour it over the coffee. Cover loosely and allow the liquid to cool enough to handle. Strain it through several layers of cheesecloth or through a coffee filter. Extract as much liquid as possible, and set it aside.

In the top of a large double boiler, beat the egg yolks and 1½ cups of sugar. Add the coffee mixture and stir over simmering water until the custard thickens. Cool, add the cream, vanilla, and salt and chill. Freeze the cold mixture in an ice cream freezer, according to the manufacturer's directions.

Preheat the oven to 300°.

Add the butter and the honey to the crumbs, press into a buttered 10-inch pie plate, and bake for 10 to 12 minutes, or until the crust is crisp and lightly browned. Set aside to cool.

When the cream is frozen but still somewhat soft, fill the pie crust and place it in the freezer. Any leftover ice cream should be sealed tightly and frozen for later use.

Preheat the oven to 500°.

When ready to serve the pie, whip the six egg whites (approximately ¾ cup) until foamy. Gradually add the remaining ¼ cup sugar and beat constantly until the mixture is very stiff and glossy. Pile the meringue on top of the frozen pie and bake until pleasingly browned. Watch it closely! Serve immediately with a little Kahlua poured on top.

*Isham Peugh
Tanglewood Festival Chorus*

FROZEN LIME CREAM PIE

Makes two 9-inch pies

Marianne Harris, niece of former BSO cellist Louis Speyer, sends us this unusual variation of Key lime pie.

1⅓ cups graham cracker crumbs
¼ cup melted butter
¼ cup sugar
⅔ cup finely ground pecans
½ teaspoon cinnamon
6 eggs, separated
1 cup sugar

½ cup fresh lime juice (about 5 limes)
2 tablespoons finely grated lime peel
6 drops green food coloring (optional)
⅛ teaspoon salt
1 pint heavy cream, whipped
Thin slices of lime or pecan halves (for garnish)

Mix the graham cracker crumbs thoroughly with the melted butter and sugar; then stir in the pecans and cinnamon. Divide the mixture in half and pat evenly into two 9-inch pie plates, covering the sides as well as the bottoms.

Beat the egg yolks and ½ cup of sugar in the top of a double boiler and add the lime juice, peel, food coloring, and salt. Stir over simmering water until smooth and thickened. Remove from the heat and cool; then chill.

Whip the egg whites until soft peaks form, gradually add the remaining sugar, and beat until stiff and glossy. Fold the whipped cream into the chilled custard, and then into the egg whites. Pour into the pie shells and freeze for 24 hours or longer. Remove from the freezer and allow to stand at room temperature for 10 to 15 minutes before serving.

Garnish with slices of lime, decoratively twisted, or pecan halves.

Marianne B. Harris

ROSE WATER ICE CREAM

Makes about ½ gallon

One of the joys of visiting Hancock Village, which can easily be done when one is staying in the Tanglewood area, is the taste of this ice cream — it has the color and the fragrance of pale pink roses. Rose water is available at Hancock Village, drugstores, or gourmet shops.

2 egg yolks
1½ cups sugar
1 teaspoon salt
2 cups scalded milk, slightly cooled

1½ teaspoons cornstarch
4 cups light cream (see Note)
Red food coloring (optional)
Rose water

Beat the egg yolks and ½ cup sugar until light; set aside. Mix the salt and cornstarch with the remaining sugar, and stir it into the hot milk. Place over moderate heat, stir until the milk is slightly thickened, and remove from the heat: the cornstarch taste should have disappeared. Beat a little of the hot milk mixture into the beaten egg yolks, and pour this mixture back into the saucepan, beating continuously. Cool slightly, stir in the cream, and chill until ready to freeze.

Prepare the ice cream freezer, add the cold mixture, and stir in a little food coloring: it should be a very pale pink. Add rose water to taste, freeze according to the manufacturer's directions, and pack into freezer containers. The ice cream should be stored for at least 24 hours before serving.

Note
A richer ice cream may be obtained by substituting 1 or 2 cups of whipping cream for the light cream.

Hancock Shaker Village, Inc.
Pittsfield, Massachusetts

THREE-IN-ONE CREAM SHERBET

Serves 6 to 8

½ cup lemon juice
1½ cups orange juice
1 cup mashed banana

5 cups milk
1 cup heavy cream (see Note)
2 to 3 cups sugar

Place all the ingredients in a large bowl, adding sugar to taste. Stir well and refrigerate until ready to churn, at least 1 to 2 hours. Churn in an ice cream freezer or *sorbetière*, following the manufacturer's directions: it may have to be processed in two batches.

Pack the sherbet into freezer containers or decorative molds and store in the freezer. About 1 hour before serving, place the container in the refrigerator to soften the contents slightly. Unmold onto a chilled serving dish.

Note
Six cups of light cream or half-and-half may be substituted for the milk and cream.

Mrs. Thomas W. Conley

Bananas may be frozen when they are fully ripe, and kept until needed for banana bread, cake, and other uses. Children love them frozen, to be eaten like Popsicles.

COFFEE ICE CREAM DELUXE

Serves 10 to 12

1½ dozen medium-sized macaroons
½ cup brandy
½ gallon top-quality coffee ice cream, softened

Toffee crumbs (crumbled Heath bars or similar toffee)

Break the macaroons into small pieces and soak in the brandy until it is absorbed. Stir quickly into the ice cream. Refreeze in a decorative mold, a cut glass serving dish, or individual goblets. Remove from the freezer and soften in the refrigerator for about 30 minutes for individual servings, or 1 hour for the large bowl. Sprinkle with toffee crumbs just before serving.

Mrs. Edward L. Bond
Council of the BSO

GRAND FINALE CHEESECAKE

Serves 10 to 12

Born in the Middle West, Patricia McCarty won the First Silver Medal at the Geneva International Competition when she was just eighteen. She joined the Boston Symphony in 1979 as assistant principal viola. In August 1982, she married Ronald Wilkison, another member of the viola section.

Crust

1⅓ cups fine vanilla wafer crumbs
⅓ cup melted butter

⅓ cup sugar
1 teaspoon cinnamon

Filling

5 8-ounce packages cream cheese,
  softened
1¾ cups sugar
3 tablespoons flour
¼ teaspoon salt
5 eggs plus 2 yolks, at room
  temperature

¼ teaspoon vanilla extract
¼ cup heavy cream
¼ cup freshly squeezed lemon juice
  (optional)
Fresh strawberries or other fruit
  (optional)

Mix all the crust ingredients thoroughly, press into the bottom of a buttered 9-inch springform, and refrigerate while preparing the filling.

Preheat the oven to 500°.

Beat the cream cheese until light and fluffy. Combine the sugar, flour, and salt, and gradually beat into the cheese. Add the eggs and yolks, one at a time, beating well after each addition. Gently stir in the vanilla, cream, and lemon juice.

Pour the batter into the prepared crust and bake for 10 minutes; then lower the heat to 200° for 1 hour. *Do not open the oven door during this time.* When the cake is done, the center should be set so that a knife blade inserted in it comes out with a creamy coating. When it is done, turn off the oven and leave the cake there to cool gradually, with the oven door closed, for about 1½ hours, or overnight if the kitchen is cool.

Remove the cake from the oven and let it stand at room temperature until it is cool enough to refrigerate. Chill for at least 2 or 3 hours. Remove from the pan and top with fruit before serving.

Variation 1: Cheesecake Topping

2 cups sour cream　　　　　　　　*2½ teaspoons vanilla extract*
⅓ cup sugar

When the cheesecake is done but still hot, beat all the ingredients together and spread over the cheesecake. Place in a 400° oven for 10 minutes. Remove from the oven and let stand until cool enough to refrigerate. Chill before serving.

Variation 2

Commercial pie filling, such as cherry or blueberry, is an easy and colorful topping.

Patricia McCarty
BSO assistant principal viola
Boston Pops principal viola

HELEN'S HEAVENLY PIE

Serves 6

Mrs. Zimbler, who plays the double bass, is the widow of Josef Zimbler, long-time member of the cello section of the Boston Symphony. Her pie was a special favorite of former music director Charles Munch — it was he who named it.

1½ cups sugar　　　　　　　　　　*1 tablespoon grated lemon peel*
¼ teaspoon cream of tartar　　　　　*⅛ teaspoon salt*
4 eggs, separated　　　　　　　　　*2 cups heavy cream*
3 tablespoons shredded coconut　　　*1 pint strawberries*
3 tablespoons fresh lemon juice

Preheat the oven to 275°.

Sift 1 cup of sugar with the cream of tartar. Whip the egg whites until stiff but not dry and slowly add the sugar mixture, beating until the meringue is firm and glossy.

Spread the meringue on the bottom and sides of a buttered 10-inch pie plate, making the bottom ¼ inch thick and the sides 1 inch thick. Sprinkle the rim with 2 tablespoons coconut, and bake for about 1 hour, until the meringue is crisp and golden. Set aside to cool completely. Meanwhile, toast the remaining coconut over low heat in a saucepan or in a toaster oven. Set aside.

In the top of a double boiler, beat the egg yolks with the remaining sugar, and the lemon juice, lemon peel, and salt. Stir over simmering water until thick, about 8 to 10 minutes; then set aside to cool. Whip 1 cup of cream and fold it into the egg yolk mixture. Fill the meringue shell with the custard. Cover with plastic wrap and refrigerate for 24 hours.

Shortly before serving, whip the remaining cream and spread it over the pie filling. Sprinkle with the toasted coconut and decorate with strawberries.

Mrs. Josef Zimbler

VELVET CREAM CAKE

Serves 12

1 pound cream cheese, softened
3 cups heavy cream
1⅓ cups sugar

1 teaspoon vanilla extract
3 packages plain ladyfingers, split
Fresh fruit for topping

Beat the cream cheese, cream, sugar, and vanilla until very thick and smooth. Line the sides and bottom of a lightly buttered 10-inch springform with ladyfingers: it must have 2- to 3-inch-high sides. Pour in half the cheese mixture. Add a layer of ladyfingers, pour in the remaining mixture, and chill overnight.

Remove the sides from the pan and allow the cake to stand for an hour or so at room temperature before serving topped with fruit.

Mrs. Baron Hartley
Council of the BSO

COLD COFFEE SOUFFLÉ

Serves 6

1 envelope gelatin
2 cups milk
2 teaspoons instant coffee
⅔ cup sugar

¼ teaspoon salt
3 "extra large" eggs
½ teaspoon vanilla extract

Soften the gelatin in ½ cup of milk. Heat the remaining milk in a double boiler over boiling water and dissolve the coffee in it. Dissolve the gelatin in this mixture, add half the sugar, and reduce the heat.

Beat the egg yolks slightly in a large bowl with the remaining sugar and the salt. Slowly beat the hot coffee mixture into the egg yolk mixture and return it to the double boiler. Stir over simmering water until the mixture coats the spoon; remove from the heat and cool, but do not allow to set. Whip the egg whites and vanilla until very stiff, and fold into the coffee mixture. Pour into an oiled decorative mold or individual glass serving dishes and refrigerate for 4 to 6 hours or overnight. The mixture will separate into two layers, with the black coffee on the bottom. Turn out the mold onto a chilled serving platter and garnish with whipped cream and shaved semisweet chocolate. Top the individual servings with plain or whipped cream.

Mrs. Hazen H. Ayer

COLD LEMON SOUFFLÉ

Serves 8

This impressive soufflé is quick and easy to make, and holds well.

1 tablespoon gelatin
½ cup cold water
3 eggs, separated
1 cup sugar
6 tablespoons lemon juice
1 tablespoon grated lemon peel

2 cups heavy cream
1 teaspoon vanilla extract
1 tablespoon confectioners' sugar
Candied violets or rose petals
*   (optional)*

Soften the gelatin in the cold water. Beat the egg yolks and sugar until thick and light, and add the lemon juice and peel. Whip the egg whites until stiff but not dry, and whip 1½ cups of the cream.

Dissolve the gelatin over boiling water and quickly beat it into the lemon mixture. Fold in the egg whites and whipped cream, and pour the mixture into a 1½-quart soufflé dish or crystal bowl. Chill for at least 2 to 3 hours, or overnight.

At serving time, whip the remaining cream with the confectioners' sugar and vanilla. Garnish the soufflé with rosettes of whipped cream, topped with candied violets or rose petals, and serve very cold.

Mrs. John L. Thorndike

POTS DE CRÈME AU GRAND MARNIER

Serves 6 to 8

6 egg yolks
½ cup sugar
2 cups heavy cream
2 tablespoons Grand Marnier

1 tablespoon grated orange peel
⅛ teaspoon salt
Candied violets and/or mint leaves (for
*   garnish)*

Preheat the oven to 350°.

Beat the egg yolks until foamy and add the sugar gradually, beating until light and lemon colored. Stir in the cream, Grand Marnier, orange peel, and salt. Place in six or eight lightly buttered custard cups set in a pan of hot water. Bake for 40 minutes, or until the custard is just set. *Do not overcook.*

Remove from the oven and cool slightly; then refrigerate. Serve cold, garnished with candied violets and/or mint leaves.

Miss Aileen M. Farrell
Tanglewood Council of the BSO

CHOCOLATE MINT MOUSSE

Serves 6

6 ounces semisweet chocolate
¼ cup strong black coffee
2 eggs, separated
¼ cup white crème de menthe

1 tablespoon sugar
½ cup heavy cream, whipped
Fresh mint sprigs (for garnish)

Melt the chocolate over simmering water or in a microwave oven. Remove from the heat, stir in the coffee, and cool slightly. Beat the egg yolks and crème de menthe, fold into the chocolate mixture, and cool completely.

Whip the egg whites with the sugar until stiff but not dry. Fold in the whipped cream and gently add to the chocolate mixture. Turn the mousse into a serving bowl and chill for 2 to 3 hours or overnight. If the mousse is frozen, it should be removed approximately 1 hour before serving and allowed to soften in the refrigerator. Garnish with fresh mint, and serve very cold.

Mrs. William H. Radebaugh
Council of the BSO

CRÈME TANTE RENÉE

Serves 6

Mrs. Marjollet's husband was a member of the cello section of the Boston Symphony for many years. Her simple chocolate dessert looks very pretty served in individual goblets.

4 ounces dark sweet chocolate
6 eggs, at room temperature,
  separated

1 teaspoon sugar
Heavy cream

Melt the chocolate in a double boiler or a microwave oven, and set aside to cool slightly. Using a wooden spoon, beat the egg yolks into the chocolate, one at a time. Set the mixture aside and keep it warm enough so the chocolate does not set. Whip the egg whites and the sugar until they are firm and glossy. Fold a little of the egg whites into the chocolate, and then fold the chocolate into the egg whites. Pour into a deep serving dish and refrigerate for several hours or overnight. Serve with cream and vanilla wafers.

Mrs. Leon Marjollet

SYLLABUB

Serves 6 to 8

Gregarious violinist Fredy Ostrovsky, born in Bulgaria, joined the Boston Symphony in 1952. A member of the faculty of the New England Conservatory, he collects rare books. From a sixteenth-century compendium comes the following adaptation of an old and beloved recipe, which is as delicious today as it was four hundred years ago.

¼ cup Madeira or sweet sherry
¼ cup brandy
6 tablespoons superfine sugar
1 teaspoon finely grated lemon peel

3 tablespoons lemon juice
½ teaspoon almond extract
Nutmeg or cinnamon
2 cups heavy cream, lightly beaten

In a large chilled bowl combine all the ingredients except the cream and spices. Stir until the sugar dissolves and everything is well combined. Add a pinch of nutmeg or cinnamon, if desired. Add the cream and beat until peaks form. Pour into a large crystal serving bowl or individual dishes and dust lightly with additional nutmeg or cinnamon. Chill well. Serve with macaroons or crisp almond cookies.

Variation
Freeze and serve while still partially frozen.

Fredy Ostrovsky, violin

SCANDINAVIAN LEMON RING

Serves 6 to 8

Pianist Grant Johannesen was a frequent guest with the Boston Symphony for many years, particularly during Erich Leinsdorf's tenure as music director. His Scandinavian dessert is a joy to the eye and the palate.

4 eggs at room temperature, separated
½ cup sugar
6 tablespoons lemon juice
1 tablespoon grated lemon peel
1 tablespoon gelatin

¼ cup cold water
¼ cup boiling water
2 cups strawberries
½ pint cream, whipped
½ teaspoon vanilla extract

Beat the egg yolks until light and add the sugar slowly, beating until the mixture is thick and lemon colored. Add the lemon juice and peel. Meanwhile, soften the gelatin in the cold water in the top of a large double boiler. Add the boiling water, stir until the gelatin is dissolved, and set the double boiler top over simmering water. Slowly beat in the egg yolk mixture and stir for 3 to 5 minutes, until the mixture is warmed but not too hot. Remove from the heat and set aside to cool, but do not allow the mixture to set.

Whip the egg whites until stiff but not dry, and fold into the cooled lemon mixture. Pour into an oiled ring mold. Chill for several hours or overnight. Just before serving, unmold onto a chilled platter. Fill the center with fresh strawberries and/or whipped cream flavored with vanilla.

Grant Johannesen, piano

Prunes with Tea: *Poach prunes in strong sugared tea to which a little rum or lemon zest may be added. Allow to cool; then refrigerate until ready to serve.*

WINE JELLY

Serves 6 to 8

Harpsichordist and conductor Raymond Leppard has performed the music of the Bach family with the Boston Symphony both in Symphony Hall and at Tanglewood. He will meet with equal success when subscribers discover his talents in the kitchen.

2 tablespoons gelatin	*1 6-ounce jar red currant jelly*
¾ cup cold water	*1 cup sugar*
1 bottle dry red wine	*½ cup brandy*
2 teaspoons grated lemon peel	*1 cup heavy cream, whipped*
3 tablespoons lemon juice	

Soften the gelatin in the cold water. Combine the remaining ingredients except the brandy and cream, and simmer over medium heat for about 5 minutes. Remove from the heat and dissolve the softened gelatin completely in the hot mixture. Cool to lukewarm, add the brandy, and strain into a lightly oiled mold. Refrigerate for several hours or overnight, until the jelly is firm.

Unmold onto a chilled platter and serve with the whipped cream and thin crisp cookies.

Variation

Pour into parfait glasses or individual glass dishes, and serve with heavy cream or *crème fraîche.*

Raymond Leppard, harpsichordist and conductor

NEVER-FAIL PIE CRUST

Makes 4 8- or 9-inch crusts,
or 3 10-inch crusts

Harpsichordist, teacher, and singer Betsy Moyer is the wife of BSO personnel manager Bill Moyer. A former trombonist with the BSO who now
plays the recorder, he is also a composer. Her excellent basic pastry lives up
to its name. The dough is easy to handle, but it must be kept very cold.

2 cups all-purpose flour
1 cup cake-flour (see Note 1)
¾ cup lard, chilled (see Note 2)

⅓ cup butter, chilled (see Note 2)
1 egg white
½ cup ice water

Combine the flours and salt, and cut the lard and butter into the flour until
the pieces are pea-sized. Lightly beat the egg white and the water together,
and blend into the flour mixture with a fork or the fingers. Knead together
lightly and quickly and chill for at least 1 hour, or overnight.

Roll out on a lightly floured board, and cut to fit the pie plates. Bake as
follows:

For a fully cooked shell. Prick all over the bottom of the shell with a fork.
Line the shell with a sheet of aluminum foil and arrange 1½ to 2 cups of
dried kidney beans or other fairly large dried beans over the foil. Bake in a
preheated 400° oven for 10 to 12 minutes, then remove the foil and beans
(see Note 3). Continue to bake until the shell is golden brown. Cool thoroughly before filling the shell.

For a partially baked shell. Proceed as above, but cook for only 6 to 8
minutes. Remove the foil and beans, cook for 1 to 2 minutes longer, and
remove from the oven. *Do not overcook.*

For a filled double- or single-crust pie. Bake in a preheated 425° oven for 15
to 20 minutes; then reduce the heat to 350° and continue to cook for
another 20 to 35 minutes, or until the crust is crisp and well browned. The
time will vary with the filling and the size of the pie.

Leftovers may be used for small canapés, sprinkled with cheese for
cheese straws, or fitted into small muffin pans and filled with jam or fruit.

Note 1

Seven eighths cup of additional all-purpose flour, or 1 cup of presifted
"gravy" or granulated flour, may be substituted for the cake flour. Pastry
flour may be substituted for the total amount of flour.

Note 2

Lard gives an excellent flavor to pastry. The proportion of lard to butter
may be varied according to the flavor preferred. Vegetable shortening may
be substituted for the lard, in which case the amount of butter should be
increased.

Note 3

The foil and beans should be recycled: they will keep almost indefinitely. Marbles and aluminum pellets may, of course, be used, but beans are cheaper.

Mrs. William Moyer

CRANBERRY-APPLE PIE

Serves 6

World-famous baritone Sherrill Milnes has performed extensively in the concert and operatic repertories with the Boston Symphony. He also, obviously, excels in the culinary repertory. As he says, "This pie is simple to make and festive enough for special occasions like Thanksgiving and Christmas."

Pastry for a 9-inch pie shell with a
   lattice top (see Never-Fail Pie
   Crust♦)
1½ cups cranberries, washed,
   drained, and picked over
2 large apples, peeled, cored, and
   sliced
½ cup raisins

½ cup chopped nuts
1 tablespoon butter
1 cup sugar
2 tablespoons flour
2 tablespoons water
1 teaspoon cinnamon
½ teaspoon orange extract
½ teaspoon lemon extract

Preheat the oven to 450°.

Prepare the pastry shell and the lattice topping and refrigerate.

In a large mixing bowl combine the cranberries and apples with the other ingredients and mix well. Pour the filling into the pie shell, and arrange the lattice crust on top. Bake for 25 minutes, lower the heat to 350°, and bake for about 20 minutes more. When both crusts are crisp and well browned, remove the pie and cool it on a rack. Serve the pie warm or cool — never chilled — with whipped cream or vanilla ice cream.

Sherrill Milnes, baritone

YOGURT APPLE PIE

Serves 6

Pastry for a 9-inch crust (see
   Never-Fail Pie Crust♦)
½ cup sugar
2 tablespoons flour
1 cup yogurt, or half yogurt and half
   sour cream

1 egg, beaten
½ teaspoon vanilla extract
¼ teaspoon salt
3 cups apples, peeled, cored, and
   thinly sliced

Topping

⅓ cup sugar

4 tablespoons flour

½ teaspoon cinnamon

¼ cup butter, softened

Preheat the oven to 450°.

Prepare the pie crust and partially bake it for 8 to 10 minutes, and set aside to cool. Combine the sugar and flour, add the yogurt, egg, vanilla, and salt, and beat until smooth. Fill the pie crust with the apples and pour the yogurt mixture over all. Bake for 20 minutes; then remove from the oven. Meanwhile, mix the topping ingredients until they are crumbly. Spread the topping evenly over the partially baked filling and bake for 20 minutes longer, until the topping is crisp and golden and the apples are tender. Cool slightly before serving — hot, warm, or at room temperature, but never chilled.

Mrs. Eugene Doggett
Junior Council of the BSO

BEA'S CRANBERRY PIE

Makes two 9-inch pies

4 cups cranberries

2 cups apples, peeled and coarsely
  chopped

2 cups raisins

3 cups sugar

2 teaspoons cinnamon

1 teaspoon salt

3 tablespoons cornstarch

½ cup orange juice

2 tablespoons grated orange peel

Pastry for two 9-inch pie shells with
  lattice tops (see Never-Fail Pie
  Crust♦)

Preheat the oven to 425°.

Cook the cranberries, apples, raisins, sugar, cinnamon, and salt until the apples are soft and the cranberries have burst. Dissolve the cornstarch in the orange juice and stir into the cranberry mixture with the grated peel. Bring back to a boil, stirring constantly; then remove from the heat and cool. Pour into two 9-inch uncooked pie shells and cover with lattice tops. Bake for 10 minutes; then reduce the heat to 350° and bake for 10 to 15 minutes more, until the crust is crisp and golden brown.

Mrs. Howland B. Jones, Jr.
Council of the BSO

PEACH TART

Serves 8

South African–born Marita Napier is equally at home on the concert or the opera stage. Her fans will not be surprised that she is also very much at home in the kitchen. Her "tart" is really a moist and delicious cake.

4 or 5 fairly large ripe peaches
3 tablespoons lemon juice
3 tablespoons butter
¾ cup sugar
2 eggs

1 cup flour
1 teaspoon baking powder
¼ teaspoon salt
½ cup milk or light cream

Sauce
½ cup heavy cream
1 cup superfine sugar

1 teaspoon vanilla extract

Peel the peaches and cut them into thin uniform slices. Mix thoroughly with the lemon juice and set aside.

Cream the butter and ½ cup of sugar, and beat in the eggs one at a time. Combine the dry ingredients and add alternately with the milk, beating until smooth. Press the mixture into a buttered round or rectangular tart pan or quiche dish, making it as thin and even as possible. Drain the peach slices and arrange them decoratively over the crust. Sprinkle with the remaining ¼ cup of sugar, and bake the tart for 35 to 40 minutes, or until the crust is crisp and golden. Remove and set on a rack to cool slightly.

Meanwhile, make the sauce. Stir all the ingredients together until the sugar is dissolved, but do not beat. (It may be necessary to heat the cream slightly, but cool it before proceeding.)

Pour the cool sauce over the hot tart, and allow it to stand for a few minutes before serving. The tart may be served hot, warm, or cool, but never chilled.

Variation
Substitute apples for the peaches, and proceed as above.

Marita Napier, soprano

RASPBERRY RHUBARB PIE

Serves 8

This recipe for rhubarb lovers was given by the wife of former Boston Symphony Overseer Jacob Kaplan to their daughter-in-law, the wife of a present Overseer, Leonard Kaplan.

5 cups rhubarb, washed and cut into
*   1-inch pieces*
3 tablespoons tapioca
1⅓ cups sugar
¼ teaspoon salt
1 egg, beaten

2 teaspoons grated orange peel
1 tablespoon melted butter
2 tablespoons raspberry jam
Pastry for one 10-inch pie with lattice
*   top (see Never-Fail Pie Crust♦)*

Preheat the oven to 450°.

Combine all the filling ingredients and set aside for 15 minutes. Line a 10-inch pie plate with the pastry. Pour in the rhubarb mixture and cover with the lattice top. Bake for 15 minutes; then reduce the heat to 350° and bake for 30 minutes more, or until the rhubarb is tender and the pastry is brown and crisp.

Variation
Strawberry jam may be substituted for the raspberry, to make a strawberry rhubarb pie.

Mrs. Leonard Kaplan
Council of the BSO

LEMON CHESS PIE

Serves 6 to 8

Olivia Hall Luetcke played the harp on the Symphony Hall stage for a number of years, before retiring to Arkansas. It is good to have her back as a contributor to the cookbook.

Pastry for one 9-inch pie crust (see
   Never-Fail Pie Crust◆)
⅓ cup butter
1¾ cups sugar
4 eggs

2 tablespoons flour
1 tablespoon cornmeal
¼ cup milk
¼ cup lemon juice
2 tablespoons grated lemon peel

Preheat the oven to 325°.

Fit the pastry into a pie plate and refrigerate while preparing the filling.

Cream the butter, sugar, and eggs until light. Beat in the flour, cornmeal, and milk alternately, and add the lemon juice and peel. Mix thoroughly and pour into the pastry shell. Bake for 50 to 60 minutes, until the filling is set and the crust is crisp and golden brown. Serve warm or at room temperature, with or without cream.

Olivia Hall Luetcke, harp

SOUTHERN PECAN PIE

Serves 6 to 8

It is the piquancy of the orange that makes this an interesting version of an old favorite.

3 eggs, lightly beaten
¾ cup sugar
1 cup light corn syrup
2 tablespoons melted butter
2 tablespoons orange juice

2 tablespoons grated orange peel
1 cup pecan halves
1 9-inch unbaked pie shell (see
   Never-Fail Pie Crust◆)

Preheat the oven to 350°.

Combine the eggs, sugar, corn syrup, butter, orange juice, and orange peel, and beat well. Spread the pecans in the unbaked pie shell and press lightly into the crust. Pour in the filling gently. Bake the pie for 35 to 45 minutes, until the filling is barely set. Cool on a rack and serve at room temperature with whipped cream or ice cream.

Mrs. David Harmon
Council of the BSO

CANADIAN BUTTER TARTS

Makes 6 large tarts,
or 12 small tarts

These tarts keep for a week or more at room temperature, longer if refrigerated, and indefinitely if frozen.

½ cup raisins
2 tablespoons brandy, rum, or
*   bourbon*
1 recipe Never-Fail Pie Crust◆
¼ cup butter
2 cups firmly packed brown sugar

¼ cup corn syrup
2 eggs, beaten
½ cup butternuts, walnuts, or pecans,
*   chopped*
1 to 2 tablespoons lemon juice

Soak the raisins in the liquor.

Lightly grease tart shells or muffin tins with unsalted shortening and cut the pastry to fit. Press it firmly up into the pans and refrigerate until ready to bake.

Preheat the oven to 375°.

Cream the butter and beat in the sugar and corn syrup. Add the eggs a little at a time, beating well. Stir in the raisins and liquor, and the nuts; add lemon juice to taste. Fill the unbaked pastry shells two thirds full, and bake for 15 to 25 minutes, depending on the size. Watch carefully! When the tops are foamy, allow the filling to puff up; then remove the tarts immediately, so that the filling will not overflow.

Serve the large tarts with ice cream or whipped cream for dessert and the small ones plain for tea.

Mrs. Donald B. Sinclair
Council of the BSO

CREAM CHEESE TARTS

Makes 6 dozen

½ pound cream cheese, softened
½ pound butter, softened
2 cups all-purpose flour

Preserves, jam, or fruit butter, as
*   preferred*

Mix the first three ingredients very thoroughly. Divide the dough into four parts, wrap in waxed paper, and refrigerate at least 1 hour, or overnight.

Preheat the oven to 350°.

Roll out one part of the dough very thin on a well-floured surface and cut into 4-inch squares. Place about 1 teaspoon preserves in the center of each square. Bring the four corners together and twist and pinch firmly. Be sure the crust is sealed, so the filling does not leak out. Set on a buttered cookie sheet or in Teflon-coated muffin tins, and bake for 15 minutes. When the tarts are golden and can be moved easily, they are done. Remove, cool on a rack, and repeat the process until all the dough is used, with a variety of fillings.

Mrs. William C. Woodhull
Tanglewood Council of the BSO

QUEEN OF HEARTS TARTS

Makes 18 2-inch tarts

> *The Queen of Hearts, she made some tarts*
> *All on a summer day.*
> *The Knave of Hearts, he stole those tarts*
> *And took them quite away.*
> *— Alice's Adventures in Wonderland*

Composer David del Tredici's *Final Alice* was a highlight of the nation's bicentennial year for symphony audiences across the country. It is apparent that Alice remains on his mind, just as the haunting theme he wrote for her remains on ours.

1½ cups flour
Salt
4 tablespoons butter (for flavor),
  chilled
4 tablespoons lard (for texture), chilled

¼ to ⅓ cup ice water
Jam or preserves (apricot, raspberry,
  plum, or other)
Additional water

Sift the flour and a pinch of salt into a chilled bowl. Cut the butter and lard into the flour, and rub the mixture between the fingertips until it resembles fine crumbs. Sprinkle with the smaller amount of ice water, and work with the fingers until the dough holds together, adding a little water as needed to collect the flour mixture into a smooth dough. Form into a ball, wrap in waxed paper, and refrigerate for about 1 hour, or overnight.

Preheat the oven to 400°.

Roll the pastry on a lightly floured board to about ⅛ inch thick. Cut it into circles slightly larger than the buttered tart shells or small muffin tins in which the tarts will be baked. Press the circles of dough into the pans, pushing well up around the edges. Spoon a little jam or preserves into the center of each shell, and sprinkle a few drops of water on just the jam to keep it from drying out. Bake for 10 to 15 minutes, or until the pastry is lightly browned and moves freely in the pans. Remove from the pans and cool on a rack, closely guarded against marauding knaves. Serve to Alices of any age.

Variation
Bake unfilled shells (this is an excellent basic tart pastry) and half-fill the shells with Lemon Curd.◆ Top with a simple meringue and brown it quickly under the broiler. The result is a perfect lemon meringue tart.

David del Tredici, composer

LEMON CURD

Serves 6 to 8

Use lemon curd as a spread for toast, as a sauce for steamed puddings, or as a filling for cakes, tarts, and the ultimate lemon meringue pie.

1 cup sugar
6 tablespoons lemon juice
2 tablespoons grated lemon peel

4 tablespoons butter
3 eggs, beaten

Combine the ingredients in the top of a double boiler over simmering water. Stir until the mixture thickens and coats the back of a spoon. Set aside to cool slightly; then spoon into hot sterilized jars, allowing ¼ inch headroom. Seal and refrigerate until ready to use. Lemon curd will keep for several weeks in the refrigerator.

Mrs. James T. Mountz
Council of the BSO

POTPOURRI

Musicians study all their lives to perfect their musical techniques as they bring their audiences the thrill of live performances and the perfection of recordings. Behind these performers stands a vast support group, continuing a magnificent tradition of service that is uniquely American. The Friends of the Boston Symphony, both individual and corporate, are those who contribute financially to the Orchestra, while the Trustees, Overseers, and members of the various Councils constitute the corps of active volunteers who contribute time and talents as well as money. Without both groups there would be no orchestra on stage — indeed, no arts organization can survive on its earned income alone. Motivated by love, the volunteers deem themselves highly privileged to be part of the Symphony family and *(overleaf)* find themselves constantly caught up in the enormous excitement of their many projects to benefit the Orchestra.

BRANDIED CRANBERRIES

Serves 8 to 10

This sauce will keep for a long time in the refrigerator.

2 cups sugar
1 cinnamon stick
3 cloves
½ cup boiling water

1 medium-sized orange, seeded and
  chopped
1 pound cranberries
½ cup brandy

Place the sugar and spices in a large saucepan with the water. Set over medium heat and boil until the liquid is clear. Discard the spices and add the orange. Bring back to a boil, cover, and simmer for about 10 minutes. Stir in the cranberries, cover, and cook until the berries have popped. Reduce the heat and simmer slowly for 3 to 4 minutes. Remove from the heat and cool; then add the brandy. Allow to stand for at least 2 to 3 hours before serving with poultry or meat.

Mrs. Albert Funk, Jr.

CRANBERRY CONSERVE

Makes 6 half-pint jars

Perfect with the holiday bird . . .

1 pound cranberries
1 cup water
3½ cups sugar
3 tablespoons grated orange peel

1 cup peeled and diced orange, seeded
2 cups peeled and diced apple
½ cup golden raisins
½ cup chopped pecans

Bring the cranberries, water, and sugar to a boil in a large saucepan, and simmer for 5 minutes or until the berries burst. Add the remaining ingredients except the nuts, and simmer over low heat for about 30 minutes, stirring occasionally. When the mixture has thickened, remove from the heat and stir in the nuts. Pour into hot sterilized jars, leaving about ¼ inch headroom, and seal immediately. Tighten the lids as the jars cool, and store in a cool dark place. Refrigerate after opening.

Mrs. Andrew L. Nichols
Council of the BSO

SPICED GRAPE SKINS

Makes about 9 pints

This condiment will justify the effort required many times over. It makes greatly appreciated house-guest or Christmas presents. Allow it to "cure" for at least several weeks before opening.

8 pounds ripe Concord grapes,
  washed, drained, and picked over
5 pounds sugar
1 pint cider vinegar

1 large cinnamon stick
8 cloves
2 to 3 inches gingerroot, bruised
  (optional)

Squeeze the pulp from the grapes into a saucepan, and place the skins in a large preserving pan. When all the skins have been removed, bring the pulp to a boil for about 10 minutes; then remove it from the heat. Strain out the seeds, using a heavy strainer or food mill, and add the strained pulp to the grape skins. Add the sugar, the vinegar, and the spices tied in a cheesecloth bag.

Simmer the skins for about 3 hours, until the liquid reaches the jell stage. Skim if necessary, and ladle the boiling mixture into hot sterilized jars, leaving less than ½ inch headroom. Seal the jars immediately with a thin layer of paraffin. If you prefer, leave ¼ inch headroom and process in a hot-water bath: 5 minutes for half pints and 10 minutes for pints. (See any standard cookbook for canning and preserving procedures.) Tighten the lids as the jars cool, and store in a cool dark place.

Maisy Bennett
Tanglewood Festival Chorus
Council of the BSO

RHUBARB CHUTNEY

Makes 6 to 7 pints

These adaptations of a 1563 English recipe were obviously used in Colonial days. Allow the chutney to cure for at least a month before serving with curries, cold meats, or cheese.

2 pounds rhubarb, washed, peeled,
   and chopped
1 pound golden raisins
4 cups white or light brown sugar
1 lemon, seeded, quartered, and sliced
   paper-thin

3 large or 4 medium-sized cloves of
   garlic, minced
1 tablespoon salt
2 ounces gingerroot, grated
2 cups malt or cider vinegar
1 small chili pepper, or ½ teaspoon
   cayenne pepper (optional)

Combine all the ingredients in a large ·covered pan and bring to a boil, stirring frequently. Reduce the heat, cover, and simmer over low heat for 2 hours, or until the mixture has become very thick. Stir often to prevent the chutney from sticking. When it has reached the desired consistency, pour the mixture into hot pint or half-pint sterilized jars, leaving ¼ inch head-room, and seal immediately. Tighten the seals as the jars cool and store them in a cool dark place.

William Shiverick

Variation: Cranberry Chutney

Substitute 1½ pounds cranberries for the rhubarb and ½ pound dried currants for ½ pound of the raisins. Proceed as above, adding the optional chili or cayenne.

Mrs. Hart D. Leavitt
Council of the BSO

GREEN TOMATO CHUTNEY

Makes 5 to 6 pints

This is a mild chutney, a good accompaniment for any meat and an ideal use for surplus green tomatoes rescued from the frost.

4 pounds green tomatoes, peeled
1 pound apples, peeled and cored
1½ pounds onions, coarsely chopped
½ pound raisins
1 teaspoon ground ginger

6 tablespoons salt
1 teaspoon cayenne pepper
1 teaspoon allspice
1 to 1½ pints cider vinegar
2 pounds brown sugar

Chop the peeled tomatoes and apples, by hand or in a food processor. Combine all the ingredients except the vinegar and sugar in a large pan and set aside, covered, for at least 1½ hours, stirring occasionally. Place over medium heat and bring to a boil. Add the sugar and vinegar to the tomato mixture, return to a boil, cover, and simmer for 15 minutes. Pour into hot sterilized jars, leaving ¼ inch headroom, and seal immediately. Cool on a rack, tightening the seals as the jars cool, and store in a cool dark place.

Anonymous

MEG'S PEACH CHUTNEY

Makes 8 to 10 pints

8 pounds peaches, peeled, pitted, and
   diced
6 cups sugar
1 pound raisins
6 cups cider vinegar

2 cups chopped crystallized ginger or 1
   cup grated gingerroot
2 tablespoons chili powder
1 cup chopped yellow onions
4 tablespoons mustard seed
2 tablespoons salt

Place all the ingredients in a large heavy preserving pan. Stir over medium heat until the mixture boils. Simmer, uncovered, for 2 to 3 hours, until the chutney is thick but not sticky. It will set as it cools, so do not let the mixture get too thick.

Pour the chutney into hot sterilized jars, leaving ¼ inch headroom, and seal immediately. Tighten the seals as the jars cool. Store in a cool dark place.

Serve with cold meats, with cheese, and always with curry.

Mrs. Richard G. Scheide
Council of the BSO

GRANDMOTHER'S SWEET PEPPER RELISH

Makes 6 to 8 pints

24 sweet red peppers, seeded and
   minced
2 tablespoons salt

1 quart vinegar
6 cups sugar

Place the minced peppers and salt in a ceramic or stainless steel bowl, and stir until well blended. Refrigerate overnight. Next day, drain the peppers thoroughly and place them in a large preserving pan. Add the vinegar and sugar, and boil until the relish is the consistency of marmalade. This takes longer than one expects. Pour the boiling relish into hot sterilized jars, leaving ¼ inch headroom, and seal immediately. Cool on a rack, tighten the seals as the jars cool, and store in a cool dark place. Serve with meats or poultry, or with cream cheese and crackers as an appetizer.

Mrs. David Little
Council of the BSO

GREEN TOMATO RELISH

Makes about 8 pints

Virtuoso piccolo player Lois Schaefer was assistant principal flute with the Chicago Symphony before coming to Boston in 1965. Her varied career encompasses the Casals Festival in 1963 and the Boston Symphony Chamber Players' tour of the USSR in 1967. In the early 1970s, she and two Boston Symphony colleagues formed the New England Harp Trio, in which she plays the flute. Her recipe for relish is versatile and a boon to those who are inundated with green tomatoes after the first frost strikes the garden.

25 large green tomatoes, peeled	*2 tablespoons celery seed*
8 medium-sized yellow onions	*4 tablespoons white mustard seed*
2 red sweet peppers, seeded	*4 cups vinegar*
3 green peppers, seeded	*4 cups sugar*
4 tablespoons kosher salt	*⅛ teaspoon cayenne pepper (optional)*

Grind the tomatoes and onions, using the coarse blade of a food grinder, and drain overnight in a colander.

Next day, grind the peppers and combine with the tomato mixture in a large preserving pan. Add all the other ingredients and bring to a boil. Lower the heat and simmer for 15 to 20 minutes, until the vegetables are tender but not mushy. Pour into hot sterilized jars, leaving ½ inch headroom. Cap immediately, and process in a hot-water bath: 5 minutes for half pints, 10 minutes for pints. (See any standard cookbook for canning directions.) Store in a cool dark place, and serve with frankfurters or any hot or cold meat or fish.

Variation 1: Russian Dressing
Mix ½ cup each mayonnaise and Green Tomato Relish with ¼ cup chili sauce.

Variation 2: Tartar Sauce
Mix ½ cup mayonnaise with ¼ cup Green Tomato Relish and 1 tablespoon each chopped green olives and drained capers.

Lois Schaefer
Principal piccolo

SPICED ZUCCHINI RELISH

Makes 5 pints

This relish is a boon to gardeners overborne by rampaging zucchinis.

10 cups chopped zucchini, lightly packed	*2 tablespoons celery seed*
4 medium-sized onions, chopped	*2 tablespoons mustard seed*
5 tablespoons salt	*1 teaspoon cinnamon*
1 cup chopped red sweet pepper	*1 teaspoon nutmeg*
2¼ cups white vinegar	*½ teaspoon freshly ground black pepper*
1¼ cups sugar	

Combine the zucchini, onions, and salt and pack tightly in one or more large jars. Cover with water, seal the container(s), and refrigerate overnight.

Next day, drain the zucchini mixture, rinse with cold water, and drain again. Combine all the ingredients in a large preserving pan and bring to a boil, stirring constantly. Reduce the heat and simmer for 1 hour or until thickened. The total volume should be reduced to about 2½ quarts. Spoon into five 1-pint freezer containers. Cool, cover, and refrigerate for as long as three to four weeks, or freeze for longer storage.

Teddie Preston
Council of the BSO

Lemon Juice: *Heat lemons until warm to the touch in very hot water, a warm oven, or for 15 to 20 seconds in a microwave oven, and they will reward you with almost double their usual juice.*

COPPER PENNIES

Makes "a lot"

This "pickle" is a regular feature of the Marathon Café, where the workers meet to restore their strength during the BSO's Musical Marathon — an annual fund-raising event.

2 pounds medium-sized carrots (peeled
   and sliced about ⅛ inch thick)
1 medium-sized onion, sliced
½ cup wine vinegar
¼ cup lemon juice
1 cup sugar
½ cup salad oil

1 10-ounce can tomato soup
1 teaspoon salt
¾ teaspoon pepper
1 teaspoon prepared mustard
1 teaspoon Worcestershire sauce
Cayenne pepper or Tabasco (optional)

Cook the carrots and onion in a little water until almost tender (about 5 minutes). Cool under cold running water and drain thoroughly. Mix all the other ingredients in the blender and process until smooth and thick. Add cayenne or Tabasco to taste.

Place the vegetables in a large glass jar and pour in the marinade. Cover tightly and refrigerate for several days. This mixture will keep for a week or so, and the marinade may be reused as long as it is kept cold.

Mrs. Lawrence L. Clampitt
Council of the BSO

QUICK CHILI SAUCE

Makes 2 pints

Priscilla Lingham reports, "When my grandmother gave me this recipe she wrote at the bottom: 'Cost: under 50¢.' Wouldn't she be surprised now!"

1 28-ounce can tomatoes, mashed, chopped, or blended	*½ teaspoon cinnamon*
3 medium-sized onions, minced	*½ teaspoon ground cloves*
½ cup sugar	*½ teaspoon allspice*
¼ cup vinegar	*½ teaspoon freshly ground black pepper*
½ teaspoon nutmeg	*1 tablespoon salt*

Combine all the ingredients in a large stainless steel or enameled saucepan and simmer over medium heat until the onions are soft. Pour into hot sterilized jars leaving ¼ inch headroom. Seal immediately, cool on a rack, and store in the refrigerator (see Note). Serve with hot dogs and hamburgers, chicken, cold meats, or cheese.

Note

Process in a hot-water bath for 5 minutes for half pints or 10 minutes for pints, and the sauce will keep indefinitely without refrigeration. See any standard cookbook for canning directions.

Priscilla Lingham
Council of the BSO

MINCEMEAT

Makes about 6 quarts

6 pounds lean ground beef	*2 tablespoons each cinnamon, ground cloves, and allspice*
1 tablespoon salt	
Water	*1 cup molasses*
7 to 8 cups chopped peeled apples	*5 cups sugar*
3 cups cider	*2½ cups whole golden raisins*
½ cup cider vinegar	*1½ cups chopped dark raisins*
6 tablespoons lemon juice	*1½ tablespoons grated lemon peel*
1 cup orange juice	*3 tablespoons grated orange peel*
1 tablespoon each mace and nutmeg	*1½ cups brandy or bourbon*

Place the beef and salt in a large covered saucepan, and cover with water. Bring to a boil, cover, and simmer until the red color has faded. Reserve 3 cups of the cooking liquid, drain the meat, and return it and the reserved liquid to the pan. Add all the remaining ingredients, except the peels and liquor, in the order given, and bring to a boil. Lower the heat and simmer for 1½ hours; then add the peels and return to a boil. Remove from the heat and add the liquor. Pour into hot sterilized jars, and seal immediately (see Note). Tighten the seals as the jars cool, and store in a cool dark place.

Note

Processing the jars in a hot-water bath (10 minutes for pints and 15 minutes for quarts) will remove any danger of spoilage. See any standard cookbook for canning directions.

Mrs. George B. McManama
Council of the BSO

DOUBLE YOGURT

Makes 1 pint

Double Yogurt will keep at least as long as "single" yogurt, under the same conditions. Somehow, the removal of the whey tends to reduce the sharply tart taste of yogurt, making it more palatable to those who dislike sour things. But remember: do not boil *any* yogurt!

1 quart low-fat or whole-milk yogurt,
  commercial or homemade, with no
  thickening additives

Line a large strainer with a clean white cloth, four layers of cheesecloth, or a Chemex- or Melitta-type coffee filter. Pour in the yogurt, and set it aside to drain for several hours or overnight, depending on the consistency preferred. The amount should be reduced by half.

Use Double Yogurt as a substitute for sour cream, mix it with an equal amount of heavy cream for a very acceptable *crème fraîche*, spread it like cream cheese, or use it as a topping, sweetened or not, for fruit desserts. Experiment — yogurt is cheap!

The Cookbook Committee

BOILED CIDER

Makes 1 quart

Many old cookbooks speak of boiled cider as an easy and inexpensive sweetener. Now that fresh cider is available over a long season, it can be made at any time.

Boil 1 gallon fresh sweet cider down to 1 quart. Pour the boiling "syrup" into hot sterilized 1-pint canning jars, leaving ¼ inch headroom, and seal immediately. Tighten the lids as the jars cool, and store in a cool dark place. Refrigerate after opening.

Use as a sweetener for applesauce; as a flavor enhancer for mixed fresh or cooked fruits; as a basting sauce for ham, pork, or chicken; and as the basis for Apple Syrup.◆

Mrs. Thomas Gardiner, Overseer
Council of the BSO

APPLE SYRUP

Makes 1 quart

1 quart Boiled Cider◆
1 to 2 cups sugar

4 cloves (optional)
1 cinnamon stick (optional)

Add 1 cup sugar and the spices to the boiled cider and boil over medium heat until reduced to 1 quart. Add more sugar to taste and reduce again. When the syrup again measures 1 quart, pour it into two hot sterilized 1-pint canning jars. Seal immediately, and tighten the seals as the jars cool. Store in a cool dark place, but refrigerate after opening.

Use as a pancake syrup; as a substitute for honey; as a glaze for pork, ham, chicken, and cakes; to sweeten baked apples — or as the spirit moves.

Mrs. Thomas Gardiner, Overseer
Council of the BSO

GRANDMA MURPHY'S APRICOT MARMALADE

Makes 6 half-pint jars

1/2 pound dried apricots, cut into small
   pieces
2 large oranges, seeded, sliced, or very
   finely chopped
2 cups cold water

1 1-pound can crushed pineapple in
   pineapple juice
2½ to 3 cups sugar
3 tablespoons lemon juice

Place the cut-up apricots in a covered jar with 1 cup of water and soak overnight. Add 1 cup water to the chopped oranges and soak overnight.

Bring the orange mixture to a boil in a large deep pan, and simmer for 10 minutes. Add the apricots and the remaining ingredients and cook over low heat, stirring occasionally, until the jam is thick, about 1½ to 2 hours.

Pour the boiling marmalade into hot sterilized half-pint jars, leaving ¼ inch headroom, and seal immediately. Tighten the lids as the jars cool. They can be processed in a hot-water bath for 5 minutes. (See any standard cookbook for canning and preserving procedures.)

Mrs. David W. Murphy
Tanglewood Council of the BSO

RUM PLUM JAM

Makes 8 half-pint jars

2 large oranges, seeded and sliced
  paper-thin
1 large lemon, seeded and sliced
  paper-thin
1 cup water

4 cups purple Italian plums, skinned
  and sliced thin
7½ cups sugar
¼ cup lemon juice
3 ounces pectin
¼ cup dark rum

Place the citrus slices and water in a saucepan and bring to a boil. Boil hard for 10 to 15 minutes, until the peel is tender and the liquid is reduced to about ½ cup. Stir the plums, citrus peel, and sugar in a large high-sided saucepan, and bring to a rolling boil. Add the lemon juice and boil for 1 minute, stirring constantly. Remove from the heat and add the pectin and rum. Return to a rolling boil for 5 minutes, stirring constantly. Pour into hot sterilized jelly jars, leaving ¼ inch headroom, and seal immediately (see Note). Cool on a rack, tightening the seals as the jars cool, and store in a cool dark place.

Note

Jars may be sealed with paraffin or processed for 5 minutes in a hot-water bath. See any standard cookbook for canning directions.

Mrs. Samuel A. Levine
Council of the BSO

APRICOT BARBECUE SAUCE

Makes about 1 cup

For pork chops, chicken legs, veal, or strong-tasting fish such as bluefish, mackerel, or tuna . . .

½ cup apricot jam
2 tablespoons soy sauce
2 tablespoons dry sherry
2 tablespoons chopped scallions
1 tablespoon chopped gingerroot

1 teaspoon lemon juice
2 cloves garlic
Salt
Freshly ground black pepper

Combine all the ingredients in a blender and process until smooth. Correct the seasoning, and refrigerate until ready to use. Baste meat with the sauce as it cooks, and serve additional sauce, heated, in a warmed sauce-boat.

Mrs. F. Brooks Cowgill
Council of the BSO

BARBECUE SAUCE

Makes 1 quart

This all-purpose sauce for pork, poultry, or strong-tasting fish is a specialty of actress Lee Remick, who vacations on Cape Cod.

3 tablespoons tamari (Japanese soy
   sauce)
1½ cups cider vinegar
3 tablespoons grated gingerroot, or 3
   teaspoons ground ginger

1 pound brown sugar
1 large clove garlic, minced
1 46-ounce can pineapple juice

Combine all the ingredients in a large saucepan and simmer, uncovered, for about 30 minutes. Cool, cover, and store in the refrigerator.

Lee Remick Gowans

TERIYAKI MARINADE

Makes about 3½ cups

This is a Japanese-style marinade for meats, poultry, and seafood.

2 cups beef broth
⅔ cup soy sauce
½ cup red wine
¼ cup finely chopped scallions
3 tablespoons brown sugar

2 tablespoons lemon juice
A piece of fresh gingerroot the size of a
   walnut, grated, or 2 teaspoons
   ground ginger
2 cloves garlic, crushed

Combine all the ingredients in a glass jar and shake well. Refrigerate until ready to use. This marinade will keep for several weeks.

Mrs. R. Blake Ireland, Jr.

Marinating in a bag: *Place the meat, chicken, or other food in a strong plastic bag. Pour in the marinade. Squeeze out as much air as possible and seal the bag tightly. Turn occasionally to distribute the marinade.*

AMADEUS MUSTARD

Makes about 1 cup

Exercise caution: this is a *hot* mustard! Vary its flavorings with herbs such as tarragon, dill, or basil; change its spiciness by adding green or pink peppercorns; dilute it with whipped cream, sour cream, or yogurt; and use it whenever mixed mustard is called for in a recipe. It is particularly good for sandwiches, and it may be served warm or cold, with baked ham, corned beef, or cold cuts.

½ cup dry mustard
½ cup sugar

½ cup white wine vinegar
2 egg yolks, beaten

Place all the ingredients in a double boiler over simmering water and stir until thickened. Store in a covered jar in the refrigerator, where it will keep for weeks.

Anonymous Friend

HAM SAUCE

Makes about 1 pint

1 cup dark brown sugar, lightly
  packed
1 cup heavy cream

3 teaspoons flour
1 teaspoon dry mustard
Cider vinegar

Stir the sugar, cream, flour, and mustard in the top of a double boiler until well blended. Cover and cook over low heat for 3 hours, stirring occasionally. Add vinegar to taste just before serving.

Mrs. Howard M. Turner, Jr.
Council of the BSO

MUSTARD SAUCE FOR HAM

Makes about 2 cups

The smaller amount of mustard makes a gently pungent sauce; the larger amount is distinctly authoritative.

½ cup brown sugar
1 teaspoon flour
2 to 4 tablespoons dry mustard
⅛ teaspoon salt

2 eggs, well beaten
½ cup vinegar
½ cup water

Mix the dry ingredients together in the top of a double boiler. Stir in the eggs, vinegar, and water and cook over simmering water, stirring frequently, until the sauce is thick and there is no taste of flour. Cool; then chill. Serve with cold ham or tongue.

Mrs. Roger Wellington
Council of the BSO

FLORNIE'S BLENDER HOLLANDAISE SAUCE

Makes about 1½ cups

¼ pound butter
1 teaspoon flour
4 egg yolks
3 teaspoons lemon juice

½ cup boiling water
Salt
Freshly ground white pepper
Cayenne pepper (optional)

Melt the butter and flour together in a small pan or a microwave oven, and pour the hot butter into a blender. Add the egg yolks and lemon juice, and blend until foamy. With the blender running, slowly pour in the boiling water. Remove to the top of a double boiler over barely simmering water. Whisk until the sauce is thickened, and season to taste. Keep hot over warm water, or set aside and reheat gently when ready to serve.

Flornie Whitney
Council of the BSO

Lemon Balm: *Lemon balm is a very hardy, lush herb that has many uses. It adds fragrance to flower arrangements and to potpourri. It is excellent in iced tea or lemonade, instead of or in addition to mint. It may be chopped and included in salads, soups, or stuffings, and it may be used as a garnish or a flavoring for all fish, chicken, or meats that require a touch of lemon.*

MOCK HOLLANDAISE SAUCE

Serves 6

This sauce can be kept warm in the top of a double boiler while preparations for dinner continue. It will keep for several days in the refrigerator, and can be reheated. *It will not curdle.*

4 tablespoons butter (see Note)	*2 egg yolks*
2 tablespoons flour	*Cayenne and/or white pepper*
1 cup hot water	*(optional)*
1 tablespoon lemon juice	*Chopped fresh dill, parsley, tarragon,*
½ teaspoon salt	*or other herbs (optional)*

Melt the butter in a small saucepan over medium heat. Add the flour to make a roux. Stir in the hot water and cook for 5 minutes, or until the flour taste is gone. Add the lemon juice and salt and stir until smooth and thick. Beat the egg yolks until light and frothy. Slowly pour the sauce over the yolks, beating continuously. Use wherever hollandaise is indicated.

Note

For a richer sauce, up to double the butter may be used.

Mrs. Donald G. Magill
Council of the BSO

SAUCE AÏOLI

Makes 1¼ to 1½ cups

This sauce will keep in the refrigerator for a week.

4 to 6 cloves garlic
½ teaspoon salt
2 egg yolks
1 cup olive oil

3 tablespoons lemon juice
Salt
Freshly ground black pepper

Pound the garlic in a mortar with the salt until it becomes a smooth paste. Beat the salted garlic and the egg yolks together, using a whisk or an electric beater, until light and lemon colored. Add 2 tablespoons of olive oil drop by drop, beating continuously; then slowly beat in the remaining oil in a steady stream. Continue to beat until the sauce is smooth and thick. Add the lemon juice, and salt and pepper to taste.

Serve aïoli with Barbecued Shrimp,♦ or strong-tasting fish such as mackerel.

Ruth Deeley

TOMATO COULIS (Tomato Sauce)

Serves 6

This is the perfect tomato sauce to freeze or can for use all winter. It may be made in large batches.

4 tablespoons olive oil
1 medium-sized onion, minced
1 large clove garlic, minced
2 pounds ripe tomatoes, quartered
2 tablespoons minced fresh basil, or ½
    tablespoon dried oregano and ½
    tablespoon dried basil

1 tablespoon minced fresh parsley
1 tablespoon minced fresh chives
Sugar
Salt
Freshly ground black pepper

Heat the olive oil in a large heavy stainless steel frying pan. Add the onion and garlic, lower the heat, and cook slowly for 10 minutes, until the onion is transparent but not at all brown. Add the tomatoes and herbs and a pinch of sugar. Cook over medium heat for about 30 minutes, or until the tomatoes are soft. Purée the mixture, and reduce it over low heat to the desired consistency. Season to taste with salt and pepper. Serve with any dish requiring tomato sauce.

Laura G. Blau

False Basil: *Two parts coarsely chopped parsley and one part dried basil re-chopped together make an acceptable substitute for fresh basil.*

SYMPHONY BAKING POWDER

Excellent for baking powder biscuits or other recipes that are mixed and cooked immediately, this is also an emergency remedy for aged baking powder. Do not use Symphony Baking Powder in recipes that will be held a long time before cooking. Buy cream of tartar in small quantities and date the container. When it is a year old, throw it out. It may still be active but it may also let down your cake.

2 parts fresh cream of tartar　　　　*1 part cornstarch*
1 part baking soda

Sift the ingredients together several times to blend thoroughly. Seal tightly in a small glass jar. Date the jar and discard after six months. Use as specified in recipes calling for single-acting baking powder; in recipes requiring double-acting baking powder, use 1½ times the specified amount.

Mrs. Edward G. Hellier

Frozen Parsley: *Pack chopped parsley firmly into ice cube trays with the dividers in place. Remove when frozen, and store in tightly sealed plastic bags. Use in soups, sauces, or stews.*

HORSERADISH MOLD

Serves 10

A variation on a familiar theme, this pretty mold keeps well.

*1 3-ounce package lemon-flavored
　gelatin*
1 cup boiling water
1 tablespoon cider vinegar

¾ teaspoon salt
1 cup sour cream
*¾ cup freshly grated horseradish or
　drained commercial horseradish*

Pour the water over the gelatin and stir until it is dissolved. Add the vinegar and salt, and set aside until the mixture begins to set. Fold in the sour cream and horseradish, and pour into an oiled 2-cup mold. Chill for 2 to 3 hours or overnight. Unmold onto a chilled dish and garnish with sprigs of watercress or parsley.

Serve as a spread on crackers, or as a condiment with beef or ham.

Variation
Substitute lime-flavored gelatin for a pale green mold.

Priscilla B. Person

MUSTARD CREAM MOLD

Serves 6

Filled with ham salad, this is a perfect dish for very special picnics.

1 tablespoon gelatin
1 cup water
½ cup cider vinegar
⅓ cup sugar
1½ to 2 tablespoons dry mustard

½ teaspoon turmeric
¼ teaspoon salt
4 eggs, beaten
1 cup heavy cream, whipped

Soften the gelatin in the water for 5 minutes in the top of a double boiler. Set it over simmering water until dissolved, and add the vinegar.

Combine the sugar, mustard, turmeric, and salt and set aside.

Beat in the eggs and the dry ingredients and cook until slightly thickened, stirring constantly. Remove from the heat, and cool until the mixture is beginning to set. Fold in the whipped cream and pour into an oiled 1½-quart ring mold. Chill for 2 to 3 hours or overnight.

Turn out onto a chilled platter and fill the center with a pasta or bean salad, and serve for luncheon with cold meats.

Mrs. Leslie Mahony, Jr.

IRMA'S HEALTHFUL FUDGE

Makes about 40 squares

Josef Orosz was a long-time Boston Symphony trombone player, whose wife decided to quit smoking on her sixtieth birthday. She says, "I turned to fudge. It lasts indefinitely — or according to how many friends drop in knowing I have it."

2 tablespoons butter
¼ cup chopped nuts
1½ cups sugar
½ cup nonfat dry milk

⅔ cup water
25 marshmallows
12 ounces semisweet chocolate bits
1 teaspoon vanilla extract

Use 1 tablespoon butter to grease a 7-inch round or 8-by-5-inch rectangular pan; spread the nuts in the bottom. Mix the remaining ingredients except the chocolate and vanilla in a heavy saucepan, and stir over medium heat until the mixture boils. When the sugar and the marshmallows have dissolved, remove the mixture from the heat. Stir in the chocolate and vanilla and beat until the fudge is thick. Pour it into the prepared pan, being careful not to disturb the nuts, and store it in the refrigerator. Cut into small squares when it is completely cold. Take one per day.

Mrs. Josef Orosz

DILL BUTTER

Serves 8

This aromatic butter for fish is a welcome change from the ubiquitous lemon. It is also good with shellfish, chicken, or lamb.

*2 tablespoons chopped fresh dill, or 1
  teaspoon dried dill weed
1 teaspoon dill seed
2 tablespoons chopped parsley
2 tablespoons lemon juice*

*1 teaspoon paprika
½ cup butter, softened
1 teaspoon salt
Freshly ground black pepper*

Combine all the ingredients and mix very thoroughly. Spread the butter on fish steaks (halibut, swordfish, salmon, or other thick-fleshed fish) before broiling. Heat the remainder and use as sauce at the table.

Variation
Substitute fennel seed for the dill weed, and use as above.

*Mrs. F. Brooks Cowgill
Council of the BSO*

GINGER BALLS

Makes 2 to 3 dozen

Ginger balls are a fine after-dinner confection.

*8 ounces crystallized ginger, finely
  chopped
½ cup finely chopped walnuts
1 pound confectioners' sugar
¼ pound unsalted butter, softened*

*1 egg, beaten
½ teaspoon vanilla extract
Graham cracker or vanilla cookie
  crumbs*

Combine all the ingredients except the crumbs, and mix very thoroughly. Chill until firm, and form into ¾-inch balls. Roll in cookie crumbs and store, tightly covered, in the refrigerator or freezer.
    Serve very cold with fruit desserts, at afternoon tea, or after dinner.

Variation
Dip the balls in melted semisweet or bitter chocolate instead of the cookie crumbs.

*Mrs. Robert B. Newman
Council of the BSO*

ACKNOWLEDGMENTS
CONTRIBUTORS
INDEX

Acknowledgments

The Council of the Boston Symphony is deeply grateful to the people listed below, whose tireless efforts have produced this book.

The Cookbook Committee

Mrs. Thomas Gardiner,
  Chairman
Mrs. Frank Remick,
  Vice-Chairman
Mrs. George M. Alsberg
Mrs. Samuel Boxer
Mrs. F. Brooks Cowgill
Mrs. James G. Garivaltis
Miss Sylvia Gilman
Walter D. Hill
Mrs. F. Corning Kenly, Jr.
Mrs. Anita R. Klaussen

Mrs. Carl Koch
Mrs. August R. Meyer
Mrs. Jack S. Parker
Mrs. Jerome Rosenfeld
Matthew Ruggiero
Mrs. Richard F. Schanzle
Mrs. Harry Shapiro
Mrs. Robert E. Siegfried
Mrs. Arthur I. Strang
Mrs. Richard H. Thompson
Mrs. Donald Wilson

The office volunteers, testers, and writers:

Mrs. George W. Benedict
Mrs. Lawrence L. Clampitt
Mrs. Jarvis Cribb
Mrs. Alva Cuddeback
Mrs. James T. Dennison
Mrs. Alan Fenn
Mrs. C. Henry Glovsky
Mrs. John Hand
Mrs. Baron Hartley

Mrs. Stephen Heartt
Mrs. Edward G. Hellier
Mrs. Roger B. Hunt
Mrs. Béla T. Kalman
Mrs. Donald C. Kneale
Mrs. Hart D. Leavitt
Mrs. Martin Lomasney
Mrs. Charles P. Lyman
Mrs. Harry Martens

Mrs. Louis W. Mead
Mrs. Elting E. Morison
Mrs. Thomas Morse
Mrs. Hardwick Moseley
Mrs. Hiroshi Nishino
Mrs. Albert Pratley
Mrs. Robert Rafferty
Miss Jane Rosenthal
Mrs. Steven T. Russian
Mrs. Wilbert R. Sanger
Mrs. Wynn A. Sayman
Mrs. Ruth Schubert
Mrs. Ralph Seferian
Mrs. Frank P. Sherman

Mrs. Paul D. Shuwall
Mrs. George H. Simonds, Jr.
Mrs. Stephen Stone
Mrs. Charles L. Terry III
Mrs. Howard M. Turner, Jr.
Mrs. John H. Valentine
Mrs. Thomas Walker
Mrs. Raymond J. Walther
Mrs. Constance V. R. White
Mrs. Florence Whitney
Mrs. John Williams
Miss Sheila Winchester
Mrs. Erwin Ziner

Special thanks are due to the following:

Our publishers for their belief in the book, and especially Linda Glick, our editor, for her will to make the book better and for her sensitive guidance along the way.

The First National Bank of Boston for their more than generous help in having our manuscript typed and edited on their word processors.

The Symphony staff for their interest, cheerful encouragement, and ever-present practical help. Steven Ledbetter, director of publications for the Orchestra, wrote the photograph captions. Marc Mandel, editorial coordinator for the BSO, provided factual information and expertise. Thomas D. Perry, Jr., for twenty-five years manager and executive director of the Orchestra and present Trustee, contributed generously from his inexhaustible fund of Symphony history and folklore. This blend of talents is intended to give the reader a sense of the multifaceted life of this great musical organization.

Contributors

Index